Degeneration
The Dark Side of Progress

DEGENERATION

THE DARK SIDE OF PROGRESS

Edited by
J. EDWARD CHAMBERLIN
and
SANDER L. GILMAN

NEW YORK COLUMBIA UNIVERSITY PRESS 1985

Library of Congress Cataloging in Publication Data
Main entry under title:

Degeneration.

Includes bibliographies and index.
Contents: History and degeneration / Morris
Eksteins — Anthropology and degeneration / James A.
Boon — Sociology and degeneration / Robert A. Nye —
[etc.]
1. Europe—Intellectual life—19th century—Addresses,
essays, lectures. 2. United States—Intellectual
life—1783–1865—Addresses, essays, lectures. 3. United
States—Intellectual life—1865–1918—Addresses, essays,
lectures. 4. Regression (Civilization)—Addresses,
essays, lectures. I. Chamberlin, J. Edward, 1943–
II. Gilman, Sander L., 1944–   .
CB417.D44 1985   001.1   84-21495
ISBN 0-231-05196-4

Columbia University Press
New York   Guildford, Surrey
Copyright © 1985 Columbia University Press
All rights reserved

Printed in the United States of America

*Clothbound editions of Columbia University Press books are
Smyth-sewn and printed on permanent and durable acid-free paper.*

Contents

PREFACE

"Progress is / The law of life, Man is not man as yet," or at least so for Robert Browning in "Paracelsus." The myth of progress, especially as it charmed the nineteenth century, has been a stock in trade of studies in the history of ideas reaching back before World War I. There is no longer much doubt that progress is a structure which, often willy-nilly, has been superimposed on human endeavor in order to provide it with shape and meaning. But the complementary notion that there is a necessary and antithetical structure in human thought against which the concept of progress is precariously balanced has been little considered. When any attention has been given to this opposing force, it has usually been labeled "decadence" and has been observed as reposing quite quaintly in such tangential areas as literature and the arts.

The present collection of essays is an attempt to sketch against a broad background this force which complements the idea of progress in the nineteenth and early twentieth centuries. We have selected the term "degeneration" for it; and like "progress," it is a term widely employed in numerous and often contradictory contexts. There is no one area in which the concept of degeneration is dominant. It permeates nineteenth-century thought with a model (or a series of models) for decline, and it permeates nineteenth-century feeling with images of decay. Its roots are—as roots tend to be—embedded in biological models and images, but its import soon incorporated, not to say overwhelmed, the purely biological character of the paradigm. It borrows or subverts other terms, such as decadence, but it remains for the nineteenth century the most frightening of prospects, as well as at times the most enthralling.

Degeneration is a topic that has been little explored in the history of ideas, and it has never been the subject of a systematic presentation. These essays, all commissioned for this volume, present an overview of the idea of degeneration as it operated within nineteenth- and early twentieth-century thought. The essays span the natural and social sciences and the humanities. The divisions are arbitrary, reflecting more our traditional manner of dividing up western thought than the nature of the topic itself. And yet the logic of degeneration weaves themes among all the essays; ideas that appear in one reappear in others from a different perspective, or with a different emphasis.

No little reason for the power of the paradigm of degeneration is the institutional structure in which it was involved. For it was formed and functioned within institutional arrangements—such as those of medicine, anthropology, or the theater—which reflected and furthered the needs of nineteenth-century European culture to reify its own power and to institutionalize the powerlessness over which it exercised its dominion. This dominion was both literal and figurative and included the real world of the European colonies, or the shops and factories and hospitals and asylums of the cities of Europe and America, as well as the imaginative structures which gave life to many of the most powerful images of literary, dramatic, and scientific enterprise. The control that sustained these arrangements was exercised through the use of the models of progress and degeneration. The fear of losing control meant that the negative model, the model of degeneration, was a particularly powerful one, caught as it was between its own negative power as the opposite of progress, and a positive energy which gave the model a fascinating appeal on its own, an appeal not manageable by any dialectic. It lurked in the nature of the Other, whether black or homosexual, as it lurked within those who generated it.

This volume attempts to make some connections between the history of ideas and the history of perception, and in doing so to illuminate both the subject matter and the informing logic of degeneration which link many of the most important nineteenth-century intellectual and social preoccupations.

The editors extend thanks to the contributors, who kindly agreed to write essays for this volume, and then even more kindly produced them on time; to the Columbia University Press and their editor Susan Koscielniak; and to Jane Dieckmann, who copy edited the manuscript.

S.L.G.
J.E.C.

DEGENERATION:
An Introduction

Nineteenth-century obituaries sometimes used to describe the passing of the dearly beloved as a result of "simple decay of nature." The nice courtesy of the phrase marks one limit of the discussion of degeneration. The other limit concentrated on its morbid and grotesque affiliations, usually with a grim superiority. It was never an easy commerce between these points of view.

The word degeneration was itself a curious compound. First of all, it meant to lose the properties of the genus, to decline to a lower type . . . to dust, for instance, or to the behavior of the beasts of the barnyard. It also meant to lose the generative force, the force that through the green fuse drives the flower. During the nineteenth century, the pattern of degeneration was further identified in the physical as well as the natural sciences. Scientists formulated the law of increasing entropy as the second law of thermodynamics, according to which the available energy of any closed system (such as the universe) decreases over time—its "work-content" declining to a lower order, as it were. In addition, the idea of degeneration encouraged typological, just as much as it organized physical and biological, speculation; and in its more popular aspect it invited some very unscientific stereotyping. Finally, and for all of its connection with *natural* phenomena, its most powerful association was with something *unnatural*, even—or perhaps especially—when associated with natural desire or supernatural dread.

This volume of essays was undertaken as an experiment in intellectual history, and it took shape as a source book in one of the great notions of the nineteenth century. Degeneration belongs with those topics that are compelling as ideas and unnerving as realities. In a century that came increasingly to believe that the visible world is no longer a reality, and the unseen world no longer a dream, the ubiquity of degeneration had a powerful appeal. It provided a context for the interpretation of situations, and a text for speculation. It inhered in but also extended beyond the forms of life, whether microscopic or macroscopic. It focused some perennial but often unrecognized disagreements about the continuities or the discontinuities of natural history. And it is with history that our study begins, moving then to the social and natural sciences toward the arts.

Degeneration was part of a convenient dialectic for the organization of contemporary thought and feeling—a kind of fiction, if you will. But also, it was part of the inevitable structure of reality, an indisputable fact. People, nations, perhaps the universe itself, all run down, grow old and die. Those who talked about such things were usually well aware of their ambivalent obligation to the imperatives of fiction and fact; but they also accepted the convenience of fashioning their commentary according to quite tidy contraries, especially the contraries of rising and falling, going forward or going backward, regenerating or degenerating. These contraries were in part rhetorical strategies, in part logical orderings. They expressed the speaker's attitude toward his subject as much as they mirrored that subject; and they did much to determine the way in which people began to think about reality. And while the idea of degeneration was in a sense only one side of the coin, it was the magical side, for it seemed to be the image of a profound and disturbing power that operated in the universe. The theologians and the scientists of the period shared very little, but the common ground they both claimed was the perception that the only kind of account that really mattered was an account of decline and fall. Just as the nature of evil has always had a more compelling appeal to the imagination than the nature of goodness, so the idea of degeneration engaged the nineteenth-century mind with a troubling sense that here, perhaps, might be found the essential reality. In some measure, this was because with the idea of degeneration they came closest to the sanctity of types, or genuses, or species, a sanctity that was the more frantically embraced as it became more uncertain. Nineteenth-century science combined a fiercely categorical instinct with a fierce interest in the nature of things, and degeneration was a perfect focus for this. It was not only an interest in processes and forces, but also an interest in the character and permanence of the distinctions, orderings, and coherences upon which nineteenth-century thought—and in particular scientific thought—depended. Not just the autonomy of species, but their very authority as entities, was called into question by all of this.

The questions that arise with regard to degeneration are the ones that in general perplexed nineteenth-century thought. Is the astonishing authority of degeneration as an intellectual principle an authority grounded in reality, or in the imagination? Is it a part of nature, or a part of us? Do the accounts need to be considered according to categories of truth and falsehood, or of fact and fiction? or do they belong instead with the aesthetic categories of symmetry, unity, and elegance? And what exactly is the difference anyway, in a century in which scientific theories are among the most beautiful inventions of the human mind, and the discoveries about the workings of the artistic imagination among its truest? Are the laws of nature merely consistent with, or are they consubstantial with, the laws of the human imagination? or of the divine? Is the idea of degeneration a mirroring or a making? Is the reality of degeneration objective or subjective?

These are the kinds of questions that perplex any discussion, historical or otherwise; but they arise with a peculiar and persistent urgency with regard to degeneration. The question which underlies this book is why this should be so.

Degeneration seemed to develop a particular sort of conceptual autonomy. In some ways the questions about its relationship to reality or its status as an idea became less important than its authority as an organizational scheme or discursive mode. Nineteenth-century scientists worried about this kind of authority but they also exploited it with compelling assurance, especially in organizing their favorite ideas. Charles Darwin, for example, tried to extricate himself from the teleological toils of Natural Selection, and in doing so confirmed his commitment to one of his most elusive yet most authoritative figures of speech.

> Several writers have misapprehended or objected to the term Natural Selection. Some have even imagined that natural selection induces variability, whereas it implies only the preservation of such variations as arise and are beneficial to the being under its conditions of life. No one objects to agriculturalists speaking of the potent effects of man's selection; and in this case the individual differences given by nature, which man for some object selects, must of necessity first occur. Others have objected that the term selection implies conscious choice in the animals which become modified; and it has even been urged that, as plants have no volition, natural selection is not a term applicable to them? In the literal sense of the word, no doubt, natural selection is a false term; but who ever objected to chemists speaking of the elective affinities of the various elements:—and yet an acid cannot strictly be said to elect the base with which it in preference combines. It has been said that I speak of the natural selection as an active power or Deity; but who objects to an author speaking of the attraction of gravity as ruling the movements of the planets? Everyone knows what is meant and is implied by such metaphorical expressions; and they are almost necessary for brevity. So again it is difficult to avoid personifying the word Nature; but I mean by Nature, only the aggregate action and product of so many natural laws, and by laws the sequence of events as ascertained by us. With a little familiarity such superficial objections will be forgotten.

With a little familiarity such superficial objections will indeed be forgotten, and the very confusion of the literal and the figurative that Darwin cautioned against will prevail. And did prevail. The figurations of degeneration established their own imaginative autonomy in an entirely analogous way by creating an image of a process that had the authority of a natural or a divine law, and an image of a force that had the authority of a supernatural or an organic power. As an indication of this, it is easy to note a tendency to speak of the degenerate as damned, just as those who survive (being the fittest) might be described as the chosen. Insofar as degeneration, like natural selection or gravity, was perceived as both a process and a force, it provided a mode of coherence and continuity for the descriptions of phenomena.

In part, the hovering between figurations that Darwin apologized for constitutes a familiar ambivalence—not just between the literal and the figurative, but also between what D'Arcy Thompson used to call the teleological and the mechanistic, between that which operates toward some end according to a purpose or design, and that which operates from some beginning according to a logic of causal relationships and consecutive events. The uncertainty about which prevails is basically an uncertainty about what it is that we are talking about, as well as an uncertainty about what we are saying about it. Or, put differently, it is an uncertainty about whether it is a matter of knowledge or belief.

They are formidable words, knowledge and belief; but they are words by which poets and scientists alike set some store. The idea of degeneration provided a framework and a focus for knowledge about immanent natural processes in social and cultural and historical as well as biological contexts, and a locus of belief about transcendent forces affecting the pace and direction of change as well as the vitality of races and nations. The idea of degeneration provided a way of organizing impressions and of projecting desires, of formulating experience and of expressing hopes and fears, of reconciling the logics of the physical with those of the psychical worlds. In doing so, it provided an impetus for the astonishing development of new intellectual disciplines and of new institutional structures—legal, educational, administrative—to which we are still committed.

The essays in the volume were commissioned to bring together an appropriately wide range of disciplinary perspectives, and to establish through these perspectives a sense both of the topic and of the way in which the nineteenth-century mind—to use a nineteenth-century notion—organized its most troubling thoughts and feelings. This book demonstrates how the imaginative structures informing the arts were continuous with the imaginative structures informing the sciences, and how both were engaged by the notion of degeneration. It is intended as a source book not only for the history of ideas, but also for the study of the nature of history, and of one of its strongest ideas.

> The presence that thus rose so strangely beside the waters, is expressive of what in the ways of a thousand years men had come to desire. Hers is the head upon which all "the ends of the world are come," and the eyelids are a little weary. It is a beauty wrought out from within upon the flesh, the deposit, little cell by cell, of strange thoughts and fantastic reveries and exquisite passions. Set it for a moment beside one of those white Greek goddesses or beautiful women of antiquity, and how would they be troubled by this beauty, into which

the soul with all its maladies has passed! All the thoughts and experience of the world have etched and moulded there, in that which they
have of power to refine and make expressive the outward form, the
animalism of Greece, the lust of Rome, the reverie of the middle ages
with its spiritual ambition and imaginative loves, the return of the
pagan world, the sins of the Borgias. She is older than the rocks among
which she sits; like the vampire, she has been dead many times, and
learned the secrets of the grave; and has been a diver in deep seas, and
keeps their fallen day about her; and trafficked for strange webs with
Eastern merchants: and, as Leda, was the mother of Helen of Troy,
and, as Saint Anne, the mother of Mary; and all this has been to her
but as the sound of lyres and flutes, and lives only in the delicacy with
which it has moulded the changing lineaments, and tinged the eyelids
and the hands.

This is Walter Pater's celebrated description of Leonardo da Vinci's
painting of the Mona Lisa. It is a catalogue of images of degeneration,
complete with a decadent weariness, a new testament apocalyptic vision
when "the ends of the world are come," a sensuous sickness of the soul,
and a nice company of vampires, Borgias, and other suitably sinister
presences. It is also an image of eternal beauty, and an emblem of a
perennial rebirth, the spirit of the Renaissance. Birth and death went
hand in hand in the nineteenth century. Regeneration and degeneration.
The forces of nature, which rust iron and ripen corn. The forces of desire,
which ruin the flesh and raise the spirit. Or is it all the other way around?

Degeneration was one of the most uncertain of notions, and—like some
viruses—one of the most difficult to isolate. The idea of degeneration
could comfortably be caught up in tapestry of ambivalences, to be sure,
and whether it was conceived as warp or woof could be a matter of taste.
But as any account must keep insisting, degeneration was also a reality. It
was on the one hand an element of a dialectic of thought which became in
the Hegelian heyday of the second half of the nineteenth century a nice
balance to the idea of progress. On the other hand degeneration embodied
something of the structure of an evolutionary reality in which everything
moved not only toward a more advanced state but also toward death. But
perhaps first of all degeneration was simply a word.

"Nothing dies so hard as a word—particularly a word nobody understands." Harry Quilter, writing in the 1880s, was lamenting the widespread misunderstanding of the word "Pre-Raphaelitism." So of course he
wrote a book to straighten things out. This book is in a certain sense an
attempt to perform the same magic on the word degeneration. Historians
of the Pre-Raphaelite Brotherhood have found how difficult it can be to
separate the idea from the reality, and how much both are caught up in a
network of popular misconception, deliberate misconstruction, and accidental emphasis. The indeterminacy of word degeneration makes such
confusion look almost trivial.

It could certainly be said to be a word that nobody in the nineteenth century rightly understood. As is often the case, it was also a word of which many people were certain that they alone knew the true meaning. Its apparent importance as an element both in abstract speculations and in concrete situations generated a zealous corps of interpreters. But the interpretations did not always, indeed on the surface did not usually, agree.

Of course, interpretations are rather dubious things anyway. Hermes was the messenger of the gods, and in due course gave his name to hermeneutics, the science of interpretation. Hermes was also a trickster and a thief. Biblical criticism has been in his spell for a long time, mainly because of a perennial disagreement over whether the text should be read literally or figuratively. It is, as we have noted, precisely this kind of disagreement that bedevils any account of degeneration. This volume of essays is an attempt not so much to resolve the disagreement as to outline its character, and to provide the basis for a much more solid understanding of the idea of degeneration in the nineteenth century, as well as of the reality that the idea supposedly reflects. Often, needless to say, the idea was a making as much as it was a mirroring.

When the American poet William Carlos Williams took stock in 1919 of the legacy that this volume chronicles, he did so in images that betray both the fascination of the *reality* of degeneration—in this case, his own fascination as a doctor with decay and death—and the fascination of the *idea* of degeneration—his own fascination as a poet with beauty and fear. But even in saying this, it becomes obvious that the reverse may be more accurate: it may be the idea of decay and death, and the reality of beauty and fear. This is one of Williams' observations from a series of "improvisations" that he titled *Kora in Hell*.

> Pathology literally speaking is a flower garden. Syphilis covers the body with salmon-red petals. The study of medicine is an inverted sort of horticulture. Over and above all this floats the philosophy of disease which is a stern dance. One of its most delightful gestures is bringing flowers to the sick.

At the beginning of the nineteenth century, William Wordsworth said that his imagination was fostered alike by beauty and by fear. Degeneration as the nineteenth century understood it, and as the new intellectual disciplines constituted it, was in some sense the institutionalization of fear. Hope was looked after by the idea of progress, and seemed to be the tenor of the times. But fear—fear was contagious. It infected the air, and poisoned the wells.

That is the legacy. The prerogatives of the imagination, and those of reality, mirrored each other in the processes and forces of degeneration that interested the nineteenth century. In an age in which nature and nurture competed for authority, degeneration bridged the gap between the two by seeming to defy the laws of both. Defy may not be the right word. Transcend might be better.

Degeneration
The Dark Side of Progress

HISTORY AND DEGENERATION: OF BIRDS AND CAGES

MODRIS EKSTEINS
University of Toronto

Ich halte für Barberei, Vögel in Käfigen zu halten.[1]

Had George Orwell been a historian he might have said that all centuries are equal but some are more equal than others. Some witness more change, and the nineteenth century certainly falls into this category. Any discussion of the idea of history in that century must begin with some attempt to evoke the context that gave birth to both the modern conception of history and modern historians.

Perhaps the most consequential feature of the nineteenth century was the rapid increase in world population. Europe, which had taken more than two centuries prior to 1800 to double its population, more than doubled it again in the next hundred years. As factories and mass production techniques emerged in Western Europe, to provide for the vastly increasing numbers of people, cities mushroomed; in many places grim urban slums supplanted rural landscapes, often retaining, however, as a poignant comment on the scale of change, such lyrical names as Issy-les-Moulineaux, Aubervilliers, and Les Lilas, to mention some of the bleak industrial suburbs that Paris spawned in the second half of the century. In 1800 Germany had but two cities with a population over 100,000; by 1900 the number had grown to thirty-three.

If the physical conditions of life changed radically during the century, so too did man's relationship with his social environment as technology revolutionized communications. While at the beginning of the century Napoleon could travel no faster than Julius Caesar, at its end Europe was marked by an intricate one-million-kilometer spiderweb of railway lines along which moved six billion travelers a year in Britain, France, and

Germany alone; the oceans were crisscrossed by shipping lanes; and the skies were about to host the triumphant realization of man's age-old obsession with flight. As education became the social panacea of the middle classes, the literacy rate shot upward too. In England in 1810 a mere 580 books were produced; in 1901 production reached 6,000 titles. By 1914 nineteen out of twenty conscripts in the French army could write, and crosses in marriage registers had virtually disappeared in Western Europe.

Everything seemed to increase in size during the century: machines, armies, empires, bureaucracies, bridges, ships. "Dreadnought" and "Big Bertha" were the telling names Europeans applied to their most awesome weapons on the eve of World War I, the Great War as it was to be called. Everything seemed to move faster as well. Between 1876 and 1914 in their "race" for colonies, imperial powers annexed eleven million square miles of territory. On the occasion of Queen Victoria's diamond jubilee in 1897, her son-in-law, the Duke of Argyll, wrote: "we could not help remembering that no sovereign since the fall of Rome could muster subjects from so many and such distant countries all over the world."[2]

There can be little argument that the nineteenth century was one of hitherto unexcelled movement and expansion. All thought and creativity in that century was, needless to say, affected by this unprecedented activity, particularly by the exciting evidence of man's growing power over nature. And the fundamental question that confronted all men was whether this turbulence of activity was good or ill. "Where are we going?" asked Alexis de Tocqueville in *La Démocratie en Amérique*. In the face of dramatic change the moral question, whether the quality of life was improving or deteriorating, became in the Western world as a whole, though most acutely in Europe, the crucial intellectual dilemma of the century, more pressing, it seemed, than even the fundamental epistemological question of how man was to perceive that which he was trying to be moral about. All the intellectual movements of the age, from idealism and romanticism, through positivism and scientism, to symbolism and decadence, were in one way or another a response to this issue. Positivism pretended to subordinate it to scientific method, which was supposed to achieve results rather than speculation, but the moral question remained the point of departure, and its resolution the end goal, of positivist theory. Auguste Comte recognized this; his grand, unrealized dream was the enunciation of a "scientific morality."

Now the moral issue demanded, for debate let alone resolution, both an image of the future and a view of the past. Correspondingly, given the acuity of the issue, the present, in the nineteenth-century perception of time, tended to be devalued and regarded primarily as a point of transition. In industrial capitalism present time was to be used, for the sake of future rewards; past time, in turn, was useful for the sake of comparison. "The chief phenomenon of our time," said Jacob Burckhardt as a result, "is the feeling of transitoriness."[3] And John Stuart Mill pointed out that "the idea of comparing one's own age with former ages, or with our notion of those which are yet to come, had occurred to philosophers; but it never before was itself the dominant idea of any age."[4]

The classical world had thought of time as a cycle of endless recurrence. While Christianity encouraged an eschatological and hence linear view of history, as a movement toward finality, the medieval world nevertheless had no nuanced sense of time, because the future, except solely in the theological meaning of an afterlife, would be no better than the present or the past. With Vico the eighteenth century arrived at the idea of development and the contribution of the past to the present. Vico argued that for man history was the only reality because history was the creation of man, and man can only know what he himself creates. Yet, within his century Vico was an exception. Most eighteenth-century *philosophes*, with their mechanistic view of the universe and their belief that human nature was uniform, were basically present-minded; most of them ignored the idea of historical continuity and did not observe in history a process, an unfolding of interconnected phenomena. The past represented unreason, the present the struggle for reason, the future the victory of rationality.

It was the nineteenth century that, with the experience of wholesale change, produced both the modern awareness of history and the modern historian. As the Faustian notion of "becoming" rather than "being" became the central logic of the century, the historian became the indispensable explicator of this logic. The modern historian, then, is the child of the modern awareness of change. The modern historian does not deal with the past—the antiquarian might; the historian, even the most resolute empiricist, deals with the connection between the past and the present, with the process of change.

If the present, however, is so evanescent that it loses significance in favor of the future, then the link to be made is between past and future. The historian, accordingly, either because of his own inclination or on account of social pressure, finds himself in the role of seer; and in the nineteenth century many historians discovered themselves in this position, encouraged to develop a holistic vision, a secular theology of change. The polarized approach to existence—the emphasis on origins and goals—produced both grand historical enterprises and grand utopian schemes, vision of both *Universalgeschichte* and Absolute Spirit; but, at the same time, it produced Fifth Gospels, visions of the Antichrist, and an incipient nihilism—in sum a secular mood of apocalypse. History became the substitute for theology; for many it became the new theology, the *magistra vitae*, of industrial society. For Thomas Carlyle history was "not only the fittest study but the only study, . . . the true epic poem, the universal divine Scripture."[5] Leopold Ranke spoke of historians as priests. It is no accident that so many historians were the sons of clergymen.

The awareness of history was promoted most directly by observation of social and economic change, but is was reinforced by political and cultural

developments. It would be difficult to overstate the impact of the revolutionary and Napoleonic epoch on western consciousness. Not just French-
men but most Europeans were affected personally in some way by the
drama emanating from France, by the French attempt to alter radically
the structure and functioning of not only their own society but that of
Europe as a whole. In the process, as individual experience seemed to
blend with national and world history, and as revolution and war became
truly a mass phenomenon rather than a matter of conspirators and mer-
cenaries, the question of history, of how past experiences were connected
and how they related to the present, became an issue of supreme importance. Appropriately, in 1812 separate chairs for modern and ancient history were set up at the Sorbonne. Two years earlier, when the University of
Berlin was founded, history took up an equal position with other disciplines in the philosophical faculty. History thus became an autonomous
subject, no longer tied necessarily to such other disciplines as law, theology, or philosophy. The aftershocks of the great revolution, which came in
waves, in 1830, 1848, and 1871, all respectively elicited new outbursts of
historical interest. The development of modern politics, so intricately tied
to the revolutionary outbreaks, was also naturally founded on a historical
sense, an awareness of inadequacy which necessarily had to preface the
formulation of corrective ideas and measures. The statesman, said J. G.
Droysen, had to be a "practical historian."

The national awakening in Europe which was provoked by the revolutionary era and Napoleonic imperialism further encouraged a sense of
history among the broader populace, as the legacy of, among others,
Montesquieu, Rousseau, and Herder led to an emphasis on folk customs
and geographical influences. Historians played a prominent role in these
movements of ethnic regeneration, particularly in Central and Eastern
Europe. The movements for national unity in Germany and Italy and for
Slavic self-assertion in Russia fed on and bred further a historical sense, as
did of course, by the end of the century, imperialism, militarism, and a
flourishing xenophobia.

In literature, drama, and opera, historical themes preoccupied the creative imagination. Walter Scott in his Waverley novels at the beginning of
the century tried to objectify history in literature; Marcel Proust in his
great *roman fleuve,* which germinated at the end of the century, would
totally subjectify historical experience. The two approaches to the past
were not simply idiosyncratic; they expressed broader cultural attitudes;
they even paralleled the path that historians followed in their debate about
methodology during the century. In 1910, on the eve of World War I,
E. M. Forster's *Howards End* would bear, as a nostalgic epitaph to historical sense, the inscription "Only connect . . ."

The historical perspective spread into literary criticism, philology, law,
architecture, and the decorative arts. In theology the Bible and Jesus
became subjects of historical interest. As science and technology pros-

pered, they too encouraged a historical sense with the attention that they invariably paid to the stages of discovery and invention. Of all the achievements of science, Darwin's discoveries most intensified historical interest. Darwin revealed that nature was hardly the static, mechanical reality which the *philosophes* and the Hegelians considered it but a dynamic reality which too had a history; and this revelation suggested that historical scholarship might hold the key to the development of a total view of the universe including both spirit and nature. G. W. Prothero even appropriated Darwin's achievement for the historians: "what is the theory of evolution itself," he asked in 1894, "with all its far-reaching consequences, but the achievement of the historical method?"[6]

The growth of historical awareness was such a prominent feature that one can readily speak of the nineteenth century as a *saeculum historicum*. Comte began the third volume of his *Système de politique positive* with the words: "The distinctive characteristic of the present age will be the importance it assigns to history, by the light of which philosophy, politics, and even poetry will henceforth be pursued." At the end of the century Benedetto Croce, philosopher and historian, assessed his own intellectual development, but at the same time gave expression to wider sentiment when he declared: "It is a curious fate that history should for a long time have been considered and treated as the most humble form of knowledge, while philosophy was considered as the highest, and that now it not only is superior to philosophy but annihilates it."[7]

The growth in the awareness of history, not only among intellectuals but among masses of men, was, we are suggesting, commensurate with the rate of social, economic, and political change—with the development, in other words, of man's sense of himself as creator rather than simply creature. That was the positive aspect of the new interest. There was, however, a querulous side to the interest as well: the urgent need to assess in moral terms the implications of man's creations; and here doubt and anxiety were strong ingredients of curiosity. William Morris pointed out in *News from Nowhere* that "it is mostly in periods of turmoil and strife and confusion that people care much about history." J. M. Robertson has argued that the scales tipped from religious belief to skepticism in the 1840s and '50s in the western part of continental Europe and in the 1870s in Britain. The dates coincide with the appearance of some of the classics of nineteenth-century historical literature. The 1850s and '60s, in particular, are the great decades of historical writing.

Formal historical thought in the nineteenth century might be divided roughly into three broad streams.[8] There was the metaphysical or idealist approach first of all, which regarded history as a transcendental process, as spirit unfolding, beyond specific time and separate from nature. The historian's task was to discover the *Weltplan*, the eternal verities that constituted this spirit. Schiller, Schelling, and Fichte made major contributions to this approach whose theory culminated in Hegel. Virtually all historical work in the nineteenth century was influenced, in one form or another, by the metaphysicians.

Then there were the empiricists who in turn shaded into the positivist or naturalist school. The former regarded knowledge as a good in its own right; the latter looked on history as basically a part of nature whose hidden laws could be determined. What united the two groups was their practice, their emphasis on a scientific approach to history. One must proceed from observation to analysis, from the particular to the general, and then only on the basis of a critical, "scientific" use of sources. Fustel de Coulanges captured the aspirations of this approach in his claim to his lecture audience that it was not he speaking, but history through him. While Ranke's emphasis on the role of ideas in history placed him close to the metaphysicians, his lifelong insistence on scrupulous attention to detail meant that he more than any other historian helped to further the method of scientific history. In the wake of Ranke, who spanned idealism and positivism—despite the disdain he voiced for both—theory and practice in historical work began to diverge. The philosophy of history and basic historical research, which often was little more than refined philology, lost touch; and the vast majority of historians from then until this day have ignored the philosophical implications of their endeavor and have bowed simply to one part of Ranke's legacy: his exhortation to treat sources critically and to let history, in a sense, speak for itself. Generally, therefore, their effort falls into the empiricist or positivist school.

Finally, in the second half of the century, there emerged the aesthetic or "neo-idealist" approach, in which the historian became at least as important, if not more, than the subject. In this approach, to whose development Carlyle, Michelet, Droysen, and Dilthey contributed, and which found its master practitioner in Burckhardt, history, except for certain raw materials, did not exist as a fixed object in itself; it took significant shape only in the hands of a historian. Any meaning to history thus had a crucial subjective component. History was a form of literature, a form of art. The past provided the plot, the theme, the subject, the characters, but the history was in the art.

Ranke of course was not the only historian who straddled the categories. Croce, for instance, tried to bridge all three. Rarely in fact did a historian fit neatly into any one of the groups, but the three broad categories nevertheless delineate the basic patterns of historical thought in the nineteenth century. Metaphysical idealism peaked in the 1820s and '30s; empiricism and positivism were strong from the 1840s through the rest of the century, and neo-idealism found growing support as the century ended.

Because for them history had an objective reality, be it spiritual or material, and therefore had meaning, the practitioners of the first two approaches were inclined to be optimistic about both theory and method. Both fitted into the general scheme of thought which came to be known as "historicism" and which posited, as its central idea, that if one wished to understand the true nature of something, one had to understand how it had developed, how it had changed; and this effort at understanding would also invariably lead to a measure of prediction. Hegel's basic formula, that all that is rational is real and all that is real is rational, and his view of history as the development of this rationality, bespoke the general optimism. While he saw concrete existence in history as a "panorama of sin and suffering," he believed that rational man could rise above such mere existence toward essence. That his conception of rationality, freedom, and the state transcended the individual and belonged to a metaphysical realm of spirit, meant that his notion of progress also belonged to this ethereal holist sphere where historical necessity ruled out moral imperative.

Rankean empiricists poured scorn on this Hegelian metaphysical hocus-pocus which, they claimed, squeezed facts into theories; at the same time, however, despite their intent, their approach was hardly devoid of an idealistic undercurrent. Ranke's own conception of authority, monarchy, and especially the state—in which he was inclined to observe divine intervention and which he saw as the embodiment of a higher ethical purpose—had an idealistic texture which surfaced frequently in his later career and was prompted often by negative considerations, particularly his fear of the masses and revolution. While fear was an increasingly important component of Rankean thought, as the theme of the struggle between monarchy and democracy came to occupy a central position in his work, the basic impulse of his historical method and achievement nevertheless remained progressive. His ultimate concern was ultimate meaning, *Universalgeschichte:* "Historical research will not suffer from its connection with the universal; without this link, research would become enfeebled, and without exact research the conception of the universal would degenerate into a phantasm."[9]

For historical positivists man's welfare improved as he mastered his environment, as scientific discoveries and material benefits accrued. Knowledge involved a cumulative process which ultimately would allow man to understand himself and to organize society rationally. Human history, according to Comte, was a single entity, a movement toward one final type of society, and it was the role of the scientist-historian, or sociologist, to determine and further this development. The positive, as the third stage through which all knowledge had to pass, following the theological and the metaphysical, was a stage at which man abandoned the vain search for absolute knowledge and satisfied himself with laws defining relations.

Most idealists and positivists were united in looking at history as a key to the future. Not only did history have meaning; it was the job of the historian to uncover that meaning, to order and interpret experience. Ranke, although he insisted on the uniqueness of all historical events and on the priority of fact over concept, believed that assiduous scholarship might eventually reveal the hand of God. Power and morality were for him not antithetical but found their ideal fusion in the developing purpose of the state, and the historian, by studying this state and its politics, might be able to discover the divine purpose. Droysen, who objected to much of Ranke's method, nevertheless agreed that history was the unfolding of "moral forces." In the work of Marx, it might be argued, the spiritual optimism of Hegel and the scientific optimism of Comte found their synthesis.

Nietzsche pointed out that every philosophy is "a species of involuntary and unconscious autobiography,"[10] and we can now clearly see that the progressivist inclinations of both the idealist and positivist historians were rooted as much in their personal situation as in their analysis of their subject. The growing professionalization of the historical discipline—the dependence of historians on their subject for their existence and equally their dependence on the state which for the most part subsidized their enterprise—meant that history as both theory and method was bound to have a positive orientation which was also initially tied to the idea of the nation. A historian, Guizot, became minister of education in France in 1832, and he set a new example for state involvement in historical enterprise, helping to found and support financially the Société de l'Histoire de France. The federal states in the German Confederation began from 1834 on to underwrite the publication of the *Monumenta Germaniae Historica*.

Similarly, the very fact that the vast majority of professional historians came from the ranks of the bourgeoisie—Tocqueville and Acton were the most prominent exceptions—dictated that most of these historians would profess what was, for much of the century, the affirmative ethic of this propertied and educated middle class. Historians in the nineteenth century, moreover, were highly conscious of their public; in fact, it is difficult to realize today how widely read and how influential Ranke, Macauley, Guizot, and Michelet were. The great historians of the early and mid-century wrote for an educated bourgeoisie which had as yet not been completely swallowed by a pluralistic industrial society characterized by the division of labor and by specialization. Within this social grouping there was still a sense of historical unity and purpose which many historians reflected.

Of course not every historian who fell into the general categories of idealist or positivist necessarily subscribed to an optimistic world view, and some who did nevertheless experienced, as we have seen with Ranke, moments of intense fear that the teleology might in the end lack a telos. This motif of doubt, if not dominant, was still strong. The Enlightenment had viewed the past as essentially inferior to the present, and those historians, such as Macauley, who continued the Enlightenment tradition and believed fervently in progress, were inclined to view the past with a certain condescension. Romanticism, on the other hand, adopted an intrinsically negative attitute to contemporary civilization and hence considered the past as inherently superior to the modern age. Romantics became fascinated with the Middle Ages precisely because this period of history had been so neglected hitherto and was associated by the rationalists with stagnation, deterioration, and decline. The Romantics succeeded thereby in encouraging the view that every historical age possessed an inherent integrity and that historical diversity was the norm rather than the basic uniformity of human nature postulated by the *philosophes*. Chateaubriand, Novalis, Heine, and Carlyle disliked the crudely linear and antiseptic approach of much formal history and regretted the lack of attention accorded to individual will or foible, to the mythical, to the contradictory, and to the essentially inexplicable—the "Chaos of Being," in Carlyle's words. The public subscribed to many of these sentiments. Charles Dickens would not have parodied Victorian romanticism and the cult of the Middle Ages in *Dombey and Son,* published in 1848, had the views he accorded to Mrs. Skewton not been widespread: "Those darling byegone times," he had her say, "with their delicious fortresses, and their dear old dungeons, and their delightful places of torture, and their romantic vengeances, and their picturesque assaults and sieges, and everything that makes life truly charming! How dreadfully we have degenerated!"

Within the romantic grouping might also be placed the staunch religionists, such Catholics as the aristocratic Joseph de Maistre and the Vicomte de Bonald who saw in history incontrovertible proof that man was burdened inescapably with original sin and hence destined to err into repeated disasters. "The entire earth, continually steeped in blood," wrote Maistre, "is nothing but an immense altar on which every living thing must be sacrificed without end, without restraint, without respite, until the consummation of all things, the extinction of evil, the death of death."[11] In such a world historical method of course had little reason to improve: Its simple axiom was that man was a wretched sinner beyond hope. Among the firm believers were also such passionate Old Testament spirits as the Scottish Calvinist Carlyle, who berated the "torpid unveracity of heart" of his day which permitted the social evils of capitalism to occur and which denied the essential mystery of creation. Together with Ranke, Carlyle saw divine will imprinted on the historical process; because all power is ultimately divine, "Might is Right in the long run," he declared.[12] Such a view was informed by innate doubt about man's fate as a mortal being and hence about the human prospect.

The idea that Europe had entered a phase of decadence and would experience the same fate as Rome became a leitmotif of historical thinking in the first half of the nineteenth century. The Roman historian Barthold Niebuhr was terribly shaken by the revolution of 1830; he died a few months later convinced that he had witnessed conclusive evidence that Europe had entered the same phase as Rome in the middle of the third century, when, after the death of the last Severus, wars between pretenders and invasions by barbarians gradually destroyed the imperial system. The theme that Europe was following the pattern set by Rome would reach its climax at the turn of the century.

The revolutions of 1848–1849 stand as a transitional point in the development of European thought in the nineteenth century. Even though it is generally recognized that the revolutions—judged by the standards of the activists—failed, the old order could nevertheless not return to the days of the *Vormärz*. Conservatism was forced to turn to a new tactical approach which involved a good deal of compromise and a measure, many pointed out, of intellectual dishonesty. Liberalism, too, felt compelled to turn gradually from its classical principles as its adherents were squeezed between a traditional elite and a burgeoning working class. The year 1848 legitimized ideology in Europe, and ideology corrupted ideals. The economic boom of the 1850s and '60s, coming in the wake of the depression-ridden decade of the 1840s, underlined and reinforced this shift to a sobriety anchored by material considerations.

In this atmosphere of "realism" and realpolitik positivism blossomed as a movement. Now while positivism and its offshoot, scientism, with their emphasis on improvement, exuded on the whole a sense of confidence about history, their point of departure was invariably a sense of the inadequacy of existing conditions—in the case of Comte even an acute sense of social crisis. Consequently, when the economic prosperity of the 1850s and '60s turned into worldwide depression in the 1870s, confidence received a blow, disagreements and schisms surfaced in the official movement, and the notion of degeneration as the direction of history began to appear with noticeable frequency in positivist thought. In other words, optimism and a belief in progress were not inevitable companions of positivism. Nicolai Danilevsky is a case in point. He earned a degree in botany at the University of Saint Petersburg in 1849, and subsequently wrote a number of books on Darwinism and economics. His best known work, however, was *Russia and Europe,* published in 1871, in which he developed a cyclical theory of history. He propounded that all civilizations, like nature, pass through four periods from birth to death. While Slavic culture was in a phase of florescence, the West, he argued, had moved well into its decadent stage. The work became an important item in the slavophile bibliography in the 1880s, and while in its Russian context it was an optimistic document, in Western Europe, where it appeared in French translation in 1890, it of course added fuel to the flames of skepticism. So too did the growing literature of social Darwinism and eugenics, which purported to be based on scientific principles and, following the example of Gobineau's *Essai sur l'inégalité des races humaines* of 1853, argued for the most part that modern history was a protracted and dismal fall from racial purity. In the United States at the end of the century the Adams brothers, Henry and Brooks, became interested in establishing a correlation between physics and history. Referring to the laws of change in physics, they argued that

Western civilization was in a stage of dissipation and disintegration similar to that of late imperial Rome.

The reaction to 1848 gave a boost to an aggressive materialism and positivism, but it also included a marked degree of spiritual disenchantment. Alfred de Musset's *mal du siècle* merged now with a widely held impression of collective failure. World-weariness and despair combined with a sense of momentum, purveyed by the social and economic developments of the 1850s, to produce in a considerable segment of the European population a feeling of "degenerescence"—the feeling, as Metternich who had acted as the "coachman of Europe" for three decades put it, that "to advance means to descend." This was more than mere pessimism, more than a sense that history had entered a new phase of flux; the ineradicable sense of movement, combined with pessimism, meant that a great many Europeans were convinced that civilization was actually regressing.

Positivism, with its international headquarters in the Rue Monsieur-le-Prince in Paris and subsidiary centers in Chapel Street and Newton Hall in London, was an approach to knowledge that was adopted most readily, it would appear, in France and Britain. These were societies which, to be sure, experienced striking social change in the nineteenth century, but they were also societies where that change was, in comparative and historical terms, more measured than, say, in Germany in the second half of the century or Russia at the end of the century. Positivism was subscribed to by members of the middle classes who had confidence in their achievement and potential and who felt that they represented what was best and most advanced in humanity. Such a generalization is not meant to exaggerate the homogeneity of the middle classes. Industrialization and urbanization as they proceeded produced a fragmentation of this social grouping everywhere, and the new strata of technicians, clerks, and managers had social concerns and fears quite different from the older professional and entrepreneurial groups. Nonetheless, it was the rate of change that was so important and that played a decisive role in the degree of social stability. While it is clear that in the last decades of the century a new turbulence was afoot everywhere and on all fronts, the sense of the "modern," of upheaval, and of potential catastrophe was less acute in France and Britain than in Central and Eastern Europe.

Germany was a society which went through the transition from a feudal agrarian past to modern industrial existence in at most three generations, with some parts of the country experiencing the transformation in even less time. Political unity, economic power, military success, imperial acqusitions, and international esteem all arrived suddenly. While Comte's slogan for positivism, of "Order and Progress," fit the aspirations of the German elites and of much of the population as a whole, it did not, however, correspond to the turbulent reality Germans confronted. Positivism in fact found little resonance in Germany.[13]

Consequently, when in the wake of 1848 German historians lost faith in idealism, very few found a new faith in positivism. Of the fifty-seven professors at the Frankfurt parliament in 1848–1849 from non-Austrian Germany, seventeen were historians. Other historians, though not elected to the parliament, were active politically in 1848, and the profession as a whole emerged from its experience of the turmoil with the recognition that neither idealism nor empiricism offered satisfactory solutions to the question of the role of history and of the historian in contemporary society. Gervinus, Dahlmann, Droysen, and Sybel all strongly rejected Ranke's notion, for instance, "that the subject should make itself purely the organ of the object, namely of scholarship itself"; and they went on in the 1850s and '60s to formulate a theory of history in which the historian, with all the influences and impulses that he and his intellect represented, played as important and necessary a part in the writing of history as the source material. In this attempt to synthesize subject and object, members of the so-called Prussian school produced, at its worst, a *Tendenzgeschichte* of monumental banality and, at its best, a new form of political history which extended beyond individuals and events to explore the social and cultural background of the state and politics. This was not so much a revolt against as a rejection of positivism. Nevertheless the new approach laid the groundwork for that "revolt against positivism" which came principally from the peripheries of bourgeois power in Europe.

Auguste Comte defined progress as the advance from superstition to reason; Herbert Spencer defined it as the advance from simplicity to complexity; but many in Germany, Austria, Italy, and Russia were inclined to regard these developments as the reverse of progress, involving a shift from *Gemeinschaft* to *Gesellschaft,* from honesty to dissimulation, from the spiritual to the material, from fertile intuition to sterile reason. Positivism and scientism, it was felt, were the products of *civilization* rather than *Kultur,* of a rampant materialism, of superficiality and pettiness, all of which negated true spiritual culture. A new *Lebensphilosophie* was developed by some thinkers, an intensified relativism by others, and a profound pessimism engulfed still others; all of whom, however, saw in the pretensions of "scientific" history not only a lack of imagination but the extinction of creativity, values, life. In Germany in the second half of the nineteenth century historical positivism came to be regarded as a symbol of sterility and dishonesty. The criticism of it led on the whole, however, not to a coherent reorientation of social and historical thought but to a flight into subjectivism and aestheticism, and ultimately to the negation of history by many as objective knowledge.

Arthur Schopenhauer had already voiced some of these sentiments earlier. In *Die Welt als Wille und Vorstellung* (1819), *Die Freiheit des Willens* (1839), and *Das Fundament der Moral* (1840) he expressed a metaphysical pessimism that saw the world as a playground of irrational, blind forces. He mocked the Hegelian idea of a world spirit proceeding rationally through history; he sneered at the contemporary practice of history. For

Schopenhauer "the motto of history as a whole should be: *Eadem, sed aliter.*" To read into history any completeness, any progress, was to misinterpret, indeed invent, the evidence: "Clio, the muse of history, is as permeated with lies as a street-whore with syphilis."[14] Salvation should not come from history, only from within, from art, or better still from Nirvana. Schopenhauer was largely ignored by his contemporaries, but by the fin de siècle he had become a cult figure in many quarters. An audience at Harvard in the 1890s was told that he was better known than "any other modern continental metaphysician, except Kant."[15]

One of Schopenhauer's great admirers was Jacob Burckhardt, whose work was central to the development of a pessimistic historicism and, in the opinion of Friedrich Meinecke in 1948, has been of greater significance than that of Ranke in the evolution of modern historiography.[16] Burckhardt came from a prosperous patrician background. Born in Basel in 1818, he died there in 1897, and thus his life spans the century. He studied in Berlin but returned to Basel for his doctorate and, after teaching there at intervals from 1844 on, took up the chair for history in 1858. In Berlin he absorbed, alongside Ranke's empiricism, Droysen's view of history as a totality and gradually added to this brew a growing despair about the course of contemporary civilization, in Germany especially—a despair that congealed during the events surrounding 1848—to produce an intensely subjective historical vision. He escaped into the art and architecture of antiquity and Renaissance Italy because already in the 1840s he foresaw the advent of "universal barbarism" and of "everything that is hellish in human nature."[17] In September 1849, after the "springtime of peoples" had turned into the winter of bureaucratized reaction, he confessed, at the still young age of thirty-one, that he hoped "for nothing from the future; possibly we shall be granted a few half-bearable decades, a sort of Roman Empire."

Coming from a long line of distinguished city administrators and churchmen, Burckhardt was rooted in the calm, orderly existence of Swiss Calvinism. He abhorred all the dynamic manifestations of the modern age: large cities, socialists, technology, big business. Paris repelled him when he spent a summer there at the age of twenty-five. His sorties into emerging mass society revealed to him a future governed by "terrible simplifiers" and a "general levelling." The three great spiritual forces of European civilization—classical mythology, Christian dogma, and Renaissance humanism—were disintegrating in the age of revolutions. Mediocrity and anonymity would become the norm, and culture, in the traditional sense, would become a "luxury."

His most famous work, *Die Kultur der Renaissance in Italien,* written between 1858 and 1860 and completed when he was forty-two, was to be the culmination of his intellectual labors, even though he was to teach for another thirty-three years, until 1893, and live for another four years after that. He had published *Die Zeit Konstantins des Grossen* in 1852 and *Der*

Cicerone, a guide to Italian art, in 1855, but these works appear in retrospect to have been preparation for his master work. His other books were to be published posthumously from his lecture notes.

In the opening sentences of *Die Kultur* Burckhardt admitted frankly that his work was "an essay [*ein Versuch*] in the strictest sense of the word" and that others might have interpreted the same material in a completely different manner: "in treating of a civilization which is the mother of our own, and whose influence is still at work among us, it is unavoidable that individual judgement and feeling should tell every moment both on the writer and on the reader." In his later lectures he was to elaborate on this point: "The sources are inexhaustible, for they present a different face to every reader and every century, even to every different age-phase of the same individual. . . . And this is not in the least a misfortune, but simply a consequence of continuously living communication."[18] What was a misfortune, he implied, was that so few of his colleagues appreciated this. Burckhardt's abhorrence of mass man, materialism, and interest politics acted as a filter for his material, and his escape into aestheticism provided a prism which dictated the shades of coloring which the figures and events of the Renaissance received. Thus, only about one-fifth of the book was devoted to political ideas and structures, and even then both the state and war were viewed as "works of art"; the rest of the volume discussed the manners and morals, the art and literature of the age, but almost exclusively with reference to the upper classes. He insisted that his material necessitated such an approach; yet one can be certain that even had material on popular pursuits been readily available, the lower orders would not have received much attention.

Burckhardt's view of the Renaissance was, in short, more an expression of his own interests and his own worldly concerns—particularly his concern for "a world we have lost"—than an attempt to recreate, in a Rankean sense, history "as it actually happened." Moreover, the ultimate Rankean aspiration, to produce a universal history, Burckhardt regarded as a pompous and even arrogant pipedream. "It may be possible to indicate many contrasts and shades of difference among different nations, but to strike the balance of the whole is not given to human insight." To inflict on history any system, any universal meaning, any cosmic purpose, was to pervert it. History must concern itself with the pathological, with man and human nature; it must not be purposive. Here he of course iterated, from another angle, the contemporary sentiments of an emerging artistic avant-garde: the idea that the useful must by definition be ugly. "Life is so horrible," wrote Flaubert, "that one can only bear it by avoiding it. And that can be done by living in the world of Art." The association of the staid conservative Jacob Burckhardt with opinions emanating from the opium dens of the Impasse du Doyenné in Paris may require a leap in imagination, but Burckhardt's view of life and history led him to a position where he was veritably a spiritual confrère of the authors of

Mademoiselle de Maupin, Les Fleurs du mal, and *Madame Bovary.* The personal experience of beauty became everything for him—although even that, he feared, was threatened by the philistines. His method, in the long run, was no less purposive than that of the cosmologists, the idealists, and the positivists. The focus had merely shifted, from an outer to an inner reality, from a social purpose to a sacred egoism. Historical accounts, he maintained, were "mere reflections of ourselves."[19]

All of Burckhardt's major works were produced in one decade, the 1850s. Thereafter his sense of the irrelevance of history, except as a source of beauty and individual pleasure, intensified: "if anything lasting is to be created," he wrote in 1870, "it can only be through an overwhelmingly powerful effort of real poetry." Nevertheless, poetry, art, and beauty were all threatened, for the Franco-Prussian war would inaugurate an "era of wars." The news of "petroleum in the cellars of the Louvre and flames in the other palaces" led him to denounce the doctrine of the goodness of human nature, the idea of freedom, and the insidious notion of progress which he defined as "money-making and modern comforts, with philanthropy as a sop to conscience." "The only conceivable salvation would be for this insane optimism . . . to disappear from people's brains," but he saw no signs of that. By the 1880s Burckhardt was predicting only two alternatives for the future, complete democracy or "absolute, lawless despotism," the latter imposed by military usurpers "who would rule with utter brutality" and whose general password would be: *Maulhalten*—"shut up." He sensed that Germany would be the first to experience the terrible tyranny of these *Gewaltmenschen.* And what should the historian, confronted with this prospect, regard as "the most grateful task"? "Obviously: to amuse people as intensively as possible."

Burckhardt's view of history was an articulate symptom of what came to be called the "crisis of historicism," the gradual dissolution of the object and its replacement by myth and poetry. History became a "remembrance of things past," full of pathos and regret. The process, contrary to the best intentions of Burckhardt, involved a measure of dehumanization. It was an expression of extremism; it involved Burckhardt in a worship of beauty which was as absolute as any worship of Mammon. When Burckhardt berated the masses, the pretenders, the Jews, and the socialists, he devalued his own pretensions to a compassionate humanity. Art became for him more important than humanity; the realm of imagination, aestheticism, became not just a comfort but an avenue of escape. In 1886 he stopped teaching general history and devoted himself exclusively to art history.

Friedrich Nietzsche, Burckhardt's associate at Basel, delivered his inaugural lecture at the university on Homer and classical philology on May 28, 1869, with Burckhardt in the audience. Philology, he argued, could never be a pure science; it invariably had to overlap with art. "Life is worth living, says art, the loveliest seductress; life is worth seeing for what it is, says science."[20] Burckhardt, to the end, had to agree with those sentiments in theory; but his all-embracing ennui gradually overwhelmed any empirical inclination in him and reduced him to silence. The silence to which Nietzsche would be reduced was of course even more dramatic.

While Burckhardt rarely engaged in dispute with his fellow historians, despite his significant departure from the methodological standards of the Rankean era, Nietzsche rejected with virulence the approaches of historians of his age. In his early "Aphorismen über Geschichte und historische Wissenschaft," written while he was still a student in 1867, he insisted: "The historian is looking through a medium constituted by his preoccupations, those of his period and those of his sources. There is no hope of penetrating to the *Ding an sich*."[21] A few years later, in 1874, in *Vom Nutzen und Nachteil der Historie im Leben* he took the argument further, attacking the activities of scholars who believed in empirical reality not merely as an illusion but as a thoroughly destructive pursuit. By purporting to discover truth, these historians were undermining the mythical substance of life; they were destroying the idea of genius and monumentalism. There is no truth in facts, which represent actuality, only in myths and symbols, which represent life. The Hegelians, with their notion of progressively purer forms, and the positivists, with their pretensions that the quality of life was ever improving, were actually destroying life: "No, the *goal of humanity* cannot be located in its end but *in its finest specimens.*"[22] The issue is not why one should live, but how one should live. The only significance that the past could have was in the vitality and spirituality of the present, in the attainment of the "superhistorical"; but contemporary historians had no sense of that and therefore history, as substance, was being negated, and history as practice had become life-destroying antiquarianism. Nietzsche hinted here at the task that lay ahead, an *Umwertung aller Werte*, a new ethic forged on mountain tops, by *Übermenschen*. Burckhardt suffered from a lack, Nietzsche from an excess of will.

Nietzsche regarded himself as a "yea-sayer," a Dionysian affirmer of life, but in his final prescription for achieving human freedom—turning death into a conscious decision, thereby removing it from the realm of necessity—he revealed how his titanism readily translated into nihilism, how the foremost critic of nihilism was also its supreme incarnation. To affirm naked "life" is to affirm absence of meaning, is to negate the object entirely, is to destroy history.

In Turin in January 1889 Nietzsche witnessed a coachman flog a horse. He ran to the horse, embraced it, and collapsed. After being carried home and recovering consciousness he wrote a number of letters, which were to be his last coherent compositions. One was to Jacob Burckhardt, "the Professor." "In the end I would much rather be a Basel professor than God; but I have not dared push my private egoism so far as to desist for its own sake from the creation of the world. . . . What is disagreeable and offends my modesty is that at bottom I am every name in history."[23]

Burckhardt and Nietzsche represented extreme cases, within their intellectual cadre, of cultural despondency and pessimism about the state of historical studies. Neither attained any extensive public recognition during his active career. Nevertheless, despite the isolation from their society and their intellectual context which both at times felt strongly, their thought did indicate an increasingly noticeable tendency, within Germany for the most part, but also in the industrialized world as a whole, where, as the century neared its end, pessimism and a sense of decline accumulated like a heavy marsh gas. The call that Burckhardt received in 1874, but turned down, to the prestigious chair of history in Berlin, to replace Ranke, indicates that recognition from his peers was not lacking. Nietzsche's readership began to grow after the onset of his madness and then climbed strikingly after his death in 1900.

Next to Heinrich von Treitschke, the ultranationalistic celebrant of Teutonism, the most famous professional historian in imperial Germany was probably Theodor Mommsen—he was asked repeatedly to give official state addresses on national holidays and on the emperor's birthday. He had established his reputation in the 1850s with his multivolume history of Rome, and from its publication to the end of his life the most frequent question that he was asked was whether Western civilization was about to experience the fate of Rome. By the 1880s his answer was that he did see in his own society many similar features of "moral decay." The growing pessimism about his own society was accompanied by mounting skepticism about his profession. "The writer of history is perhaps closer to the artist than to the scholar," he said in a rectorial address to the university in Berlin in 1874, thus coming full circle from earlier positivistic inclinations; and his later correspondence contained frequent disparaging remarks about the unimaginative journeymen who abounded in the profession.[24] If Germans dominated the theoretical side of historical work throughout the nineteenth century, this was never more obvious than as the century neared its end. Following the lead given by Droysen, such thinkers as Dilthey, Simmel, Windelband, and Rickert turned the philosophy of history into an increasingly popular field of inquiry. The drift of this work questioned the ability of the historian to understand the past, asserted that all knowledge of the past must be related to the present, and suggested that therefore the objectivity of history disappears. Dilthey argued that the study of history led to self-knowledge, a self-knowledge that then radiated back into history to give it meaning: The subject-object dichotomy disintegrated, and thus "history makes one free." Yet, at the end of his life Dilthey was left with the existential predicament: free for what? *Die Anarchie der Weltanschauungen* was the tragic balance he confronted.[25] The path of introspection and relativism led ultimately to a yawning chasm, symbolized by Burckhardt's silence and Nietzsche's madness.

On the popular level developments in Germany were similar. Julius Langbehn's *Rembrandt als Erzieher*, which was published in 1890 and ran through thirty-nine editions in its first two years, urged Germans to turn their backs on their materialist preoccupations and, following the example of Rembrandt, to turn their lives into heroic works of art. "Schiller superscribed his first book: *in tyrannos*; he who would direct a general address to the Germans today should superscribe it: *in barbaros*. They are not barbarians in coarseness, but in culture. . . . The whole culture of today is Alexandrine, historical, backward-looking." Degeneracy, he said, was the German condition, and historians with their empiricist outlook had contributed, as much as anyone else, to the malaise. Professors as a whole, proclaimed Langbehn, were a German national disease: "The specialist has given away his soul; one might say, indeed, that the Devil is a specialist, just as God is certainly a universalist."[26] Langbehn's impact was reinforced by Houston Stewart Chamberlain, whose enormously successful *Grundlagen des neunzehnten Jahrhunderts* was published in 1899. He derided any pretense to objectivity among historians as "academic barbarism"—*wissenschaftliche Bildungsbarbarei;* history, if it was to be of any interest, had to be another form of poetry. While Chamberlain advocated a life based on myth, legend, and art—of which the purported Wagnerian synthesis of art and life in the *Gesamtkunstwerk* was the prototype—his entire neurotic endeavor was founded on a sense of personal failure. He was an Englishman who became a German, a sickly man who fawned upon the *Übermensch*, and, of particular interest here, a budding scientist of considerable promise who never completed his doctorate and became a *Feuilletonist* and self-proclaimed historian instead. His racially motivated *Lebenslehre* notwithstanding, many reputable intellectuals heaped praises on his work, George Bernard Shaw among them, who urged all those who wished to keep abreast of the best in current historical literature to read Chamberlain's *Foundations*.[27]

Intellectually, Germany was hardly the "encircled," isolated state which her imperial leadership claimed her to be politically by the end of the century. In 1875 83 percent of the professors in Russia had received their first degrees in Germany.[28] In 1895 one-half of the historians in the United States had received some part of their training in Germany.[29] Gabriel Monod, the first editor of the *Revue Historique*, founded in 1876, could call Germany "this second homeland for all men who study and think," recalling his mentor Michelet's remark: "Germany is the bread of life for strong minds."[30] British historical studies, too, were strongly influenced by German historicism. Stubbs, Seeley, Acton, and Maitland made repeated acknowledgment of their indebtedness to German historical thought. "As a rule," wrote Seeley, "good books are in German."[31] Thus it is not surprising that the doubt about the purpose and method of historical work evident in Germany should radiate from that country to the world as a whole.

In Russia the thesis of the decaying West was one of the ideological pillars of both the slavophile and the populist movements, which grew in significance proportionately to the social and economic change introduced from the West. Building on the work of Schlözer and Schelling, both of whom had predicted early in the century a great destiny for Russia, such writers as Homyakov, Dostoevsky, and Leontiev argued that occidental Europe had betrayed its past and had repudiated true culture in favor of atheistic, materialistic civilization. Russia's historical purpose, said some, was to revive European civilization, but the more extreme slavophiles wanted to divorce Russia from the West entirely. The desire that Russia establish an authentically spiritual culture was of course the positive impulse behind slavophilism, but there was an equally strong negative consideration as well: the fear that Russia was being dangerously infected by soulless Western ways. The veneration of the peasant commune and the promotion of the idea of a federation of all Slavic peoples came to be regarded as the means of negating negation. The apocalypticism and despair in the Russian revolutionary tradition bordered in many quarters on Nietzschean nihilism. "Better to perish with the revolution than to seek refuge in the almshouse of reaction," wrote Alexander Herzen to his son.[32]

The turbulent *affaire de cœur* which the French had with the Russians from the early 1890s to World War I was prompted in large part by strategic and political considerations, which were in turn provoked by a sense of vulnerability in the face of growing German power, but there was also in the relationship a good measure of intrinsic doubt about *l'idée française*. The wave of popularity that Russian culture enjoyed in France, from the success of Tolstoy and Dostoevsky to the frenetic acclaim accorded the *Ballets Russes* when they arrived in Paris in 1909, suggests a profound yearning for the spirituality and new forms which the Russians offered. The epithet "barbaric" was employed constantly by French critics to describe the Russian imports but almost always with a *frisson* of delight. The Russians, on the other hand, were hardly offended by such terms. Alexandre Benois, the Russian painter and designer, captured the blend of arrogance and condescension present in the attitude of Russian artists in France when he described the success of the 1909 Russian season in Paris. "We have shown the Parisians what theater should be. . . . This trip was clearly a historic necessity. We are, in contemporary civilization, the ingredient without which it would corrode entirely."[33] Many in the West of course exulted in the rising tide of "barbarism" which was associated with vitalism and regeneration. For William Morris it carried hope that the world might become "beautiful and dramatic" again.[34]

Europe, at the fin de siècle, was a civilization triumphant. A small cape of the Asiatic continent controlled the globe. In world-historical perspective that achievement was truly stunning. The control was based largely on a belief in science, rationalism, and progress. The evidence for that control speaks for itself, and thus to argue that a sense of degeneracy and decline was dominant in Europe as a whole at the end of the century would be nonsensical. Pessimism, as Nietzsche recognized, was still "untimely." Nevertheless, the achievement was accompanied by a backwash which gained in size and momentum in relation to the vessel as it slowed. And by the end of the century the vessel clearly had slowed; of that there was no doubt anywhere. Ludwig Büchner, the early scientific materialist, commented in 1898 that an enormous gap had emerged between scientific and technical progress on the one hand and moral behavior on the other.[35] He himself felt that the gap could be bridged, but a presentiment of doom or, at the very least, the expectation of a radical reorientation gripped the minds of many. Nationalist movements in the colonies were gaining strength. The Italians had trouble subduing the Ethiopians in 1895–1896; Spain was driven from Cuba and the Philippines in 1898; Britain struggled to defeat the Boers; and, when, five years into the new century, Russia was soundly trounced by Japan, who could any longer confidently assert European world hegemony? Henry Adams noted in February 1910, from Washington, that the pessimism of Malthus, Marx, and Schopenhauer was "openly preached now on all sides," and when he arrived in Europe that summer he was struck by the imminence of a "moral débâcle," which, he predicted, would be complete in ten, possibly even five years: "The risk of a general disappearance of all civilized society has become a nightmare in Europe. Even the newspapers discuss it constantly."[36] Oswald Spengler conceived his *Untergang des Abendlandes* in 1911 in the wake of the Moroccan crisis.

A parable, related in the *New Statesman* in 1913, told of a passenger, on an express train that had made an unexpected stop at a suburban station, who decided that he would descend from the train. "You can't get off here," said the conductor to the passenger who was already standing on the platform. "But," came the reply, "I *have* got off." "The train doesn't stop here," insisted the conductor. "But," said the former passenger, "it *has* stopped."[37] Most passengers of course failed to follow, much less comprehend, the initiative of the rebel. Faith in European civilization and in history, its collective meaning and purpose, was still strong. It was to take the first world war to tip the balance toward doubt for many and the holocaust of the second to complete the "journey to despair." When James Joyce had Stephen Dedalus say that history had become "a nightmare" from which he was "trying to awake," he echoed Schopenhauer's earlier assessment that history is "the long, difficult and confused dream of mankind."[38]

It was again the Germans who systematically took historicism, vitalism, and relativism to their twentieth-century conclusion of absolute philosophical nihilism, a nihilism that would be translated to the political arena by National Socialism. For Ernst Jünger, Carl Schmitt, and Martin Heidegger, *Geschichte* had been negated and only *Geschichtlichkeit* remained. Life consisted now *only* of movement, action, process; existence rather than essence; form rather than content; struggle without meaning. H. A. L. Fisher, who had studied in Göttingen before the war, was on similar shifting ground when he wrote the preface to his *History of Europe* in 1934 and made a declaration which probably has been quoted more often than any other single theoretical statement written in this century by a historian: "Men wiser and more learned than I have discerned in history a plot, a rhythm, a predetermined pattern. These harmonies are concealed from me. I can see only one emergency following upon another as wave follows upon wave."

Twentieth-century culture has become alienated from history and has adopted an ahistorical, even anti-historical, form. Schopenhauer had suggested that history is to mankind what reason is to the individual. When Dada said, "La vie est une chose vraiment idiote," it rejected both reason and history. *Irre regieren Irre* insisted a graffito recently on a wall in front of the Römer, the former residence of the Holy Roman Emperors, in Frankfurt.[39] If all is madness then there can of course be no history. A century and a half earlier the young Russian Hegelian, Stankevich, had written quite the opposite: "There is only one salvation from madness—history."[40]

"In little more than two centuries," Susan Sontag has reflected, "the consciousness of history has transformed itself from a liberation, an opening of doors, blessed enlightenment, into an almost insupportable burden of self-consciousness."[41] In view of the collapse of external reality, Egon Friedell was led to assert in 1931 that "history does not exist,"[42] and many have joined in that refrain since. But if history has been called into question, most professional historians are not even aware that a problem exists. The vast majority have long since ceased to worry about meaning in history. The empiricists plough on, adding, they claim, to our knowledge, little concerned with implications and even less concerned with public impact; a vast army of scholars in the employ of facts. The public, while on occasion still responsive to bold synthesis, has also lost interest in the meaning of history: The speed and complexity of existence, which in the industrializing society of the nineteenth century at first encouraged historical awareness, now in our "post-technological society" elicit a pervasive confusion and ennui. One author has spoken, as a result, about the "loss of history" characteristic of our own age.[43] W. H. Auden, in *The Double Man*, addressed such an age, an age without History:

The situation of our time
Surrounds us like a baffling crime.

NOTES

1. "I believe it to be a barbarism, to keep birds in a cage." Jacob Burckhardt, *Historische Fragmente,* in *Gesamtausgabe* (cited hereafter as *GA*), Albert Oeri and Emil Dürr, eds. (Stuttgart: Deutsche Verlags-Anstalt, 1929), 7:227.

2. Max Beloff, *Imperial Sunset.* Vol. 1: *Britain's Liberal Empire, 1897–1921* (New York: Knopf, 1970), p. 20.

3. Burckhardt, *Historishe Fragmente,* in *GA,* 7:421.

4. J. S. Mill, "The Spirit of the Age" (1831), in *Essays in Politics and Culture,* Gertrude Himmelfarb, ed. (Garden City, N.Y.: Anchor-Doubleday, 1962), p. 1.

5. G. P. Gooch, *History and Historians in the Nineteenth Century* (London: Longmans, 1913), p. 302.

6. G. W. Prothero in *The National Review,* December 1894, p. 461, quoted in Lord Acton, *The Study of History* (London: Macmillan, 1895), p. 131.

7. Benedetto Croce, *History as the Story of Liberty,* Sylvia Sprigge, tr. (London: Allen and Unwin, 1941), p. 35.

8. Hayden V. White, "On History and Historicism," introduction to Carlo Antoni, *From History to Sociology,* H. V. White, tr. (London: Merlin, 1962), pp. ix–xxviii.

9. Fritz Stern, ed., *The Varieties of History* (Cleveland: Meridian-World, 1956), p. 62.

10. Friedrich Nietzsche, *Jenseits von Gut und Böse,* in *Werke,* Karl Schlechta, ed. (Frankfurt am Main: Ullstein, 1972), 3:17.

11. Joseph de Maistre, *Les Soirées de Saint-Pétersbourg* (Paris: Pélagaud, 1854), 1:32, 214; 2:32.

12. Pieter Geyl, *Debates with Historians* (Cleveland: Meridian-World, 1958), p. 62.

13. W. M. Simon, *European Positivism in the Nineteenth Century* (Ithaca, N.Y.: Cornell University Press, 1963), ch. 9.

14. Arthur Schopenhauer, "Über Geschichte," *Die Welt als Wille und Vorstellung,* in *Arthur Schopenhauer Werke in zwei Bänden,* Werner Brede, ed. (Munich: Hauser, 1977), 2:44–53; and Egon Friedell, *A Cultural History of the Modern Age,* C. F. Atkinson, tr. (New York: Knopf, 1954), 3:7.

15. Josiah Royce, *The Spirit of Modern Philosophy* (1892, rpt. New York: Braziller, 1955), p. 228.

16. Friedrich Meinecke, "Ranke and Burckhardt," in *German History: Some New German Views,* Hans Kohn, ed., Herbert H. Rowen, tr. (London: Allen and Unwin, 1954), p. 143.

17. This and other quotations from Burckhardt's correspondence come from *The Letters of Jacob Burckhardt,* Alexander Dru, ed. and tr. (London: Routledge, 1955), p. 97 and passim.

18. Burckhardt, *Weltgeschichtliche Betrachtungen,* in *GA,* 7:15–16.

19. Burckhardt, *Historische Fragmente,* in *GA,* 7:225, 426–27; and *Weltgeschichtliche Betrachtungen,* in *GA,* 7:4.

20. Ronald Hayman, *Nietzsche* (New York: Oxford University Press, 1980), p. 109.

21. Hayman, p. 86.

22. Friedrich Nietzsche, *Unzeitgemässe Betrachtungen*, in *Werke*, 1:270.

23. *The Portable Nietzsche*, Walter Kaufmann, ed. and tr. (New York: Viking, 1954), pp. 685–86.

24. Theodor Mommsen, *Reden und Aufsätze* (1905, rpt. Hildesheim: Olms, 1976), p. 91; Alfred Heuss, *Theodor Mommsen und das 19. Jahrhundert* (Kiel: Hirt, 1956), pp. 92–93, 111.

25. Gerhard Masur, *Prophets of Yesterday* (London: Weidenfeld, 1963), p. 167.

26. The volume was initially published anonymously, *Rembrandt als Erzieher* (Leipzig: Hirschfeld, 1890), pp. 1–2, 69–70, 95–96, and passim. See also the excellent discussion of Langbehn by Fritz Stern, *The Politics of Cultural Despair* (Berkeley: University of California Press, 1961).

27. Geoffrey G. Field, *Evangelist of Race: The Germanic Vision of Houston Stewart Chamberlain* (New York: Columbia University Press, 1981), pp. 177, 262.

28. James C. McClelland, *Autocrats and Academics: Education, Culture, and Society in Tsarist Russia* (Chicago: University of Chicago Press, 1979), pp. 61–62.

29. J. Franklin Jameson, "The American Historical Review, 1895–1920," *American Historical Review* (1920), 26:2.

30. Claude Digeon, *La Crise allemande de la pensée française (1870–1914)* (Paris: Presses Universitaires de France, 1959), p. 374; and Gooch, p. 169.

31. Klaus Dockhorn, *Der deutsche Historismus in England* (Göttingen: Vandenhoeck, 1950), p. 217 and passim.

32. Alexander Herzen, *From the Other Shore*, Moura Budberg, tr. (London: Weidenfeld, 1956), p. 3.

33. Alexandre Benois, "Lettres artistiques: Les Représentations russes à Paris," typescript in the papers of Gabriel Astruc, 30/11–14, with ascription "Journal de St. Pétersbourg, 2 July 1909," in the Dance Collection, New York Public Library.

34. Nikolaus Pevsner, *Pioneers of Modern Design*, rev. ed. (Harmondsworth: Penguin, 1960), p. 24.

35. Walter Wiora, "'Die Kultur kann sterben': Reflexionen zwischen 1880 und 1914," in Roger Bauer et al., eds., *Fin de siècle* (Frankfurt am Main: Klostermann, 1977), p. 50.

36. *Letters of Henry Adams*, W. C. Ford, ed. (New York: Houghton Mifflin, 1938), 2:535, 551, 553.

37. Gerald Gould, "Art and Morals," *The New Statesman*, August 23, 1913, pp. 625–26.

38. Arthur Schopenhauer, *Ein Lesebuch*, Arthur and Angelika Hübscher, eds. (Wiesbaden: Brockhaus, 1980), p. 168.

39. Photograph reproduced in *Die Zeit*, January 8, 1982.

40. James H. Billington, *The Icon and the Axe* (New York: Vintage, 1970), p. 325.

41. Susan Sontag, *Styles of Radical Will* (New York: Farrar, 1976), p. 14.

42. Friedell, 3:467.

43. Alfred Heuss, *Verlust der Geschichte* (Göttingen: Vandenhoeck, 1959).

2

ANTHROPOLOGY AND DEGENERATION: BIRDS, WORDS, AND ORANGUTANS

JAMES A. BOON
Cornell University

A recent issue of the journal *Archipel* cites current examples of the Western habit of representing Indonesia by simplified extremes: whether images of its most famous tourists' paradise or reports about its most notorious hellhole for political prisoners. In the stereotypes of the French media, Indonesia thus becomes "a distant world, at once attractive because of its exotic landscapes and repulsive because of the rigors of its regime: a simplified vision that could be expressed schematically with the *binôme* 'Bali-Buru.'"[1] This sensational conjunction of the presumable "isle of the gods" (*pulau dewata* in Indonesia's domestic tourism slogans for Bali) and the actual isle of inhuman incarceration is a *vision simplifiée* that Indonesia now provides as a representation of itself.

Archipel's contemporary polar image (half of which the Indonesian government would wish to conceal) comes at the end of a long history of formulations by outsiders that schematized Indonesian peoples, obscured their complexities, and made them appear both alluring and repelling. *Archipel* adds a word of qualification to today's popular French idea of "Bali-Buru": "between these two extremes, that there is no question of avoiding, there exists the entire history and the density of everyday life of a population numbering some 130 million." Similar observations apply to past representations of Indonesia, even scholarly ones, including those enduring ethnological stereotypes this paper surveys and samples. Even when past observers managed somewhat to penetrate the *épaisseur* of a people's everyday life, they seldom failed to reinsinuate polar schemes, as if to excuse (if only to their readers) having lingered too long over drier details. In ethnology, as in mythology, the appeal has proved often to stem from the enticing extremes.

Regenerative Degeneracies

Because of its very pervasiveness, the concept of degeneracy is difficult to isolate in the intellectual history of anthropology. In her influential *Early Anthropology in the Sixteenth and Seventeenth Centuries* (1971), Margaret Hodgen's discussion of the issue focuses on Renaissance and Reformation figures like Johann Boemus, the German Hebraist whose *Omnium Gentium Mores* (1520), translated into English as the *Fardle of façions* (1555), syncretized the Bible and ethnological information from travelers, missionaries, and traders. Works by Sebastian Muenster (*Cosmographica*, 1544), Thomas More (*Utopia*, 1516), and the French jurist Jean Bodin (best known as a forerunner of environmental determinism)—representatives of diverse religious factions during the sixteenth century—shared Boemus' dilemma of restoring authority after confidence in the accuracy of Scripture had been shaken. Boemus' notion of degeneracy tied to human diversity helped consolidate issues in ethnological interpretation for centuries to come. While mankind suffered the Fall in Genesis, evil became manifest *as diversity* only with the flood:

> according to his reworking of the Scriptural narrative, it was Ham, a son of Noah, not Cain, who severed the Adamic bond. It was he who vanished into Arabia. . . . During these migrations, even the language was altered, "and knowledge of the true God and all godlie worshippe vanished out of mind"; so that in the end those who went to Egypt founded the worship of the sun and moon, while many others became so uncivil and barbarous "as hardly any difference be discerned between them and brute beasts." . . . distance, weakening the slender threads of memory and the process of transmission "of minde to minde without Letters," led to the decline of ancient institutions. With this process of degeneration, a state of barbarism descended upon the sons of Ham.[2]

As Hodgen indicates, this "theory of the degeneration of savagery" stemmed from "the ancient and medieval belief, still viable during the Renaissance, that the world and man were subject to inevitable and progressive decay" (p. 378). But the Renaissance equation of degeneracy and diversity led observers increasingly to refine and elaborate the symbols of corruption; later, various Enlightenment figures would project the stigmas onto lower categories of their taxonomies of mankind, rather than onto doctrinal opponents in sectarian disputes.

Hodgen lodges notions of degeneracy in Renaissance-Reformation pessimism reinforced by the Age of Discoveries. But her evidence shows how difficult it is to stipulate their eras or areas. From the German Boemus in 1520 one can leap to the remarkable study on degradation in the tongues of men by the Britisher B. Brerewood in 1614; one can then jump to the renowned Frenchman Lafitau (*Mœurs des sauvages amériquains*, 1724) for whom "the problem of variation in religion remained orthodox and unchanged. . . . The religion of the Indians of North America was thus the result of decay" (p. 268). Eventually one finds nineteenth-century American proslavery agitators, such as J. C. Nolt and G. R. Glidden, who "reiterated the old story that the blacks failed to belong to the same creation as the whites, that their organization doomed them to slavery and precluded their improvement." Hodgen adds that American Indians were likewise branded unimprovable by means of a particularly convoluted reasoning: "Indian archeological monuments were interpreted as the work of people greatly superior to the rude tribes found by Europeans in these regions, and were taken, therefore, as indications of degeneration" (p. 381).

This representative selection, which can look like a simple series of influences, in fact conceals crucial transformations in the notion of degeneracy itself (if indeed it is an isolable concept): from the bottom human rung in an all-enfolding, plenitudinous Great Chain of Being (largely a model of morality) to a qualitative sectioning of humanity into disparate species (largely a model of physicality). Such variation is a central concern of Hodgen's study but as a historian she wants to disclose a strict development. She assumes the history of ideas unfolds as conventional historians imagine the history of events unfolds: abruptly and in bold periodizations. Her task, then, is to spotlight its substantive eras. Having once evoked the vague, lingering, gloomy ancient and medieval doctrine of corruption in which "the savage was only a little more corrupt than anybody else" (p. 278), she outlines sharp discontinuities, creating two more stages. One she locates in works at the end of the seventeenth century:

> The break came . . . with Sir William Petty's abortive essay entitled *The scale of creatures* (1676–77), Sir William Tyson's *Orang-outang, sive homo silvestris; or, the anatomy of a pygmie* (1708), and Carl Linnaeus' *System of nature* (1735). After the publication of these books mankind was no longer considered a perfect whole, standing alone and indivisible in an unassailable central position in the hierarchy, with the animals classified and ranked below him and the angels classified and ranked above. In both biological and ethnological inquiry the discovery of "missing links" became the order of the day. It became the task of the naturalist to effect a rapprochement between man and the ape and of the student of man to compose an acceptable social or cultural hierarchy as an extension of the biological. (p. 418)

The next stage she overdramatizes as a muted revolution in ideas, without explaining how this "event" could have been so clear-cut, given the earlier dawn of the "missing link" idea. In Hodgen's tradition of the emergence of evolutionism in the 1860s, we can almost hear a *Zeitgeist* go "Bang":

> Overnight, as it were, and in the almost uncanny silence of unquestioning agreement, the hierarchical concept of nature, which once was

taken to be an orderly arrangement of forms in space, became a progressive sequence in time. The savage, who in the context of the medieval schematization of the universe had been given a merely logical and spatial antecedence to European man, was now endowed with temporal or historical priority. Meanwhile, the doctrine of degeneration, which had so long darkened the human spirit, seemed to give way quite suddenly to its opposite, the doctrine of progress. For the zoological world the temporalized hierarchy became natural history, or the evolutionary series; and for the cultural world it became culture history, or the developmental or evolutionary cultural series. (p. 451)

Hodgen here risks underestimating the complexity of nineteenth-century attitudes, when she assumes that the rise of a doctrine of progress automatically implies cancellation of degeneracy. (Indeed, below we find a kind of bifocal view of Europe as both extremes in no less an evolutionist than A. R. Wallace). In her account, the history of ethnological ideas seems devoid of internal contradictions, and the rhythm of its movement appears cataclysmic. One might say that Hodgen's march of the idea of degeneracy itself conforms to a model of degeneracy.

I doubt that intellectual history happens this way. And certainly intellectual historians should not unquestioningly depict things this way. It may prove more accurate to think of shifting matrices rather than doctrines: divinity/degeneracy distinctions (or even divinity/degeneracy/decadence distinctions), each side capable of elaboration and transformation, but always in implicit reference to the other. The West's so-called doctrine of degeneracy has possibly been applied to exotic cultures in a fashion more prismatic than cataclysmic. In its indirect manifestations no stage—Great Chain of Being, implicit missing links, separable species, evolutionary sequence—need ever be left behind, just as none is altogether absent from the start.[3]

It is this more dialectic, evasive, even surreptitious rhythm that characterizes ideals of degeneracy/divinity in fundamental Western texts on Indonesia. To demonstrate this point, I shall highlight two moments from the history of a complex ethnological discourse. We first glance at the earliest records of Western contact with Malay speakers. We then leap to a nineteenth-century genre: the first-person travel narrative, represented by A. R. Wallace's meandering natural history, *The Malay Archipelago*. This bizarre book of cultures and nature drew on earlier "descriptive histories" (an important variety of comparative study that limitations of space preclude our considering). Yet the genre aimed to please with adventure tales, and adventure required personal contact with signs of divinity/degeneracy. Wallace's text demonstrates that even a tome dedicated "to Charles Darwin, author of *The Origin of Species*," transgressed the boundaries of the evolutionary school's doctrine of degeneracy as depicted by Hodgen. Indeed, Wallace's popular book restored rumors of Renaissance-style divinity/degeneracy; where evidence for the rumors was sparse in ethnography, certain animal species from nature could be used to implicate cultures, as it were, by contamination.

A Prologue of Pigafetta

We owe so many names the world over to Antonio Pigafetta, from "Patagonians" to the antipodal "Ave de paraiso", from the "Big-footed" devil worshippers of Tierra del Fuego to the feathery divines of the "odorous Moluccas." The last-named creatures appear repeatedly over four and a half centuries of Western texts on Indonesian lands and peoples, particularly its clove-producing islands: "Tarenatte, Tadore, Mutin, Machian and Bachian."[4] One vivid example of such accounts, which looks back to Pigafetta's *Prima Viaggio* (1525), appears in John Crawfurd's lively and influential *Descriptive Dictionary of the Indian Islands* (1856):

> PARADISE, (BIRDS OF). The first mention made of these remarkable birds is by Pigafetta, who informs us that the king of Bachian, one of the true Moluccas, gave the companions of Magellan a pair of them, along with a slave, and two bahars, or near 1000 pounds weight of cloves, as a gift to the emperor Charles the Fifth. "He gave us besides," says he, "two most beautiful dead birds. These are about the size of a thrush, have small heads, long bills, legs a palm in length, and as slender as a writing quill. In lieu of proper wings they have long feathers of different colors, like great ornamental plumes. Their tail resembles that of a thrush. All the other feathers, except those of the wings, are of a dark color. They never fly, except when the wind blows. They informed us that these birds came from the terrestrial paradise, and they called them *Bolondinata*, that is 'birds of God.'" . . . The name of the bird as given by Pigafetta in this account of it, is properly *burungdewata;* and I have no doubt was correctly enough written by the author but corrupted in transcription. It is the Malay name, and signifies "bird of the gods"; that is, of the Hindu *deutas* or deities. . . . Before the arrival of the Europeans, the Malay and Javanese traders seem to have brought the birds of Paradise to the western emporia of the Archipelago from the Spice Islands, most probably for sale to the Chinese, for such an article would not have been in demand either by Hindu or Mahommedan consumers.[5]

Consider, then, these birds of paradise, undesired by Hindus and Muslims, sought after by Chinese and Europeans, but doubtless for different reasons. Pigafetta seems to connect the birds intimately with the evidence of kingship he enthusiastically reports from these actual fortunate isles. His accounts suggest that nature itself turns divine in this peculiar locale—"that entire province where cloves grow . . . called Malucho." In this topsy-turvy climate the cloves are gathered twice a year, "once at the nativity of our Savior, . . . and the other at the nativity of St. John the Baptist."[6] In the scheme of Renaissance similitudes possibly tucked into Pigafetta's text, nature joins society in testimony to the divinity of this unique place: heavenly birds coincide with cloves and with kings rather than cannibals. In the very paragraph cited by Crawfurd, Pigafetta proceeds to associate the omen of the birds (of a singular deity!) with a proper alliance of kings: "they call them *bolon diuata*, that is to say, 'birds of God.' On that day each one of the kings of Maluco wrote to the king of Spagnia [to say] that they desired to be always his true subjects" (12:105). Crawfurd's *Dictionary*, of course, does not perpetuate Pigafetta's Renaissance interpretation; yet those fragmentary signs and symbols within the names Pigafetta bestowed remain; and Crawfurd's summary anticipates the culmination of tales Pigafetta initiated in Wallace's *Malay Archipelago* (1869), by which time bagging a bird of paradise was an adventure de rigueur for explorers of the exotic East Indies. Alas, nature, and the Indonesian cultures that again in nineteenth-century narratives appear to echo its various modes, will reveal other faces as well, including degenerate ones.

The subtle situation of degeneracy in stereotypes of Indonesia is part of the story I have to tell. But first we should consider how from the beginning, although the Moluccas seemed divinely endowed, the diabolical lurked offstage.

Pigafetta had arrived with Ferdinand Magellan off Ternate and Tidor in 1521. Throughout the three-year voyage (1519–1522) it was Pigafetta's task to write. By 1525 he published an account that included the first extensive Malay word list in a European language. While he possibly compiled it to further Western trade contacts, no one really knows quite why or exactly how Pigafetta wrote.[7] We are not even sure when the vocabulary was inscribed, although the "most prudent opinion is that he composed it after his return to Europe, utilizing miscellaneous notes taken in different places."[8] We know even less about his sources: how much did he rely on Magellan's slave Enrique, a Malay-speaking Sumatran? Does the "Vocaboli de Questi Popoli More" conceal under its "Moorish" label a Molluken-Maleisch, or is it a trade-language Malay tinged with Filipino? Asianist linguists, philologists, and lexicographers today scrutinize Pigafetta's 426 entries to guess what the words spoken in 1521 must actually have been. (To my knowledge no modern dragoman has been warned off by the coincidence that Pigafetta's term #331, which poses *girobaza—juru bahasa* in contemporary Malay spelling—as "interpreter," is immediately preceded by the Malay *gila, al mato* or madman!).

I want to raise questions about Pigafetta's list by sifting its words through four categories outlined by Kenneth Burke in his *Rhetoric of Religion*.[9] Most entries are "words for the natural," including things, material operations, body parts, flora, fauna, items of material culture. Among these are terms for the eight winds and for fifty-four numbers from one to one million. Pigafetta includes scattered adjectives (tired, angry), verbs (to trade), and assorted simple expressions from "Don't be afraid" to "Oh, how it stinks!" A few entries cover what Burke calls "words about words": for example, *berapa bahasa tahu?*, "How many languages do you know?" (*Quanti lingagi sai?*). "Words for the socio-political realm," primarily reciprocal social relationships, are better represented. We find unmarried/married (*bujang/sudah berbini*) and friend/enemy (*saudara/sobat*). Earlier, starting with item eleven, there is a list of kinship terms: father, mother, child, brother, cousin (*saudara sepupu*), grandfather, father-in-law, son-in-law.

This brings us to Burke's final category, "words for the supernatural." And oddly enough, it brings us as well to the beginning of Pigafetta's list. Here are the initial entries:

God (al suo Ydio)	Allah
Christian	nasrani (naceran)
Turk	rumi
Muslim Moor	islam
Heathen	Kafir (Caphre)
Mosques	mesdjid
Priests	maulana, katib, modin
Wise Men	orang pendeta (horin pandita)
Devout Men	(mossai)
Their Ceremonie	sembahyang didalam mesdjid

Contrary to the desire of modern scholars, we know little about this list, save the list itself. We do, however, know something about Renaissance arts of interpretation, whereby scriveners considered the world, and the life and language in it, a closed book. We can surmise that Pigafetta wrote as Magellan voyaged: circularly. In crossing from the Old World to the New and on back to the Old, he probably saw and heard according to conventions less like linguistic empiricism and more like Great Chains of Being. Certainly it is according to the latter conventions that he organized his word lists.

Next comes something we do know about Pigafetta, although little has been made of the fact. Pigafetta compiled four word lists: besides the 426 Malay items, 160 Philippine terms from a "heathen" (*gentili*) people of Zubu; eight words from a Brazilian tribal language (millet, flour, fish-hook, knife, comb, scissors, good/better), and ninety words from the Patagonians of Tierra del Fuego. In terms of simple information, taking the Brazilian list as our standard, we know eleven times as much about the Patagonians, twenty times about the Philippine population, and fifty-two times about the Malays. But any quantification of information obscures, indeed belies, the critical dimensions of Pigafetta's lists. Because modern scholarship segments itself into geographical areas, Asianists have ignored Pigafetta's New World words, just as Americanists have passed by his insular Asian vocabularies. But I suspect that the lists have as much to do with each other as with what they purport to report.

Certain items are standard; even the brief Brazilian list includes fish-hook (in Malay *mata kail*), and the longer lists reveal strings of terms in standard order: after Patagonian armpit and Malay heart, both have nearly identical runs—in Malay teat, stomach (here Patagonian has bosom), body, penis (Patagonian adds testicles), vagina, communication with women, buttocks (Patagonian lacks this entry), thighs, etc. Our concern, however, is with nonstandard items. Some entries—"wood eaten by beavers" on the Malay list, for example—seem too specific to recur. Other nonstandard aspects of the list may be more meaningful. Recall that the Malay words commence with Allah and the text on the Moluccas presents elaborate courts full of splendors and intrigues: tales of designing queens, pretenders to thrones, processions of praus with 120 oarsmen in tiers, rowing to the sound of gongs beneath banners of parrot feathers "filled with girls to present them to [a king's] betrothed" (1:80). (Even the heathen Philippine list includes before its numerals the term *raja* [*raia*] "for a king or captain-general"). Then compare at once Pigafetta's "Words of the Patagonian giants." It opens with body parts and, a few verbs aside, restricts itself to simple objects; until the last two items that resound down the history of ethnological imagery: *Setebos* "for their big Devil" (*al diauolo grande*); *cheleule* "for their small ones" (*ali picoli*).

That the Malay list commenced with Allah, sectarian divisions, and names of religious specialists does more than identify the Moluccans as "Moorish people." Joined with the text on kingship, it suggests legitimate monarchs, some of them distinctly "Moro," such as the king of Giailolo; others less so. But the religion is ordered in proper alliances of kings: "That king told us that since we were friends of the king of Tadore, we were also his friends, for he loved that king as one of his own sons" (2:85). As soon as the account leaves the Moluccas, Pigafetta's narrative grows less grandiose, more *pizzicato*. Just after the word list, we pass into fragmented tales of realms antithetical to kingship: an island inhabited by a race "as small as dwarfs"; Sulach, whose heathen inhabitants "have no king, and eat human flesh"; another lofty island whose "savage and bestial" inhabitants "eat human flesh . . . have no king, and go naked"; and alas, Buru, "inhabited by Moros and heathens. The Moros live near the sea, and the heathens in the interior. The latter eat human flesh."

The conventions in Pigafetta opposing bedeviled heathens to divinely ordained kings are clear. The Moluccan monarchs are now in league with the king of Spagnia rather than the ruler of Portagalo. Again: "Each one of the kings of Maluco wrote to the king of Spagnia [to say] that they desired to be always his true subjects" (2:105). It was these same kings who kept at bay the degenerate forces of nearby islands and who presumably thwarted such forces within their own lands. In Pigafetta's entire account, however, the ultimate contrast to the kings of Ternate and Tidor is the group of diabolical, antipodal Patagonians half a world away. Not that the New World is altogether devoid of kingly signs: the text on Brazil includes a word for their king (*cacich*). But like the *degeneracy* imagery in Indonesia, these hints of *divinity* in the Americas remain scattered, if not invisible. New World ethnological stereotypes are centralized around the imagined degeneracy of Patagonians. Thus, Pigafetta, particularly in the order and contrasts of his word lists, inscribed Indonesia and Patagonia as ethnological antitheses.[10]

In short, these early accounts epitomized Indonesia in terms of its favored locale: scene of cloves, mace, paradise birds, and proper kingship. In this part of the globe, the marks of degeneracy—cannibalism and nakedness—remained dispersed or unseen. But in future accounts, produced under different historical circumstances, attributions of degeneracy would encroach once more on the ethnology of Malay-speaking lands.

Between Wallace's Lines

Indonesian studies as we know them today first developed in a late eighteenth and early nineteenth-century genre of English-language "descriptive histories." Fundamental books by William Marsden on Sumatra, Stamford Raffles on Java, and John Crawfurd on the archipelago at large flirted with various ideas of decay; but even these three connected works by near-contemporary co-patriots fracture Hodgen's stages of degeneracy theory and raise doubts about any possibility of an integral doctrine.[11] I must reserve commentary on this genre for another study; still, we should note that the first-person narratives discussed below developed after and in light of compendia by philologist-historians. The connections between the two genres are subtle and diverse. One can appreciate certain indirect linkages from a peculiar preface by Sir Arthur Keith (M.D., D.Sc., LL.D., F.R.S.) to the final work (1927) by Charles Hose (Hon. Fellow Jesus College, Cambridge; member of the Sarawak [Borneo] State Advisory Council; formerly Divisional Resident, and member of the Supreme Council of Sarawak). I cite this revealing passage merely to suggest the motives connecting scientists like A. R. Wallace to previous scholar-administrators like Stamford Raffles and to apologize in part for the transgression against historicity we will commit in leaping from sixteenth-century Pigafetta to nineteenth-century Wallace. Herewith Sir Arthur Keith, introducing Charles Hose's *Fifty Years of Romance and Research, or a Jungle-Wallah at Large*:

> Nature has given [Charles Hose] an endowment she bestows on few—
> the power of remaining young in heart and in outlook as years mount

up. It is because he has retained his boyish spirit of adventure and his freshness of vision that he has been able to give zest to his narrative. There is in it something of Robinson Crusoe, something of *Treasure Island*, something of White's *Selborne*, something he caught in his boyhood from the romances of Walter Scott, something he drank in as a youth from Stamford Raffles, from the Rajahs Brooke, and from another who remained a boy at the age of ninety-one—Russel Wallace. That spirit of boyish adventure and youthful outlook he carried with him to Borneo, and it abode with him there. It was because he had the power of becoming a child again that it was possible for him to enter into the native mind and see the world as Nature's savages see it— minds which swarm with spirits of all kinds—spirits which have to be obeyed or propitiated. How stupid we white men often are! We have to know each other very intimately for many years to discover the motives of conduct, and yet we can persuade ourselves that in half an hour, by a few questions, framed in imperfectly understood words, we can fathom the secrets of a native people whom we wish to rule. Charles Hose never made this mistake; he approached the tribes as one boy approaches another, and in the course of time came an exchange of secrets, and this exchange gave Dr. Hose the key to successful government.[12]

Thus the history of texts, particularly of *reading* them, ties Defoe, to Raffles, to Scott, to Wallace, to Hose, producing a discourse intermittently tinged by stereotypes from Pigafetta.

The crowning nineteenth-century first-person ethnological narrative is Wallace's *Malay Archipelago*. Strangely enough, although read by such officials as Charles Hose along with books by Scott and others, Wallace's bizarre text has come to be regarded as empirical. Perhaps a blinding light from the dedication to Darwin has caused scholars to "conventionalize" the work. Perhaps tales of the origins of the theory of natural selection have been substituted for actual experience of the volume: Did Wallace achieve his creative paradigm shift on Ternate or Gilolo (scene of Pigafetta's cannibals!)? Did he mysteriously converge with his rival's ideas by reflecting on the Moluccas as Darwin had reflected on the Galapagos? Here I seek to redress this imbalanced reading, or not-reading, of Wallace's tome in favor of its pecularities. I would not wish to suggest that the entire study coheres around the degeneracy/divinity imagery that seasons it from the outset. I merely recommend reconsidering pat assumptions concerning *The Malay Archipelago*'s messages. Certainly to regard the work as a routine natural history is to ignore eerie undercurrents.[13]

Standard summaries of Wallace's book begin with his opening apology for the lapse of time between its publication in 1869 and his actual travels ending in 1862. This apology, however, does not begin the book. The first U.S. edition (1869), for example, begins on its cover's spine, upon which perches a gilded bird of paradise, its plumage trailing toward the Harper and Brother's imprint. In the front is embossed a winsome, doe-eyed *mias* (orangutan), whose tresses overflow the circular frame (which truncates a

fuller illustration from the text); its gaze confronts in innocent benevolence the reader about to commence his voyage. Two frontispieces follow,
both now famous ethnological icons. The first depicts a struggle labeled
"Orang-utang attacked by Dyaks." One of the five muscular, near-nude
hunters falls back as his enraged prey tears flesh and tendons from his
biceps; comrades sprint to his aid, wielding spears and axe. The second
picture reveals lolling "Natives of Aru shooting the great bird of paradise." Two youthful archers cradled in the crux of branching trees
effortlessly fell their abundant victims being fetched by a helper below.
One last feathered marvel graces the title page:

> The Malay Archipelago
> The Land of the Orang-utan and the Bird of Paradise
> A Narrative of Travel with Studies of Man and Nature

Wallace confesses himself to be a writer of the most strategic kind: "The
chapter on Natural History, as well as many passages in other parts of the
work, have been written in the hope of exciting an interest in the various
questions connected with the origin of species and their geographical
distribution" (p. vii). It is the variety of interest Wallace hoped to excite
with the opening illustrations, and the extended moments deep into his
text referring back to them, that I wish to open as a question. The puzzling theme we shall trace is the hinted affinity between man and nature,
or more precisely between certain excesses in each.

The boundary between man and nature is just one of the lines at issue in
The Malay Archipelago. Wallace, of course, is best known as co-discoverer
of natural selection and as sole discoverer of Wallace's Line, the profound
geological rift dividing insular Southeast Asia into two natural worlds:
Indic on the one hand and Australia-like on the other:

> The great contrast between the two divisions of the Archipelago is
> nowhere so abruptly exhibited as on passing from the island of Bali to
> that of Lombock, where the two regions are in closest proximity. In
> Bali we have barbets, fruit-thrushes, and woodpeckers; on passing
> over to Lombock, these are seen no more, but we have abundance of
> cockatoos, honeysuckers, and brush-turkeys, which are equally un-
> known in Bali, or any island further west. (p. 25)

Anything that smudges the lines is untidy. Wallace regrets reports of "a
few cockatoos at one spot on the west of Bali, showing that the intermin-
gling of the productions of these islands is now going on." Needless to say,
cultures mingle even more. It seems a discourtesy to nature's regions that
the Balinese have established themselves in Lombok as well. Not just for
this most spectacular line, but for all sorts of lesser lines, Wallace notes
the failure of distributions of flora, fauna, races, and cultures to respect
boundaries nature seemingly intended. His text illustrates with peculiar
intensity that half hope by natural historians that things would divide

neatly, coupled with repeated confirmations that—whether in matters of geological divisions and species, race, and region, or physical form and moral character—"the same line does not limit both" (p. 30).[14]

The theme of man and nature in Wallace extends beyond issues of natural selection and vagaries in distribution and diffusion. He depicts more than simple contradictions (or discourtesies) between natural regions and the dispersal of cultures. In special moments we shall savor, Wallace suggests an affinity between human and animal groups, but at the point where the latter transforms into nature's most wondrous extremes.

Wallace penned many natural history articles for the scientific community, but he stitched together *The Malay Archipelago* for popular consumption. When citing Raffles' earlier, stately tomes, he remarks that "few Englishmen are aware of architectural remains in Java because they have never been popularly illustrated" (p. 114). This deficiency he hopes to remedy; throughout he writes for "the ordinary Englishman" for whom "this is perhaps the least known part of the globe" (p. 13). Although things are not set out in strictly chronological order and an occasional standardized essay is tucked into his text, Wallace organizes the whole as a first-person travel narrative. One obvious advantage to this format is its fluidity and ease of digression. Digression had, of course, been prevalent in Renaissance discovery literature (recall Pigafetta) and in varieties of early nineteenth-century descriptive histories discussed above. Even outright chronicles by strategy-minded historians—such as Horace St. John's mid-century *Indian Archipelago*—occasionally indulged in paeans to the birds of paradise: "All the birds are beautiful enough. . . . More beautiful than any are the birds of paradise—*discolorés maximes et inenarrabiles*—fabled to be the messengers of God, who fly toward the sun, but overpowered by the fragrance of the isles over which they pass, sink to the earth and fall into the hands of man."[15] The same scholar who decried "despotic, decrepid native governments" could thus pause to reinject notes of Linnaeus and Pliny in his discourse. But first-person narrative, freed from an artifice of historiography, managed better than chronicles like St. John's to build suspense and surprise.

An extreme example is *Travels in the East Indian Archipelago* (1869) by shell-collector A. S. Bickmore, a work exactly contemporary with Wallace's but lacking its scientific pretensions.[16] Bickmore accumulates information on customs and usages from circumcision to polygamy. He adorns his readable account with opium smokers, deer hunts, the inevitable birds of paradise, and several episodes about the cannibal Battak, one drawn from Marsden's account of a native from Nias whose murder of a Battak was revenged by his being "cut in pieces with the utmost eagerness while yet alive, and eaten upon the spot, partly broiled, but mostly raw." The study laces select items from past accounts with details from Bickmore's own travels. He includes a "page of romance" about a young officer's amorous adventures. Later we are spirited into the scene of a "mazy waltz" on a brilliantly lighted portico with a festoon of flowers at a wedding festival in Palembang: "I prepared to meet the Resident in full dress. He . . . at once commenced introducing me to the host and hostess, the bride and bridegroom, and all the assembled guests. The chills and burning fever, from which I had been suffering, vanished, and in a moment I found myself transferred from a real purgatory into a perfect paradise" (p. 530).

The book's final pages contain one last glimpse of purgatory in a daring "struggle for life," with an illustration labeled "killing the python" plus three pages of caption:

> In the bottom of the boat, aft . . . I espied, to my horror, the great python closely coiled away. . . . Suffering the acutest agony from the deep wound I had already given him, he raised his head high out of the midst of his huge coil, his red jaws wide open, and his eyes flashing fire like live coals. I felt the blood chill in my veins as, for an instant, we glanced into each other's eyes, and both instinctively realized that one of us two must die on that spot. . . . The next time he darted at me I gave him a heavy cut about fifteen inches behind his head, severing the body completely off, except about an inch on the under side, and, as he coiled up, this part fell over, and he fastened his teeth into his own coils. . . . The long trail of his blood on the deck assured me that I was indeed safe, and, drawing a long breath of relief, I thanked the Giver of all our blessings.
> This was my last experience in the tropical East. (pp. 539–42)

Although Wallace included his own "python" adventure, complete with sensational illustration (pp. 304ff.), his narrative devices are altogether less blatant than Bickmore's. Occasionally he seasons his portraits of cultures with the kind of vivid simile he usually saved for natural species, as in an uncharacteristically circumstantial description of a Javanese ritual:

> The next morning . . . the two lads, who were about 14 years old, were brought out, clothed in a sarong from the waist downward, and having the whole body covered with a yellow powder, and profusely decked with white blossoms in wreaths, necklaces, and armlets, looking at first like savage brides. They were conducted by two priests to a bench placed in front of the house in the open air, and the ceremony of circumcision was then performed before the assembled crowd. (p. 114)

But most of Wallace's discursive flair is reserved for orangutans and paradise birds. The orangutan chapter, first of three dealing with Dyaks, concludes with striking features of the creature's distribution: "It is very remarkable that an animal so large, so peculiar, and of such a high type of form as the orang-utan, should be confined to so limited a district—two islands [Borneo and Sumatra], and those almost the last inhabited by the higher Mammalia" (p. 72). More lines. But the chapter is primarily de-

voted to a sequence of episodes during his stay in Sarawak, whose renowned ruler, Sir James Brooke, abetted the indefatigable Wallace (on
twenty-six nights he once managed to collect 1,386 moths) in his "search
of shells, insects, birds, and the orang-utan" (p. 46). The intensive narrative highlights differences in each encounter. A selection of excerpts on
the "great man-like ape of Borneo" readily demonstrates the circuitous
route to standardized information in Wallace:

> On April 26th . . . we found another. . . . It fell at the first shot, but
> did not seem much hurt, and immediately climbed up the nearest tree,
> when I fired, and it again fell, with a broken arm and a wound in the
> body. The two Dyaks now ran up to it, and each seized hold of a hand,
> telling me to cut a pole and they would secure it. But although one arm
> was broken, and it was only a half-grown animal, it was too strong for
> these young savages, drawing them up toward its mouth notwithstand-
> ing all their efforts. . . . It now began climbing up the tree again, and,
> to avoid trouble, I shot it through the heart. (pp. 51–52)

> This little creature was only about a foot long, and had evidently been
> hanging to its mother when she first fell. . . . I fitted up a little box for
> a cradle. . . . It enjoyed the wiping and rubbing amazingly, and when I
> brushed its hair seemed to be perfectly happy. . . . Finding it so fond
> of hair, I endeavored to make an artificial mother, by wrapping up a
> piece of buffalo-skin into a bundle. . . . The poor little thing would
> lick its lips, draw in its cheeks, and turn up its eyes with an expression
> of the most supreme satisfaction when it had a mouthful particularly to
> its taste. . . . If [not sufficiently palatable] food was continued, it
> would set up a scream and kick about violently exactly like a baby in a
> passion. . . . after lingering for a week a most pitiable object, [it] died,
> after being in my possession nearly three months. (pp. 53–57)

> Very soon, however, one of the Dyaks called me and pointed upward,
> and on looking I saw a great red hairy body and a huge black face
> gazing down from a great height, as if wanting to know what was
> making such a disturbance below. I instantly fired, and he made off at
> once, so that I could not then tell whether I had hit him. . . . Running,
> climbing, and creeping among these, we came up with the creature on
> the top of a high tree near the road, where the Chinamen had dis-
> covered him, and were shouting their astonishment with open mouth:
> "Ya, ya, Tuan; Orang-utan, Tuan." [A full page of repeated shots
> later:] . . . we all began pulling at the creepers . . . down he came with
> a thud like the fall of a giant. And he was a giant, his head and body
> being full as large as a man's. . . . His outstretched arms measured
> seven feet three inches across. . . . On examination we found he had
> been dreadfully wounded. Both legs were broken, one hip-joint and
> the root of the spine completely shattered, and two bullets were found
> in his neck and jaws! Yet he was still alive when he fell. The two
> Chinamen carried him home tied to a pole, and I was occupied with
> Charley the whole of the next day, preparing the skin and boiling the

bones to make a perfect skeleton, which are now preserved in the
Museum at Derby. (pp. 58–60)

Each episode is many times longer than these abbreviated versions; they
are filled out with some comments on ethnozoology and corrections of
measurements estimated in earlier sources. But by and large they celebrate the extraordinary strength of the manlike *mias*. Even Wallace's regretted infant specimen, when skinned and preserved after finally passing
away, turned out to have broken an arm and leg when clinging to its
mother, shot dead in her sheltered treetop (p. 57). Symbol of unimaginable endurance (and touching tenacity), the orang turns truculent only
when threatened. The beast, concealed in nature, becomes manifest when
disturbed.

It is worth following the cue from Wallace's title and frontispieces by
juxtaposing this image from Borneo with counterpart adventues in Aru.[17]
(The "connected form" of descriptions of birds of paradise is in the more
conventional natural history of chapter 38, where information from the
adventure stories is repeated with less climactic commentary; the work
thus contains two versions of the same information.) Aru itself presents
those mingled racial, linguistic, and cultural characteristics of the kind
that both disturb and somehow attract Wallace. He observes that the
complicated mixture of races would "utterly confound an ethnologist,"
and he puzzles over the combination of Papuan physiognomy with delicate
European features but dark skin and hair that argues against Dutch intermixture. He then detects some Portuguese words—*jafui, porco*—in their
language and concludes that early Portuguese traders had deposited "the
visible characteristics of their race": "If to this we add the occasional
mixture of Malay, Dutch and Chinese with the indigenous Papuans, we
have no reason to wonder at the curious varieties of form and feature
occasionally to be met with in Aru" (pp. 453–54).

It is the lines of contrast and evidence of intermixtures in both physical
traits and linguistic features that interest the natural historian, not the
natives or languages themselves. Unlike their predecessors in comparative
philology, scientists like Wallace plotted lexical distributions with little
accompanying interest in translation: "And the [Aru people] certainly do
talk! Every evening there is a little Babel around me: but as I understand
not a word of it, I go on with my book or work undisturbed" (p. 453).

Even in the alloyed isles of Aru, Wallace seeks "nicely-balanced relations of organic and inorganic nature." While he seems to desire the same
balance in the orders of human nature, without the confusion of diffusions
and mixtures, a curious ambivalence enters the picture. Consider first
Aru's nature. The island habitat presents a perfected form hitherto seldom
witnessed by Europeans. Wallace encounters first the *burung raja*—in
which his Aru hosts saw nothing more "than we do in the robin or the
goldfinch"—and then the great paradise birds. He evokes a naturalist's
epiphany, moving from sound to vision:

> At early morn, before the sun has risen, we hear a loud cry of "Wawk—
> Wawk—wawk, wok—wok—wok," which resounds through the forest,
> changing its direction continually. This is the Great Bird of Paradise
> going to seek his breakfast. Others soon follow his example; lories and
> parroquets cry shrilly, cockatoos scream, king-hunters croak and bark,
> and the various smaller birds chirp and whistle their morning song. As
> I lie listening to these interesting sounds, I realize my position as the
> first European who has ever lived for months together in the Aru
> Islands, a place which I had hoped rather than expected ever to visit. I
> think how many besides myself have longed to reach these almost fairy
> realms, and to see with their own eyes the many wonderful and beauti-
> ful things which I am daily encountering. (pp. 449–50)

At this charmed moment Wallace seems still to subscribe to his new-found conviction that "surely all living things were *not* made for man. Many of them have no relation to him" (p. 449). This insight accompanied his sense of the inevitable doom that civilization spelled for the "nicely balanced organic relations" he was privileged to glimpse. Ironically, civilization would extinguish "these very beings whose wonderful structure and beauty [civilized intellect] alone is fitted to appreciate and enjoy" (pp. 448–49). But his conviction is short-lived; with the heavenly, early-morning medley ringing in his ears, the routine reemerges: "But now Ali and Baderoon are up and getting ready their guns and ammunition, and little Baso has his fire lighted and is boiling my coffee, and I remember that I had a black cockatoo brought in late last night, which I must skin immediately, and so I jump up and begin my day's work very happily" (p. 450).

Wallace summarizes paradoxes of distribution in Aru and New Guinea in chapter 38, where he offers a mercantilist view of organic species that recalls sixteenth-century observations on mace, cloves, and other natural rarities: "It seems as if Nature had taken precautions that these her choicest treasures should not be made too common, and thus be undervalued" (p. 574). Back in the narrative proper matters remain more ambivalent. Again, although civilization portends the birds' demise, it seems wantonly wasteful for nature to manifest its perfection in creatures existing only in a place "with no intelligent eye to gaze upon their loveliness." Later we learn that something special is manifest in Aru's human inhabitants as well. Wallace's adventure culminates neither in his personal epiphany nor in documentation of the many specimens collected, but in a slightly ecstatic passage providing an elaborate caption to that second frontispiece (explained in much abridged fashion in chapter 38). The Aru hunting technique is designed to avoid bloodstains on the plumage. (We see portrayed a kind of "herbal" hunting in stark contrast to Dyak methods, as ferocious as that enraged orang the natives hack and spear.) But the Aru illustration implies more than techniques of preserving valuable skins:

> The birds had now commenced what the people here call their
> "sacaleli," or dancing-parties, in certain trees in the forest, which are

not fruit trees, as I at first imagined, but which have an immense head
of spreading branches and large but scattered leaves, giving a clear
space for the birds to play and exhibit their plumes. On one of these
trees a dozen or twenty full-plumage male birds assemble together,
raise up their wings, stretch out their necks, and elevate their exquisite
plumes, keeping them in a continual vibration. Between whiles they
fly across from branch to branch in great excitement, so that the whole
tree is filled with waving plumes in every variety of attitude and motion
(See Frontispiece). . . . The bird itself is nearly as large as a crow. . . .
At the time of its excitement, however, the wings are raised verticall·'
over the back. . . . The whole bird is then overshadowed by them, the
crouching body, yellow head, and emerald-green throat forming but
the foundation and setting to the golden glory which waves above.
When seen in this attitude, the bird of paradise really deserves its
name, and must be ranked as one of the most beautiful and most
wonderful of living things. (pp. 466–67)

This magnificent *sacaleli* scene is not all. After a comment about his
specimens and a blank line suggesting a change of topic, Wallace proffers
yet another epiphany, this time over a human correspondence to Aru's
perfected nature:

Here, as among most savage people I have dwelt among, I was delighted with the beauty of the human form—a beauty of which stay-at-
home civilized people can scarcely have any conception. What are the
finest Grecian statues to the living, moving breathing men I saw daily
around me? The unrestrained grace of the naked savage, as he goes
about his daily occupations, or lounges at his ease, must be seen to be
understood; and a youth bending his bow is the perfection of manly
beauty. (p. 467)

Thus, an apparently anecdotal picture of hunting routines conceals a
conjunction of aesthetic ideals: nature's paradise birds and culture's Aru
bowsmen, both caught in the act and at the moment of their respective
perfections. This natural species with its divine resonance elevates alloyed
Aru toward a similar state of beauty. And Wallace's narrative offers this
apex of man and nature boundless homage.

From this explicit point in Wallace we might briefly wonder back to
Borneo: does a similar correspondence infuse the Dyak picture? The
Dyaks (by which term Wallace includes the Iban) fair relatively well in his
ethnological generalizations. They appear superior in both mental capacity and moral character to the Malays who plunder them. Although their
"half-savage state" makes them apathetic and dilatory, they have shown
the good sense to back the late, lamented Rajah Brooke:

In forming a proper estimate of Sir James Brooke's government, it
must ever be remembered that he held Sarawak solely by the good-will
of the native inhabitants. He had to deal with two races, one of whom,
the Mohammedan Malays, looked upon the other race, the Dyaks, as

savages and slaves, only fit to be robbed and plundered. He has effectually protected the Dyaks, and has invariably treated them as, in his sight, equal to the Malays, and yet he has secured the affection and good-will of both. Notwithstanding the religious prejudices of Mohammedans, he has induced them to modify many of their worst laws and customs, and to assimilate their criminal code to that of the civilized world. That his government still continues, after twenty-seven years—notwithstanding his frequent absences from ill-health, notwithstanding conspiracies of Malay chiefs, and insurrections of Chinese gold-diggers, all of which have been overcome by the support of the native populations, and notwithstanding financial, political, and domestic troubles—is due, I believe, solely to the many admirable qualities which Sir James Brooke possessed. (p. 104)

Yet the stability achieved remains fragile. Wallace's narrative links the potential ferocity of a roused orang and the physical power of the half savages that share its habitat. It would seem that neither the Aru nor the Dyak emblem simply identifies a population with its animal neighbors. Rather, each fauna pulls its human counterpart toward its extreme characteristic: lyrical divinity on the one hand, bestial might (beneath apparent docility) on the other: avial grace versus animal urge. It is difficult to know whether Borneo, like Aru, suggests the possibility of a culture becoming nature's simulacrum, but certainly the murmur is there.

Wallace's work concludes with a socialist complaint about the "deficient morality" that is the "great blot of modern civilization, and the greatest hindrance to true progress" (p. 597). He deems many savages inferior intellectually but superior morally, and he finds Europe's urban masses "worse off than the savage in the midst of his tribe" (p. 598). Moreover, "thickly-populated England," full of proprietors, is still in a "state of social barbarism . . . as regards true social science" (p. 599). Wallace's socialist stance makes England itself a barbarian-civilized mixture; even in his homeland dividing lines are shaky. And again he seems most concerned with the interstices of his own categories, what Mary Douglas calls, in the realm of symbolic classifications, "dirt." The plea for Europe's masses is tucked into Wallace's final chapter on archipelago races where he strictly and conventionally contrasts Malays and Papuans. Ideally, again, the lines are clear:

It appears, therefore, that whether we consider their physical conformation, their moral characteristics, or their intellectual capacities, the Malay and Papuan races offer remarkable differences and striking contrasts. The Malay is of short stature, brown-skinned, straight-haired, beardless, and smooth-bodied. The Papuan is taller, is black-skinned, frizzy-haired, bearded, and hairy-bodied. The former is broad-faced, has a small nose, and flat eyebrows; the latter is long-faced, has a large and prominent nose, and projecting eyebrows [contrast this to Raffles' chinless Papuan]. The Malay is bashful, cold, undemonstrative, and

quiet; the Papuan is bold, impetuous, excitable, and noisy. The former
is grave and seldom laughs; the latter is joyous and laughter-loving—
the one conceals his emotions, the other displays them. (p. 590)

But these crisp distinctions smudge; these lines too blur. Recall again the
"savage Malays" of orangutan land and elsewhere: "The savage Malays are
the Dyaks of Borneo; the Battaks and other wild tribes of Sumatra; the
Jakuns of the Malay peninsula; the aborigines of Northern Celebes, of the
Sula Islands, and of part of Bouru" (p. 585).

Wallace's narrative concludes as it has proceeded: in a continual tension
between desired orderly divisions and their enticing chinks. Moreover, we
have seen how notions of divinity/degeneracy emerge where nature seems
to transcend itself. Thus Wallace both resists and celebrates transgressed
boundaries; his story moves less within the confines he would establish
than between them, finally concluding with the social barbarism of the
civilizing West. He assumes that a popular readership would be more
readily lured across different Indonesian and Malay cultures if transfixed
by a polar image. Where the image was lacking in cultures, it could always
be borrowed from nature. He thus restores some of the flavor (but not, of
course, the world view) of Pigafetta's sixteenth-century account from the
heyday of the Great Chain of Being. The extreme symbols for typifying
Malay-speaking cultures arise from Wallace's selective schematization of
the area's exotic fauna. We may as well designate the device what it was: a
totemism in Western ethnological discourse; yes, a *totemism* propounded
in the name of evolutionist science.[18]

Conclusions

Just as peculiar activities become normative in every culture, so strange
sorts of texts become standard in ethnological pursuits. Nothing is less
empiricist, more convention laden, than certain components of "natural
histories" that once assumed responsibility for representing Indonesian
cultures. By seizing such works not at their hearts but at their somewhat
obsessive digressions, we can better assess the source of their appeal, the
oddness of their format, and the complexity of their discourse. Tracing
circuitous hints of degeneracy/divinity in such texts helps expose hidden
continuities among different ethnological genres. Even our too-confident
sense of disjunction between pre-Enlightenment varieties of description
(Pigafetta, for example) and scientific ones (Wallace, for example) grows
bothered. From the earliest Western sources Indonesia was spared the
encompassing stigma of degeneracy (as diabolicalness) that became associated with certain New World populations. The divinity of Indonesian
kings outshone suggestions of cannibalism. Yet with the West's double
lens of divinity/degeneracy already in place, even where kingship reigned,
symbols of decay slithered about, sure to reemerge.

Unsettling moments in Indonesian ethnology point to the advisability of enriching Margaret Hodgen's model of the history of anthropological ideas while maintaining her sense of variations in any doctrine of degeneracy. The texts we have perused suggest how various are the discursive modes in which cultural or racial decay can be imputed. It may even be the fact that rumors of degeneracy last longest where the doctrine is most fragmentary. Fleeting transitions are more difficult to purge than bold declarations. A concluding remark in Hodgen's study may help clarify what is most distinctive about the Indonesian case:

> The main difficulty . . . for all social evolutionists was to hit upon that nonliterate people which was demonstrably the lowest, nearest the beast, and hence oldest. On this matter agreement has never been achieved. In an earlier period of ethnological controversy, now beginning to be forgotten, Cook, Fitzroy, and Wallis were said to be in favor of the Fuegians, as was true also for Karl Marx and Charles Darwin; "Burchell maintained that the Bushmen [were] the lowest. D'Urville voted for the Australians and Tasmanians; . . . one French writer even [suggested] that monkeys were more human than Laplanders."[19]

Neither Indonesian cultures themselves nor the history of their documentation cooperated very well with this negative quest. Earlier "missing link" formulations tended to usher the famous orangutan (orang hutan = forest dweller or wild man) toward the human as much as to push human groups down. Reputed cannibalism cropped up in the literate Battak of Sumatra; headhunting was hard to isolate. And notorious amok-running and ritual suicide (as in the courts of Bali and Java) occurred at every level of civilization and "savagery." As Crawfurd's *Dictionary* took pains to explain:

> AMUCK. The muck of the writers of Queen Anne's time; who introduced the word into our language. In Malay it means a furious and reckless onset, whether of many in battle, or of an individual in private. The word and the practice are not confined to the Malays, but extend to all the people and languages of the Archipelago that have attained a certain amount of civilization. Running a-muck with private parties is often the result of a restless determination to exact revenge for some injury or insult; but it also results, not less frequently, from a monomania taking this particular form, and originating in disorders of the digestive organs.[20]

No two criteria of degeneracy—physiological, psychological, cultural—pointed precisely in the same direction. No nonliterate people perfectly filled the bill of the Renaissance's "diabolical," the Enlightenment's taxonomic "missing link," or the social evolutionist's "beastliest and oldest." Over the centuries Indonesian cultures refracted charges of degeneracy whose symbols proved difficult to "fix."

Yet rumors of decay persisted at the peripheries: between the seams of arguments and at points where ethnological texts might otherwise have altogether unraveled. During that peculiar set of historical circumstances we call the nineteenth century, from its place in the margins degeneracy continually infiltrated Western assessments of Indonesia's cultures—exotic yes, but in actuality neither divine nor declined, or no more so than anything else human. Categories like divinity/degeneracy, which do not exactly develop, can nevertheless permute. In a way Indonesia has remained perceived as a land of extremes—up to and including "Bali-Buru"—because ethnological ideas often operate like myth: exhibiting "a 'slated' structure, which comes to the surface, so to speak, through the process of repetition."[21]

An Envoi of Verne

Traces of Western responses to Indonesian cultures and nature appeared in works devoted to lands well beyond the realm of Malay-speakers. A lingering note of degeneracy imagery—appropriate finale for our disturbing story—was sounded in a famous fiction of 1874. Did this winning work draw inspiration from Borneo and Sumatra's manlike orangs, or did it merely adapt ideas from Linnaeus' tantalizing tales of troglodytes, those "missing links" in a comfortable Enlightenment taxonomy who "have a language of their own which they speak in a whistle, so difficult, that scarce any one can learn it except by long association with them. . . . In many places of the East Indies they are caught and made use of in houses as servants.[22] From either source or both of them, Jules Verne's enchanting robinsonnade introduced its own *homo sylvestris,* duly domesticated:

> The settlers then approached the ape and gazed at it attentively. He belonged to the family of anthropoid apes, of which the facial angle is not much inferior to that of the Australians and Hottentots. It was an orang-outang [one of the anthropoid apes] . . . possessed of almost human intelligence. Employed in houses they can wait at table, sweep rooms, brush clothes, clean boots, handle a knife, fork, and spoon properly, and even drink wine . . . Buffon possessed one of these apes, who served him for a long time as a faithful and zealous servant. . . .
> "A handsome fellow!" said Pencroft; "if we only knew his language, we could talk to him."
> "But master," said Neb, "are you serious? Are we going to take him as a servant?"
> "Yes Neb," replied the engineer, smiling. "But you must not be jealous."[23]

In a book about a *Mysterious Island* in the Pacific (eventually called by its castaways "Lincoln," complete with a lake named "Grant"), four enlightened Yankees and a freed slave—escaped by balloon from their capture in Richmond during the siege of 1865—set about to build a world from scratch. In Verne's story no Eve intrudes; yet his narrative voice, renowned today for its forward vision and technological prophecies, cannot resist seasoning the tale with a nostalgic *topos* from the desultory history of ideas of degeneracy. Again, whether Verne developed these passages from reading about Borneo, about troglodytes, or about both is unclear; nor would it matter. The orang is "Jup," the ex-slave is "Neb":

> By this time the intelligent Jup was raised to the duty of valet. He had been dressed in a jacket, white linen breeches, and an apron, the pockets of which were his delight. The clever orang had been marvelously trained by Neb, and any one would have said that the Negro and the ape understood each other when they talked together. Jup had besides a real affection for Neb, and Neb returned it. . . . he endeavored to imitate Neb in all that he saw him do. The black showed the greatest patience and even extreme zeal in instructing his pupil, and the pupil exhibited remarkable intelligence in profiting by the lessons he received from his master. (p. 297)

Neb is loyal to Jup, and Jup to Neb. Verne shored up a Chain of Being by evoking subtle affinities between two creatures that certain classifications declared marginal. Thus an Indonesian orang exported to a Pacific atoll served once more to foster hints of cultural or racial degeneracy, in an adventure destined to become a children's classic. Such are the odd and oozy twists characteristic of nineteenth-century ethnological discourse.

What an unlikely cast of characters emerges when we hold fast to the tail of "degeneracy," as one episode leads to another across discovery literature, descriptive histories, naturalists' quests and fantastic voyages. We have on the brighter side Pigafetta's "Ave de Paraiso," but also Wallace's giant *mias* carcass he informs us he called "Charley," and Verne's orang "Jup" (short for Jupiter) in some kind of similitude with manumitted Nebuchadnezzar (who "only answered to the familiar abbreviation of Neb"—p. 24). Representatives of exotic extremes often find themselves bestowed with proper names; and in the case of Charley, Neb, and Jup with nicknames: special kinds of words coined in the West's ethnological discourse to label, or rather to subjugate, the unknown.

NOTES

1. *Archipel*, (1978), 16:3–5. Colleagues and students too numerous to list have influenced this study. I have benefited from resources in Cornell University's Department of Anthropology, Southeast Asia Program, and Olin Library with its incomparable John M. Echols Collection.

2. Margaret T. Hodgen, *Early Anthropology in the Sixteenth and Seventeenth Centuries* (Philadelphia: University of Pennsylvania Press, 1971), p. 234.

3. An extremely interesting collection that, I think, confirms this view is Edward Dudley and M. E. Novak, eds., *The Wild Man Within: An Image in Western Thought from the Renaissance to Romanticism* (Pittsburgh: University of Pittsburgh Press, 1972). While their volume mainly covers "wild man" imagery from the Renaissance to Romanticism, its threads weave through the entire history of Western discourses of self/other. The classic account of "The Great Chain of Being" is Arthur O. Lovejoy, *The Great Chain of Being: A Study of the History of an Idea* (1936; rpt., Cambridge: Harvard University Press, 1964), a major source for Hodgen's discussion; extensive commentary on Lovejoy's arguments has appeared over the years in the *Journal of the History of Ideas* and other periodicals.

4. Antonio Pigafetta, *Magellan's Voyage Around the World*, James A. Robertson, tr., 2 vols. (Cleveland: A. H. Clerk, 1906), 2:71. I leave place names in this translation's spellings. I consider sexual episodes in Pigafetta in a paper in preparation on females and males (e.g., sisters and brothers) in Indonesian myths. "Odorus Moluccas" is an epithet in Melville's *Moby-Dick*. See James A. Boon, *Other Tribes, Other Scribes: Symbolic Anthropology in the Comparative Study of Cultures, Histories, Religions, and Texts* (New York: Cambridge University Press, 1983).

5. John Crawfurd, *A Descriptive Dictionary of the Indian Islands and Adjacent Countries* (London: Bradbury & Evans, 1856), p. 32.

6. Pigafetta, 2:87.

7. See John M. Echols, "Presidential Address, Dictionaries and Dictionary Making: Malay and Indonesian," *Journal of Asian Studies* (1978), 38:11–24.

8. Alessandro Bausani "The First Italian-Malay Vocabulary by Antonio Pigafetta," *East and West* (1960), N.S.11: 229–48.

9. Kenneth Burke, *The Rhetoric of Religion: Studies in Logology* (Berkeley: University of California Press, 1970). Burke's categories are designed to accentuate "logology," devoted to words about things and gods, rather than to things and gods themselves. He directs us to "polar" or dialectic definitions in the realms of society, polity, and theology—precisely the province of ethnological discourse.

10. On symbolic dimensions in stereotypes of Patagonians, see James A. Boon, "Comparative De-enlightenment: Paradox and Limits in the History of Ethnology," *Daedalus* (1980), 109:73–91. I have traced other signs of kingship (in such scribes as Pigafetta and compilers-commentators as Jacobean Samuel Purchas) in Boon, *Other Tribes*, ch. 5.

11. William Marsden, *The History of Sumatra*, 3d ed. (London, 1811); Thomas Stamford Raffles, *The History of Java* (Kuala Lumpur: Oxford University Press, Oxford in Asia Historical Reprints, 1817/1965); John Crawfurd, *History of the In-*

dian Archipelago, Containing an Account of the Manners, Arts, Languages, Religions, Institutions, and Commerce of its Inhabitants, 3 vols. (London, 1820, repr. 1967, Frank Cass).

12. Hose's own books—especially this self-absorbed retrospective on his career and the unparalleled continuity of Sarawak's administration—merit a full study of their discursive properties. Clearly the nineteenth century held on in Hose until 1927. The "stars" of *Fifty Years of Romance and Research* (London: Huchinson, 1927) include a native ruler (the "Rob Roy of Sarawak"), Hose's adoring wife Poppy, and a mispreserved, bloated, giant orangutan head she valiantly delivered to Cambridge's Dr. Duckworth. (Readers of this work attentive to what it mirrors of English life of the times will have no trouble locating ample evidence of degeneracy!)

13. Alfred Russel Wallace, *The Malay Archipelago* (New York: Harper, 1869). The place of Wallace in evolutionary theory is briefly reviewed in D. R. Oldroyd, *Darwinian Impacts* (Atlantic Highlands, N. J.: Humanities Press, 1980). It includes Wallace's own account of his visionary flash concerning "the survival of the fittest" while ill and "prostated . . . for several hours every day during the cold and succeeding hot fits" (p. 107). That Wallace persisted in viewing the human mind as "the only divine contribution to the history of life" (Stephen J. Gould, *Ever Since Darwin* [New York: Norton, 1977] p. 25) is as troubling to historians of biological sciences as it is pertinent to Wallace's ethnological imagery. Recent works on Wallace, largely on his contribution to natural selection, are listed in Oldroyd, *Darwinian Impacts*, p. 274.

14. The border between Bali and Lombok is a striking point in Wallace's text as well as in his geography. He inserts an anecdotal account (pp. 186–95) of a (Balinese) raja in Eastern Lombok who outfoxed his subjects when they proved reluctant to pay their taxes and tried to deceive their rulers' census takers. In the Dutch translation of Wallace, *Insulinde: Het Land van den Orang-Oetan en den Paradijsvogel.* P. J. Veth, tr. (Amsterdam: Van Kampen, 1870), this tricky tale is called "eene volkstelling," but not labeled "folktale" in his original. It reads like the moral reverse of similar episodes in Multatuli's *Max Havelaar*, Roy Edwards, tr. (London: Heinemann, 1967), the great satire of 1860 (aimed against Dutch colonialism) that Wallace pointedly derided. Wallace finds that Multatuli's (alias Edward Douwes Dekker) work "has been excessively praised . . . for its supposed crushing exposure of the inequities of the Dutch government of Java. Greatly to my suprise I found it a very tedious and long-winded story, full of rambling digressions, and whose only point is to show that the Dutch Residents and Assistant Residents wink at the extortions of the native princes" (p. 107). Whether to counteract Multatuli's case or no, Wallace includes his story of a raja on Lombok, suggestive of a benevolent authority rather than the harsh oppression depicted by Multatuli (whose satirical work *is* digression and nothing but digression, precisely in accord with its genre!).

15. Horace St. John, *The Indian Archipelago: Its History and Present State,* 2 vols. (London: Longman, 1853).

16. A. S. Bickmore, *Travels in the East Indian Archipelago* (New York: Appleton, 1869).

17. For a recent summary of archaeological and historical evidence about the inhabitants of Aru (and of coastal Sumatra), see A. C. Milner, Edward McKinnon,

and Tengku Luckman Sinar S. H., "A Note on Aru and Kota Cina," *Indonesia* (1978), 26:1–42.

18. Totemic codes employ different natural species to signify social divisions. The modern classic demonstrating that totemism is not restricted to a level of social development or a primitive type of society is Claude Lévi-Strauss, *Totemism*. Rodney Needham, tr. (Boston: Beacon Press, 1963). His study, originally titled "Totemism Today," reviews anthropological investigations of tribal totemic practices and suggests that to divide the world into totemic versus nontotemic populations is itself a kind of "totemism."

For additional background on Wallace's natural historical research, with lively chapters on his work in Indonesia and Sarawak and his interest in varieties versus species in human populations, see John Langdon Brooks, *Just Before the Origin: Alfred Russel Wallace's Theory of Evolution* (New York: Columbia University Press, 1984); unfortunately, this book appeared after the present article was completed. For comments on Wallace's "hard hyper-selectionist line," his optimism about humanity's eventual emancipation from suffering, and his "conventional Christian solution," see Stephen Jay Gould, *The Panda's Thumb* (New York: Norton, 1982). Wallace's interest in spiritualism largely postdated his travels in the Malay Archipelago; relevant studies are too copious to cite here.

19. Hodgen, *Early Anthropology*, p. 510.

20. Crawfurd, *Dictionary*, p. 12.

21. Claude Lévi-Strauss, *Structural Anthropology* (New York: Anchor Books, 1963), p. 226.

22. J. Burke, "The Wild Man's Pedigree," in Dudley and Novak, *Wild Man Within*, p. 268; cf. Lovejoy, *Great Chain*.

23. Jules Verne, *The Mysterious Island* (Cleveland: World, 1957), pp. 280–81.

3

SOCIOLOGY AND DEGENERATION: THE IRONY OF PROGRESS

ROBERT A. NYE

University of Oklahoma

The disenchantment of our century with progress predisposes us to two potential errors with respect to the previous one. We risk underestimating the breadth and the profundity of fin-de-siècle *perceptions* of decline, and we are likely to survey the past only for the first signs of the terrors that have haunted our own century, a kind of Whiggish history in reverse. While it is an indisputable truth that the roots of twentieth-century despair lie in the nineteenth century, the inhabitants of that era did not regard the evidence for decline as a simple harbinger of future chaos, but as an expression of pathologies long in preparation. This is not to deny the power or the appeal of the idea of progress, at least before 1914; even if we deny progress the most complete hegemony over nineteenth-century thought, we cannot refuse it a role of great influence. Rather, I wish to argue, the concept of decline was conceptually inseparable from that of progress.

I wish to make the point that two binary oppositions dominated sociological discourse in the nineteenth century: progress/decline and social/individual. As I hope to show, the exponents of a science of society found it impossible to discuss the progressive aspects of social evolution without considering the negative effects that accompanied it, and that threatened to stall or even reverse the "normal" condition of advance. What is more, in their efforts to identify the general laws that governed *social* life, sociological theorists could not neglect altogether the *individuals* who inhabited the social system. This was because the consensual basis of social organization, which these theorists were at pains to identify and explain, could be disrupted in a variety of ways by individuals in conflict. Individual conflict had to be incorporated into sociological theory because, as

Edward Shils has written, "it constantly raised the problem of 'defective consensus.'"[1]

It is also important to make the *historical* point that the origins of social theory are inextricably bound up with the emergence of the concept of the modern individual. As Georg Simmel pointed out at the beginning of this century, the concept of the individual underwent a crucial change around 1800, from a kind of indistinguishable and atomistic "similarity" to a strong valuation of the "absolute peculiarity" of the individual personality rooted in "the collective, . . . concrete totality of the living species."[2] Despite the remarkable strength of the eighteenth-century variant of the individual and the social in the form of British utilitarianism, the more organic nineteenth-century model provided the starting point for the earliest essays in sociological theory. But in adopting organic or hierarchical models of society, nineteenth-century theorists did not ignore or minimize the role of individuals in social evolution. On the contrary, sociological theorists were heavily dependent on precisely the sort of individual "peculiarity" of which Simmel wrote to make their systems work. Indeed, individual variation was in a certain sense a *condition* of social evolution that developed in reciprocity with society itself. As a consequence, the two binaries which I have argued guided sociological thinking in the nineteenth century are interrelated, so that progress/decline was influenced by the nature of the social/individual, and vice versa.

This point is worth making because of the abiding tendency in the history of social theory to consider the individual and society as opposing principles in sociological explanation, the weight given to the one necessarily taking away from the other. They have also been regarded as a paradigm for the relative force of heredity (the individual component) and environment (the social component) in social evolution. But until the advent of neo-Darwinian genetics just before World War I, sociologists did not make distinctions between individuals and society in such a rigid manner. Even where they paid lip service to Weismann's germ theory after 1885, European social theorists did not decisively break with Lamarckian notions of inheritance. Applied to social theory, Lamarck's concept of heredity had the effect of placing the individual and society on a continuum, wherein individual acquisitions could be fixed and stored in the social organism, and where the evolution of the social unit expressed its growth in the persistent differentiation of individual functions.

Another rather curious influence helped to reinforce the connection between individual and social phenomena in sociological theory, and to provide indirect support for the important concept of environmentally induced acquired characteristics. I am referring to the extraordinary impact that phrenology had on several important nineteenth-century thinkers. F. J. Gall and J. C. Spurzheim advanced the idea that the brain was the "organ of the mind," housing all higher mental life, including temperaments and emotional proclivities, in certain delineated faculties. Their doctrine met with strong "official" resistance in the 1820s and 1830s from the dominant associationist psychology in Europe, but in the long run the thoroughly materialistic assumptions of phrenology proved attractive to such neurophysiologists as Paul Broca and Hughlings Jackson;[3] in the short run it had a powerful effect on evolutionary psychology and on social theory.

Contrary to our received ideas about phrenology, Gall, and especially Spurzheim, did not believe that the "innate" and inheritable facilities were nonmodifiable. Indeed, they stressed the role that environment and "exercise" of the faculties played in developing certain favorable human qualities, which could be passed subsequently to the offspring. The optimistic aspects of the doctrine exercised an irresistible appeal on social and medical reformers in both England and France in the 1830s and 1840s.[4] Mental pathologists also found phrenology useful as a diagnostic and a therapeutic tool. Mental illness was considered a consequence of the overuse or underuse of certain faculties, and mental health, logically enough, was the effect of their regular but moderate exercise. As Roger Cooter has written, the moral underpinnings of Victorian "hygiene" were clearly evident in the work of British phrenologists: "Slothfulness and overindulgence were alike at the root of much insanity. It was necessary, therefore, that the public should be educated against perpetuating these vices that would damage their health and (because of the belief in social hereditarianism) the mental health of future generations. The virtues of sobriety, chastity, self-improvement, and moderation in all things were thus recommended."[5] Phrenology was adopted by Comte and Spencer and played an important role in their work and the work of their heirs. Once fixed solidly in the larger setting of social evolution favored by these authors, phrenology then reentered the mainstream of psychiatric and neurological thinking.[6] Dressed out in evolutionary clothes, the idea of modifiable and inheritable moral faculties was able to have a strong influence on *both* social and psychiatric theory in the late nineteenth century, in a manner that was admirably suited to the spreading of ideas about degeneration.

I propose first to discuss these developments in the work of Auguste Comte and Herbert Spencer, then to demonstrate the continuity of outlook in French and British sociology at the end of the century. Limitations of space preclude exploring other continental writers in detail, but a strong case could be made for the influence of degeneration theory on a number of European "social biologists," on Robert Michels and Vilfredo Pareto, and on Simmel, Oswald Spengler, and even Max Weber.[7] I will stress the historical reasons why social theorists found degeneration such a compelling theme. Though degeneration is very much a *European* reaction to urbanization, industrialization, and the democratization of political life, there was also a unique *national* appeal in certain countries. Thus, Germany's rise to great power status provoked anxious reassessments about national health in France and Great Britain at the end of the century.

The reputation of Auguste Comte has experienced a greater number of wild fluctuations than a thinker of his originality deserves.[8] Even during his lifetime, as the example of John Stuart Mill demonstrates, Comte was at first praised as an intellectual liberator and later reviled as the advocate of authoritarian despotism.[9] Behind the uneven course of his career is the belief that Comte's work has two separate stages of development. The first, "sensible" phase is the era of the *Cours de philosophie positive* (1830–1842); this is usually segregated from the later multi-volume *Système de politique positive*, which appeared in the 1850s when Comte was under the "spell" of the ghost of Clotilde de Vaux.[10] Without taking sides in this controversy, I shall confine my analysis to the "sensible" Comte of the *Cours*.

To assure an autonomous scientific status for their discipline, sociological theorists have often excluded from the list of worthy predecessors all those writers who openly or surreptitiously relied on individual psychology to explain social action. In this view Comte is usually retained as an important precursor of "sociologism" because he banned the introspective and unsystematic psychology of the day from his system.[11] Comte certainly missed no opportunity to heap abuse on "unscientific" psychology; he attempted to build his system of social laws directly on human biology, which formed the cornerstone in his scheme of "social physics." But in replacing psychology with biology in his system Comte did not thereby dispense with individuals. He simply traded a form of human nature which was intractable for one that articulated more satisfactorily with his concept of social development. The "biology" on which Comte heavily relied was the phrenology of Franz Joseph Gall, at the height of its popularity when Comte was writing the *Cours*.

Much of the *Cours* was devoted to the demonstration of mankind's historical progression from the lowest levels of social organization through an ascending order of civilization characterized by increasing complexity and functional differentiation. Comte identified the now celebrated three stages of development—the theological, the metaphysical, the positive—as the stages through which mankind must pass before reaching a final apotheosis in the "positive society." Each stage displayed different forms of social organization, religious expression, forms of thought, and even logic. Crucial to Comte's notion of social evolution was the gradual emergence of a scientific hierarchy of knowledge, embraced and augmented by increasing numbers of individuals as Western man moved ineluctably through consecutive stages of development. When finally completed, this hierarchy of the sciences, surmounted by sociology, would command uni-

versal intellectual and moral adherence, ending once and for all the revolutions and intellectual anarchy of human history.

The role played by individuals in this process has not been adequately
appreciated. As Comte explained in the lesson of the *Cours* on "social
dynamics":

> The general result of our fundamental evolution does not consist only
> in ameliorating mankind's material conditions of life through the con-
> tinuous effects of his actions on the exterior world; but also and espe-
> cially to develop, by an increasingly preponderant *exercise*, our most
> eminent *faculties*, while at once stimulating the various social instincts
> . . . and augmenting spontaneously the habitual influence of reason
> over man's conduct.[12]

In his lesson on the "intellectual and moral, or cerebral, functions,"
Comte acknowledged his debt to Gall's ideas. He made it clear that the
exercise of a faculty will lead to its growth, while disuse brings about
atrophy (3:564–65). In the evolution of mankind the "frontal" part of the
brain, wherein reside the analytical and reasoning powers, has shown the
greatest degree of growth and has exerted an increasing and beneficent
influence over human affairs (4:460–61). Comte vigorously defended
phrenology against the charge that Gall's system was utterly deterministic. On the contrary, he argued, the "philosophical problem of education"
must now be the sole province of "cerebral physiology (3:566)." Clearly
Comte regarded the brain as endowed with an extraordinary plasticity and
as the seat, not only of the reasoning powers, but of the sentiments constituting the social "instincts," a fact entirely compatible with Gall's
system.

The mechanism by which Comte accounted for the growth of the cerebral faculties was in its essence a process of Lamarckian adaptation. This
point has been consistently misunderstood because Comte himself seems
to occasionally adopt Cuvier's conception of fixed species, which contra-
dicts, to say the least, Lamarck's idea of biological *transformisme*.[13] There
is no gainsaying, however, the important influence Lamarck's thinking
plays in Comte's concept of individual and social evolution. The very
"idea of life," Comte writes, supposes the "necessary correlation" of "an
appropriate organism in a suitable milieu." All vital phenomena are the
product of the "reciprocal actions" of these two factors, and health is best
maintained when their relations are in "equilibrium" (3:209–10). As
Lamarck had done, Comte drew particular attention to the relation between structure and function in biological adaptation, taking as his analytic motto: "Given the organ or the organic modification, find the function
or the act, and reciprocally (3:211). Elsewhere, Comte made it clear that
advanced species adapt to variations in the environment through a kind of
willful and conscious effort, which becomes "habitual" to the "individual,

and even to the race, reproducing itself spontaneously" (3:548–49). On human evolution he cites the biologist H. Ducrotay de Blainville: "Instinct is fixed reason; reason is mobile instinct" (3:549).

Comte believed that the way in which the brain acquired and integrated new skills and sentiments was an important part of the general process of social evolution. His mistrust of the atomistic and mechanical models dear to English political economy certainly disposed him to favor a mode of transformism which stressed notions of equilibrium and organic economy, a bias he shared with most nineteenth-century French social and biological theorists.[14] But there are clear signs that he regarded the evolution of the individual mind as the sine qua non of all progress and the very foundation of his hopes for an orderly future society. At the least, a certain level of biological capacity for rational and sociable behavior in individuals would prevent backsliding in the whole social organism. As he wrote in the *Cours*, the positive philosophy will certainly triumph because "to it alone belongs the possibility of developing in us an unshakable vigor and a reflective constancy directly drawn *from our own nature*, and without external assistance"[15]

As all students of Comte's work realize, his optimism was not of the firmest stuff. He worried in the *Cours* about the "fatal" possibility of an "imminent dissolution" in the present social order, taking some consolation in the thought that the next "organic" phase would be organized on a more "progressive and more consistent" level (4:16). Indeed, he read the history of society as a record of oscillations between "critical" and "organic" phases, in which a gradual ascent could be marked, though at a terrible cost in human lives and institutions. Comte alluded in his system, therefore, to a number of mechanisms, at both individual and social levels, which he imagined explained the episodes of social "dissolution" scattered throughout the history of civilization.

Comte believed, as did many of his contemporaries, that population growth was a factor leading to division of labor and social differentiation, especially in cities where the most rapid rate of social progress could be documented. Consistent with his theory of the parallelism of individual and social progress, he identified the urban areas as the sites of greatest concentration of "intellectual and moral" development in society. He acknowledged the potentially disastrous effects of overpopulation (and, by extension, underpopulation) on the continued function of this process, but believed Malthus' fears to be absurdly exaggerated (4:455–56). Comte did draw attention, however, to the mortality rate as a crucial factor in the necessary equilibrium in society between "innovation" and "conservation." A high mortality rate eliminated too many old and conservative individuals, to the benefit of youthful rebels, but too low a mortality risked the ossification that can occur when the ideas of the young are not permitted an adequate hearing.[16] In this area alone—characteristically portrayed as a struggle of ideas—Comte believed in the fruitfulness of an "indispensable and permanent struggle." Comte equally believed progress in all eras to have depended on the existence of an elite class which disposed of the leisure time to "speculate," for he warns ominously that only the presence of this class had allowed us to evolve "beyond the level of apes" (4:486).

At the individual level, Comte reveals his debt to what Georges Canguilhem has identified as the ruling idea in French biology in the nineteenth century, namely the idea that "pathological" vital phenomena are but extreme rates of function at one end or another of the continuum of "normal" activity.[17] He refers to certain "spontaneous perturbations" in living organisms, and to changes in vital function provoked by the milieu to explain how, on certain occasions, organisms may develop pathologies that are not mere "curiosities" but "true maladies."[18] Comte seems to be allowing here for a development in the individual organism that would have, on his theory of reciprocity, a negative effect on the social organism. His willingness to identify these potentially disruptive agents of progressive social evolution makes it difficult to interpret Comte's system as unambiguously optimistic in nature. Indeed, with respect to Comte's influence later in the century, the pessimistic uses to which his theories were put weigh heavily in the balance against those which maintained hope.[19] In the end, the part of Comte's contribution to sociological theory which I wish to emphasize, and which is usually overlooked in favor of his so-called sociologism, is nicely summarized in a remark of Gertrude Lenzer:

> What Comte in effect did was to intercalate between the study of biological and social phenomena the study of brain functions. Only from our present vantage point can this ingenious device be properly appreciated. It was in this way that he posited the individual person as being controlled by biological and physiological mechanisms on the one hand, and as open to control by means of social forces and mechanisms on the other.[20]

Herbert Spencer was the other major nineteenth-century social theorist to be thoroughly influenced by Gallian phrenology. Spencer became a devout follower of phrenological doctrine after hearing Gall's disciple Spurzheim lecture at Derby in 1830.[21] Confirmed by the mood of Spencer's youthful dabblings, phrenology in its British setting was markedly optimistic in outlook, its chief exponents stressing self-help, material progress, and moral improvement. Spencer read Comte in the early 1850's and though he later denied all influence, he may have been impressed with the compatibility of a biology of mind and social evolutionism in Comte's system.[22] Spencer had embarked on his life-long career as amateur social scientist with the publication of *Social Statics* in 1850. He had already adopted the evolutionary perspective on which all his mature work would be based. As has been fully appreciated, Spencer's concept of evolutionism was thoroughly Lamarckian. He integrated the rather generalized concept of natural selection propounded by Darwin into his work written after 1859, but he was aroused to defend the Lamarckian hypothesis in his extreme old age after Weismann's formulation of the mutational heresy in the mid-1880s.

Spencer was most decidedly an exponent of "methodological individualism." Although his sociology contained general laws of social development, these were nearly wholly determined by or deduced from the nature and actions of individuals.[23] Appropriately, the first major subject to which Spencer applied his Lamarckian evolutionism was a systematic psychology. Though the *Principles of Psychology* of 1855 looked ahead to the social theory, it also addressed itself to the untying of some old knots in epistemology. As Robert Young has shown, though Spencer had become a convert to associationism, he did not therefore abandon the phrenological ideas of his youth. His psychology was an effort to combine these two traditions within a single evolutionary matrix. Though there were occasional difficulties at the level of empirical explanation, Spencer's system represented a major conceptual advance in psychological epistemology. His system explained sensationalism and the associational basis of conscious mental life, as well as the existence of certain natural (innate) endowments whose presence could not be accounted for by sensational experience alone. Spencer accomplished this feat by positing a "racial" or group evolutionary experience, a kind of average effect of the historical exposure of a body of individuals to a particular set of environmental conditions.[24] According to Spencer, both "physical and psychical peculiarities" are hereditarily transmitted, "which by infinite repetition in countless successive generations have established these sequences as organic relations."[25]

Spencer's formula for expressing the mechanism of transmission is the "adjustment of inner relations to outer relations," a close approximation of the Lamarckian notion of an adaptive "organic economy." This is how Spencer applied this concept to the evolution of instinct, which had been the Achilles heel of associationist psychology:

> Let it be granted that the more frequently psychical states occur in a certain order, the stronger becomes their tendency to cohere in that order, until they at last become inseparable; let it be granted that this tendency is, in however slight a degree, inherited, so that if the experiences remain the same each successive generation bequeaths a somewhat increased tendency; and it follows that, in cases like the one described, there must eventually result an automatic connexion of nervous actions, corresponding to the external relations perpetually experienced. (p. 439)

Spencer's point is that a hierarchy of instincts and "psychic" sentiments exists in the organism based on the degree of "indissolubility" each possesses. An instinct, or any "combination of psychical states," is the more indissoluble the more frequently it has been repeated in the course of organic evolution. The "highest" instincts, on the contrary, having been less often repeated, are less determinate ("undecided" in Spencer's word), and so merge "insensibly" with "something higher," by which Spencer means conscious and voluntary mental acts (pp. 442–43). In typical nineteenth-century fashion Spencer illustrates his argument by appeal to "evidence from abnormal variations":

> The plexuses which coordinate the defensive and destructive activities, and in which are seated anger, are inherited from all antecedent races of creatures, and are therefore well organized . . . But the plexuses which, by connecting and coordinating a variety of inferior plexuses, adapt the behavior to a variety of external requirements, have been but recently evolved; so that, besides being extensive and intricate, they are formed of much less permeable channels. Hence when the nervous system is not fully charged, these latest and highest structures are the first to fail. (p. 605)

In Spencer's mechanistic model of brain and nerve function, blood nutrients and blood pressure account for the observable macroscopic effects in behavior. Mental disorders are therefore the consequences of bad nutrition, of engorgements or deficiencies in blood pressure due to rates of cerebral and motor actions, or of the presence of "morbid matter" in the bloodstream arising from constitutional disease, alcohol, drugs, or other intoxicants (pp. 606–12). In all these instances the paradigm of intoxication applies, so that "the highest nervous actions are the first to be arrested; and that the artificial paralysis implicates in descending order the lower, or simpler, or better-established nervous actions (p. 611). Spencer allowed for the operation of similar processes in his sociology.

J. D. Y. Peel has effecively demonstrated the differences between the Darwinian and Spencerian models of social evolution. The Darwinian model, agnostic about the *direction* of species change, held evolution to be a consequence of the survival of those best adapted to some physical environment. Spencer's Lamarckism led him to the view that the environment to which individuals had to adapt was comprised of the collectively acquired "social state" in addition to the basic physical elements in the Darwinian scheme. Mediated by the presence of social "instincts," the struggle for life in Spencer's evolution was less vicious, preserving space for teleological elements and considering "selection" to be a process preserving individuals whose acquired characters advanced adaptation to an increasingly integrated and harmonious "social state."[26]

As we have seen in the *Psychology*, however, Spencer's evolutionary model allowed for the possibility of individual regression and the appearance of individual pathologies. Since, despite the optimistic teleology he built into his evolutionism, Spencer's concept of adaptation was essentially *ecological* in nature, he was forced to address himself to all those influences in the environment that might nurture the appearance of social pathologies. By 1873, when he finished *The Study of Sociology*, his early optimism was beginning to give way to concern.

Spencer was gravely worried about the negative effects of welfare-state socialism on evolution. He believed the expansion of the sphere of state interference carried with it the danger of physical and mental defects of a *biological* order. Spencer argued that there was a natural equilibrium between fertility and mortality in a society. If one diminished mortality by removing or mitigating some of its causes, fertility would increase, but only by preserving feeble individuals who would normally have perished in the struggle for survival. In the end, these individuals and their descendants would be less able to withstand "fresh diseases" or sources of mortality arising from unexpected quarters, with the effect that more would die, thus bringing mortality and fertility back into equilibrium.[27] The preservation of enfeebled individuals also takes its toll, Spencer insisted, on the "mental applications" of the fit, who, in their efforts to supply the necessities of life for the weak, "are subject to an overdraw upon their energies." In various ways this exertion tends "to arrest the increase of the best, to deteriorate their constitutions, and to pull them down towards the level of the worst" (pp. 343–44).

Spencer was convinced, in 1873, that though there had been a *quantitative* improvement in the population in his lifetime (a great number of people living longer lives) there had been a *qualitative* decline. He remarked on how many new diseases were met with nowadays than in earlier stages of human development, and observed "how few thoroughly-strong people we meet, and how prevalent are chronic ailments notwithstanding the care taken of health" (pp. 342–43). The Lamarckian acquisition of characters thus also worked in reverse as "a deliberate storing-up of miseries for future generations. There is no greater curse to posterity than that of bequeathing them an increasing population of imbeciles and idlers and criminals" (pp. 344–45). If society no longer provides an environment in which adaptive changes will foster the growth of the virtues of self-reliance and independence, it is doomed. Thus, "enforce these conditions, and adaptation to them will continue. Relax these conditions, and by so much there will be a cessation of the adaptive changes. Abolish these conditions, and, after the consequent social dissolution, there will commence (unless they are re-established) an adaptation to the conditions then resulting—those of savage life" (p. 349).

It may be fairly said that Spencer made a definite allowance for evolutionary regression in his sociology. Indeed J. D. Y. Peel defends him vigorously against the charge that he was a naive proponent of unilinear progress. Not only did Spencer not deny historical proof of regressions, averring that they might be as frequent as progressions, but he held that progress and decline proceeded in oscillations, with progress, when it occurred, being of a divergent and redivergent rather than a linear character.[28]

In France, Spencer's thought was readily assimilated into the native Lamarckian tradition. Théodule Ribot, who was the most influential psychologist in France before the time of Pierre Janet, introduced Spencer's evolutionary psychology to French thinkers in *La Philosophie anglaise contemporaine* (1870). Ribot joined the work of French pathological medicine, including the work of B.-A. Morel and his disciples, with Spencer's evolutionary outlook in his important thesis of 1873, *L'Hérédité psychologique*. Here Ribot explained how individual faculties and aptitudes reflected the environmental experience of the entire race or species, and were passed on to later generations in the genotype. In a series of monographs on mental pathology written in the 1880s, Ribot maintained that the lower passions and instincts had a prior adaptive role in human evolution than the qualities of reasoning and self-control, and so were more firmly rooted in contemporary mental structure.[29]

These central ideas were simply ramified in the major works of mental pathology during the remainder of the century.[30] In practice, French psychiatrists treated heredity and milieu as factors of equal importance and as mutually reinforcing elements in the etiology of mental illness. British psychiatry, moved by the same theoretical considerations, also struck a pragmatic middle way between heredity and milieu. Like their French colleagues, Charles Mercier and Henry Maudsley regarded mental disease to be a failure of inhibitory control by "higher" functional levels over the "lower" and more primitive levels of the central nervous system.[31]

The advantage of this blending of mental pathology and evolutionary psychology was its ability to explain the *origin* of morbid mental states as "adaptive" pathologies that were then fixed in the organism. As in the format proposed by B.-A. Morel in the *Traité des dégénérescences* (1857), the first generation concealed the adaptation as a "tendency" or "predisposition," but later generations experienced it as a debilitating physical condition of morbid type.

In the absence of some countervailing external force, the syndrome developed an autonomous hereditarian momentum, exhibiting its advance in worsening behavior and physical signs. The weakened capacity for "resistance" made the individual organism vulnerable to diseases and hostile environments. The "moral" effects expressed themselves as will pathologies, that is, as a catastrophically reduced ability to resist "impulsions" of instinct, the blandishments of sensual allure, the wine shop, or easy money.[32] I have shown elsewhere how psychiatrists, criminologists, and other social scientists in France treated crime, madness, alcoholism, prostitution, suicide, and the declining birthrate as effects of widespread degeneration.[33] As these pathologies infected increasing numbers of *individuals*, they contributed to the general worsening of the *social* milieu by acting as pathogenic environmental influences on healthy persons. Symptoms thereby assumed the status of causes in degeneracy theory, becoming so hopelessly confounded with one another and with the syndrome itself that they were in practice interchangeable.[34]

Degeneracy theory had a special appeal in France. Statistics revealed that after 1850 the nation was suffering from a variety of internal ailments. The French birthrate was dramatically lower than other European states, actually falling below the mortality rate in certain years after 1890.[35] The French led all of Europe in per capita alcohol consumption at the end of the nineteenth century; strong cases were made for the rise in crime rates, particularly assault and homicide. Much was also made of a rise in the population of insane asylums from 49,589 in 1871 to 100,291 in 1911.[36] Organic diseases appeared to many medical observers to be on the increase: tuberculosis and syphilis were "discovered" by hygiene and public health experts near the end of the century, lending impetus and cogency, in the case of the latter affliction, to the arguments of purity crusaders who connected it to prostitution and pornography in this "golden age of venereal peril." Doctors estimated that 13 to 15 percent of Parisian males and one million individuals nationwide were infected with venereal disease, which in its chronic form of "parasyphilis" was believed to be inheritable.[37] Degeneration theory enabled one to see in the criminal, the alcoholic, or the suicide a symbol of France's tenuous grip on great-power status. This mode of thinking encouraged the appraisal of social problems from the point of view of national interest, thrusting, as it were, the issues of domestic health and external security into an identical frame of analysis. As we shall see later, this dialectic also operated in Britain after 1890 or so.

France's foremost sociologist, Emile Durkheim, was profoundly aware of his nation's sad dilemma and addressed its problem in his work. In *The Division of Labor in Society* (1893), Durkheim proposed a model of social evolution similar in many respects to Herbert Spencer's.[38] Durkheim advanced the Lamarckian argument that the growth of the division of labor shapes the brain and nervous system of humans as they adapt to social arrangements of increasing speed and complexity: "The nerve cords . . . are the canals which life has hewed for itself while steadily flowing in the same direction"[39] In meeting the challenges of "civilization" the human brain becomes "more voluminous and more delicate," suffering "difficulties and privations" that less refined brains do not feel (p. 273). Man must pay another price for enlarging his intellectual capacity. Since the organism functions at any time on a fixed quantity of vital force, an excessive expenditure of effort by a single faculty creates a "deficit" in the "budget" of the organism. This rupture of internal equilibrium causes the atrophy of other organ functions, notably muscular force and reproductive power. Durkheim argues that though these qualities are "recent" acquisitions of the organism, and do not have the "fixity or rigidity" which only a long hereditary sequence can produce, they nonetheless assume "definite forms" in which they become "imprisoned little by little" (p. 231).

Durkheim applied this general approach to his work on social pathology through the 1880s and 1890s. In a little-known paper of 1888, Durkheim treated the relationship of suicide and birthrates. He affirmed the pathological nature of large increases in suicides, and inquired whether or not one could conclude similarly about changes in birthrates, especially where it could be shown that they varied regularly with suicide rates. He placed the question immediately in a geopolitical context, arguing that a low birthrate is a tragedy for a society, but "it is in addition a pity and an evil for individuals. Not only is a society which grows regularly stronger and more capable of maintaining itself against rival societies, but its members themselves have a greater chance to survive. Their organism has more vigor, more force of resistance."[40] Durkheim identified the common cause underlying both these pathological conditions as a disruption of the equilibrium of "vital force" which served as the stable milieu in which individuals lived. Then, in an effort to establish the primacy of sociological causation, for which he campaigned in all his work, Durkheim had resort to a typical neo-Lamarckian explanation, merging biological and social realms:

> It is true that the departments where there are most suicides and least births are also those which have the most insane. But that proves only that madness, like suicide and the birth-rate does not result uniquely from individual and accidental variations, but, for a good part, from social causes. Tainted nervous systems do not multiply themselves in a group only by means of unfortunate cross-breedings and hereditary predispositions, but also from the bad sociological conditions in which they find themselves placed. *Organic causes are often social causes transformed and fixed in the organism. There are thus social causes common to suicide and natality which are able to explain their relation.*[41]

In his classic *Suicide* (1897), Durkheim continued his battle against wholly psychiatric explanations of self-destruction. He made the point he had already raised in 1888, namely that insanity "is partly a social phenomenon."[42] It is not entirely enlightening, as Gurvitch and others have done, to accuse Durkheim of having constructed a "false dichotomy" between the "individual" and the "social," and to claim that he failed to recognize the "reciprocity" of their mutual influence.[43] It would be more accurate to say that, far from locating society and the individual in separate ontological realms, he merged those realms to a point where the boundaries between them, for the purposes of social causation, practically disappeared.

In a similar fashion, Durkheim refused to make hard and fast distinctions between normal and pathological phenomena, holding that one could only, in the fashion of the physiologists, measure quantitative differences along an infinite scale of variations. As a consequence, "suicides do not form, as might be thought, a wholly distinct group, an isolated class of monstrous phenomena, unrelated to them by a continuous series of intermediate cases. They are merely the exaggerated form of common practices."[44] By the same token, in the motivations of suicides, there is a "gradual shading from normal and deliberate acts to illusions and automatic impulses" (p. 66). To make this biological conception of the normal and the pathological work smoothly in his theory of suicide, Durkheim borrowed the popular clinical idea of neurasthenia from psychiatry. Neurasthenia, according to Durkheim, lies in the "intermediate stages" between mental alienation and a "perfect equilibrium" of intelligence. The neurasthenic is not insane, and is capable of deliberation, but is nonetheless a type commonly found among suicides. He is extremely sensitive and impressionable, his nervous system is in a "weakened state," and his feelings are always in "unstable equilibrium" (p. 69).

As it is a lesser form of insanity, Durkheim asks, may we not study neurasthenia to see whether it varies with the social suicide rate? Since statistics on neurasthenia were not known, Durkheim proposed an "indirect" solution in perfect accord with degeneration theory: "Since insanity is only the enlarged form of nervous degeneration, it may be granted without risk of serious error that the number of nervous degenerates varies in proportion to that of the insane, and consideration of the latter may be used as a substitute in the case of the former" (p. 70).

Durkheim then attempts to demonstrate that there is an *inverse* relation between suicide rates and insanity, using sexual, religious, and national differentials. But, astonishingly, his conclusion is not to dismiss neurasthenia as a causal influence on suicide, but to detach it from insanity and claim it as a secondary social cause for self-destruction. Neurasthenics, in short, have no *intrinsic* predisposition to suicide; indeed they are not "essentially a-social" in nature:

> Other causes must supervene upon their special organic condition to give it this twist and develop it in this direction. Neurasthenia by itself is a very general predisposition, but capable of assuming the most varied forms according to circumstances. It is a field in which most varied tendencies may take root depending on the fertilization it receives from social causes.[45]

Durkheim clinches his argument by showing how this model explains who commits suicide:

> The hypercivilization which breeds the anomic tendency and the egoistic tendency also refines nervous systems, making them excessively delicate; through this very fact they are less capable of firm attachment to a definite object, more impatient of any sort of discipline, more accessible both to violent imitation and to exaggerated depression. Inversely, the crude, rough culture implicit in the excessive altruism of primitive man develops a lack of sensitivity which favors renunciation. In short, just as society largely forms the individual, it forms him to the same extent in its own image. Society, therefore, cannot lack the material for its needs, for it has, so to speak, kneaded it with its own hands. (p. 323)

These neuropathic individuals, whose mental constitutions are shaped by the social conditions of "hypercivilization," do not kill themselves simply because they are neuropathic; instead, as Durkheim has demonstrated throughout his book, they kill themselves because they are driven to do so by suicidogenic currents which are social in nature and which "call" their victims from among those neurasthenics because these individuals offer "less resistance" to them. One can explain this or that suicide by appeal to a clinical diagnosis of neurosis or alcoholism, but one can explain suicide rates only by reference to social conditions.

In Great Britain by the 1880s and 1890s, the evolutionary ideas of Spencer and Darwin had—willy-nilly—been grafted onto the dominant liberal paradigm in order "as evidence, metaphor or law, to demonstrate that competition was the motor of advance in the natural and social world alike."[46] The best-known manifestation of this tendency in British liberalism was the eugenics movement, which flourished between 1900 and 1914. But eugenical thinking cannot be accounted for along strictly political lines: eugenists numbered liberals, socialists, and even a few conservatives in their midst, and their opponents showed a similar political diversity. The most articulate opponents of the eugenics movement could be found in the small but energetic British sociology community.

British sociology cannot be identified with a school, as was true of French sociology in that era, nor were there any giants who personally shaped the contours of the emerging discipline. Indeed, Abrams has argued that British sociology borrowed heavily from continental social science because it conceived that its task was to build a solid defense against the pernicious influence of Herbert Spencer.[47] Spencer presumably failed to influence the development of the theoretical tradition he helped to found because of his blatant attack on ameliorism and improvements in the environment. Emerging British sociology was located somewhere on the left wing of the Liberal party, which began to tilt in the direction of welfare-state interventionism in the 1890s. L. T. Hobhouse, J. A. Hobson, and others defended the two main scientific ideas on which the philosophy of the liberal welfare state was based: the efficacy of environmental reforms and the growth of altruism in the course of social evolution. If we set these views in opposition to those espoused by the eugenists, namely the counterproductive effects of environmental reforms and the enduring value of rugged individualism, we seem to have a clear-cut political dispute with equally tidy divisions in the parallel realm of evolutionary science.

Unfortunately, these neat distinctions were not very well maintained in practice, on either the scientific or the political level. We are told that in order to become a "plausible political creed" eugenics had to await the emergence of a scientific theory of heredity which precisely explained how physical and intellectual qualities were transmitted.[48] In G. R. Searle's view this stage was not finally reached until the "rediscovery" of Mendelian genetics in 1899 and its theoretical elaboration by deVries, Bateson, and others in subsequent years. But all eugenists were not so willing to treat 1899 as a great scientific watershed. Elements of pre-Mendelian genetical theories, and even some retouched Lamarckism, could be found in the works of eugenical writers. Degeneration theory, whose origins are closely connected to Lamarck's idea, was also an indispensable part of their ideology.

The liberal social scientists, on the other hand, were obliged to finesse the issue of Mendelian genetics so that it would do minimal damage to their reformist and environmentalist aspirations. In their efforts to make the best case for the formative influence of the milieu, reformist sociologists often adopted degeneration theory as a supporting argument. As the liberal economist Alfred Marshall put it in 1908, "If it is true that good wheat sown year after year on barren soil degenerates, why should it not be true that the social life of many generations of parents—quite independent of selection—affects the nerves, and the quality and the character of later generations."[49] The liberals could not, in the end, deny the scientific status of Mendelian genetics, nor, as events later proved, was the notion of abrupt mutations in the genotype uncongenial to twentieth-century liberalism.[50] In some ways the outcome of the argument over the precise mechanism of hereditary transmission was beside the point. The idea of degeneration had a powerful appeal to British men and women in the period after 1885 no matter what their politics or their views on genetics. This was so because the basic concept had become part of both social science lore and popular culture for sound *historical* reasons. It appeared to account for developments in British life about which there was widespread public concern.

Gareth Jones has persuasively documented the Victorian change of attitude toward cities in his *Outcast London* (1971). From a place of creative opportunity, upward mobility, and transitory impoverishment, the metropolis after 1870 was widely regarded as the breeding ground of a subhuman class of permanently pauperized beings known as "the residuum." What Jones calls "the theory of urban degeneration" was created to replace the outmoded notion that poverty and its attendant evils were a product of rampant lower-class hedonism.[51] This theory held that drink, idleness, and improvidence were *symptoms* not simply causes of a syndrome of poverty whose actual causes were rooted in the pathological ecology of the urban slum. Concern about the "residuum" was at fairly low ebb until around 1900, when the reverses of the Boer War and the issue of fitness of the recruits revived public interest. It is difficult for us today to appreciate fully the extraordinary panic produced within the educated classes by the spectacle of Boer armies resisting an Imperial Army which had conquered half the world. With the great majority of the organs of public opinion in an uproar, an official Committee on Physical Deterioration issued a soothing report in 1904 playing down the danger of permanent damage.[52] But, as Samuel Hynes has pointed out, far from stilling anxieties of this kind, the report was generally taken as proof of the seriousness of the biological situation, and the word "deterioration" was used interchangeably with "degeneracy" and "decadence."[53] More importantly, the smoldering concern of the 1880s and 1890s burst into a nationwide debate on the sources of imperial greatness. Suggestions were aired about segregating the "residuum," and a decade-long crusade began that sought to regenerate the "national efficiency" of the Victorian era.[54]

Logically, the recommendations about housing and urban hygiene in the report of the Committee on Physical Deterioration might be taken as a victory for the environmentalists. But the general atmosphere encouraged the growth of eugenical organizations and publications, and lent scientific legitimacy to the work of Francis Galton and Karl Pearson in the Eugenics Laboratory.[55] Leaving aside the matter of "positive" or "negative" eugenics, the core of the eugenist argument was that there was a grievous "fertility differential" between the well-off and healthy, who limited their births, and the diseased and destitute masses of the poor, who bred like rabbits. Owing to the improvident generosity of modern welfare, many more of the allegedly defective offspring of the poor survived to reproduce more of their own kind, replacing, in the words of Karl Pearson the "survival of the fittest" by the "survival of the most fertile."[56]

But, in spite of their reliance on Mendelian genetics, eugenists could not dispense with the concept of degeneration. The most popular eugenical formula for describing Britain's biological quandry was "racial degeneration." The various qualities of alcoholism, tuberculosis, or mental illness were widely reported as part of the syndrome Karl Pearson called "general degeneracy," in which these "symptoms" were regarded as "interchangeable."[57] This condition was hereditary and was magnified in the offspring of two infected parents. What eugenists seem to have done here is to have reified degeneracy. They appropriated the symptomatic syndrome with its progressive, hereditary consequences, but they abandoned the self-adjusting equilibrium model which made degeneracy a product of dynamic interaction between individuals and their environments. Thus such studies as Richard L. Dugdale's on the infamous Juke family, which was based in part on Lamarckian premises, were converted into arguments for hereditarianism by subsequent commentators.[58]

Many eugenists and hereditarians also endorsed a kind of closet Lamarckism, which allowed them to smuggle in the back door what had been expelled with great fanfare out the front. John Berry Haycraft wrote in the immediate pre-Mendelian era, but based his austere hereditarianism on Weismann's theory of the absolute separation of soma and germ cells. He did not find it inconvenient, however, to aver that alcohol was transported by the bloodstream to the "germinal" cells and could "debilitate" the offspring produced by them. The resulting "incapable" possessed a lower threshhold to "exciting factors" or "intoxicants" in the environment to which he might succumb.[59] In his *Heredity and Selection in Sociology* (1907), George Chatterton-Hill, after attacking Lamarckian theory, propounded the theory that alcohol, and such diseases as tuberculosis and syphilis, could have a direct effect on the "germ" cells by means of blood circulation. This led to a "constitutional weakening" in the offspring, which Chatterton-Hill calls a "general pathological condition" predisposing its victim to "epilepsy, insanity, crime, and neurasthenia."[60] Chatterton-Hill wrote that alcoholics were the "typical product of modified social conditions, tainted with the external stigmata of his vice, incapable of doing anything settled, going every year to swell the host of good-for-nothings and loafers, of criminals, and the other waste products of society."[61] Alongside an appeal for the implementation of eugenics, Chatterton-Hill observed that modern life "has multiplied the risks of danger by creating new diseases and sources of degeneracy as fast as it has invented new methods for combating old ones" (pp. 542–43). Degeneration *redivivus*.

L. T. Hobhouse, with E. A. Westermarck, one of Britain's first academic sociologists, is generally regarded as the most effective opponent of the eugenists among the so-called liberal reformers.[62] In his *Social Evolution and Political Theory* (1911), he offered a systematic critique of social evolution conceived as a biological process, and generally amplified the notion, found in germ form in Spencer, that progress could be measured in terms of the growth of a *sui generis* "social mind" in which the highest collective values of civilization resided. However, the book is far from being either a thorough repudiation of eugenics or an unambiguous resuscitation of some notion of progress with the biological element removed. First, Hobhouse acknowledged the scientific force of the new mutation theory. From this ground he admitted that the biological health of the race was a factor in human progress, but held it was an independent variable that could influence the overall progress only in a limited degree.[63] He concentrated his criticism of eugenics on its ability to discern truly what in the biological character of man was useful or harmful to social evolution. Thus, he denied that tuberculosis could be made out to be a negative factor, and he did his best to extricate both poverty and insanity from the nexus of biologically grounded hereditary traits (pp. 44–51). However, he did not thereby dismiss the program of "negative" eugenics on either scientific or ethical grounds. Indeed, he acknowledged the value of the segregation of some of the insane, feeble, syphilitics, and alcoholics, and wrote, in connection with the "feeble-minded" that "the evidence, I understand, is rather that it is a form of general deterioration not correlated with any specially good qualities by way of compensation" (p. 46).

But Hobhouse could not resist, much as with some eugenists, the temptation to reintroduce the morbid effects of environmental influence on the organism. He quotes the biologist J. Arthur Thomson, that the germ-plasm could be shaped by "a deeply saturating influence," concluding that the "indirect and subtle" effects of environment could not be ruled out.[64] Evidently Hobhouse could not fully break with the old Lamarckian notion that man and milieu were linked in a dialectical relationship that was productive of both positive and negative effects. He was at pains to show that social evolution revealed evidence of increasing amounts of self-determination, but held that man was by no means free to "make of himself whatever he pleases" (pp. 157–58). Accordingly, stagnation and even retrogression were entirely possible, and even undoubted advances were often balanced off by unfortunate consequences (pp. 163–65).

Despite Abrams' contention about the anti-Spencerian qualities of British social thought, most elements of Spencer's social evolutionism were clearly present in the debates over eugenics. For both sides negative environments could produce harmful and hereditary biological effects. Neither party could conceive of social progress without being also heedful of the ill effects generated by new social formations.

As we have seen, sociologists throughout the nineteenth century found degeneration theory indispensable in their work. It effectively accounted for the terrible human costs of modernization, expressed in the perceived growth of "urban" diseases, of alcoholism, crime, insanity, suicide, and various sexual perversions. Integrated into sociological theory, the idea of degeneration was able to resolve the apparent paradox of misery amidst growing plenty, of individual pathologies in a vigorous and highly integrated social organism. But, displaying its debt to its medical and biological origins, degeneration theory ordained that there were certain natural limits in the ability of the social organism to withstand the spread of infected individuals. Reverses in the fortunes of states and societies were possible, and perhaps inevitable. Progress was most tenuous and most vulnerable at its moments of greatest triumph, an irony that haunts us still in our own century.

NOTES

1. Edward Shils, "Tradition, Ecology, and Institution in the History of Sociology," *Selected Papers of Edward Shils* (Chicago: University of Chicago Press, 1980), 3:230.

2. Georg Simmel, *The Sociology of Georg Simmel*, Kurt H. Wolff, tr. (New York: Free Press, 1950), p. 80.

3. For these influences, see Robert M. Young, *Mind, Brain, and Adaptation in the Nineteenth Century: Cerebral Localization and its Biological Context from Gall to Ferrier* (Oxford: Clarendon Press, 1970), esp. pp. 9–53, 197–223.

4. These aspects of phrenology have been discussed in some recent work: Roger Cooter, "Phrenology and British Alienists, ca. 1825–1845," in Andrew Scull, ed., *Madhouses, Mad-Doctors, and Madmen: The Social History of Psychiatry in the Victorian Era* (Philadelphia: University of Pennsylvania Press, 1981), esp. pp. 66–75; Angus McLaren, "A Prehistory of the Social Sciences: Phrenology in France," *Comparative Studies in Society and History* (January 1981), 23(1):13–16.

5. Cooter, pp. 78–79.

6. Young has effectively shown how Hughlings Jackson and, through him, Ferrier, was influenced by Spencer's *Principles of Psychology*, which presented phrenological ideas in an evolutionary-adaptational context. See Young, pp. 197–206.

7. I discuss the influences of individual and "collective" psychology on some of these thinkers in *The Anti-Democratic Sources of Elite Theory: Pareto, Mosca, Michels*, Sage Papers in Contemporary Political Sociology (London and Beverly Hills: Sage Publications, 1977).

8. See, on these fluctuations, Gertrud Lenzer's remarks in *August Comte and Positivism. The Essential Writings*, Gertrud Lenzer, ed. (New York: Harper and Row, 1975), pp. xviii–xxxi.

9. Mill's *Auguste Comte and Positivism* (1865) relates the progress of this relationship, but it is also summarized briefly in the "Autobiography" (New York: New American Library, 1964), pp. 155–56. See also Lenzer, ed., *Auguste Comte*, pp. xxvi–xxxi.

10. For the view that Comte was mentally disturbed while writing the *Système*, see Stanislaw Andrewski, ed., *The Essential Comte*, Margaret Clarke, tr. (London: Croom Helm, 1974), introduction. Lenzer takes the opposite view that Comte may not be perfectly appreciated until all "stages" are seen in common focus (p. xv).

11. Pitirim Sorokin, *Contemporary Sociological Theories through the First Quarter of the Twentieth Century* (New York: Harper and Row, 1964), pp. 433–54.

12. August Comte, *Cours de philosophie positive*, 4th ed. (Paris: Baillière, 1869), p. 446. My emphasis.

13. Lucien Lévy-Bruhl, writing in the golden age of French neo-Lamarckian biology, acknowledged this difficulty, arguing that Comte was "much influenced" by Lamarck, adopting Cuvier's hierarchy of fixed species for the "formal" reason that it corresponded fully with the "positive" and static hierarchy of knowledge that Comte believed was imminent. Lucien Lévy-Bruhl, *La Philosophie d'Auguste Comte* (Paris: Alcan, 1900), p. 210.

14. See the exhaustive survey of the French scientific community's rejection of natural selection in Yvette Conry, *L'Introduction du Darwinisme en France au XIXe siècle* (Paris: Vrin, 1974).

15. Comte, 4:488–89. My emphasis.

16. Comte, 4:451–52. In this passage Comte's debt to the idea that "phylogeny recapitulates ontogeny" is clearly revealed, despite Lévy-Bruhl's insistence that he had not read Von Baer, in Lévy-Bruhl's *La Philosophie d'Auguste Comte*, pp. 208–09. For other references to this process see Comte, 4:446–47.

17. He refers here to Broussais, one of the chief exponents of this view in French physiology. Comte, 4:232. See Canguilhem, *Le Normal et le pathologique*, 3d ed. (Paris: Presses Universitaires de France, 1975).

18. Comte, 3:234–35. He goes on to say that some organic anomalies "whose origin is only older and less known . . . are by nature more incurable" (pp. 236–37). Lévy-Bruhl also allows this possibility in the *Cours;* see *La Philosophie d'Auguste Comte*, p. 239.

19. Comtists have historically responded pessimistically to revolutionary episodes in French history. See Emile Littré, *Conservation, révolution, positivisme* (Paris, 1852); see also the extraordinary book by Comte's disciple Georges Audiffrent, a would-be neurologist, whose book *Des maladies du cerveau et de l'innervation d'après Auguste Comte* (Paris: Leroux, 1874), drew pessimistic conclusions about post-Commune France. Audiffrent's huge study is a compression of Comte's sociology into an updated phrenological psychiatry, proving, I think, that if Comte himself moved from biology to sociology, it was also possible to go back the other way.

20. Lenzer, pp. xiv–xv.

21. J. D. Y. Peel, *Herbert Spencer. The Evolution of a Sociologist* (New York: Basic Books, 1971), pp. 10–11.

22. Peel, pp. 14–15.

23. Peel, esp. pp. 154–55.

24. For a full discussion of this point, see Young, pp. 172–79.

25. Herbert Spencer, *The Principles of Psychology,* 2nd ed. (London: Williams and Norgate, 1870), p. 422.

26. Peel, pp. 145–48, 154–55.

27. Herbert Spencer, *The Study of Sociology* (New York: Appleton, 1874), pp. 339–42.

28. Peel, pp. 156–57. Peel also emphasizes Spencer's growing conservatism, his interest after 1880 in playing down the possibility of further advantageous adaptational acquisitions in favor of the simple retention of the stored-up benefits of past progress (p. 145).

29. *Maladies de la mémoire* (1881), *Maladies de la volonté* (1883), *Maladies de la personnalité* (1885). As Ribot wrote in 1883 of volition: "Volition is not an event coming from no one knows where; it drives its roots into the depths of the unconscious and beyond the individual into the species and the race. It comes not from above, but from below: it is a sublimation of the lower instincts" (*Maladies de la volonté*, p. 150).

30. For instance, Dr. Henri LeGrande du Saulle, *La Folie héréditaire* (Paris, 1873); Dr. Alexandre Axenfeld, *Des Névrosés* (Paris, 1879); J. Déjérine, *L'hérédité dans les maladies du système nerveux* (Paris, 1886); Charles Féré, *La Famille névropathique* (Paris, 1894).

31. On these developments see Laurence J. Ray, "Models of Madness in Victorian Asylum Practice," *Archives Européennes de Sociologie* (1981), 20(2):229–64; Michael J. Clark, "The Rejection of Psychological Approaches to Mental Disorder in Late Nineteenth-Century British Psychiatry," in Scull, esp. pp. 283–88.

32. See Paul-Maurice LeGrain and Valentin Magnan, *Les dégénérés* (Paris: Rueff, 1895), p. 79. On the dominant "organicist" psychiatry of the period 1880–1914, see Paul Sérieux, *Valentin Magnan* (Paris: Masson, 1921); Robert Castel, *L'Ordre psychiatrique: L'Age d'or de l'alienisme* (Paris: Editions de Minuit, 1976), pp. 266–94; Henri Baruk, *La Psychiatrie Française de Pinel à nos jours* (Paris: P. U. F., 1967), pp. 94–124.

33. "Degeneration and the Medical Model of Cultural Crisis in the French Belle Epoque," in Seymour Drescher et al., ed., *Political Symbolism in Modern Europe: Essays in Honor of George L. Mosse* (New Brunswick, N. J.: Transaction Press, 1982), pp. 19–41. These issues are also treated in my *Crime, Madness, and Politics in Modern France: The Medical Concept of National Decline* (Princeton, N. J.: Princeton University Press, 1984).

34. The medical literature is extensive. We can cite only the most influential here: Dr. Charles Féré, *Dégénérescence et la criminalité* (Paris: Flammarion, 1888); Dr. Emile Laurent, "Les Maladies de la volonté chez les criminels," *Annales Médico-Psychologiques* (May 1891), pp. 434–50; Emile Laurent, *L'Anthropologie criminelle et les nouvelles théories du crime*, 2d ed. (Paris: Société d'Editions Scientifiques, 1893); Dr. H. Thulié, *La Lutte contre la dégénérescence et la criminalité*, 2d ed. (Paris: Vigot, 1912); Dr. Paul Masoin, *Alcoolisme et criminalité* (Paris, 1891); Dr. Paul-Maurice LeGrain, *Dégénérescence sociale et alcoolisme* (Paris, 1895); G. L. Duprat, *La Criminalité de l'adolescence* (Paris: Alcan, 1909) and *Les Causes sociales de la folie* (Paris: Alcan, 1900); Dr. Paul Jacoby, *Etudes sur la séléction chez l'homme*, 2d ed. (Paris: Baillière, 1905).

35. André Armengaud, *La Population française au XIXe siècle* (Paris: P. U. F., 1971), pp. 47–108.

36. See Michael R. Marrus,"Social Drinking in the *Belle Epoque*," *Journal of Social History* (Winter, 1974), 7(2):315–47; "Résumé rétrospectif," in *Annuaire Statistique* (Paris, 1937), 52:47–48; and "Assistance, asiles d'aliénés," *Annuaire Statistique*, 1913 (Paris, 1914), p. 33.

37. See Gérard Jacquemet, "Médicine et 'maladies populaires' dans le Paris de la fin du XIXᵉ siècle," *Recherches* (Dec., 1977), 29:245–83; Alain Corbin, *Les Femmes de noce: Misères sexuelles et prostitution au XIXᵉ et XXᵉ siècles* (Paris: Aubier, 1978), pp. 387–88.

38. I have discussed the model Durkheim constructs elsewhere in detail. See "Heredity, Pathology, and Psychoneurosis in Durkheim's Early Work," in *Knowledge and Society* (1983), 4:103–42.

39. Emile Durkheim, *The Division of Labor in Society*, George Simpson, tr. (New York: Free Press, 1933), p. 366.

40. Durkheim, "Suicide et natalité: Étude de statistique morale," *Revue Philosophique* (1888), 26:460.

41. Durkheim, pp. 461–62. My emphasis.

42. Emile Durkheim, *Suicide. A Study in Sociology*, John H. Spaulding and George Simpson, tr. (New York: Free Press, 1951), p. 58, n. 2.

43. See Anthony Giddens, "The Suicide Problem in French Sociology," *Studies in Social and Political Theory* (London: Hutchinson, 1977), pp. 328–29.

44. Durkheim, *Suicide*, p. 45.

45. Durkheim, *Suicide*, p. 77. As proof of the "ambiguous power" of neurasthenia, Durkheim offers the extraordinary example of the affinities between French and Russian writers, notably their delicate nervous systems and "lack of mental and moral equilibrium." But, he argues, different social consequences flow from these similar organic conditions: Russian literature is idealistic, "excites faith and provokes action," while "ours prides itself on expressing nothing but deep despair and reflects a disquieting state of depression" (p. 77, n. 30).

46. Stefan Collini, *Liberalism and Sociology: L. T. Hobhouse and Political Argument in England, 1880–1914* (Cambridge: Cambridge University Press, 1979), p. 26.

47. Philip Abrams, *The Origins of British Sociology: 1834–1914* (Chicago: University of Chicago Press, 1968), p. 67.

48. G. R. Searle, *Eugenics and Politics in Britain, 1900–1914* (Leyden: Noordhoff, 1976), pp. 5–6.

49. Quoted in Reba N. Soffer, *Ethics and Society in England: The Revolution in the Social Sciences, 1870–1914* (Berkeley: University of California Press, 1978), p. 92.

50. See the discussion in Everett Mendelsohn, "The Continuous and the Discrete in the History of Science," *Journal of Social Reconstruction* (1980), 1(1):23–25; also, Peter J. Bowler, "Hugo De Vries and Thomas Hunt Morgan: The Mutation Theory and the Spirit of Darwinism," *Annals of Science* (1978), 35:55–73.

51. Gareth Stedman Jones, *Outcast London: A Study in the Relationship between Classes in Victorian Society* (Oxford: Clarendon Press, 1971), pp. 127–31, 281–89.

52. On the initial reaction and debate see Searle, *Eugenics*, pp. 20–33.

53. Samuel Hynes, *The Edwardian Turn of Mind* (Princeton: Princeton University Press, 1968), pp. 22–24.

54. Jones, pp. 330–36, gives an account of the administrative and popular focus on the urban areas; also G. M. Searle, *The Quest for National Efficiency, 1899–1914* (Oxford: Oxford University Press, 1971).

55. Searle, *Eugenics*, pp. 9–19.

56. Karl Pearson, "Reproductive Selection," in *The Chances of Death and Other Studies in Evolution* (London: Edward Arnold, 1897), p. 102.

57. Searle, *Eugenics*, pp. 27–30.

58. Searle, *Eugenics*, p. 30. See the reference to the Juke study by John Berry Haycraft, *Darwinism and Race Progress* (London: Swan Sonnenschein, 1895), p. 90.

59. Haycraft, pp. 70–76.

60. George Chatterton-Hill, *Heredity and Selection in Sociology* (London: Adam and Charles Black, 1907), pp. 69–72.

61. Chatterton-Hill, p. 277. See also pp. 169–71, 259–73, 285–305.

62. Summaries of his views are plentiful, if slightly misleading. See Abrams, pp. 126–35; Collini, pp. 202–08; and John E. Owen, *L. T. Hobhouse, Sociologist* (London: Nelson, 1974), pp. 111–52.

63. L. T. Hobhouse, *Social Evolution and Political Theory* (London: Macmillan, 1911), pp. 37–39.

64. Hobhouse, pp. 62–64. The book from which Hobhouse quotes is Thomson's *Heredity* (London: Progressive Science Series, 1908).

4

SEXOLOGY, PSYCHOANALYSIS, AND DEGENERATION: FROM A THEORY OF RACE TO A RACE TO THEORY

SANDER L. GILMAN
Cornell University
Cornell Medical College

No realm of human experience is as closely tied to the concept of degeneration as that of sexuality.[1] The sexual connotation of the pejorative use of the word "degenerate" had its very source in a vision of mankind that defined and then examined the pathologies of human experience. The concepts of human sexuality and degeneracy are inseparable within nineteenth-century thought. Both evolved together and provided complementary paradigms for understanding human development.

Early Analogies of Sexuality and Degeneration

A glance at the history of human sexuality as understood by the human sciences in the late eighteenth and early nineteenth centuries illuminates a fascination with the pathological rather than the normal.[2] As much of the work on human sexuality was undertaken by medical practitioners who saw the pathological as the subject of their calling, it is of little surprise that their central focus in examining human sexuality was the problem of deviancy, and for the late eighteenth century and early nineteenth century the major deviancy was masturbation. The initial interest in masturbation as a sexual pathology appeared in the early eighteenth century, and its impetus was clearly theological. Indeed, the first widely circulated tractate on the subject, *Onania, or the Heinous Sin of Self-Pollution* (1726?), reads, not as much like a series of medical case studies as like the testimony of sinners presented in the newest church on Grub Street, the Tabernacle of Public Opinion. Indeed, the standard study of this subject assumes from the nature of the text that its author was probably a "clergyman turned quack."[3] Whether this conclusion is necessary can be left to individual judgment, but clearly the earliest popular or pseudomedical interest in sexuality was in the light of its illustration of the corruption of sexuality expressly when it occurs in the child. The cases portrayed in *Onania* exclusively deal with children or young adults who began masturbating as children. The deviancy of masturbation was an indicator of the potential for perversion inherent in mankind through the corruption of the fall from grace.

The first comprehensive nosology of human sexual pathology, Heinrich Kaan's *Sexual Pathology* (1844), departed from the basic view of human sexuality as perceived through this model of masturbation.[4] Kaan presented a definition of sexual pathology that argued for a universal, comprehensive perception of sexual pathology as proven by childhood sexual deviancy (pp. 47–48). Kaan's analogy between the sexuality of primitive man and that of the child is a crude type of chronological primitivism, similar to that argued by Hegel.[5] The child is the primitive form of man; the primitive is proof of man's earlier attitudes toward sexuality. In this conflation of types of sexual Otherness the germ of the concept of sexual degeneration is present. Hidden within each individual, capable of being triggered by his fantasy in opposition to his rational mind, is the tendency toward perversion. Perversion is the basic quality ascribed to the sexuality of the Other. Individual perversion is thus seen as a proof of the potential for the perversion of the group. Kaan, for example, even in postulating specific etiologies for masturbation in the hereditary, geographic, and environmental context of any given individual, presents a mini-history of human sexuality in his discussion of the ubiquitousness of sexual deviancy.

The worm hidden within man and society is also the leitmotif for B.-A. Morel's definition of "degeneration."[6] Morel argued that the degenerate bore the scars of his fall from grace.[7] He presented a straightforward categorization of the primitive as the proof of deviancy, much as did his contemporary Count Gobineau. The use of the anthropological model, Morel's greatest contribution to psychiatry, mirrored his understanding not only of man's individual development but his societal development. Here the presence of the degenerate is an anagoge for the eternal potential for the fall from grace.[8] It is found in the child, whatever the child's manifestation, either as primitive or as pathology.

Both Kaan and Morel share more than a generalized sense of chronological primitivism based on a theological perception of the fall from grace. Both draw on a model, that of the cretin, in which all the factors found in the models of deviant sexuality and degeneracy appear. B.-A. Morel initially formulated his concept of the degenerate through his study of the cretin.[9] Kaan's major predecessor in Germany, an author whose work is little examined in studies of the history of human sexuality, was Johannes Häussler, whose work entitled *On the Relationship of the Sexual System to the Psyche in General and to Cretinism in Particular* appeared in 1826.[10] The figure of the cretin provided a common locus for various aspects of Otherness found in the literature on masturbation as well as in the studies of the transmission of psychosexual pathologies. For the masturbator in his final state of collapse, his mind gone, his strength sapped, totally lethargic, is perceived as a type of mental defective. The literature of masturbatory insanity never clearly delineates what is cause and effect, imbecility or masturbation.[11] Morel presents parallel cases in his supplementary atlas. He introduced this case as one of two which he had selected from among the multitude of cases he had amassed. The case and its mode of presentation is illustrative of that type of material which Morel believed to show the generalized typology of the cretin:

> Marguerite Gros, twenty-three years old, from the village of Marcas, appears like a ten-year-old girl. She is not quite 977 mm tall and weighs about 20 kg. Noticeable is the lack of any sign of puberty and the retention of all her milk teeth. Her genitalia are no more developed than those of a seven or eight-year-old child. The pubis is totally hairless. The feeling of shame seems not yet to have been awakened.
>
> The examination of Dr. Destrade, the family doctor, who accompanied me on my visit, actually seemed to cause her no embarrassment. Twenty-four teeth are present and Destrade had determined, as I did that these were milk-teeth. This girl, whose organic development had come so completely to a stop, also had a very limited intelligence. She is unable to say how old she is nor does she know the value of various coins.[12]

The cretin here is the child and the primitive. The cretin's physiognomy is that of the child, her sexual attitude that of the child and the primitive.[13] The unrestrained sexuality of the cretin, the cretin's childlike appearance, the geographical and familial isolation of the cretin provided the ideal cases upon which to base the portrayal of retrogressive sexuality. For Morel, as indeed for Kaan, the presence of shame is the proof of adult and therefore civilized sexual behavior. The cretin stands apart from civilization, as does the deviant, in a world inhabited by the sexual Other, the primitive and the child.

Sexual Politics and Degeneration

The "scientific" study of human sexuality is the equivalent of the "scientific" study of human history. Jakob Santlus, in his *Psychology of*

Human Drives (1864), saw the origin of the "cultural history" of mankind in the combined "sexual and spiritual creativity" of mankind. Needless to say he remarked this in his tracing of the development of the history of human sexuality from the muck *(Schmutz)* of pre-Christian myth to the "ethical perfection" of Christianity.[14] Christianity's introduction of the feeling of shame or modesty was viewed in the mid-nineteenth century as the major indicator of the move from the primitive to the civilized. And just as three decades later Ernst Haeckel was to see the development of human society in the light of his embryological model of ontogeny recapitulating phylogeny, so too did those mid-nineteenth-century thinkers concerned with the development of sexuality from the child into the adult, the detailed course of human history.

One further qualification to this model was added by Rudolf Virchow, who, in his *Cellular Pathology* (1858), also drew on the analogy between the structure of the organism and the structure of the state.[15] For Virchow the interaction of the cells in the body was equivalent to the interaction of citizens in the body politic. Disease arose from only two sources: an active external source ("irritation") and a passive internal source. The latter he labeled "degeneration." So within the human body as well as within the body politic forces are constantly at work which expose hidden weaknesses of the body and can cause its eventual collapse.

The concept of sexual degeneracy as a political force in the flow of human history was expressed at mid-century in J. J. Bachofen's *Mother Law* (1870). While *Mother Law* does not overtly discuss the medical aspects of human sexuality but rather the development of history in the light of human sexuality, it does analyze the question of sexual degeneracy. Rather than a concern with models of masturbatory or cretinous degeneracy, the question of sexual degeneracy appears in relationship to the Amazon and becomes one of the major sources of early twentieth-century feminist criticism of Bachofen's model of history. For Bachofen perceived the movement from the hetaeristic age, of the age of exploitative promiscuity through matriarchy to eventual domination of the patriarchy as proof of the maturation of human society. Within this seemingly linear movement of history are ambiguous eddies, such as the violence of the Amazon, labeled by Bachofen as "savage degeneration."[16] The state of the Amazon, the cruel and unnatural domination of the male by the woman warrior, was a sign of an aberrant but necessary stage in human development. Its presence in all cultures echoed Kaan's discussion of the ubiquitousness of human sexual pathology (p. 105). Bachofen saw the origin of this form of deviancy as the result of psychic aberration. Unlike Kaan it is not the dominance of the irrational but rather the natural result of the dialectic of political repression (pp. 105–06).

Hegel's master-slave dyad had been used by John Stuart Mill in 1869 to describe the status of the woman in a male-dominated society.[17] However, seeing this as the rationale for the Amazon's nature is a remarkable shift in

Hegel's position. For Hegel had used the Amazon as the nadir of sexual degradation. In his *Lectures on the Philosophy of Religion* Hegel presented an anecdote concerning the fabulous state dominated by women, which told of a world of the Amazons even more destructive than Kleist's *Penthesilea*:

> Tradition alleges that in former times a state composed of women made itself famous by its conquests: it was a state at whose head was a woman. She is said to have pounded her own son in a mortar, to have besmeared herself with the blood, and to have had the blood of pounded children constantly at hand. She is said to have driven away or put to death all the males, and commanded the death of all male children. These furies destroyed everything in the neighborhood, and were driven to constant plunderings, because they did not cultivate the land. Captives in war were taken as husbands: pregnant women had to betake themselves outside the encampment; and if they had born a son, put him out of the way. This infamous state, the report goes on to say, subsequently disappeared.[18]

Hegel used this image of the Amazons not primarily to illustrate the history of the degenerate sexuality of the female but of the horrors which can take place among the blacks, whom Hegel describes not only as "pre-historic," that is, outside of the concept of history, but also as an "infantile nation."[19] Bachofen's discussion places the Amazon back into history but at a moment of degeneration. But degeneration is not merely retrogression to a more primitive mode of sexual expression; on the contrary he sees in this moment of degeneracy a progressive force. Society can be improved through a dialectic in which the antithesis is "savage degeneracy" (p. 105). This sense of the creativity inherent in the primitive underlies yet another perception of the nineteenth century concerning the close analogy between sexual deviancy and the nature of the state. The state can be undermined or revolutionized by retrogressive models of sexuality and the state bears within its own history this potential just as does the body. The state must have the means to control or harness this force. For Bachofen this can be seen in his view of the necessary progression from the Amazonian reaction against the bondage of woman in the hetaeristic state to the matriarchy. From lawlessness through lawlessness to mother law.

The arena of mid-nineteenth-century thought in which the analogy of the political and sexual models of degeneracy was most clearly played out was that of public health. Eduard Reich can stand as a representative writer in this area for the German-speaking lands. Reich, a medical doctor turned polyhistor, wrote a remarkable series of books during the latter half of the nineteenth century, books that were widely read and translated and were quite influential in public health reform. These books had one common leitmotif—the study of human history illustrates the repression of sexuality—and advocated the movement of sexuality from the private into the public sphere. For Reich the basic problem confronting society in the late nineteenth century was the question of the public control of human degeneracy, specifically through the control of sexual activity. Beginning with his study of the *History, Natural Laws, Laws of Hygiene in Matrimony* (1864) Reich saw the movement of mankind from the promiscuity of primitive man to modern institutions of matrimony as a means of eliminating potential causes of illness and perversion.[20] In his work *On Immorality* (1866) his historical means of understanding marriage was applied to the root causes of the potential of degeneracy, which however he still saw within the limits of the masturbatory mode.[21] Such deviant behavior, according to Reich, demanded the intervention of the state before the entire society succumbed to immorality. In 1868 Reich wrote one of the first major German studies—*Degeneracy of Man: Its Source and Prevention*.[22] Among the other causes of degeneracy in the individual as well as of the eventual collapse of the state, according to Reich, is the moral climate of society. For, as in Bachofen's view, an immoral state causes the corruption of its members. One of Reich's examples, not surprisingly, of the immorality of the state is the institution of slavery. He saw slavery not in Hegel's extrapolation of the master-slave dyad, but rather in the more specific model of black slavery, an issue that had defined this problem during the first half of the nineteenth century. Slavery can lead to degenerate sexuality as it can lead to other forms of degeneracy.

What can the state do to prevent this degeneracy from appearing and thus undermining the state itself? It can, of course, eliminate those features that further degeneracy, such as slavery, but it can and must police itself to prevent the excesses that lead to sexual degeneration. The public control and supervision of prostitution with its attendant reduction in the spread of venereal disease was one important arena of state intervention, but Reich also saw control of the form of government as a vital area of intervention.[23] Indeed, he ended his work on degeneration with a discussion of the potential degenerative effect of democracy and monarchy. In democracy degeneration can occur when wealth is unequally distributed and the state strives to expand itself too greatly through war, which leads to a "worsening of morals." Under a monarchy, the prime threat is the rigidity of the class structure and the "all too great striving for money."[24]

Reich's view that social and moral illness are inexorably linked was already echoed in the French discussion of racial and social degeneracy during the 1860s. Both Morel and Gobineau saw the analogy between class and race as a valid one. Class mobility was perceived as almost as dangerous as "hybridization" or, to use the mid-nineteenth-century term, of American racial pseudoscience, "miscegenation." Indeed the attraction of the Other as a sexual being in nineteenth-century fiction was enhanced by the Other being either another race or another class.[25]

The analogy between history and sexuality was most influential in its presentation as the opening chapter of Richard von Krafft-Ebing's *Sexual Psychopathology* (1888). This chapter, entitled "Fragments of a System of the Psychology of Sexual Life," is a skeletal history of mankind according to sexual principles. Like Bachofen, Krafft-Ebing perceived the history of mankind in stages of social development extrapolated from the stages of his sexual development. He began with the most "shameless" level of human development, seeing in contemporary "primitive" societies proof of the biblical view of the earliest stages of human society.[26] In his sketch of human sexuality Krafft-Ebing relied heavily on Edward Westermarck's *History of Human Marriage*.[27] Westermarck, however, saw a continuity of human institutions, such as monogamous marriage, as a means of overcoming aberrant promiscuity. For Krafft-Ebing the second state is the movement from the swamp, to use Bachofen's term, of universal promiscuity to a male-dominated world of human law (p. 25). It is only with Christianity that the concept of abstraction is introduced into human sexual activity:

> Christianity raised the union of the sexes to a sublime position by making woman socially the equal of man and by elevating the bond of love to a moral and religious institution. Thence emanates the fact that the love of man, if considered from the standpoint of advanced civilization, can only be of a monogamic nature and must rest upon a stable basis. Even though nature should claim merely the law of propagation, a community (family or state) cannot subsist without the guarantee that the offspring thrive physically, morally and intellectually. From the moment when woman was recognized the peer of man, when monogamy became a law and was consolidated by legal, religious and moral conditions, the Christian nations obtained a mental and material superiority over the polygamic races, and especially over Islam (pp. 25–26).

This movement from chaos to human law to divine law is the basic view of history found in Hegel. It reappears in various guises in Bachofen, Reich, and in such later writers about human sexuality as August Forel. It is this paradigm that Lewis H. Morgan (1877) and Friedrich Engels (1884) adopt in their extension of the argument that the human control of human sexuality is but another means of state control.[28] Krafft-Ebing, unlike Westermarck, added yet another feature to the discussion of the history of human sexuality—the potential of degeneration. He, like Bachofen and Reich, saw the potential for degeneration as omnipresent and under the influence of the state. In contrast to earlier views he sees advanced rather than primitive cultures as the generators of degenerate sexuality (pp. 27–28). The fluctuation, which Bachofen perceived within the dialectic of history and Reich sees within the potential faults of the state, is also articulated by Krafft-Ebing. Here there is a reversal of Virchow's basic analogy which views man as being like society; here society is like man.[29] It contains the potential for decay within its systems, and its decay is manifested in the deviancy of the basic human drives. But decay is not embodied in the Amazon or in the prostitute, but in the Other as homosexual.[30] Already in Reich's views, as in the early literature on masturbation, the potential for other deviancies, including homosexuality, was present within the effect of childhood masturbation on adult sexuality. Krafft-Ebing, who saw childhood masturbation as an extremely minor and rare manifestation, discounts masturbation. He replaces it with homosexuality as the exemplary sexual degeneracy. The homosexual is the prime violator of "natural drives."

The idea of the basic drives as the structures of natural law is an eighteenth-century concept. Indeed, both Reich and Krafft-Ebing refer to Friedrich Schiller's poem "The Worldly Wise," in which Schiller sees the "drive for Hunger and Love" as that "which holds the structure of world-philosophy" together.[31] The basic drives can be perverted through the state, and this manifests itself through perversion, which in turn undermines the state. Bachofen's positive model is thus made manifest. Degeneracy, especially degenerate sexuality, is a positive force as it moves mankind to the necessary changes in forms of human interaction. Society thus benefits from its own repression as it dialectically causes changes within itself. Even Engels, who adapts this basic model, sees in the development of female gender identity within capitalism the negative result of the exploitation of the woman within the family structure and thus as the seed for revolutionary change. Engels, while rejecting the basic analogy between the history of man and the history of his sexual development and replacing it with an analogy to the development of the economic systems on which his societal structures are based, still retains the basic dialect paradigm concerning sexual repression and its potential. Bachofen, Reich, and Krafft-Ebing incorporated the predominant view of the sexual basis for human society and the dilatory effects of society, a view that is given medical validity through the creation of a disease entity which manifested the sexual pathology of nineteenth-century society.[32]

Freud and Degeneracy

Sigmund Freud, like many of his contemporaries, even those not trained in science, saw the world in terms of the biological model.[33] After Darwin the description of the biological world became what the chemical model had been to the eighteenth century and the psychoanalytic model would be for the twentieth century—the source of a universal explanation of causality through analogy. For late-nineteenth-century history proceeded as if it were biology. Such biologists as Ernst Haeckel were so convinced by the power of their explanatory model that they wrote philosophies of history as if the analogies seen to biology were literal.[34] Historians, especially conservative ones, such as Houston Stewart Chamberlain, littered their works with the crudest parallels to biological development.[35] Within all of these theories of history the problem of degeneracy held a major role in providing the explanation for the negative moments of history, just as it did in contemporary biology.

It is Freud's earliest work on neurological diseases in childhood that the concept of degeneracy is first articulated. Freud, whose work on cerebral diplegia and multiple sclerosis put him in the forefront of thinkers on the neurological diseases of childhood, went to Paris in 1885–86 specifically to study the "secondary atrophies and degenerations that follow on affections of the brain in children."[36] While the term "degeneration" was used within the strict neurological sense given by Virchow, it is this early linkage between the concept of degeneration and childhood illness that colored Freud's thinking during this period. While in Paris his interest moved, under the tutelage of Jean Martin Charcot at the Salpêtrière, from this original problem to the problem of hysteria. In his essay on neurosis (1894) Freud distinguished between degenerative neurosis, which had a primarily psychological etiology, and hysteria:

> In fact, hysterical illnesses even of troublesome severity are no rarity in children of between six and ten years. In boys and girls of intense hysterical disposition, the period before and after puberty brings about a first outbreak of the neurosis. In infantile hysteria the same symptoms are found as in adult neuroses. Stigmata, however, are as a rule rarer, and psychical changes, spasms, attacks and contractures are in the foreground. Hysterical children are very frequently precocious and highly gifted; in a number of cases, to be sure, the hysteria is merely a symptom of a deep-going degeneracy of the nervous system which is manifested in permanent moral perversion. As is well known, an early age, from fifteen onwards, is the period at which the hysterical neurosis most usually shows itself actively in females (1:52).

Most earlier work on childhood hysteria, as well as on the other endogenous illnesses catalogued by nineteenth-century medicine, had seen all childhood psychopathologies as proof of an inherent failing in the child.[37] Using the model of insanity *ex onania*, the weakness was seen within the child and was usually triggered by outside causes. Hermann Smidt, in his dissertation on childhood hysteria (1880), argued for such a purely somatic manner of understanding the appearance of hysteria in children.[38] In Freud's earliest work a questioning of the somatic etiology of childhood psychopathologies was introduced. Nevertheless the concept of "degeneracy" remained linked to childhood, to illness, and to childhood sexuality.

The French tradition ran parallel to this view. Jean Martin Charcot saw all neurosis including hysteria as "neuropathic" and Pierre Janet's view only refined this, seeing in the neurotic an inability to synthesize, which he called a "psychical stigmata," and evidence of the "degeneracy of hysterical individuals."[39] Freud maintained that the neurotic individual has some type of "pathological disposition," although such a disposition was in no way identical with individual or hereditary 'degeneracy'" (3:48). Freud saw the roots of such pathologies existing prenatally. But he also equated the French formulation of this view, a view that had almost universal acceptance, with the concept of degeneration itself. Indeed, in all the later retrospective discussions of the history of psychoanalysis, Freud felt it necessary to draw the distinction between this earlier, more rigid manner of understanding the etiology of neurosis and his own views.[40] Quite often he will use the term "dégénéré" rather than the equivalent German term (*Entartung*) to stress the French origin of this concept.

During this period, in his detailed correspondence with Wilhelm Fliess, the problem of sexual degeneracy as the model for psychopathogy appeared as a major factor in their exchange. Freud attempted, in his draft outline "On the Etiology and Theory of the Major Neurosis," to distinguish between those psychopathologies that are the product of degeneracy and those that are the product of disposition (1:187). Both categories placed the sources of the illness within the patient, the latter demanded an external stimulus before the illness manifested itself. Even with this modification, degeneracy remains the primary etiology. But Freud had postulated the role of trauma in the initial stages of some psychopathologies. In a letter to Fliess, dated May 21, 1894, Freud still reduced the roots of all neurosis to four primary sexual etiologies, and degeneration remained central to all four categories (1:188). Degeneracy remained the basis for the sexual etiology of neurosis. But degeneracy and disposition were too rigid for Freud as they excluded the possibility of psychological influence. Freud simply equated degeneracy with inherent genetic error and by August 1894 began to move away from the concept of degeneracy as the root of sexual "enfeeblement" and toward the need for some type of psychological motivation for neurosis (1:196, see also 3:48). Yet, in his paper on anxiety neurosis (1895), the first major attempt by Freud to undermine the concept of neurasthenia with its strong linkage to the role of degeneracy, Freud still gave credence to Paul Julius Möbius' category of "hereditarily degenerate individuals" as one of the etiologies for neurasthenia (3:90, 1:106). In his paper on this question, "Heredity and the Neurosis" (1896), he still retained "syndromes constituting mental degeneracy" as a valid category, but excluded obsessions from it (3:146). This was a qualification of his rejection of degeneracy in the beginning of his paper on "Obsessions and Phobias" (1894), which stressed the special place these neurosis had outside the category of degeneracy (3:74). But there too Freud retained the idea that degeneration does not exist and that certain psychopathologies must be attributed to it.

Freud worked on the concept of degeneracy, trying to recast it for his own needs. In January 1897 he wrote to Fliess completely restructuring the concept of degeneracy.[41] He moved from an understanding of somatic "disposition," the relationship between inherent somatic factors and some type of psychological stimulus, to give the concept of degeneracy a greater psychological quality (1:240–41). Degeneracy can be the inheritance of behavior patterns from one generation to another. The existence of such earlier psychological structures played a major role in Freud's recasting of the moment of degeneracy from prenatal influence to early childhood experience:

> An idea about resistance has enabled me to put straight all those cases of mine which had run into fairly severe difficulties, and to start them off again satisfactorily. Resistance, which finally brings work to a halt, is nothing other than the child's past character, his degenerate character, which (as a result of those experiences which one finds present consciously in what are called degenerate cases) has developed or might have developed, but which is overlaid here by the emergence of repression. I dig it out by my work, it struggles; and what was to begin with such an excellent, honest fellow, becomes low, untruthful or defiant, and a malingerer—till I tell him so and thus make it possible to overcome this character. In this way resistance has become something actual and tangible to me, and I wish, too, that, instead of the concept of repression, I already had what lies concealed behind it. (1:266–267)

Character and not biology structures Freud's understanding of degeneracy. Character is linked with the fantasy world of masturbation, following Kaan, and the concept of degeneracy has a specifically sexual context, as it does in late nineteenth-century discussions of neurasthenia.

It is in the *Studies on Hysteria* (1895), written together with Joseph Breuer, that Freud comes to terms with the pejorative implications of the term "degeneration." His patients, even though hysteric, are in no way congenitally predisposed to hysteria (2:104, 161). In the case of "Fräulein Elisabeth von R." Freud rejected the label of degenerate for the hysteric. Indeed this prefigured much of Freud's later discussion of the role the concept of degeneracy should play in the diagnosis of psychosexual pathologies. In "Little Hans" (1909) Freud's argument created a rhetorician who condemns the child as hopelessly mired in the swamp of his own ancestry:

> But before going into the details of this agreement I must deal with two objections which will be raised against my making use of the present analysis for this purpose. The first objection is to the effect that Hans was not a normal child, but (as events—the illness itself, in fact—showed) had a predisposition to neurosis, and was a young "degenerate"; it would be illegitimate, therefore, to apply to other, normal children conclusions which might perhaps be true of him. I shall postpone consideration of this objection, since it only limits the value of the observation, and does not completely nullify it. . . .
>
> I think, therefore, that Hans's illness may perhaps have been no more serious than that of many other children who are not branded as "degenerates"; but since he was brought up without being intimidated, and with as much consideration and as little coercion as possible, his

anxiety dared to show itself more boldly. With him there was not place for such motives as a bad conscience or a fear of punishment, which with other children must no doubt contribute to making the anxiety less (10:100, 141).

By 1917 this voice, condemning all through the use of the term "degeneracy," is the voice of "psychiatry" as opposed to the voice of the psychoanalyst:

> Psychiatry, it is true, denies that such things mean the intrusion into the mind of evil spirits from without; beyond this, however, it can only say with a shrug: "Degeneracy, hereditary disposition, constitutional inferiority!" Psycho-analysis sets out to explain these uncanny disorders; it engages in careful and laborious investigations, devises hypotheses and scientific constructions, until at length it can speak thus to the ego:—"Nothing has entered into you from without; a part of the activity of your own mind has been withdrawn from your knowledge and from the command of your will" (17:142).

Degeneracy is the label for the Other, specifically the Other as the essence of pathology (3:280). It is the sense of hopelessness and helplessness which is captured by the label of degenerate. Thus Freud rejected clinical psychiatry's label of the sexually deviant as the degenerate, again through the rhetoric of the prototypical "psychiatrist." In his paper of female homosexuality (1920) one of Freud's last uses of the term "degenerate" appears in this context (18:149). The authority of medicine is the condemning voice Freud mockingly quotes to illustrate its own limits:

> Perhaps you would like to know in advance, having in mind our earlier talks, what attitude contemporary psychiatry adopts toward the problems of obsessional neurosis. But it is a meagre chapter. Psychiatry gives names to the different obsessions but says nothing further about them. On the other hand it insists that those who suffer from these symptoms are "degenerates." This gives small satisfaction; in fact it is a judgement of value—a condemnation instead of an explanation. We are supposed to think that every possible sort of eccentricity may arise in degenerates. Well, it is true that we must regard those who develop such symptoms as somewhat different in their nature from other people. But we may ask: are they more "degenerate" than other neurotics—than hysterical patients, for instance, or those who fall ill of psychoses? Once again, the characterization is evidently too general. Indeed, we may doubt whether there is any justification for it at all, when we learn that such symptoms occur too in distinguished people of particularly high capacities, capacities important for the world at large. It is true that, thanks to their own discretion and to the untruthfulness of their biographers, we learn little that is intimate about the great men who are our models; but it may nevertheless happen that one of them, like Emile Zola, may be a fanatic for the truth, and we then learn from him of the many strange obsessional habits to which he was a life-long victim.

> Psychiatry has found a way out by speaking of "dégénérés supér-
> ieurs." Very nice. But we have found from psycho-analysis that it is
> possible to get permanently rid of these strange obsessional symptoms,
> just as of other complaints and just as in people who are not degener-
> ate. I myself have succeeded repeatedly in this (16:260; see also 3:201
> and 7:160).

The locus of this voice of authority is problematic. Is this merely the
French medical tradition, with its general acceptance in Germany, against
which Freud is arguing, or is this an internalized element of Freud's own
system of belief which he is striving to overcome? If it is the latter, the
internalized voice of the biologist in a struggle with the psychoanalyst,
then other residual elements of this conflict should be found in Freud's
work.

Hidden within this rejection of the origin of psychopathology within
the heredity of the individual is a fascination that links the role of heredity
to sexual pathology. The pejorative sense of "degeneration" which Freud
saw in the use of this label distanced the essence of the Other. Freud
observed medical science's need to differentiate between the normal and
the degenerate as a means of drawing the line between the perfect self and
the perverse Other (9:45). This observation, in Freud's essay on Jensen's
Gradiva (1906), crystallized the problem which runs parallel to his own
rejection of the medical/biological concept of the degenerate.

In *The Interpretation of Dreams* (1900) Freud continued to evolve a
model of infantile sexuality as the basic developmental model of mankind.
This view of chronological primitivism traced the movement of the infant
from "egoist" to "moralist," a view compatible with earlier views of the
acquisition of shame as the wellspring of morality:

> For we may expect that, before the end of the period which we count
> as childhood, altruistic impulses and morality will awaken in the little
> egoist and (to use Meynert's terms . . .) a secondary ego will overlay
> and inhibit the primary one. It is true, no doubt, that morality does not
> set in simultaneously all along the line and that the length of non-moral
> childhood varies in different individuals. If this morality fails to de-
> velop, we like to talk of 'degeneracy,' though what in fact faces us is an
> inhibition in development (4:250).

Degeneracy comes to have for Freud the sense of a faulty designation for
the sexually pathological, inherent, immutable (7:50). With his *Three Essays on the Theory of Sexuality* (1905) the seemingly separate strands of
childhood sexuality, the etiology of neurosis, perversity, and degeneracy
merge, and the major shift prefigured in the above passage becomes evident, the shift from the model of sexuality to its historical analogy
(7:138–39). While Freud attributed his shift in interest to Iwan Bloch's
semipopular studies of sexuality in history, clearly Freud is to no little
degree influenced by the contemporary debates concerning the nature of

homosexuality and the role of hereditary predisposition in the development of the homosexual.[42] Yet Freud's discussion of degeneracy in this passage is as a disease of civilization, parallel to the discussions of neurasthenia during the late nineteenth century. For Freud perversity is not necessarily degenerate (except in the ultimate sense that polymorphous perversity is inherent in all infants) but degeneracy is an illness of civilization (see 7:160). There are yet further contemporary overtones in this passage on degeneration and civilization.

Freud adapts a view of trauma in his view of sexual psychopathology that would seem much more at home in Ibsen's *Doll's House* in the figure of Dr. Rank, or in the central figure in *Ghosts*, Oswald Alving. It is the trauma of civilization, the illness that characterizes it and condemns it, syphilis. For Freud civilization in its most degenerate sexuality passed the fear of syphilis, syphilophobia, from generation to generation (7:236). The hidden decay of syphilis, its mythic relationship to sexuality (assumed but not yet scientifically proven), its ability to destroy across generations, made it one of the late nineteenth-century paradigms for degenerative sexuality. Freud had already made this fear the subject of one of his illustrative anecdotes in *The Interpretation of Dreams* (1900) (4:300–01). Freud transferred sexual pathology, from the private, masturbatory sphere to the public, venereal one. Eduard Reich, as well as many other writers on public health during this period, projected at least some of their anxiety concerning sexuality and sexual pathology from masturbation to syphilis, moving from a degenerate endogenous model to a degenerate exogenous one. In masturbation the evil lies within the degeneracy of the individual; in syphilis, within the degeneracy of the Other, the prostitute. Sexuality can become contaminated through an external source, rather than from any inherent failure of the individual. Late nineteenth-century discussions of the prostitute centered around the question of whether she was inherently degenerate (the view of Lombroso) or whether she merely has a disposition for prostitution, which is triggered by her economic circumstances (the view of Parent-Duchatelet).[43] Freud's views favored the former, as his understanding of sexuality stressed its inherent nature. Libido theory, with its view of the inherent polymorphous perversity of the infant, is not far removed from the view that perversity is the disposition of all human beings, including the prostitute (7:192). This extrapolates from the view that a special subclass of degenerates carry the stigmata of perverse sexuality rather than its rejection.

But sexuality is not "degenerate." In reversing the paradigm of degeneracy, sexuality becomes, in Freud's thinking, the antithesis of degeneracy. Freud undermined the view that sexuality in most of its forms leads to decay. He traced the descent of a ciliate infusorian unto the 3059th generation and observed that it showed "no signs of . . . degeneration" (18:47).[44] Freud continued with an analogy in *Beyond the Pleasure Principle* (1920), seeing in this absence of decay the vitalism inherent in sexuality:

> Let us, however, return to the self-preservative sexual instincts. The
> experiments upon protista have already shown us that conjugation—
> that is, the coalescence of two individuals which separate soon after-
> wards without any subsequent cell-division occurring—has a strength-
> ening and rejuvenating effect upon both of them. In later generations
> they show no signs of degenerating and seem able to put up a longer
> resistance to the injurious effects of their own metabolism. This single
> observation may, I think, be taken as typical of the effect produced by
> the sexual union as well. (18:55, see also 1:187)

Thus Freud's earliest and his last use of the concept of degeneracy employed Virchow's sense of inner decay of the cell. Freud, however, reversed his perception of the pathological nature of sexuality and its
importance within the degenerative model.

Freud needed to draw on historical data to more clearly delineate his
views concerning perversion from generation theory. The cyclical occurrence of perversion only within highly developed cultures still implied
degeneration. In 1917, in the *Introductory Lectures,* he reformulated his
reading of Bloch from 1905, seeing perversion as a universal presence,
limited neither in its historical manifestation nor in its geographic locus.[45]
The degenerate cannot exist within human nature. Freud had already
stressed this in his dismissal of the false rhetoric of psychiatry, which used
the concept of the degenerate to defame the Other. In the striking opening
paragraph to his "Thoughts for the Times on War and Death" (1915)
Freud had attributed this labeling of the Other as degenerate to the
"anthropologists":

> In the confusion of wartime in which we are caught up, relying as we
> must on one-sided information, standing too close to the great changes
> that have already taken place or are beginning to, and without a glim-
> mering of the future that is being shaped, we ourselves are at a loss as
> to the significance of the impressions which press in upon us and as to
> the value of the judgements which we form. We cannot but feel that no
> event has ever destroyed so much that is precious in the common
> possessions of humanity, confused so many of the clearest intel-
> ligences, or so thoroughly debased what is highest. Science herself has
> lost her passionless impartiality; her deeply embittered servants seek
> for weapons from her with which to contribute towards the struggle
> with the enemy. Anthropologists feel driven to declare him inferior and
> degenerate, psychiatrists issue a diagnosis of his disease of mind or
> spirit. Probably, however, our sense of these immediate evils is dispro-
> portionately strong, and we are not entitled to compare them with the
> evils of other times which we have not experienced. (14:275)[46]

It is indeed to the French anthropological tradition of modern psychiatry with its pseudoscientism that the term degeneracy is most indebted. In
dismissing this label as false rhetoric, Freud is able to move the category
of degenerate from its sexual context and place it, where it belongs, in the

realm of political rhetoric. The degenerate for Freud is not merely a biological category but also one that implies a specific understanding of the historical process.

Summary

History, sexuality, and degeneracy are inexorably linked within the thought of the late nineteenth century. Through Hegel's model of history in which each age succeeds and replaces, on a higher level, the one that preceded it, the understanding of human sexuality was perceived in a teleological manner. Welded to this movement from the concrete to the abstract is another paradigm. The theological model of the Fall as the wellspring of history with its culmination in Christ's sacrifice served as an explanation for human degeneration (from the preadamic state) and re-generation. These historical analogies were perceived within the model of human development as understood in the nineteenth century. If the most advanced stage of human sexuality following the redemption of Christ is that of the adult, male European, rather than the child, or the Other (woman, black) as child, it is proof of the most primitive stage of human history, the stage of primitive sexuality. The sexuality associated with the Other, labeled as perverse as it was seen as retrogressive, was soon linked with all other modes of sexuality other than those prescribed for adult Europeans. The child's masturbation is perverse. The Other's sexuality is perverse because it is childlike. Here the linkage among all modes of deviant sexuality can be found. Masturbation, homosexuality, promis-cuity (in primitive societies), prostitution (in advanced societies) are all degenerate forms of adult sexual experience, since they are ascribed to the Other.

The projection of deviant sexuality onto the Other during the nine-teenth century was understood in theological as well as teleological terms. The aberrant sexuality of the child was proof of man's fall from grace. It seldom manifested itself, as mankind had been saved through Christ's sacrifice, but its rare appearance was proof of the potential within each adult of regression to the state before redemption. Here the idea of the degeneracy of the Jew fitted quite nicely. Hegel could not understand the Jews' tenacity at existing following their contribution to a specific stage of Western culture. Nineteenth-century science tried to explain the special quality of the Jew, as perceived by the dominant European society, in terms of a medicalization of the Jew.[47] This categorized him at a stage of sexual development that was understood as primitive and perverse and therefore degenerate.

It was, however, not merely the child, the woman, the homosexual, the Jew, who was seen in terms of degenerate sexuality. Embedded within all nineteenth-century concepts of the Other is the concept of class and the sense of the inherent potential of class conflict. Hegel took the rhetoric for his model of the "master-slave" dyad from the nineteenth-century focus on black slavery. Inherent in the slave-owners' perception of the institution was the "paranoid" fear of slave uprisings.[48] This sense of the seizure of power by the Other is inherent in all images of Otherness. The idea that revolutionary change is accompanied by the most horrible of sexual excesses finds its liberal echo in thinkers such as Bachofen and its conservative denial in thinkers such as Westermarck. In the very formulation during the nineteenth century of institutions such as prostitution and marriage is a clear link between the potential for revolutionary change and aberrant sexuality.

The city becomes the icon of "modern life" and the locus of degenerate sexuality. This continuation of the Rousseauian paradigm of the contamination of "idyllic" life through the imposition of social institutions continues throughout the nineteenth century and isolates the potential fear of revolt to one specific locus of "modern life," the city.[49] The city, as opposed to the image of the garden, is yet another image of the fall from grace. The city—an icon of the rejection of redemption, of Abraham's failure in Sodom and Gomorrah, of the Jerusalem of Herod—permeates the image of civilization and is represented as the breeding ground of perverse and unnatural sexuality.

Within the biologization of medicine during the nineteenth century the prime focus on human sexuality was on its pathological aspects. Normal reproduction and human sexual potential were defined in terms of pathology. Since sexual pathology was a standard means of labeling the Other, the normal was defined through the most powerful of analogies, that of deviant human sexuality. The power possessed by society in defining the Other was here linked to the power of the explanatory model of human biology. Models of human sexuality used the paradigm of degeneracy as a means of labeling the nature of the Other. The ambiguity of power, with the potential of losing power and thus becoming the Other, was shared by the biologists as well as by other members of society. The magic of an explanatory model that answers all problems disguises, but does not eliminate, its potential impeachability. Thus images of degenerate or atavistic sexuality are used to qualify the image of the Other. Such disease entities as neurasthenia are invented, by which the Other's illness is characterized as sexual degeneracy. The sense that such illnesses are inherent in a separate class of the Other and stand apart from the normal is seen in the labeling of such diseases as inherited, and therefore outside the world of the observer. The labels given to this icon of degenerate sexuality, whether masturbation, hysteria, neurasthenia, congenital syphilis, or even incest, all have one thing in common. In all cases the etiology and the symptomology are identical. They all begin in some type of sexual deviancy and result in perversion. The concept of the Fall is present here. The proof of the Fall is in the existence at the present time of a special group, of the Other, which illustrates the Fall in their necessary, eternal repetition of the Fall.

Sigmund Freud was in a very special position to question this model of degeneracy. The late sixteenth century saw the organization of large numbers of individuals who had been stigmatized through the projections of the majority. Jews, women, homosexuals reified the majority's fear of losing their dominance in defining the normal by demanding the label of "normal" for themselves. The role of the child as the paradigm of Otherness had to be reexamined and Freud was able to draw the very paradigm of the Fall, of degeneration, into question. He was helped to no little degree by his perceived peripherality to Western cultural and scientific traditions.[50] As an "Eastern" Jew in "Western" Vienna, he saw himself as the Other, at least in his perception of the world. This "myth" of persecution was more than the question of the specific treatment of the single individual; it was inherent in the rhetoric of Western society, a rhetoric also present within the scientific model of degeneracy. What is most interesting in Freud's struggle with the concept of degeneracy is that he was never able to abandon it completely, even when he saw its inherent implications. Indeed, much of the impetus of his latter works on history, *Totem and Taboo* (1912–13) and *Civilization and Its Discontents* (1930), were rooted in variations on the theme of degeneracy, either in its reversal or in the use of aspects of the model (such as incest) as the foundation of a model of historical development. The explanation of the dark center of human history, like the mirage of degeneracy, turns out to be an inner fear of that hidden within us and projected onto the world. The productive power of Freud's necessary grappling with the model of degeneracy produced a deeper understanding of the implications of the rhetoric of science for him and sent him to the power of language as a means of understanding not only the individual but society. Freud, like his great contemporary adversary Karl Kraus, repudiated the model of degeneracy, because both saw within themselves the qualities ascribed to the Other. As the wellspring of these projections is universal, their discovery is not surprising. But they also sensed the potentially destructive power of such projections linked to the political power of an explanatory model such as biological degeneracy. Central to the model and to the understanding of the Other is the definition of the Other in sexual terms, for no factor in nineteenth-century self-definition was more powerful than the sense of the sexually pathological. The stigma of the Fall, of the rejection of Christ's redemption, is the stigma of sexuality, hidden within oneself and projected onto the Other. "Degenerate" remains for the nineteenth century the central term of sexual opprobrium categorizing the inner nature of the Other. It remains so even today.

NOTES

1. The following works were of special help in formulating this paper: Anne-marie Wettley, *Von der "Psychopathia sexualis" zur Sexualwissenschaft*, Beiträge zur Sexualforschung, 17 (Stuttgart: Enke, 1959). This work appeared in abridged form in Annemarie and Werner Leibbrand, *Formen des Eros: Kultur- und Geistesgeschichte der Liebe* (Freiburg: Karl Alber, 1972), pp. 569–86. The following essays by An-nemarie Wettley-Leibbrand were also of interest: "Bemerkungen zum Entar-tungsbegriff im Hinblick auf den Alkoholismus und die sexuellen Perversionen," *Archivo Iberoamericano de Historia de la Medicina* (1959), 9:539–42, and "Zur Prob-lemgeschichte der 'dégénérescence,'" *Sudhoffs Archiv*, (1959), 43:193–212. Other useful works on the concept of degeneration were: Georges Genil-Perrin, *Histoire des origines et de l'évolution de l'ideé de dégénérescence en médecine mentale* (Paris: Alfred Leclerc, 1913), Richard D. Walter, "What Became of the Degenerate? A Brief History of a Concept," *Journal of the History of Medicine and the Allied Sciences*, (1956), 11:422–29; Francesco Parenti, "Psiche e degenerazione (Nascita ed evoluzione di una teoria)," *Pagine di storia della medicina* (Rome), (1965), 9:45–53; Françoise Castel, "Dégénérescence et structures: Réflexions méthodologiques à propos de l'œuvre de Magnan," *Annales Médico-Psychologiques* (1967), 125:521–36; Emilo Balaguer Perigüell, "El somaticismo y la doctrina de la 'degeneración' en la psiquiatría valenciana del siglo XIX," *Medicina Espagnola*, (1969), 62:388–94; Colin Martindale, "Degeneration, Disinhibition, and Genius," *Journal of the His-tory of the Behavioral Sciences* (1971), 7:177–82.

2. On the relationship of the history of sexuality to the concept of degeneracy see Michel Foucault, *The History of Sexuality*, Vol. 1: *An Introduction*, Robert Hurley, tr. (New York: Vintage, 1980). See also Eugen Holländer, *Askulep und Venus: Eine Kultur- und Sittengeschichte im Spiegel des Arztes* (Berlin: Propyläen, 1928); Jill Conway, "Stereotypes of Femininity in a Theory of Sexual Evolution," *Victorian Studies*, (1970), 14:47–62; Milton Rugoff, *Prudery and Passion* (London: Rupert Hart-Davis, 1972), pp. 98–102; Norbert Elias, *The Civilizing Process: The History of Manners*, Edmund Jephcott, tr. (New York: Urizen, 1970), pp. 169–89; Vern L. Bullough, *Sex, Society and History* (New York: Science History Publishers, 1976), pp. 112–25; Peter Gay, *The Bourgeois Experience: Victoria to Freud*. Vol. 1: *Education of the Senses* (New York: Oxford University Press, 1984); Eric Trudgill, *Madonnas and Magdalens: The Origins and Development of Victorian Sexual Attitudes* (New York: New American Library, 1974); Vern L. Bullough, *Sexual Variance in Society and History* (New York: Wiley, 1976); Georges Lanteri-Laura, *Lecture des perver-sions: Histoire de leur appropriation médicale* (Paris: Masson, 1979); Fraser Harrison, *The Dark Angel: Aspects of Victorian Sexuality* (London: Sheldon Press, 1977); Dietrich von Engelhardt, "Sittlichkeitsdeliquenzen in Wissenschaft und Literatur der 2. Hälfte des 19. Jahrhunderts," in H. Hess, ed., *Sexualität und sozialle Kontrolle* (Heidelberg: Kriminalistik Verlag, 1978), pp. 141–68; G. Williams, "Unclean Sex and the Unclean Sex: Some Victorian Paradoxes, *Trivium*, (1978), 13:1–17; J. J. Sauri, "Nacimento del concepto de perversion," *Revista Neuro-Psi-quiatrica*, (1979), 42:71–85; J. A. Banks, "The Attitude of the Medical Profession to

Sexuality in the 19th Century," *Society for the Social History of Medicine,* (1978), 22:9–10; Esther Fischer-Homberger, *Krankheit Frau und andere Arbeiten zur Medizingeschichte der Frau* (Bern: Hans Huber, 1979). The basic interrelationship between models of human sexuality and the model of degeneracy as perceived during the nineteenth century is discussed by Phyllis Grosskurth, *Havelock Ellis: A Biography* (New York: Knopf, 1980), pp. 116ff. See also R. A. Padgug, "Sexual Matters: On Conceptualizing Sexuality in History," *Radical History Review,* (1979), 20:3–24.

3. E. H. Hare, "Masturbatory Insanity: The History of an Idea," *Journal of Mental Science,* (1962), 108:2. See also Karl-Felix Jacobs, *Die Entstehung der Onanie-Literatur im 17. und 18. Jahrhundert* (Diss.: Munich, 1963).

4. Heinrich Kaan, *Psychopathia sexualis* (Leipzig: Leopold Voss, 1844). See Foucault, pp. 63, 118. My translation. All works are cited to available translations; other translations are mine.

5. See my essay "Hegel, Schopenhauer and Nietzsche See the Black," *Hegel-Jahrbuch,* (1981), 16:163–88.

6. Central to any contemporary reading of Morel is the comprehensive study by Ruth Friedlander, "Bénédict-Augustin Morel and the Development of the Theory of Dégénérescence (The Introduction of Anthropology into Psychiatry)" (Ph.D. dissertation, University of California, San Francisco, 1973). Friedlander stresses the break that Morel's work made with earlier uses of the term "degeneration." As this is simply a shift within the same paradigm, I have maintained the older term "degeneration" here. See also Peter Burgener, *Die Einflüsse des zeitgenössischen Denkens in Morels Begriff der "dégénérescence,"* Züricher Medizingeschichtliche Abhandlungen, N. R. 16 (Zurich: Juris, 1964).

7. This passage is a contemporary English translation and paraphrase from Morel's 1857 *Traité des dégénérescences physiques, intellectuelles et morales de l'espèce humaine* which appeared as a series during 1857 in *The Medical Circular* (London), here March 25, 1857, Edwin Wing, ed. and tr. This represents the contemporary impression of what was important within Morel's work.

8. The merger of theoretical and medical literature during the nineteenth century was possible only by the presumed identity of these basic models. See P. J. C. Debreyne, *Essai sur la théologie morale, considérée dans ses rapports avec la physiologie et la médecine* (Brussels: M. Vanderborght, 1846), pp. 62–69, and Felix Antoine Philabert Dupanloup, Bishop of Orleans, *De l'éducation* (Paris: Charles Douniol, 1863), 3:399–402. Both texts use contemporary scientific material for their theological discussions of the nature of childhood sexuality.

9. Friedlander, pp. 134 ff. F. Merke, in *Geschichte und Ikonographie des endemischen Kropfes und Kretinismus* (Bern: Hans Huber, 1971), gives a detailed discussion of the central role played by the model of the cretin in nineteenth-century medical thought.

10. Johannes Häussler, *Über Beziehungen des Sexualsystems zur Psyche überhaupt und zum Cretinismus ins Besondere* (Wurzburg: Strecker, 1826). For some reason Merke does not discuss Häussler's work, but it plays a role in Hans Giese, ed., *Die sexuelle Perversion* (Frankfurt: Akademische Verlagsgesellschaft, 1967).

11. On this confusion of cause and effect see my essay "Den Geisteskranken sehen: Henry Mackenzie, Heinrich von Kleist, William James," *Confinia Psychiatrica,* (1979), 22:127–44.

12. Morel, *Traité des dégénérescences.* . . . *Atlas des XII Planches* (Paris: J. Baillière, 1857), p. 22.

13. See my essay "Freud and the Prostitute: Male Stereotypes of Female Sexuality in fin-de-siècle Vienna," *Journal of the American Academy of Psychoanalysis* (1981), 9:337–60.

14. Jakob Santlus, *Zur Psychologie der menschliche Triebe* (Neuwied: Heuser, 1864), pp. 68–69. On the politics of sexuality see Carl E. Schorske, *Fin-de-siècle Vienna: Politics and Culture* (New York: Vintage, 1981), pp. 181–207; Richard Hamann and Jost Hermand, *Stilkunst um 1900* (Frankfurt: Fischer, 1977), pp. 26–178; George L. Mosse, "Nationalism and Respectability: Normal and Abnormal Sexuality in the Nineteenth Century" (1982), 17:221–46; Reinhard Koselleck and Paul Widmer, eds., *Niedergang*, Sprache und Geschichte 2. (Stuttgart: Klett/Cotta, 1981); as well as Isabel V. Hull, "Reflections on George L. Mosse's 'Nationalism and Respectability,'" *Journal of Contemporary History*, (1982), 17:247–68.

15. See the English translation by Frank Chance, Rudolf Virchow, *Cellular Pathology as Based upon Physiological and Pathological History* (New York: Robert M. De Witt, [1860]), p. 40. Virchow rejected the rhetoric of degeneracy throughout his later work, see esp. his essay "Descendenz und Pathologie," *Archiv für pathologische Anatomie und Physiologie* (1886), 103:1–14. Virchow's views are in no way unique. The key term "atavism" was coined by the economist Walter Bagehot, *Physics and Politics* (Boston: Beacon, 1956), in the early nineteenth century to describe the Hobbesian return to the primitive state. This view was continued within medical biology by John Hughlings Jackson. See James Taylor, ed., *The Selected Writings of John Hughlings Jackson* (New York: Staples, 1958).

16. All references are to the English translation by Ralph Manheim, *Myth, Religion, and Mother Right: Selected Writings of J. J. Bachofen*, Bollingen Series 84 (Princeton: Princeton University Press, 1967), here p. 105. See Sir Galahad [Berta Eckstein-Diener], *Mütter und Amazonen: Ein Umriss weiblicher Reiche* (Munich: Albert Langen, 1932), pp. 239, 276–90, for a major political critique of Bachofen's concept of the Amazon.

17. Mill's *Subjection of Women* (1869; written in 1861) simply continued a view basic to early nineteenth-century thought; see M. H. Abrams, *Natural Supernaturalism: Tradition and Revolution in Romantic Literature* (New York: Norton, 1971), pp. 356–72. An interesting note on the power of this image: Friedrich Nietzsche evidently rediscovered it in his reading of Mill's essay in Sigmund Freud's 1880 translation.

18. G. W. F. Hegel, *Lectures on the Philosophy of Religion*, E. B. Spiers, tr. (New York: Humanities Press, 1962), 1:101.

19. This reference is in Hegel's *Philosophie des Geistes* in Hermann Glockner, ed., *Sämtliche Werke* (Stuttgart: Fromann, 1927ff.), 10:73–74.

20. Eduard Reich, *Geschichte, Natur- und Gesundheitslehre des ehelichen Lebens* (Cassel: J. C. Krieger, 1864).

21. Eduard Reich, *Über Unsittlichkeit: Hygienische und politisch-moralische Studien* (Neuwied: J. H. Heuser, 1866).

22. Eduard Reich, *Über die Entartung des Menschen: Ihre Ursachen und Verhütung* (Erlangen: Ferdinand Enke, 1868). Other works of interest by Reich are: *Studien über die Frauen* (Jena: Hermann Costenoble, 1875); *Die Abhängigkeit der Civilisation von der Persönlichkeit des Menschen und von der Lebensbedürfnisse* (Minden: J. C.

C. Bruns, 1883); *Geschichte der Seele, die Hygiene des Geisteslebens und die Civilisa-tion* (Minden: J. C. C. Bruns, 1884).

23. Prostitution became the central point about which major questions of the "private" versus the "public" sphere were focused. For a summary of the problem see my essay "Freud and the Prostitute."

24. Reich, *Entartung*, pp. 519–22.

25. Gordon W. Allport, *The Nature of Prejudice* (Garden City, N.Y.: Doubleday, 1958), p. 315. The discussion of Gobineau is indebted to the unpublished book manuscript by Professor Annette Smith of the California Institute of Technology, "Gobineau et l'histoire naturelle" (1981).

26. Richard von Krafft-Ebing, *Psychopathia Sexualis: A Medico-Forensic Study*, Harry E. Wedeck, tr. (New York: Putnam, 1965), p. 24. "Shamelessness" is a major category for the development of civilized sexual behavior in Bachofen's system. He refers to Hyginus' label of Oedipus as *"impudens"* as a label for the "unregulated tellurian sexuality of the swamp" (p. 180). Here too shamelessness demands some type of control.

27. Edward Westermarck's *The History of Human Marriage* (London: Mac-millan, 1903) is the major conservative document of the nineteenth century con-cerning human sexuality. He so wished to project European sexual standards on history that he argued that promiscuity, postulated by such thinkers as Bachofen as the original form of human sexuality, is an aberration among "savages" caused by the influence of "civilization" (pp. 66–70).

28. Engels, basing his work on Morgan's anthropological studies among the Iroquois and on Bachofen, saw the development of human sexuality in three stages: wildness, with unlimited sexual partners (promiscuity); barbarism, with a limited number of sexual partners (*Paarungsehe*); and civilization, with one sexual partner (monogamy). However, he saw this history as a destruction of the productivity of the gens with the state replacing the gens, and the abrogation of the rights of the woman and her reduction to the role of the producer of children as heirs for the male. See the detailed introduction by Eleanor Burke Leacock to Friedrich Engels, *The Origin of the Family, Private Property and the State*, Alec West, tr. (New York: International, 1972).

29. See R. G. Collingwood, *The Idea of Nature* (Oxford: Oxford University Press, 1945), p. 13, for a discussion of history as a model for nineteenth-century biology.

30. The literature on the homosexual emancipation movement of the late nine-teenth century is extensive. See the following bibliographies for a general overview: J. Foster, *Sex Variant Women in Literature: A Historical and Quantitative Survey* (New York: Vantage, 1956); N. Garde, *The Homosexual in Literature: A Chronologi-cal Bibliography, Circa 700 B.C.–1958* (New York: Village Press, 1959); W. Legg and A. Underwood, *An Annotated Bibliography of Homosexuality* (Los Angeles: Institute for the Study of Human Resources, 1967); *A Gay Bibliography: Eight Bibliographies on Lesbian and Male Homosexuality* (New York: Arno, 1975); Gene Daman, *The Lesbian in Literature: A Bibliography* (Reno, Nev.: The Ladder, 1975); Linda C. Dowling, *Aestheticism and Decadence: A Selective Annotated Bibliography* (New York: Garland, 1977); Martin S. Weinberg and Alan Bell, *Homosexuality: An Annotated Bibliography* (New York: Harper and Row, 1972); Verne Bullough, et al., *An Annotated Bibliography of Homosexuality* (New York: Garland, 1976); William

Parker, *Homosexuality Bibliography: Supplement 1970–1975* (Metuchen, N.J.: Scarecrow, 1977). Of importance for my study has been James D. Steakley, *The Homosexual Emancipation Movement in Germany* (New York: Arno, 1975). The debate concerning the applicability of degeneracy to the homosexual was central to such writers as Magnus Hirschfeld. See his "Ursachen und Wesen des Uranismus," *Jahrbuch für sexuelle Zwischenstufen*, (1903), 5(1):142–59, for his rebuttal of Möbius. However, Hirschfeld did share the "biologistic" paradigm of sexuality discussed in this essay, to the extent that he named the lecture hall in his Institute for Sexual Science (Berlin) the Ernst Haeckel Hall.

31. The idea of the "basic drives" as elements of "natural law" is discussed by Otto von Gierke, *Das deutsche Genossenschaftsrecht*, 4: *Die Staats- und Korporationslehre der Neuzeit* (Berlin: Weidmann, 1913).

32. "Degeneration" as a label is rarely used today except within the limited area of cell pathology. The concept has been absorbed into modern medicine and biology with the label "endogenous," which was introduced into psychiatric terminology by Möbius in 1892. The parallel terminology (degenerate/endogenous) made it possible for the concept of degeneration to exist even after the political associations of the term made its use in post-World War II science an impossibility. See Achim Mechler, "Degeneration und Endogenität," *Der Nervenarzt*, (1963), 34:219–26, and James C. King, *The Biology of Race* (Berkeley: University of California Press, 1981[2]).

33. This section and the next are intended to serve as a corrective to Frank J. Sulloway, *Freud, Biologist of the Mind: Beyond the Psychoanalytic Legend*, (New York: Basic Books, 1979), esp. pp. 289–97, 423. Sulloway's attempt to present nineteenth-century biology as "science" as apart from its pseudoscience aspects draws his very conclusions into question. But even more centrally, he rarely attempts to offer reasons for Freud's myth making and when he does they are often simplistic. In addition to Sulloway, the following essays were important in the formulation of this section: Hermann Glaser, "Die 'kulturelle' Sexualmoral und die moderne Nervosität," in his *Sigmund Freuds Zwanzigstes Jahrhundert* (Munich: Carl Hanser, 1976), pp. 51–168; Alexander Schusdek, "Freud's 'Seduction Theory': A Reconstruction," *Journal of the History of the Behavioral Sciences* (1966), 2:159–66; Heinz Schott, "Traum und Geschichte: Zur Freudschen Geschichtsauffassung im Kontext der *Traumdeutung*," *Sudhoffs Archiv* (1980), 64:298–312; Samuel Jaffe, "Freud as Rhetorician: *Elocutio* and the Dream-Work," *Rhetorik* (1980), 1:42–69. Of little use, despite its title, is the speculative essay by Jean-Marc Dupen, "Freud and Degeneracy: A Turning Point," *Diogenes* (1977), 97:43–64. The longer work announced in the essay has evidently not appeared.

34. See Emanuel Radl, *Geschichte der biologischen Theorien seit dem Ende des siebzehnten Jahrhunderts* (Leipzig: Engelmann, 1905), and Roderick Stackelberg, *Idealism Debased: From völkisch Ideology to National Socialism* (Kent, Ohio: Kent State University Press, 1981).

35. The appearance of the hybrid theory in Chamberlain's *Die Grundlagen des neunzehnten Jahrhunderts* (Munich: Bruckmann, 1899[14]), 1:406–9 as a way of denying the Jews the label of a "pure race" by labeling them as a hybrid with blacks continues an identification between blackness and Otherness which has very old historical roots in Germany, but which is here given biological form. See my *On Blackness without Blacks: On the Image of the Black in Germany* (Boston: G. K. Hall, 1982). Chamberlain cites "Siegmund" Freud in his discussion of the nature of

sexual repression in the formation of neurosis in a virulently anti-Catholic discussion of Loyola. Recently a major study of Chamberlain has appeared, Geoffrey G. Field, *Evangelist of Race: The Germanic Vision of Houston Stewart Chamberlain* (New York: Columbia University Press, 1981).

36. All references to Freud's works are to *The Complete Psychological Works of Sigmund Freud*, Standard Edition, James Strachey, ed. (London: Hogarth Press; New York: Macmillan, 1953–1974), here 1:8. Hereafter, parenthetical references to volume and page numbers of the Standard Edition are given in the text.

37. Paul Julius Möbius, *Geschlecht und Entartung* (Halle: Carl Marhold, 1903), presents a typical summary of these earlier views. See Esther Fischer-Homburger, pp. 32–48, on the image of the hysteric, and the brilliant new work by Patricia Meyer Spacks, *The Adolescent Idea: Myths of Youth and the Adult Imagination* (New York: Basic Books, 1981).

38. Hermann Smidt, *Über das Vorkommen der Hysterie bei Kindern* (Diss., Strasbourg, 1880). See K. Codell Carter, "Infantile Hysteria and Infantile Sexuality in Late 19th-Century German Language Medical Literature," *Medical History* (1983), 26:186–96.

39. See Standard Edition, 2:87, 104, 294; 3:21, 46, 51, 249; 11:21; 12:207. See also the general discussion in Henri Ellenberger, *The Discovery of the Unconscious: The History and Evolution of Dynamic Psychiatry* (New York: Basic Books, 1970).

40. Standard Edition, 12:207, but compare 7:254 and 263.

41. Fliess' influence on Freud's thought was far reaching but fitted very much within the general "pseudoscience" tradition inherent in nineteenth-century biology; see Peter Heller, "A Quarrel over Bisexuality," in Gerald Chapple and Hans H. Schulte, eds., *The Turn of the Century: German Literature and Art, 1890–1915* (Bonn: Bouvier, 1981), pp. 87–116.

42. See Iwan Bloch's *Beiträge zur Aetiologie der Psychopathia sexualis* (Dresden: H. R. Dohrn, 1902–03) and his *Das Sexualleben unserer Zeit in seinen Beziehungen zur modernen Kultur* (Berlin: Marcus, 1907), as well as the work of Magnus Hirschfeld. These volumes are part of an attempt to achieve a political solution to the question of homosexuality by recruiting science on the side of liberalism.

43. The great debate about prostitution in the nineteenth century was between the economic determinists, who relied on the work of Alexandre Jean Baptiste Parent-Duchatelet, *De la prostitution dans la ville de Paris* . . . (Paris: Baillière, 1836), and the biological determinists, represented by Lombroso. On Lombroso see Klaus Hofweber, *Die Sexualtheorien des Cesare Lombroso* (Diss., Munich, 1969).

44. For the context of these remarks see Fredrick B. Churchill, "Sex and the Single Organism: Biological Theories of Sexuality in Mid-19th Century," *Journal of the History of Biology* (1979), 12:139–77.

45. Standard Edition, 16:307, see also 16:320; 18:243; 23:152.

46. See Larry Stewart, "Freud before Oedipus: Race and Heredity in the Origins of Psychoanalysis," *Journal of the History of Biology* (1977), 9:215–28, and King, *The Biology of Race*.

47. On the context for this see my essay "Jews and Mental Illness: Medical Metaphors, Anti-Semitism and the Jewish Response," *Journal of the History of the Behavioral Sciences* 20 (1984); 150–59.

48. The pressures involved in understanding stereotyping as a dynamic process are best described in David Brion Davis, *The Slave Power Conspiracy and the Paranoid Style* (Baton Rouge: Louisiana State University Press, 1970). A survey

concerning the various approaches to anti-Semitism in recent scholarship has just appeared—Alphons Silbermann, *Der ungeliebte Jude: Zur Soziologie des Antisemitismus* (Zurich: Interfrom, 1981). Of great value on the linkage of images of Otherness is Hans Mayer, *Aussenseiter* (Frankfurt: Suhrkamp, 1975).

49. See Burton Pike, *The Image of the City in Modern Literature* (Princeton: Princeton University Press, 1981).

50. My reference here is to Sulloway, p. 592, and his references, tabulated in his index, to the twenty-six "myths" concerning Freud. Sulloway does not even attempt to understand the necessity of such myth-building as a means of existing in the world. This is especially true of the second "myth," "The Myth of Anti-Semitism."

5

BIOLOGICAL DEGENERATION: RACES AND PROPER PLACES

NANCY STEPAN
Columbia University

From the late eighteenth century until well into the twentieth, the idea of "degeneracy" was central to the biological sciences—to the study of variation, the pattern and mode of inheritance, and above all to the debate about the definition of "species."[1] The study of "degeneration" in human races seemed especially critical to these issues by providing information about the extent of racial variation in physical and psychological traits in the human species and the changes brought about by reproduction, especially those from crosses between very different "races."

"Degeneration": A Compelling Racial Metaphor

Racial degeneration was critical to these debates in part because it supplied them, if unconsciously, with their social and political meanings. Originally, scientists assumed that all human races belonged to the same species, and that environmental influences caused a "degeneration" away from a primordial form to create the different racial varieties in the world. By mid-century, however, the concept of degeneration had been reformulated in the direction of a more pessimistic and typological view of human variety. Scientists now argued that races formed distinct types which no amount of environmental degeneration could transform into each other. Nevertheless, the metaphors and modes of analysis associated with the original meaning of racial degeneracy were not lost. Certain races were assumed to be in and of themselves "degenerate types." The dean of French biology, Georges Cuvier, for example, argued that certain races could never be stimulated by their physical or social environment to achieve greatness—to become, in essence, "whitened," physically, mentally, or morally. The Negro race, in particular, he singled out for study, being marked by a "compressed cranium" which doomed it to stagnation. It was, Cuvier said, "the most degraded human race, whose form approaches that of the beast and whose intelligence is nowhere great enough to arrive at regular government."[2] Cuvier's use of the sign of a "compressed" cranium indicates the importance attached to the skull, head, and brain in racial science and to the definition of degenerate types. The jutting jaw characteristic of the ape, and the behaviors of the "uncivilized" peoples of the world, were other "signs" of inferiority.

Degeneracy as a *process* also had a place in the typological science of racial difference. It now meant a decay within the limits set by racial type. Thus a Negro placed outside his "proper" place in nature—in too stimulating an intellectual or social environment, or in a climate unsuited to his "tropical" nature—could undergo a further "degeneration," causing the appearance of atavistic or evolutionarily even more primitive behaviors and physical structures.

Racial biology, in short, by mid-nineteenth century was a science of boundaries between groups and the degenerations that threatened when those boundaries were transgressed. As slavery was abolished and the role of freed blacks became a political and social issue, as industrialization brought about new social mobility and class tensions, and new anxieties about the "proper" place of different class, national, and ethnic groups in society, racial biology provided a model for the analysis of the distances that were "natural" between human groups. Racial "degeneration" became a code for other social groups whose behavior and appearance seemed sufficiently different from accepted norms as to threaten traditional social relations and the promise of "progress."[3] By the late nineteenth century, the urban poor, prostitutes, criminals, and the insane were being construed as "degenerate" types whose deformed skulls, protruding jaws, and low brain weights marked them as "races apart," interacting with and creating degenerate spaces near at home.[4]

The meanings attached to racial "degeneracy" and the technologies they encapsulated became constituent elements, therefore, of the doctrine of social decay that emerged by the late nineteenth century. It was a doctrine that, in its polar opposition to the doctrine of social progress, seemed almost necessary to the latter, by providing a measure of the distance progressive individuals and groups had traveled from their biological and historical beginnings.

Non-Cosmopolitan Man: Races out of their Proper Places

For the racial biologists, a question that required answering was what happened to races when they moved out of their designated places in the economy of nature. Increasingly, as Western Europeans became more pessimistic about the possibilities of progress and more inclined to think in exclusive terms, scientists claimed that the fate of races when they transgressed their boundaries was a "degeneration" that could be so extreme as to cause racial extinction. A large literature developed on this theme, whose interest far transcended the apparently specialized topic of anatomical race.

The idea of the racial type, of its "proper place," and of the degenerations that occurred when "out of place" demanded a rejection of the thesis of "cosmopolitan" man. As quasi-polygenist ideas of race took hold in biology, belief in the infinite adaptability of man, in his cultural and physical cosmopolitanism, was replaced by the more negative theory of noncosmopolitanism. On the basis of analogies between human races and animal species, it was argued that races, like animal types, tended to be confined to definite localities of the earth. The British geologist and friend of Darwin, Charles Lyell, commented in his "Species" journal, "Each race of Man has its place, like the inferior animals."[5] A race's ties to its geographical, national and social place was aboriginal and functional; it gave strength to races in their proper places. Movement out of their proper places, however, caused a "degeneration."

Two themes, in particular, were sounded in the typological theory of racial degeneration. One was the degenerations caused by the movement of freed blacks into the geographical and social spaces occupied by whites and into the political condition of freedom. Negroes were now made, by biological definition, a tropical "species" naturally found in hot places like Africa. Their movement out of the tropics caused a "degeneration" away from their type; by a curious reversal of earlier conceptions of degeneration, Africa, far from being the cause of tropical degenerations such as laziness and unbridled sexuality, was now conceived as the very place where blacks did best. It was only in the temperate areas of the world, belonging to the white man, that degenerations such as those manifested by disease and depravity were believed to occur. The language of "acclimation" and "non-acclimation" became incorporated into the generalized theory of degeneration. The social and political realities giving the biological theory of black social degeneration its sanction deserves exploration.

Contrariwise, the "proper" place of the white race was now defined as the temperate, "civilized" world of Europe. When the white race moved out of its "natural" home, it too underwent a process of biological degeneration—it became "tropicalized." The relationships between racial typology, the idea of degeneracy, and colonial ideology obviously bears investigation here.

The problem of the proper place of the Negro in the Americas, not surprisingly, was a major concern of the American biologists. Most racial theorists in the United States shared, by the 1840s and 1850s, the typological orientation of the European scientists. Some were, in fact, far more polygenist and extreme in their views than the Europeans. Led by the craniologist Samuel Morton before his death in 1851, by the Swiss biologist Louis Agassiz, who had come in America to lecture in 1846 and remained for the rest of his distinguished career as the country's outstanding naturalist, and by such figures as Josiah Nott, George Gliddon, and J. Aitken Meigs, a physician from Philadelphia, scientists began to use polygenist arguments to defend the thesis that each of the human races were anatomically distinct and therefore intellectually and morally unique.[6] Given the importance of slavery and the abolition movement in the 1840s and 1850s, the Negro was singled out for special attention.[7] His special traits and his role in the nation were of prime importance.

Morton converted to polygenism in the 1840s, using detailed craniological measurements to argue the innate inferiority of blacks and other races. He turned to ancient Egyptian materials for evidence that for all of recorded history Negroes had not changed their type and had always served others as slaves.[8] Polygenism meant to Morton an "original adaptation of the several races to those varied circumstances of climate and locality which, while congenial to the one are destructive of the other."[9]

The thesis of primordial racial distinctions and noncosmopolitanism provided support for the theory that blacks were fundamentally "out of place" in the Americas and were doomed to degenerate as they moved northward into white, temperate territory, and as they moved socially and politically into freedom. The thesis that, as Van Evrie claimed, "the Negro is as much a product of the tropics as the orange or the banana" was an expression of the fervent desire of white physicians and biologists to foreclose a multiracial society, to prove that the Negro was unassimilable in the United States, and to insist on the necessity of distance.[10] It helped perpetuate the status quo at a time when emancipation threatened to change it.

An exaggerated and succinct statement of the theory of the "natural" places of human races was made by Agassiz in 1850 and again in 1854, the latter as a contribution to the racialist compendium on race edited by Nott and Gliddon called *Types of Mankind*.[11] Agassiz was prompted by his personal distaste for contact with the Negro, and by his biological theory of the fixity and separate creation of animal species, to suggest that races originated and were at home in distinct areas of the world. By creation, the African was tied to the tropical climate of Africa, his whole physiology and zoology making him suited and healthy there. Geographical distribution was a convenient metatphor for the distance Agassiz and others desired to exist among peoples that seemed strange and "inferior" to them. He proposed that the geographical boundaries between animal species and the distribution of mankind into distinct zones were primordial "facts" of nature. Such a theory of "natural racial zones" allowed Agassiz to suggest that the African did not originate in the same place as the white race, and the black was in no way a "degenerate white." Instead, each race could claim its own "degeneracies." In his article on geographical distribution Agassiz also managed to imply that the Negroes' role in the temperate, northern areas of the United States was unnatural and that liberty and moral responsibility were directed by God to fulfill the great "harmonies established in nature." In other words, God did not intend the Negro to be free, enfranchised, and living close to the whites in the north.

Nott and Gliddon, in turn, argued that though Negroes fared well in the hotter, southern latitudes of the United States, north of forty degrees latitude they steadily deteriorated. "Their type is not in reality changed or obliterated, but they undergo a degradation from their physical state analogous to the operation of a disease."[12]

After the Civil War and the emancipation of the slaves, the question of boundaries between whites and blacks became ever more urgent. What was to be the role of the freed blacks? Were they to take their place on terms of equality with whites, mingle with them, cross sexually with them? Few Americans thought so. The old belief that freed blacks were, of all blacks, the "most corrupt, depraved, and abandoned element in the population," was now given a biological rationale.[13] It was not the environment of slavery, nor just the cold, but freedom itself that was an unnatural environment for blacks, causing them to degenerate in a rapid fashion. Census data, most of it highly unreliable, was brought forward to show that "natural improvidence and social conditions" hastened the degeneration of blacks toward extinction.[14] Haller shows how Miller used the census data from 1860 to 1890, for instance, to prove that freedom brought "a beautiful harvest of mental and physical degeneration," so that the Negro became "a martyr to an heredity thus established."[15] The theory of racial extinction was a useful myth which concealed deep fears about the "blackness within" American society and the harm that might come to whites from too close a moral and physical contact between themselves and "degenerate" blacks.[16]

One of the most determined uses of census data to prove the degeneration and eventual extinction of blacks was that by Hoffman, a statistician and economist whose work was influential at the turn of the nineteenth century.[17] The model of extinction for Hoffman was the Indian, who had virtually disappeared. Hoffman was sure the Negro would follow suit, not merely because the superior Anglo-Saxon race invariably dominated inferior races, but because of the high mortality rate of the Negro compared to whites. The high mortality rate was a racial trait, but one provoked by unsanitary conditions, ignorance of the laws of health, and general poverty. The Negroes' drift into urban areas in the north was especially dangerous; it was usually in fact "a drift into an early grave."

Negroes suffered particularly from venereal disease, due to sexual immorality and excess, and to consumption, which became deeply rooted as a hereditary disease and exacerbated the Negro's decay. Improved sanitary conditions would have little effect on the Negroes' degeneracy, according to Hoffman; he quoted the report of the U.S. Surgeon General's Office for 1889, which ostensibly showed that under conditions of environmental equality with whites, blacks suffered unequally from disease and high mortality. Everything pointed to the "undermined constitution, a diseased manhood and womanhood, in short . . . a race on the road to extinction."[18] The political meaning of the biological theory of the degenerating and disappearing Negro was that the white race need have no fears from the blacks, for the white race, far from degenerating, throve in the geographical and political climate of the United States. The medical doctor J. Allison Hodges echoed what had become by the late nineteenth century a cliché of medical-biological science, namely, that freedom itself caused degeneration in the Negro. The Negro suffered excessively from venereal disease and consumption, diseases Hodges claimed had been nonexistent when the Negro was under the discipline of slavery. Freedom was an unnatural environment which removed constraints and plunged the Negro into "natural" and innate excesses and indulgence of the racial appetites. Morbid tendencies took hereditary root, making the Negro susceptible to illness and laying the foundation for degeneration in his mental life. Negroes reverted, under freedom, to their primitive state of savagery and sexuality, revealing the ancient features of the race by a process of reversion.[19] To the evolutionists, the degeneration of races out of their proper places was nature's way of "weeding out the weak" in the struggle for survival.[20]

In Europe, the main concern of scientists when it came to acclimation was the fate of the white race in the tropics. Was the "tropicalized" white race a degenerate type? How could white people maintain their "proper" place in an alien physical and cultural environment? What should their relations with native races be?

Curtin has shown that fear of the tropics was a product not only of the strangeness of Africa—its intense heat and humidity, the unfamiliarity of its fauna, flora, and its inhabitants—but also of the extraordinarily high mortality rates whites suffered from such tropical diseases as malaria and yellow fever. The apparently "natural" (though in fact acquired) resistance of Negroes to yellow fever fueled the belief in distinct racial susceptibilities and resistances to diseases and, with it, racial typology in biology.[21] It also helped to give some credibility to the thesis that Africa was the very place in which the Negro, though by nature a "degraded" type compared to whites, did best, while the white race was "out of place." Long after improvements in practical hygiene and medical treatment of disease had lowered the mortality rates of whites in Africa, the thesis of white degeneration in the tropics gave scientific weight to the importance of maintaining the correct psychological and social distance from the very places into which the white race, by its putatively "natural" vigor, ambition, restlessness, and dominance, was moving.

Vogt, for instance, quoted a variety of European sources for evidence that movement into the tropics caused whites to become diseased and anemic, to have high mortality rates and decreased fertility by the second or third generation.[22] There was, according to the physicians who began to produce a very large medico-racial literature on acclimation, special danger of intellectual and sexual degeneration caused by the physical and social climate of the tropics. The American sociologist William Ripley, in his book *The Races of Europe* published in 1899, which provided a thorough summary of European biological thought on race, said that the first result of a change in climate was an upset in the regular habits of the soldier or colonist. The temperate youth became a heavy drinker, for example. With alcoholism went sexual excess and "vicious habits" caused by a subtle "surexcitation of the sexual organs" from the heat. In the presence of a servile and morally underdeveloped native population, the result was sexual immorality on the part of whites. The appetites in general were overstimulated and overindulged, which caused indolence. Here was a biological "reminder" to avoid sexual mixing and the sexual freedoms so feared by the Victorians.[23]

The theory of tropical degeneration also gave support to the notion of the importance of maintaining the social mores of the home country. Biologists spoke of the need to keep the colonies going by fresh supplies of whites to make up for the diminished fertility most physicians believed the tropics caused in whites, but also of the need for whites to keep close ties with the homeland, to refresh their depleted energies, to restore their "type," and to repair the degeneracy acquired abroad. On the other hand, the message from the biologists was that colonization of the tropics by whites was in the long run inevitable because the white race, by its very nature, was aggressive and migratory. The American physician Meigs claimed that, though the white race suffered bad health and a sacrifice of life in the tropics, it could live there, but only as a master race. It could not undertake physical labor, which had to be left to the natives.[24]

A new twist to the theme of the degenerate European abroad was added toward the end of the nineteenth century, when competition between the European nations for colonies began to intensify. Did some European "races" have advantages over others, as far as acclimation was concerned, and if so, how would this affect the political balance of power? This was indeed the main theme of Ripley's chapter on acclimation in his book on race in 1899. To Ripley, acclimation was no longer of concern merely to theories of unity or plurality; unity was in principle accepted, as was the reality of racial differences. The issue of immediate consequence, he argued, was whether a single generation of European emigrants could live and perpetuate themselves in equatorial regions. Could they settle, preserve their own civilization there, or would they revert to the "barbarian stage of modern slavery"—to "a servile, native population, that alone could live and work in such regions?"[25] Ripley referred to the concern of the British biometrician Karl Pearson that the Mongolian "hordes" showed great superiority in their capacity to accommodate to new climates. Ripley said that it was well recognized that any move into new climates had bad effects, and that races also seemed to have different resistances to disease that might affect patterns of settlement.

The main burden of Ripley's chapter, however, was to evaluate the available data on the differential adaptability of the various "races" of Europe to the tropics. The evidence as to the infertility of the European in the tropics was conflicting, but mortality statistics did suggest that in new climates the Teutons seemed to suffer more compared to other European races. Indeed, according to Ripley's review of European medical and biological authorities, there was general agreement among scientists that the Latin, darker races did best in the tropics, followed by the French, with the Anglo-Saxons and Teutons doing least well. The French were in fact "divided against themselves," since the Provençal fraction of the nation did better than the Teutonic branch of the nation. Ripley wondered whether the fact that the Provençals also had survived better the rigors of the cold, as soldiers during Napoleon's Russian campaign, was due to the admixture of Jewish blood, as Wallace had suggested. Of all European races, the Jews were conceded by biologists to be the most cosmopolitan, able to adapt and thrive in all places.[26] Ripley's remarks show not only the way the myth of the "wandering Jew" was "naturalized" in biological discourse, but also how the idea of black inferiority worked its way into the discussion of the European races and was adapted to the needs of noncosmopolitanism, so that by implication only the darker Europeans did well in the alien tropics.

The theory of the "tropicalized" white race was an expression of the ambivalence still felt by European physicians and biologists at the end of the nineteenth century about colonial settlement, rather than of new medical and biological knowledge. For, as Ripley indicated, it seemed paradoxical yet biologically true that the very peoples who worked hardest to establish colonies, the Teutons and Anglo-Saxons, were the least able to cope successfully there. The implicit message seemed to be that the Anglo-Saxons' very refinement required the greatest possible physical, social, and sexual distance from the peoples they increasingly governed abroad. It was a theory of social control and separation which harmonized well with the British and German colonial policy of maintaining sharp boundaries, socially, between themselves and "natives," compared to the more assimilationist patterns of colonization of the Portuguese and French.

Proper Sexual Places: The Degenerate Racial Hybrid

Of all the boundaries between peoples, the sexual one was the most problematic to the Victorian mind. In the area of racial thought, there had been since earliest times a prurient interest in the strange sexual customs of alien peoples, especially the African. Did African women, for instance, mate with the great apes who came out of Africa? Were the sexual organs of the African larger than those of whites? Did a tropical climate encourage an unbridled sexuality that resulted in promiscuity?[27] It was not surprising that anthropological accounts of strange peoples provided a surrogate pornography for Europeans.

At the same time as the sexuality of strange peoples fascinated, it also repelled. There was a deep social aversion to "bad breeding," and to "impurity of blood." There was a worry that the incorrect mingling of classes, or ethnic groups, would produce a social chaos that would break the traditional boundaries between groups. In the eighteenth century, the idea of the Great Chain of Being was used to suggest that the separation of human beings into distinct classes and races was itself "natural."[28] If nature separated humans into ranks, mixing between them was "unnatural." There was a dislike, especially, of mingling between blacks and whites. It was sometmes asserted that the Negro's sexuality allured only white women who were wanton, or were working class.[29] Other biologists maintained that the anatomical differences between the sexual parts of the blacks and whites made mating across racial lines difficult and therefore rare, especially the mating of white women with blacks.[30] The convenience of this particular myth, at a time when legislation against racial intermarriage had been established in several of the British colonies of America, is obvious.

Scientists, therefore, inherited a set of negative ideas about racial mixture which over time they built into the theory of biological race degeneration. The first students of race knew that in fact intercourse between all races and classes was biologically possible and fruitful. The definition of a biological species in the eighteenth century, established by Buffon, was that members of the same species were interfertile.[31] On these grounds humans formed a single species. The problem was to reconcile the actual interfertility of all humans with the social dislike of intermixing. The solution was to redefine the meaning of the key word "species" and to reformulate the theory of sexual degeneration. In doing so, racially minded biologists explored the limits by which the meaning of the term "species" could be stretched, until Darwin, who himself inherited the long racial debate, extended the term indefinitely by showing that species were not closed units but units that merged with varieties and that changed over time. The idea of degeneracy associated with the debate over racial mixing survived even Darwin's reformulation, as we shall see. The result was an extremely flexible biological theory of species and fertility, protean in its capacity to incorporate and interpret all the social and racial variations possible on the theme of mixing, a theory that could indeed well express the social worries people had about sexual distance. The theory that improper racial mixing resulted in degeneracy had a very long life, surviving countless changes in biological theory. It provided a model of degeneracy of extraordinary influence on later theories of degeneracy quite outside biology. Here was a place where biology clearly rationalized and "naturalized" the intense concern people felt about improper unions, while giving, along the way, a new sense of the difficulties of defining "species."

Biologists took their cue in the eighteenth century from the fact that crosses between distinct species are indeed rare. In nature, individuals belonging to the same species are fully fertile when crossed with each other, but crosses between individuals of different species tend to be either infertile or yield offspring that are infertile. The classic example is, of course, the mule. To the eighteenth-century biologist, species were, therefore, stable entities, created by God at the beginning of time, and capable of transmitting their traits to their offspring with only minor variations. The barriers to mixing between species seemed nature's way of preserving order. Prichard, the leading student of biological races in Britain in the early part of the nineteenth century, said that mixing between different species of living things would cause "universal confusion" and was "contrary to the established order of nature." There seemed to be a natural "repugnance" or "antipathy" to such unions that went far beyond physiological incompatibility.[32] Lawrence called crosses between species "un-natural unions" that took place only under man's power and required continual supervision. Nature, he wrote, has provided "barriers of instinctive aversion, of sterility in the hybird offspring, and in the allotment of species to different parts of the earth, against any corruption or change of species in wild animals."[33]

Clearly human beings did not fit this model of "hybridization." Wherever they had gone they had mixed freely with each other—the Dutch with the Hottentots and Polynesians, the Spanish with the Indian, and the Anglo-Saxon with the African. Everywhere these unions had been fertile.

Yet as the social distaste for such unions grew, and as biologists began to conceptualize human races not as changeable varieties but as unchangeable types, it became increasingly possible to incorporate human crosses into the theory of hybridization and hybrid degeneration. In the process of incorporation, a wide-ranging investigation of animal hybrids in domestication and in the wild was undertaken, some of it involving experimental breeding. The ways in which the simple rule of inheritance—that like bred like—was interrupted by hybridization were explored, though not until Mendel were the numerical laws of inheritance unraveled, and even then it was only in 1900 that his work was rediscovered and understood. Nevertheless, the debate about species, varieties, races, mongrelization, hybridization, and degeneration provided the foundation for the revolution in biology brought about by Darwin. It was a revolution fueled, at least in part, by racialism and given shape by social meanings.

The British anatomist Sir William Lawrence is an interesting transitional figure in racial biology, for though he was formally a monogenist, he rejected environmental explanations of racial change, and viewed human races as fundamentally distinct varieties whose crossings were, like those between animal species, "un-natural unions." Crossing brought about a physical and moral "deterioration" of the European, he believed, while it improved and enabled the dark varieties. Once introduced into whites, black blood was like a "stain" that was not easily removed. For instance, said Lawrence, when a mulatto backcrossed with whites, the blackness was absorbed into the white in three generations, so that the offspring were perfectly white in color. Yet such offspring were not, in Jamaica, entitled to the legal protection of whites because there still existed a "contamination of dark blood, though no longer visible." It revealed itself, thought Lawrence, by a special smell in the individual.[34]

Lawrence's opinion of the deterioration of the white caused by racial mixing was widely quoted by polygenist biologists, and indicated the direction in which biology was moving. While Lawrence had referred to human mixtures as mulattoes and mongrels, biologists were now willing to call human races "species" and the products of their unions as "hybrids." The language of hybridization, of "aversion," "antipathy," and "repugnance," of "degeneration" and "deterioration," was now appropriated by biologists for the discussion of human beings.

To justify the application of the model of hybridization, however, it was necessary to show first, that distinct species sometimes crossed and had fertile offspring in the animal world analogous to human "species" when crossed; second, that human "species" had varying *degrees* of fertility when crossed, not perfect interfertility.

The redefinition of species and human hybridization was pushed far in some American biological works, because in the United States the dislike of black-white unions was so strong. Legislation against racial intermarriages had arisen early in the colonies, though the existence of a large mulatto population testified to the sexual exploitation of black women by white men and the lack of any biological barriers to such mixture. Originally, the status of the mulatto was unclear and varied from area to area. In some places, mulattoes were free and tolerated, while in others they were enslaved. After the Civil War and emancipation, however, attitudes toward mulattoes became more negative, and mulattoes were drawn into the two-color system of racial classification which has existed until the present.[35] There was an increasing need in the middle of the century for a biological theory that would show mulattoes to be degenerate types destined for self-destruction.

The polygenist Nott argued as early as 1843 that human races were in fact distinct species producing not a mulatto when crossed, but a true "hybrid," which was "a degenerate, unnatural offspring, doomed by nature to work out its own destruction."[36] Nott's work prompted Samuel Morton, the dean of craniological studies, to take up the theme. In 1851, Morton attacked the conventional definition of species, which was unsuited to his personal and social "need" to increase the distance between blacks and whites. He argued that the definition based on fertility was inadequate.[37] In this he was a good company, for even the monogenists Prichard and Lawrence in Britain and conceded that on occasion hybrid unions between species did occur which were fertile, which meant that the interfertility of human races could not by itself be used to prove their unity.

By 1851, the year he died, Morton had adopted the term "primordial organic forms" to describe human races; he believed that they shared with animal species a moral and physical repugnance against mingling which was overcome only by proximity and by the "moral degradation consequent to the state of slavery." Such repugnance, he claimed, was proverbial in Europeans where Negroes had been introduced, but was also natural to Africans. However, he admitted that just as in animals, the possibility of hybridization varied from species to species. In some remote species of the same genus, hybrids were never produced; allied species and more proximate species also existed in which fertile offspring could be found. The implication was that some human mixing was satisfactory while others were not.[38]

The signs of mulatto degeneracy were several. In 1843 Nott claimed that mulattoes were the shortest-lived of all human races, intermediate in intelligence between black and white, but less capable of undergoing hardship than blacks, with the women especially being frail and given to infertility. Originally Nott believed that all black-white unions were in the long run unproductive, so that mulattoes would eventually self-destruct as a type if prevented from backcrossing with the white or black parental stocks. Thus segregation would ensure the end of the mulatto population. Later, in *Types of Mankind,* Nott adopted Morton's distinction between fertile and less fertile crosses. He added the new "observation," based on his knowledge of New Orleans, that crosses between such "dark" European races as the French, Italian, Spanish, and Portuguese with Negroes were more successful than crosses between blacks and Anglo-Saxons and Teutons. They gave a hardier and more prolific stock.[39]

Yet even in prolific unions, the peculiarities of each race never, in his view, became completely fused so as to obliterate the types of either. No truly homogeneous race was produced, but instead one or the other of the race type "cropped out" from time to time. Although in the crosses between dark Europeans and blacks the dark could disappear in a few generations, by crossing back to whites, in Anglo-Saxon crosses with blacks the mulattoes died before the "stain" of blackness could be washed out by amalgamation. Meanwhile, degeneration produced a type that, as the product of two races adapted to different climates, was suited to neither the hot nor the cold regions of the United States, though it did acquire the racial resistance to yellow fever of the Negro.

Other scientists also commented on the incomplete fusion that occurred when two very different races crossed. Meigs, in his contribution to the second large work of the American polygenist school, *Indigenous Races of the Earth*, published in 1857, quoted from the British book *Crania Britannica:* amalgamation depended on the original proximity of the races. When the races were "remote," as blacks and whites were, then the hybrid products were weak, short-lived, prone to disease, and perishable. Only when races were very close in type could there be perfect "moral amalgamation," and even here, nature at times evinced her "unsubdued resistance by the occurrence of families bearing the impress of one or other of their original progenitors." In short, union was incomplete and hybrids unstable. In general, in mulattoes, said Meigs, the sagittal sutures of the brain were missing, and the lateral expansion of the head ceased in infancy, making the mulattoes narrow-headed and degenerate. Each additional foreign element in a race made fusion more difficult, and allowed odd forms to crop up in a most unacceptable manner; Meigs suggested the reader examine the population of any large city, such as London, Constantinople, or New York for a quick proof of the point. The instability of the hybrid was due to the deep-seated antipathy in its very nature, causing a "mysterious degradation of vital energy." Even when mulattoes were absorbed back into the white population, they left their impression on a conquering or exterminating race "in the shape of malformations—modifications of the skull, stature and intelligence." There was an inherent instability, an inherent tendency to decay. Mulattoes formed not a new race, but were rather a "confusion of form." "Nature asserts her dominion on all heads in a deterioration and degradation the fatal and depopulating consequences of which is appalling to contemplate."[40]

In Europe, just as class divisions had helped prompt racial speculation in the early nineteenth century, now classes and other social groups were in the process of being socially reconstructed as alien races in the midst of society who threatened civilization with racial degeneration and adulteration of the stock. Was the European race, the progressive race by definition, destined to undergo its own decay within, from the unnatural confusion of different races and classes?

The anatomist Robert Knox was explicit and dogmatic. Crossbreeding between races, he argued, produced no new types, no permanent varieties, for mulattoes were not self-supporting. As a result, the mulattoes in Spanish America would over time be eliminated, and the entire population would retrograde to its indigenous type, a people whose vital energies had "mysteriously run its course." The mulatto had no place in nature but was destined to decay.[41]

The classic, and most extreme statement of European racial degeneration by mixing in mid-century, was that by Gobineau in his *Inequality of Race*, published between 1850 and 1853. European society was termed a racial hybrid brought about by the inevitable mixing of distinct races. The result was always a degeneration, the loss of superior racial traits, and the decline of civilization. Thus Greece had sunk from the heights of civilization, and France was in the process of sinking. According to Biddiss, race and class were "secular symbols of group loyalty" and adulteration of race and class the mechanism of degeneration.[42]

Few biologists in Europe were comfortable with Gobineau's extreme pessimism. French biologists were unwilling to concede, for instance, that France was already degenerate and had no hope of progress. Paul Broca preferred to distinguish between suitable and unsuitable unions. In a book on human hybridity, he argued that closely related races were "eugenesic" and capable of producing fertile offspring, but as races became more distant from each other, fertility and the quality of the mulattoes declined. This approach to racial crossing allowed Broca to claim that no modern European nation was made up of a "pure" race, but that France was "mixed and prosperous."[43]

The thesis of hybrid degeneracy also found a home in the new evolutionary biology.[44] John Lubbock, Darwin's friend and a prolific writer of popular, evolutionary biology, quoted Darwin as saying that "crossed races of men are singularly savage and degraded," and that "when two races, both low on the scale are crossed, the progeny seems to be eminently bad." Darwin concluded that the "degraded state of so many half-castes is in part due to reversion to a primitive and savage condition, induced by the act of crossing, as well as to the unfavourable moral conditions under which they generally exist."[45] Lubbock commented that he was inclined to think that indeed much could be attributed to the unfortunate circumstances under which half-breeds often lived, and that half-breeds between native Indian women and servants from the Hudson Bay company "being well treated and looked after, appear to be a creditable and well-behaved set."[46]

In Germany, the polygenist evolutionist Carl Vogt also distinguished, as did most biologists in the second half of the nineteenth century, between crosses of "allied" races and more "distant" ones. He argued that crosses between white males and black females were indeed prolific and resulted in mulattoes that were prolific with either parental stock. Proof that mulattoes were prolific inter se was, he believed, lacking, because of the preference of mulattoes to cross back with one or the other parental stock. A cross between a Negro male and a white female, he believed, was less prolific "for anatomical reasons, which appear to be well-founded." With prolific mulatto stock, such as existed between Latin stock and Negroes, the first effect was "perfectly raceless masses" without constant type, because of continuous recrossings, though Vogt thought that perhaps a new race might develop over time and that in some cases such a race might be superior to either the aboriginal stock or the creoles. Yet even in these cases, Vogt believed that mixing would never entirely obliterate the original differences.[47]

The French scientist Paul Topinard also synthesized the ideas of Broca and other scientists by distinguishing between the perfect fecundity of contiguous races and the slightly reduced fertility of less close races. The eugenesic peoples of Europe, Topinard wrote, had produced a valuable mongrel people, as had the eugenesic Asians who had crossed among themselves. Yet even so, Topinard believed there were numerous examples in many mongrels of "interrupted, collateral or atavistic" inheritance, suggesting that fusion between the disparate elements in the races had been less than complete and harmonious.[48]

At the end of the nineteenth century, in his summary of European racial science, Ripley concluded that the weight of biological evidence showed that mulattoes were "pathologically intermediate."[49] Almost alone among the leading biologists in Europe, the French anthropologist Armand de Quatrefages remained steadfast in his monogenism, consistently maintaining that human races throve by crossing, "even when separated by profound differences."[50]

Ripley's compendium of anthropological knowledge about human races was published in 1899, the year before Mendel's work on heredity was rediscovered. Within a short time the new science of "genetics" was born and knowledge of heredity greatly expanded. Yet, even as the vocabulary of hybrid degeneracy changed, the fundamental ideas did not. Provine, for instance, in reviewing the ideas of the American geneticists on racial hybrids, shows that the Mendelian Charles Davenport, who pioneered the Mendelian analysis of unit traits in human beings, believed that crossing between different races produced new combinations of Mendelian traits that were unfavorable in the offspring. Davenport thought that a tall race crossed with a short race, for example, might produce a hybrid with a large frame and small viscera, or a short frame and too large a circulatory apparatus.[51] He believed that a mulatto would combine the intellectual inadequacy of the black with the ambition of the white, which would make him "unhappy to himself and a nuisance to others." Racial crossing was now a "Mendelian disharmony." In 1918, Harry Johnston wrote what Provine calls the most widely quoted textbook in America on genetics for the next fifteen years; he included a chapter on the mixing of races in which he claimed that racial antipathy was an inborn, biological mechanism for preventing races from degenerating. Edward East, the geneticist from Harvard, repeated Broca's distinction between eugenesic and agenesic crosses in the language of Mendelism. Crosses between races close to each other were fruitful and healthy, he maintained, but between distant races the hybrids "would break apart those compatible physical and mental qualities which have established a smoothly operating whole in each race by hundreds of generations of natural selection"[52] As late as

1937, Cedric Dover, in a book called *Half-Caste* designed to attack the prejudice against mulattoes as unfounded on the basis of modern biology, and which carried a foreword by the British geneticist Lancelot Hogben, said the mulatto was presented, in a "prodigal literature," "mostly as an undersized, scheming and entirely degenerate bastard. His father is a blackguard, his mother a whore. . . . But more than all this, he is a potential menace to Western Civilization, to everything that is White and Sacred and Masjusculed."[53]

Degeneracy: The Racial Influence

By mid-century the idea of degeneracy was beginning to take hold in fields outside race biology—in medical pathology, psychiatry, and criminology. The fear was growing that degenerations within civilized peoples threatened civilization itself. In the study of degeneration, the racial style of biological analysis was available for more general use, providing interesting analogies and identities. Racial stereotypes increasingly became a convenient place for the projection of new social anxieties and racial degeneration now became a part of a more general theory of "morbid anthropology."

Some sense of the ways the themes of racial degeneration were woven into the larger fabric of socio-biological degeneracy in the late nineteenth century can be gathered from an examination of the work of an American dental surgeon, Eugene Talbot, whose book *Degeneracy: Its Causes, Signs and Results* was published in the Contemporary Science Series (edited by Havelock Ellis) in 1898.[54] The book is in many ways paradigmatic of the medical-racial style of degeneracy theory at the turn of the century. It was typical of its time in its reliance on Lamarckian notions of heredity and in the extraordinary inclusiveness with which the term "degeneracy" was used. To Talbot it meant, in fact, any and every conceivable kind of illness, social pathology, deviance, abnormal psychological state or physical condition. In Talbot's formula, even an apparently healthy and wholesome individual could be harboring, unknowingly, a degenerate condition. Degeneracy in this sense was a pervasive, subtle decay of the individual or group, a deviation from a standard of normality, which was caused by some transgression of social, moral, or physical rules and which became established in the hereditary constitution of the individual.

Since races were well-known exemplars of degenerate types in themselves, they provided important points of comparison and analogy. Degenerate individuals were often found to resemble lower races in important physical signs and in moral and intellectual behaviors. According to Talbot, for example, criminals showed abnormal states in their instinctive faculties, which resulted in uninhibited behavior like that in lower races, or like that of the "moral idiots" in the best races. The "law of physique" in degenerates was like the law of "type" in races, causing traits to be perpetuated over time, so that degenerate families acquired a "racial" likeness because they came from a community of individuals that retrograded from generation to generation. Juvenile criminals, wrote Talbot, often had unnaturally shaped heads, and were stupid, like lower races, and like mulattoes they lacked vital energy. The urban poor or "persistent paupers" formed another degenerate class and were clear examples of "race degeneration." Prostitutes were like a race, showing arrested development, morbid heredity, and stigmata of physical and mental kinds, such as skull deformities. Sexual perverts were to him representative of a "still blacker phase of biology" (pp. 18, 319–23).

Since degeneracy was a "semiotic" science par excellence, it borrowed many of its signs from racial biology, as well as the techniques of measurement. The small head shape, the narrow skull, the prognathous jaw, the prematurely closed sutures were all signs of lower races and the stigmata of degeneracy in higher races—indications that an individual from a higher race had deviated from the ideal standard. Talbot included in his book an entire chapter on degenerate crania, showing that in degenerate people the sutures closed improperly, or the heads were small, like those of lower races. He even compared ape, Negro, and European skulls as Camper had done in the eighteenth century, in order to display the craniological stigmata of degeneracy, renaming the Negro a "criminal," degenerate type (pp. 181–83). Prognathism was another racial sign applied both to entire races, such as the Chinese and Japanese, and individuals of higher races, as marks of degeneracy.

The theory of climatic and sexual racial degeneracy was also absorbed into Talbot's schema. The intermixture of races was assumed by Talbot to produce degeneration. He acknowledged that there were exceptions; that, for example, the mulatto Dumas family in France was distinguished and healthy, but the mulattoes in Haiti and Louisiana had, he noted, relapsed into voodooism and cannibalism. He thought mulattoes were particularly inclined to produce "morbid proclivities" and "retrogressive tendencies." In the mulatto, the struggle for existence between the reproductive elements and the mental usually resulted in the success of the reproductive, as in the Negro and the ape. Thus Talbot suggested, once again, the old myth of the sexually promiscuous and immoral black, and the close association between the black and the ape. Peoples out of their proper climatic spaces also degenerated. The European in the tropics, Talbot argued, could easily become a tramp or a pauper, and could accelerate the degenerative process by illicit relations which resulted in degenerate offspring (pp. 92–103, 140).

Though essentially Lamarckian and reformist in tone, Talbot's book showed some signs of the growing worry medical scientists had about the containment of degeneracy. The leading theorist of degeneracy on the continent in the middle of the century, Morel, had viewed hereditary degeneration as self-limited, arguing that by the third generation degenerate stock had so reduced its fertility as to extinguish itself. The thesis of self-limiting degeneracy paralleled the myth of the decline and eventual extinction of the blacks and mulattoes in the United States. Like the racial myth, the thesis of degenerate extinction was often held in conjunction with the equally compelling yet less happy myth of uncontrolled and growing degeneracy. Talbot himself expressed some concern that no discipline or reform could eliminate the congenital criminal class, the sexual perverts, or the constitutional prostitutes (p. 317). The Lamarckian model of biological and social inheritance, which allowed for the environmental reform of individual heredity, was beginning to lose favor. The time was ripe for "eugenics," the ultimate biological theory of racial degeneration and regeneration.

In the non-Lamarckian, pessimistic eugenics movement of the early twentieth century, many of the old themes of racial degeneracy, such as those of hybrid degeneracy and the overpowering influence of degenerate stocks, found a new home.[55] What was new was the emphasis given to heredity itself and to the importance of correct breeding. Since civilization was believed to prevent the operation of natural selection, which in the normal course of events eliminated degenerate individuals and stocks, the only solution, according to the eugenists, was to prevent the overproduction of degenerates by segregation and sterilization of the "unfit." It was as though racial hybridization and segregation had become a metaphor of the kinds of degenerations threatening society, and the kinds of separations needed to contain classes and individuals in their proper social and physical spaces. There was a fear of the "universal sickening of the people, of a progressive degeneration of the civilized nation."[56] As Rosenberg comments, eugenics and the vogue of Mendelism "crystallized and added impetus to well-established intellectual and emotional concerns."[57]

The End of Racial Degeneracy?

The racial biology based on the idea of fixed, morphological types, which could be ranked in a great chain of social worth, was remarkably tenacious in biology. Equally tenacious was the associated thesis of racial degeneration, whether expressed in biological or social terms. Indeed, it was not until the 1930s that scientists began to express serious doubts about typological racial biology, and it was not until the 1940s and World War II that scientists, in the effort to disassociate themselves from what they saw as Nazi perversions of racial science for political ends, began radically to change their minds about race and racial degeneration. It took an additional ten to fifteen years after the war for a new, genetically based, populational view of human variation to become established in science, one that drastically reformulated the problem of human diversity and that left little room for the thesis of noncosmopolitan races, racial degeneracy and typology.[58]

Attacks on racial typology and the theme of racial hybrid degeneracy began in a piecemeal fashion, starting early in the twentieth century in fact. In 1911, for instance, the American physical and cultural anthropologist Franz Boas asserted that the antipathy to race crossing was not biological but social in origin, and that biologically speaking, crosses were not inferior.[59] By the 1920s, other scientists had begun to second Boas, while social scientists began to explore the social as opposed to the biological causes of racial inequalities and the fear of miscegenation. Even so, as we have seen, biologists continued on the whole to maintain, in the new language of Mendelian genetics (a genetics particularly concerned with the issue of hybridization), that while mulattoes were fertile, they were also inferior in many respects to the white race. Even the sociologists transferred to social discourse a sense of the peculiar social pathology of the mulatto.[60] In his classic work on race, *An American Dilemma*, published in 1944, the Swedish sociologist Gunnar Myrdal commented on how black inferiority and mulatto degeneracy were "contrast conceptions," serving psychologically as the "antithesis of progress."[61]

Provine, in his detailed study of the geneticists' views of racial hybrids, shows that not until the first UNESCO *Statement on Race*, published in 1950, did biologists for the first time since the early nineteenth century reject publicly the well-worn themes of noncosmopolitan races and "hybrid" degeneration. The *Statement*, which was based on a collective effort by geneticists, biologists, and anthropologists to define clearly for the public the modern scientific understanding of the meaning of the term "race" and racial differences, reaffirmed the early monogenists' thesis of the biological unity of the human species. It also reasserted the adaptability of all human beings, mentally and physically, and denied there was evidence that the biological effects of racial crossing were pernicious.

Provine also shows that the change in biological opinion about racial hybrid degeneration involved no radical change in the data about racial hybrids in the period 1930 to 1950. Instead, the change was as much one in social and political outlook as it was in science.[62] Indeed, looking back over the entire history of biological degenerationism one is stuck forcefully with the shaping of racial science by social expectations and with the extraordinary range of interactions between the social and the biological. These interactions were almost always indirect rather than direct, in that the science involved more than mere rationalizations of social and political beliefs. We have seen, in fact, that racial biology had, if not always internal consistency, at least a coherent history of its own. Nevertheless, interactions between the social and the biological were easy and possible. This was so not just because the Lamarckian model of inheritance, which was so integral a part of degeneration theory in the nineteenth century, did not separate the social and the biological in inheritance; after all, the interactions continued well into the non-Lamarckian, Mendelian period of racial biology in the twentieth century.

Instead, the interactions were feasible and commonplace because of what the historian Robert Young calls the "common context" of much social and biological thought about human nature.[63] Young notes that "close study of the documents has made it clear that it is difficult, and ultimately impossible, to maintain the conventional distinction between the science of the period and the interacting factors which are usually considered to provide its context."[64] Rather there was a common social and biological context out of which emerged, in Young's case, the nineteenth-century debate over "man's place in nature," and in the case studied here, the nineteenth and early twentieth-century debate about biological degeneration. This common context made the history of racial biology and degenerationism from the start a "biosocial" or "socio-biological" history. This common context made it quite proper, and indeed "natural," for example, for the biologist Lankester, when writing about the possibility of evolutionary retrogressions, to analyze animal and societal parasitism as though they were exemplifications of the same biosocial process.[65] Rosenberg's dictum that "social context, not empirical research or internal logic, determined the contours of hereditarian thought," can well be applied to the entire story of biological, racial degenerationism described in these pages.[66]

NOTES

1. The importance of "degeneration" to biological theory in the first half of the nineteenth century is suggested by the use of degenerationism in the work of Lamarck and Darwin. In his analysis of transmutation, Lamarck did not speak first of the increasing complexity of animals as one moved "up" the animal chain, but of the increasing "degradation and simplification" the naturalist encountered in following the animal chain downward; see J. B. Lamarck, *Zoological Philosophy*, Hugh Eliot, tr. (New York: Hafner, 1963), esp. pp. 68–69. An entry in Darwin's notebooks in 1838, stating that there was "not *gradual* change or degeneration from circumstances, if one species does change into another it must be *per saltum*—or species may perish," indicates Darwin's search for an alternative mechanism to degeneration by which one species might be transformed into another. For this entry, see Nora Barlow, ed., *Charles Darwin and the Voyage of the Beagle* (London: Pilot Press, 1945), p. 263.

2. Georges Cuvier, *The Animal Kingdom Arranged in Conformity with Its Organization* (New York: Carvill, 1931), pp. 10, 52.

3. Stephen J. Gould, in *The Mismeasurement of Man* (New York: Norton, 1981), examines how race, sex, and class stood as "surrogates" for one another in biological determinism; see esp. p. 80.

4. On prostitutes and degeneracy, see Judith R. Walkowitz, *Prostitution and Victorian Society: Women, Class, and the State* (Cambridge: Cambridge University Press, 1980), pp. 36–37.

5. See Leonard G. Wilson, ed., *Sir Charles Lyell's Scientific Journals on the Species Question* (New Haven and London: Yale University Press, 1970), p. 347.

6. The American school of racial biology and anthropology is described by a number of authors, including William Stanton, *The Leopard's Spots: Scientific Attitudes Towards Race in America, 1815–1859* (Chicago: University of Chicago Press, 1960); John Haller, *Outcasts from Evolution: Scientific Attitudes of Racial Inferiority, 1859–1900* (Urbana: University of Illinois Press, 1971); and George M. Frederickson, *The Image of the Black in the White Mind* (New York: Harper and Row, 1971). Frederickson is particularly useful for his long discussion of degenerationism in American thought.

7. Stanton, p. 78.

8. Morton's life and work is reviewed by Henry S. Patterson in "Memoir of the Life and Scientific Labors of Samuel George Morton," in J. C. Nott and George R. Gliddon, eds., *Types of Mankind* (Philadelphia: Lippincott, Gambo, 1854), pp. xvii–lvii.

9. Samuel G. Morton, "Hybridity in Animals, Considered in Reference to the Question of the Unity of the Human Species," *American Journal of Sciences and Arts*, 2d ser. (May 1847), 3:40.

10. Quoted in Frederickson, p. 138.

11. Louis Agassiz, "Geographical Distribution of Animals," *Christian Examiner*, 4th ser. (March 1850) 13:181–204; and "The Diversity of the Human Races,"

Christian Examiner, 4th ser. (July 1850) 14:110–45; and "Sketch of the Natural Provinces of the Animal World and Their Relation to the Different Types of Man," in Nott and Gliddon, *Types of Mankind*, pp. lviii–lxxvi.

12. "Geographical Distribution of Animals and the Races of Men," in Nott and Gliddon, *Types of Mankind*, pp. 63–64.

13. Frederickson, pp. 4–5, 35–36; the quotation is from p. 15.

14. Frederickson, pp. 249–53, and Haller, pp. 40–68.

15. Haller, p. 46.

16. For further discussion consult Joel Williamson, *New People: Miscegenation and Mulattoes in the United States* (New York: Free Press, 1980).

17. His career is reviewed by Haller, pp. 60–68.

18. Frederick L. Hoffman, "Vital Statistics of the Negro," *The Arena* (April 1892), 29:520–42.

19. J. Allison Hodges, "The Effect of Freedom upon the Physical and Psychological Development of the Negro," Annual Address, *Transactions of the American Medico-Psychological Association* (May 1900), 7:88–98. See also F. Tipton, "The Negro Problem from a Medical Standpoint," *New York Medical Journal* (May 22, 1886), pp. 569–572.

20. Frederickson, p. 257.

21. Philip D. Curtin, *The Image of Africa: British Ideas and Action, 1780–1850* (Madison: University of Wisconsin Press, 1964), 1:83–84, comments on the importance of the medical experience of Europeans in Africa to racial biology.

22. Carl Vogt, *Lectures on Man: His Place in Creation, and in the History of the Earth* (London: Longman, Green, Longman, and Roberts, 1864), pp. 429–30.

23. William Z. Ripley, *The Races of Europe: A Sociological Study* (New York: Appleton, 1899), pp. 561–64.

24. J. Aitken Meigs, "The Cranial Characteristics of the Races of Men," in J. C. Nott and George R. Gliddon, eds. *Indigenous Races of the Earth, or, New Chapters of Ethnological Enquiry* (Philadelphia: Lippincott, 1857), p. 53.

25. Ripley, ch. 21, "Acclimatization: The Geographical Future of the European Races," pp. 560–90. See also T. H. F. Kohlbrugge, "The Influence of a Tropical Climate on Europeans," *Eugenics Review* (April 1911–Jan. 1912), 3:25–36.

26. Ripley, pp. 582–89, gives the comparative aptitudes for acclimatization of the various European races, see p. 581 for the fertility of the Jews.

27. Winthrop D. Jordan, *White Over Black: American Attitudes Toward the Negro, 1550–1812* (New York: Norton, 1977), pp. 30–40, 150–54, 238–39.

28. Nancy Stepan, *The Idea of Race in Science: Great Britain, 1800–1960* (London; Macmillan, 1982), pp. 6–12.

29. See Curtin, 1:46–47, and Jordan, p. 151.

30. Johann Friedrich Blumenbach, in *The Anthropological Treatises* (London: Anthropological Society of London, 1863), p. 249, discussed the size of the sexual organ of male Africans.

31. James Cowles Prichard, *Researches into the Physical History of Man*, George W. Stocking, Jr., ed. (Chicago: University of Chicago Press, 1973), pp. 7 and 10.

32. Prichard, pp. 7 and 10.

33. William Lawrence, *Lectures on Physiology, Zoology, and the Natural History of Man* (London: James Smith, 1822), p. 182.

34. Lawrence, pp. 200–04.

35. Williamson deals at length with the development of the two-color system of racial classification in the United States between 1850 and 1915; see *New People*, pp. 61–109.

36. Josiah C. Nott, "The Mulatto, a Hybrid," *American Journal of Medical Science* (1843), 5:256.

37. Samuel G. Morton, "Value of the Word Species in Zoology," *American Journal of Science and Arts*, 2nd ser., (May 1851), 11:275–76.

38. Prichard, pp. 8–13, and Lawrence, pp. 180–82. For his definition of races, see Morton "Value." For the remark on moral degradation, see Morton, "Hybridity in Animals," p. 211.

39. For Nott's review of his own thoughts on the subject, see his chapter "Hybridity of Animals, Viewed in Connection with the Natural History of Mankind," in Nott and Gliddon, *Types of Mankind*, pp. 373–407.

40. Meigs, pp. 250, 252–53.

41. Robert Knox, *The Races of Men* (Philadelphia: Lea and Blanchard, 1850), pp. 53–54.

42. Michael D. Biddiss, *Father of Racist Ideology: The Social and Political Thought of Count Gobineau* (London: Weidenfeld and Nicolson, 1970), p. 109.

43. Paul Broca, *On the Phenomena of Hybridity in the Genus Homo*, Carter Blake, ed. (London: Longman, Green, Longman and Roberts, 1864); quotation on pp. 21–22.

44. Darwin himself maintained, as did most biologists, that hybridization in itself was not a test of species, because well-recognized animal species did on occasion cross. Yet he also believed that evolution by natural selection would produce sterility between incipient species. The role of hybridization in evolution was too difficult a problem for Darwin to solve, given the absence of an adequate genetic theory.

45. John Lubbock, *The Origin of Civilization and the Primitive Condition of Man* (New York: Appleton, 1870), p. 354.

46. Lubbock, p. 354. Robert E. Bieder, in "Scientific Attitudes toward Indian Mixed-Bloods in Early Nineteenth Century America," *Journal of Ethnic Studies* (Summer 1980), 8(2):17–30, shows how positive views of Indian mixed-bloods gave way to negative ones by the 1840s and 1850s.

47. Vogt, pp. 436–42.

48. Paul Topinard, *Anthropology* (London: Chapman and Hall, 1878), pp. 367–83; quotation from p. 381.

49. Ripley, p. 570.

50. Armand de Quatrefages, "The Unity of the Human Species," *Popular Science Monthly* (May–Oct. 1872), 1:71.

51. William B. Provine, "Geneticists and the Biology of Race Crossing," *Science* (Nov. 23, 1973), 182:790–96.

52. All quotations from Provine.

53. Cedric Dover, *Half-Caste* (London: Secker and Warburg, 1937), p. 13.

54. Eugene S. Talbot, *Degeneracy. Its Causes, Signs, and Results* (London: Walter Cott, 1898), p. 20.

55. Many eugenists, in fact, continued to think in terms of Lamarckian inheritance, emphasizing, as had earlier degenerationists, the accumulated, negative effects of bad habits and environment on the hereditary constitution. See, for

example, C. W. Saleeby, "Racial Poisons II: Alcohol," *Eugenics Review* (April 1910–Jan. 1911), 2:30–52.

56. William Hirsch, *Genius and Degeneration. A Psychological Study* (New York: Appleton, 1896), p. 320.

57. Charles E. Rosenberg, *No Other Gods: On Science and American Social Thought* (Baltimore and London: Johns Hopkins University Press, 1976), p. 49.

58. These changes are described in Stepan, chs. 6 and 7.

59. Franz Boas, *The Mind of Primitive Man* (New York: Free Press, 1965), pp. 240–41.

60. See, for instance, Edward Byron Reuter's *The Mulatto in the United States* (Boston: Richard G. Badger, 1918), which, though sociological in emphasis, nevertheless treats mulattoes as a separate and "deformed" social class requiring explanation.

61. Gunnar Myrdal, *An American Dilemma: The Negro Problem and Modern Democracy* (New York: Pantheon, 1972), 1:100.

62. Provine, p. 796.

63. Robert Young, "Malthus and the Evolutionists: The Common Context of Biological and Social Theory," *Past and Present* (1969), 43:109–45.

64. Robert Young, "The Historiographic and Ideological Contexts of the Nineteenth-Century Debate on Man's Place in Nature," in Mikuláš Teich and Robert Young, eds., *Changing Perspectives in the History of Science: Essays in Honour of Joseph Needham* (Dordrecht: Reidel, 1973), p. 348.

65. Edwin Ray Lankester, *Degeneration. A Chapter in Darwinism* (London: Macmillan, 1880), p. 60.

66. Rosenberg, p. 32.

6

MEDICINE AND DEGENERATION: THEORY AND PRAXIS

Eric T. Carlson
Cornell Medical College

The attention to decadence in French literature burst forth in 1857 in a slim volume of poems entitled *Les Fleurs du mal*. The product of Charles Baudelaire, it illustrated a trend to the darker, more evil, disorganized part of man. A similar theme, although with a different focus, appeared the same year in a book by a physician, Bénédict-Augustin Morel, that forcefully brought the concept of degeneration to the medical profession.[1]

Morel (1809–1873) was born of French parents in Vienna. Although impoverished, he received a medical degree in 1839 with a thesis influenced by the naturalism of Henri Blainville and the search by Franz Joseph Gall to find laws of nature in comparative physiology and pathology, a search across time in history and across various cultures. These factors would play an important role in the strong anthropological component that would pervade degeneration theory. To further his education in psychiatry, Morel obtained a position under Jean-Pierre Falret at the Salpêtrière after his friend Claude Bernard had arranged an introduction.

While sharing living quarters with Claude Bernard, Morel extended his psychiatric studies to broader issues. He studied the works of Buffon, Cuvier, and the neurophysiological researches of Flourens and attended the lectures of Henri Marie de Blainville on natural history. In 1844 he took a melancholic patient abroad and studied the psychiatry of Germany, Switzerland, Belgium, Holland, Great Britain, and Italy. While in Berne, Switzerland, he became interested in the problem of cretinism and later wrote on the subject.[2]

After his return to France, he continued his research, which intensified when he became director of an asylum. By 1857 he was able to report his findings in his highly influential book *Traité des dégénérescences physiques*, *intellectuelles et morales de l'espèce humaine* (Paris: Baillière, 1857), followed three years later by his *Traité des maladies mentales* (Paris: Masson, 1860). His last publications appeared in 1871, two years before his death from complications of diabetes. In one he responded with indignation to a publication by Carl Starck on the signs and causes of degeneration in the French people. The application of Morel's principles to the entire French population was too much for the author of this wide ranging theory.[3]

Morel proposed two fundamental laws for degeneration theory: the law of double fertilization (or the impact of heredity) and the law of progressivity. The former may follow somewhat in the tradition of Moreau de Tours in that there was a dual heritage, a heredity from both mother and father, but Morel did not separate the contribution of each into physiognomy and character as Moreau had done.[4] Instead, he stressed what might be called the "law of double jeopardy," the risk that followed from a psychological inheritance from both parents, each of whom could contain the seeds of destruction.

His law of progressivity, expounded in his 1860 textbook on psychiatry, had a great impact on psychiatric as well as later social and anthropological thought. It stated that in hereditary transmission from generation to generation not only was the "bad seed" passed along, but each new generation received a heavier and more destructive dose of whatever the evil influence was. This postulation was largely hypothetical, as no one had any inkling at this time what the process could be, although it was thought to be biological and to involve the respective sperm and ovum. This destructive accumulation eventually gathered such force that it led to the extinction of the family line. Morel gave detailed examples of this process, which appeared disheartening in its inevitability. The first generation was characterized by a nervous temperament and a tendency toward cerebral vascular congestion, accompanied by irritability, a quick temper, and resulting violent behavior.[5] The second generation ran the risk of illnesses of the central nervous system: cerebral hemorrhages, epilepsy, and the neurotic disorders of hysteria and hypochondriasis. The third generation felt the gathering malevolent force toward insanity. Its members would appear to be eccentric, disorderly, and dangerous. The accumulated defects reached lethal proportions in the following generation and the family line was, or soon would be, gone. Infants were born with markedly reduced vitality, demonstrated a congenital weakness of their faculties, and were sterile, imbeciles, or idiots. If this generation managed to reach adolescence, it was likely to develop a mysterious decline that Morel named dementia praecox. Writers who followed embellished this list, adding variations in sequence and timing. Perhaps the most common arrangement was alcoholism near the beginning to the middle of the chain, and a greater emphasis on insanity and idiocy at the end.

I shall investigate Morel's theory by looking at the causes he espoused and by examining brief histories of the concepts of degeneration and heredity. I shall then review the signs or stigmata that suggest the presence of degeneration or its predisposition. There follows a lengthy discussion of the application of these ideas to psychiatry proper and of such various related topics as criminality and the association of genius and insanity.

History

Causation

Reading Morel on causation quickly reveals a strong environmental bent. His treatise on degeneration could be fairly described as a text on environmental biology and social psychiatry. Certainly heredity was also included. There are sections on how to understand heredity based on the work of his teacher Buchez. In addition, Morel reviews the evidence for degeneration in plants in chapter 5, and goes on to discuss cross-fertilization in plants and animals and, finally, between the races of mankind. In this chapter, he also presents the conditions under which the reverse of degeneration—or what he calls regeneration—could occur. Much of the book centers on what Morel called intoxicants and allied products, and these discussions have a strong chemical tinge.

Included first were a number of natural substances that humans used for their pleasureable effects, which became addictive or, at least, habit forming. Alcoholism received the main attention. At this point in his book, Morel wrote an interesting section on the degenerative effects on the infants of alcoholic parents. Typically he discussed the influence on the nervous system, anatomical changes, and behavioral modifications, but also the impact on the nation's economy. Three other "vegetable poisons" received his attention: opium, hashish, and tobacco. He next turned his attention to the mineral poisons. Although he mentioned copper, phosphorus, mercury, and arsenic, he focused on the physical and psychological effects of lead poisoning and later on illnesses that arose from clearly recognized syndromes that were only partly understood. One was ergotism, which Morel connected with weather conditions and the degradation of cultivated grains. The other was pellagra, which clinical observations indicated would commonly arise in groups of humans who subsisted almost entirely on maize. The last disorders reviewed seemed to be related to the geology of the earth—the appearance of marshy areas and the impact of different kinds of soils.

Morel's discussions of psychological and social factors in degeneration were wide ranging. He not only considered transcultural factors (such as the effects of opium on the Chinese or alcoholism among the Swedes), but compared results from studies in savage societies (such as the American Indian) to those considered civilized. He also considered what the absence of revealed religion meant in certain cultures. Finally, in relation to the civilized society of Western Europe, he discussed the effects of factory conditions on workers, the illnesses commonly seen in industrial centers and among mine workers, and the deleterious effects of immorality.

A major problem for degeneration theory is its vagueness. It is therefore used imprecisely and applied to all kinds of situations. All physicians have had experience with patients whose disease made them worsen, deteriorate, or degenerate. This is understandable with acute illnesses, but chronic, unexplained, progressive illnesses are more puzzling. Diabetes is one example. If such a disease appeared to run in a family, then one might speculate that it is hereditary and degenerative, but not necessarily progressive through generations. Even after Morel's special use of "degeneration," writers appeared to use the word with both biological and moral meanings. When the word "degeneration" entered popular literature, it had moral implications and was often used to condemn or defame certain groups.

The moral implications go far back. One is reminded of the Old Testament. First there is the doctrine of the Fall of Man, which is so important to the history of Christian thought. Because of man's disobedience to God, God in his retribution introduces a bodily disposition toward illness and death and condemns future generations to this dismal bodily end. This theme also appears in the biblical story of the threat of an angry and jealous God to transmit the sins of the father unto the third and fourth generation.[6]

Degeneration as a biological and medical concept seems to come largely from French thought. Precursors can be found in the influential eighteenth-century writings of Buffon (Georges Louis Leclerc), who theorized that the animals of the new world showed signs of degeneracy. His follower Abbé Raynal took Buffon's ideas one step farther by suggesting that man was also susceptible to the pernicious and degenerating climate of North America. The Americans were apparently not too distressed when he described some of the alleged unsavory behavior of the American Indians as a sign of degeneration, but they reacted when he extended his criticism to the emigrated white man. Benjamin Franklin responded with twitting humor, while Thomas Jefferson attempted a lengthy refutation in his *Notes on Virginia,* in which he attributed the popularity of the obviously incorrect thesis to "vivid imagination and bewitching language." The impact of these writers on nineteenth-century medicine is unknown, but there is no question about the attention to the concept of growing degeneration.[7]

Philippe Pinel, in the first edition of his famous textbook on psychiatry asked, "May not melancholia of several years standing degenerate into mania?"[8] His affirmative answer used the case history of a man under his care who had been melancholic for eight years and then went into a maniacal excitement. Pinel did not build any theory based on this observation, which better fits the idea of deterioration and does not suggest family progressivity.

By the 1840s, degeneration as a word and as a concept was appearing more frequently. In 1842, Bertulus spoke about the dangers of degeneration for those who lived under unhygienic conditions in large cities.[9] It was not only the poor, living under squalid conditions in the cities, who were at risk, as W. M. Bush of England pointed out when he wrote "Juvenile Delinquency and Degeneration in the Upper Classes of Society" in 1849.[10] Bush discussed the roles of "defective organization" and "defective nervous energy." He wrote about the many nervous signs that appeared in the young who faced various school demands and other pressures, but he did not bring heredity into his discussion.

The concept of heredity may be found in the Bible and in the writings of the Greek philosophers, suggesting that it is as old as written history. Hippocrates, for example, struggled to understand two methods of disease transmission. People living in the same household often appeared to be most susceptible. One class of illness seemed more immediate and acute and suggested contagion as a factor.

Chronic diseases presented a somewhat different exploratory problem. Again, it had been noted in classical writings that some diseases seemed to appear more frequently in certain families. Tumors and cancers, idiocy, and alcoholism were mentioned early. Closer to our time more attention was paid to gout and diabetes.

Familial transmission now seems to be the issue, but this presented yet an additional set of problems for the medical theorist. Even Hippocrates thought that some kind of biological material was collected from the body and transmitted sexually through the semen. In this way he could explain the inheritance of diseases and of what we now call acquired characteristics. Charles Darwin had a similar explanation and apparently his hypothesis of pangenesis did not differ much from the Hippocratic tradition—a sure indicator that not much biological progress had been made in the basic understanding of inheritance over the last two millennia. This would have to wait until the twentieth century for clarification.

It was in botanical studies in the late 1600s that progress in scientific heredity showed a temporary spurt. Plant hybridization was advanced by the systematic researches of Joseph Gottlieb Kolreuter in Germany in the 1760s. His work was familiar to both Darwin and Mendel in the next century. Kolreuter noted that crossbreeding tended to be accompanied by greater vitality, an observation confirmed by Darwin, who also noted that inbreeding led to a decline.[11]

In the nineteenth century, heredity was the subject of increased attention and speculation in the writings of a growing cadre of psychiatrists. In their attempts to be scientific, they even began to apply primitive statistical methods to the analysis of their data. French psychiatry took over the role of international leader during the early nineteenth century and provided the soil from which the theory of degeneration would spring.

Philippe Pinel was the dominant figure in psychiatry from the French Revolution until his death in 1826. From that position, he contributed to the increasing emphasis on heredity in psychiatric illnesses, although he believed in environmental and psychological causes. In the second edition of his famous psychiatric text, he inserted a brief paragraph in which he admitted that the histories of mania or madness occurring over several generations in the same family made it difficult to deny the existence of hereditary transmission.[12]

Shortly thereafter, in England, Joseph Adams wrote a book entitled *A Treatise on the Supposed Hereditary Properties of Diseases* (London, 1814). Adams stressed that the appearance of familial diseases did not necessarily mean that the diseases were actually inherited. A few could be, but most presented only an inherited susceptibility, a predisposition, on which some exciting cause acted to produce the resulting illness. Gradually this emphasis on a hereditary predisposition took hold and became predominant in psychiatric theory. This view left ample room for the role of environment and of psychological causes.

Returning to the French psychiatric scene after 1815, Pinel was gradually supplanted in power and influence by his pupil Jean-Etienne Esquirol. Esquirol wrote extensively and taught most of the major leaders of French psychiatry of the next generation. In 1838, he collected his extensive ideas from the previous thirty years in a highly influential text, *Des maladies mentales*. Esquirol believed a hereditary predisposition was most common among the rich mentally ill, but was in only sixth place among the poor. Esquirol mentioned the appearance of signs for this predisposition, a topic that would later be of considerable interest and importance. He broadened the areas within the person that could be affected: the physiognomy and the external form of the body in general. He also moved into the psychological sphere by speaking about predispositions in the intellectual realm, in the emotions, in habits, and even in "moral character." In a study of 1,375 patients at his asylum, the Charenton, Esquirol found 337 with a positive family history or 24.5 percent with evidence for a hereditary factor.[13]

Much more attentive to heredity from a research point of view was Moreau de Tours, who in 1850 showed that inbreeding in animals led to a poorer product in the offspring. Jacques Joseph Moreau wrote his thesis in 1830 on the effect of physical factors on the intellectual faculties. This orientation led to his studies (1852) on the hereditary role in epilepsy. In addition, he proposed a similar role in mental illness, hysteria, alcoholism, and a general irritability and excitability of the nervous system. He continued to study predisposition, looking for appropriate signs over the next few years, and extended his studies to imbecility and idiocy.[14]

Signs and Stigmata

Signs and symptoms have always been of interest to medicine—signs being the objective findings for the presence of disease while symptoms were the subjective complaints of the patient. Stigmata, traditionally a theological term, had been used when early Christians branded themselves with nail and spear marks to resemble those of Christ. With the personal experience of St. Francis of Assisi in the thirteenth century and of St. Catherine of Siena a century later, miraculous stigmata were noted. The stigmata of degeneration, in a way, represent the reverse of such experience, as if an evil mark had been placed on the sufferer, if not by the devil, then by biology. Morel apparently used the term "stigmata" only two times, but he studied his families thoroughly for evidence of signs and symptoms.

Two historical traditions contributed to the emphasis on stigmata: the stress on physiognomy (Lavater) and phrenology (Gall and followers) and the clinical studies of mental defectives, cretins, and criminals. Studies on cranial capacity and facial angles followed and became one foundation of physical anthropology. Blainville, Morel's teacher, also studied the lack of symmetry in the head and ears. The study of symmetry continued throughout the century and led to a study of composite photographs of the left versus the right side of the face. As early as 1863 Morel had established a photographic studio in his asylum to aid him.

These beginnings led to an intensification of psychopathological studies in both neurology and psychiatry. By 1900, the list of potential physical stigmata had lengthened and included all parts of the body. Morel also looked for evidence of mental signs and stresses and for the "unbelievable susceptibility and impressionability" in the affected.[15] The tendency for intellectual and emotional functions to get out of balance with each other led to extensive behavioral disturbances. This emphasis on functions led later writers to speak of physiological and mental stigmata, even though this confused the usual separation of the objective-subjective dichotomy. A list in a popular 1899 textbook on neurology and psychiatry widely used in the United States illustrates this dichotomy:[16]

Physiological Stigmata.
    Anomalies of motor function:
        Retardation of learning to walk.
        Tics.
        Tremors.
        Epilepsy.
        Nystagmus.
    Anomalies of sensory function:
        Deaf-mutism.

    Neuralgia.
    Migraine.
    Hyperesthesia.
    Anesthesia.
    Blindness.
    Myopia.
    Hypermetropia.
    Astigmatism.
    Daltonism.
    Hemeralopia.
    Concentric limitations of the visual field.
Anomalies of speech:
    Mutism.
    Defective speech.
    Stammering.
    Stuttering.
Anomalies of genito urinary function:
    Sexual irritability.
    Impotence.
    Sterility.
    Urinary incontinence.
Anomalies of instinct or appetite:
    Uncontrollable appetite (food, liquor, drugs).
    Merycism.
Diminished resistance against external influences and diseases.
Retardation of puberty.

Psychic Stigmata.
    Insanity.
    Idiocy.
    Imbecility.
    Feeble-mindedness.
    Pavor nocturnus.
    Precocity; one-sided talents; disequilibration.
    Eccentricity.
    Moral delinquency.
    Sexual perversion.

A related psychological enumeration had been developed by the Italian psychiatrist Cesare Lombroso. First published in Italian in 1894, it was not available in English until 1901.[17] Lombroso's list, however, was skewed toward his studies of genius and degeneration.

Although the attention to clinical studies of signs and symptoms led to considerable understanding of many areas of human functioning, there was growing recognition of the limits of this descriptive approach. In

1896, for example, Adolf Meyer reported on the objective figures collected from his live patients and, especially, his autopsy studies, and observed: "The number of observations is relatively so small that it is hardly
ripe for general conclusions."[18] Meyer requested more studies, claiming
that not enough was known about the laws of heredity and of growth and
development. "Why do we find families with stigmata of degeneration
going from bad to worse, and others grow up again and develop healthy
and prospering children?" Meyer asked. He then called for greater attempts at controlling and understanding the other variables: nationality,
locality, and conditions of family life.

Applications to Psychiatry

Psychiatric Diagnosis

One of Morel's immediate legacies, considered in detail in his 1860
volume, was hereditary insanity. He presented four classes, the details of
which need not concern us here. In general, they paralleled his law of
progressivity. Intellectual disturbances, absent in the lower orders, pre-
dominate in the first stages.

In France, Morel's proposals provoked such a critical discussion at the
1860 meeting of the Société Médico-Psychologique that his former teacher
Jules Falret came to his defense. The history of the French debate on
hereditary insanity from 1860 through Jacques Joseph Valentin Magnan
and his students and the meeting of the French psychiatric society in 1886
have been reviewed by Genil-Perrin. The struggle to refine and define
various syndromes of mental illness became an active inquiry in psychiatry in general, particularly in France and Germany.

Morel's proposal of a syndrome of dementia praecox illustrates the effect of this ferment on diagnostics. Dementia, from Pinel on, had been a
syndrome seen either in the elderly or in patients with various chronic
manias. Clearly associated with the middle aged or older, it was not expected in the young. Morel was struck by the sight of adolescents who had
developed satisfactorily and who suddenly started to deteriorate in their
teens. Here was a mysterious force at work that fitted his degeneration
concept. Little did he know what an illustrious and controversial idea he
had launched.

The Germanic psychiatrists gradually extended Morel's diagnosis. In
1871, Ewald Hecker described a confused youthful exuberance associated
with an often colorful and impressive silliness which he named
hebephrenia. In 1874, Karl L. Kahlbaum added descriptions of a strikingly opposite behavior in young people, withdrawal into a mute, immo-
bile state. These patients often demonstrated a peculiar way of respond-

ing, one of waxy flexibility; moved into various positions they would automatically hold the pose. Kahlbaum named this condition catatonia. In 1896 Emil Kraepelin collected his careful observations of the course of many patients' illnesses into one diagnostic grouping, dementia praecox. Eventually others added simple subgroupings a well as a paranoic division of cases that usually developed in early middle age. The next step took place in 1911 in Switzerland when Eugen Bleuler redefined this whole category as schizophrenia.[19]

Degeneration also became entangled with another popular diagnostic category of the 1880s—neurasthenia. Introduced by the writings of an American neurologist, George M. Beard, first in 1869 and then in three books (1880, 1881, and 1884), it rapidly became popular. Although today we recognize that much in it is inconsistent hodge-podge, the category served a useful purpose in exploring human beings who suffered from emotional and functional disorders, later diagnosed as neurotic and psychogenic. Although these people rarely needed hospitalization and did not usually deteriorate, they fit quite easily into the larger degenerative picture as being in the earlier stages of this progressivity. Most writers tended to see neurasthenia as a disease of the successful, stressed, and overworked person in a rapidly changing modern civilization. Beard particularly viewed it as the inevitable by-product of an American society proud of its achieving ferment. As such it was viewed as progress rather than regression.[20] At the same time, the weakness and loss of will that accompanied neurasthenia could be represented as a degenerative loss of energy. Gilbert Ballet, in 1908, stated that stigmata were so common among neurasthenics that degeneration must be considered a possible cause.[21] On the other hand, Max Nordau, the pseudonym for Max Simon Südfeld, made abulia or lack of will a basic symptom of the degenerative effects of de-energizing the higher brain centers.[22]

Psychiatric speculation about degeneration extended into many scholarly areas. What follows illustrates the broad application of the notion of degeneration to such popular subjects as alcoholism, mental retardation and its extension to criminal behavior, and the question of whether or not a genius is a variant of a degenerate.

Dipsomania

Dipsomania became a popular term in the nineteenth century and illustrated the spreading view that drunkenness was not willful but an illness, a particular form of mania. It followed from Esquirol's concept of monomania and was paralleled by such terms as kleptomania, pyromania, and even graphomania.[23]

Morel considered alcoholism a degenerative state and many who came after him agreed. In France, Jacques J. V. Magnan took the lead, and because he was one of the most powerful forces in French psychiatry, his writings had wide impact. Magnan had first studied the effects of toxic chemicals and then researched their impact on experimental animals. In 1874, he published his observations on alcoholism. For Magnan, dipsomania was an episodic syndrome representative of a profound mental condition in which heredity played a large part.

Magnan's focus on alcoholism was not isolated in the psychiatry of the day. In the history of substance abuse, waves of enthusiastic use seem to alternate with concern and with attempts to control the problem. For example, in the early 1800s, Benjamin Rush played an essential role in the temperance movement in America. Later, Isaac Ray wrote of the risk of inheriting alcoholism when parents were intoxicated at the moment of conception.[24] In similar fashion, writers at the end of the century again saw alcoholism as a field for prevention and treatment. The avoidance of alcohol was favored by Swiss psychiatrists, first Auguste Forel and then his student Eugen Bleuler. Magnan's counterpart in Germany, Emil Kraepelin, also joined the fight. Alcoholism fits in nicely with Morel's idea of progressivity.

In his study of one hundred cases of chronic alcoholics in the 1880s Thomas D. Crothers reported an incidence of alcoholism in over 50 percent of the ancestors. In addition, Crothers discovered that 30 percent of these ancestors showed signs of degenerative diseases. The assumption of an association between heredity and dipsomania had grown so great by the middle of the decade that the Woman's Christian Temperance Union briefly published a magazine call the *Journal of Heredity*.[25] The Dugdale study of the Juke family, with its high percentage of criminals, also revealed the association with alcoholism. Of seventy-one family members, forty-five or 63 percent were alcoholics. Of these, only three were in good health, ten were diseased, and twenty-nine, licentious.[26] Drunkenness produced despair for the next generation; but as a bad environment also was considered a factor, there was hope that much could be prevented if the parents stopped their own drinking.[27] Enthusiasm for prevention played an important role in the literature on mental retardation and crime and in the formation of the eugenics movement.

Mental Retardation

The application of degeneration theory to mental retardation was facilitated by the existence of clear-cut, severe conditions, frequently recognized in infancy and associated with physical changes that fulfilled the need to find evidence for stigmata. Growth of interest in and research on idiocy and imbecility paralleled similarities concerning insanity throughout much of the nineteenth century.

Discovery of the wild boy of Aveyron in 1798 led to the studies of Jean M. G. Itard. Itard, in turn, taught Edward Sequin, who established one of the earliest successful schools for training the mentally retarded in 1837, a school which became a model. In the United States, the first private and state institutions were established in 1848. The first specialized school for the education of cretins was opened in Switzerland in 1842 by J. Guggenbuhl. This was part of an enthusiastic movement that hoped proper training could return large numbers of retarded persons to useful roles in society.

The movement gradually developed difficulties at the end of the century, partly because of the degeneration theory of Morel; more important, however, was the impact of the evolutionary theories of Charles Darwin. The hypothesis of natural selection and of Herbert Spencer's "survival of the fittest" easily applied to the degenerates who were retarded. They cluttered up society and interrupted the progress of civilization.

A negative social evaluation of the retarded came after careful investigation of families. The earliest and most famous was the prototype for all those that followed—the study by Richard L. Dugdale. His great opportunity came in 1874 when he was a member of a committee instructed to visit a total of thirteen county jails. When he found six members of the same family in jail at the same time, he decided to investigate further. His initial study appeared in the annual report of the Prison Association for 1875. After this work was expanded and issued as a separate volume in 1877, it was widely read and quoted. Its title: *The Jukes: A Study in Crime, Pauperism, Disease, and Heredity.*

By starting with his six convicts, and adding from an ever-widening net of genealogical information, he was able to locate 834 members of the family ranging over five generations. He estimated that the family had close to twelve hundred members. Dugdale wondered if the nearly four hundred members not traced may have been healthier ones who escaped.

Dugdale, those who followed him, and even contemporary readers were deeply impressed by the misery, illness, and social pathology demonstrated in this one family. Criminality was Dugdale's primary focus. There had been 250 arrests and trials in the family, with 140 convicted. Of this group, 60 were known to be habitual criminals, and 7 were murderers. In an independent study of 233 general criminals, Dugdale found that among those who had committed crimes against persons, 40.5 percent had a history of a neurotic family stock. The rate for all crimes was 23.2 percent, further evidence for a hereditary factor.

Dugdale also reviewed the assocation of the Juke family with pauperism and its effects on the children, as well as the role of alcoholism and the sexual behavior of the women in the family. Of the whole Juke family, 22 percent were paupers; among the women the incidence was seven and one-half times that of the general population, among the males nine times as much. Dugdale also calculated the costs of providing welfare for the family and found that 180 adults had either been in the poorhouse or received outdoor relief. The highest rate of pauperism, 56.5 percent, was found, as might be predicted, in the sick and disabled.

Sexual behavior had its effects on the children. Of those born into the family, 23.5 percent were illegitimate. With illegitimacy there was an "environment of neglect," and, there were 30 prosecutions for bastardy. In his "Further Studies of Criminals," Dugdale found his non-Juke criminals had a frightening history from childhood. Forty-five percent of the families were intemperate, but their children may have been fortunate to have had a family at all, for 41 percent of the felons were orphans. Nearly half (47 percent) had a history of a neglected childhood. While the men of the family were criminals and alcoholics, the women were noted for their casual sexual behavior and living arrangements, especially considering the mores of the mid-Victorian era. Eighteen ran brothels, while 128 were prostitutes, twenty-nine times the rate in society. Of these, Dugdale said forty were diseased. Dugdale called the behavior of the women harlotry. If it meant loose and immoral women who had casual relations with men, then Dugdale found that 52 percent of the marriageable Juke women were harlots.

Without question Dugdale found much pathology in his Juke family; similar modern studies give similar results. Dugdale, however, did not adopt a degeneration hypothesis, although he did accept the role of heredity, balanced by the role of the environment. He was open-minded about the role of each factor. While hereditary taint seemed to be present to Dugdale, he did not consider it universal, inevitable, or progressive. People who used his book for their own purposes took that position. In the area of mental retardation, for example, later writers cited him in support of their hereditarian views on feeblemindedness, even though he clearly reported only one feebleminded case in the entire Juke family.

The study of defective ancestry had received early support from Morel, as we have seen, and was recommended by Francis Galton in 1865. But it was not until the early twentieth century that such research reached its height. The second famous family study was by the eminent American specialist on mental retardation, Henry H. Goddard, in a book of 1912 entitled *The Kallikak Family.*[28] Studies of five other families followed in the next four years, one of which was an extension of the original Juke report. Goddard had found a family descended from a respected soldier of the American Revolution who supposedly produced two lines of descendants—one from his wife and another from a liaison with a servant girl presumed to be retarded. One side of the family produced healthy offspring and, predictably, the other children, the product of the affair, were contaminated. Hence the given name Kallikak, a condensation of the Greek words for good and bad. The bad side produced many mentally defective children. Goddard and the five researchers who followed him concluded that mental defect followed from tainted heredity, which such writers as Goddard and Charles Davenport erroneously concluded to be a product of a simple Mendelian recessive trait. By 1915, Goddard could confidently report that two-thirds of the feebleminded were the products of weak-minded parents. Estabrook, in his 1916 followup of 2820 Jukes, was equally convinced of the association when he reported that 50 percent of the Jukes were feebleminded, including all the criminals.[29]

The stage had been set for an almost phobic concern about the destructive potential of the retarded to society. Walter E. Fernald, another medical leader in mental deficiency in America, wrote in 1913: "The feebleminded are a parasitic, predatory class, never capable of self-support or of managing their own affairs. They cause unutterable sorrow at home and are a menace and danger to the community."[30] Prevention became the great hope for the solution of this problem, and eugenics became the movement that was going to make it possible. Eugenics was a term coined by Galton in 1883 and his inspiration led to the founding of the movement in England in 1904. It spread rapidly to the United States, with a two-pronged emphasis on the prevention of further retardation in the susceptible, and, more important, positive encouragement for reproduction by the superior human stock. The negative, preventive side led to laws restricting marriage, the use of segregation, and the introduction of legal sterilization.[31]

This whole movement gained strength with the development by Alfred Binet and Theodore Simon in 1905 of widely accepted mental tests. The tests were the outgrowth of numerous attempts in the previous decade by such psychologists as Galton and McKeen Cattell. Introduced into the United States by Goddard in 1908, they led, in 1910, to a new, graded definition of mental deficiency based on mental ages: the idiot (0 through 2 years), the imbecile (3–7), and the moron (8–12). The tests were widely used in the American army draft in World War I, which led to a rapid reevaluation of their accuracy and validity when it was found that close to 50 percent of the American public was mentally retarded! In addition, the genealogical studies were reconsidered and found wanting in research design, especially in the criteria for classification. The main correlation now was found to be with poverty. It seemed obvious at this juncture that any family could be submerged by the poor living conditions these people faced. The process of reevaluation was so rapid that by 1924 Fernald renounced his position of eleven years earlier. With these changes in theory about the cause of mental retardation, degeneration disappeared. Though the role of heredity diminished, it was not dropped. It led eventually to emphasis on biochemical research and the discovery of such syndromes as phenylketonuria, which causes hereditary retardation.

Criminals

Related to degeneration and psychiatry is the question of crime. Criminals and the mentally retarded provided a rich ground for spotting anatomical variations. Gall, for example, did much of his phrenological research on prisoners. They were available, often had demonstrated flagrant behavior, and, if they were to be executed, provided useful autopsy material for brain studies. It is no wonder that Morel included them among his degenerates and that his theory played an important role in the development of criminal anthropology.

Cesare Lombroso, the Italian psychiatrist, is usually given credit for founding this field. As he made degeneration theory the center of his criminal theory, it is reasonable to assume that he knew the writings of Morel. However, as George Mora points out, he never cited him.[32] Lombroso believed the criminal was born that way, already stamped by heredity, and showing possibilities of a wide range of stigmata. His ideas were first presented in *Delinquent Man* (1875), and later in *The Female Offender.*

Lombroso's works, widely translated and reprinted, influenced thinking in the United States. Apparently the first American article on criminal anthropology was written in 1888 by William Noyes, an assistant psychiatrist at the Bloomingdale Hospital in New York City.[33] It presented unalloyed Lombroso. Americans took the atavistic view that the criminal was a throwback, a kind of primitive savage existing in the midst of modern civilization. A related view, that the criminal represented arrested development, was adopted by the psychologist G. Stanley Hall and his students, among others. Whether the criminal demonstrated atavism, an active reversion to an earlier biological type, or arrested development, which blocked any progress beyond primitive capabilities, the outcome was the same. The Americans applied themselves enthusiastically to degenerative studies; they explored cranial capacity and sought all kinds of evidence of anatomical and physiological stigmata. At the same time, they considered many emotional and environmental factors.

Charles J. Guiteau assumed an importance in 1881 when he assassinated James A. Garfield, the president of the United States. In spite of what would be considered obvious insanity today, he was brought to trial, found guilty, and executed. Much about Guiteau appealed to the degenerationists. His appearance was enough to convert a disbeliever—strangely misshapen and asymmetrical, he quickly became a gold mine for the searcher of stigmata. His strange ideas and behavior made many people have second thoughts about his sanity, once they experienced the relief of his execution. One writer concluded that Guiteau was "a degenerate of the regicidal class."[34] D. Hack Tuke, writing in 1885 about the problem of criminals from the preconception of atavism, queried: "What is to be done with the man who, from no fault of his own, is born in the nineteenth instead of a long-past century? Are we to punish him for his involuntary anachronism?"[35] His article dealt with moral insanity.

Moral insanity was an enormous issue at Guiteau's trial, with experts lined up on both sides of the question. Although moral insanity was a confused and confusing doctrine, there was a growing acceptance of the idea that mental illness might not represent delirium only, to use as a prototype, when intellectual disturbance was evident. Newer versions of the doctrine found that the intellect could remain essentially intact while there were emotional and behavioral disturbances. Attention to the emotions led toward neurasthenia, psychasthenia, anxiety states, and neuroses in general. Studies of behavior focused on impulsiveness and compulsiveness, and, more important, on any behavior unacceptable to society. Such behavior included dipsomania, as well as kleptomania, pyromania, and other kinds of criminal activity. Were people who exhibited such behavior morally insane and therefore not responsible? "Moral," coming from the French, brought uncertainty because it not only referred to the emotions, but also had strong behavioral and ethical overtones.

Jules Falret, writing about moral insanity on the French scene in 1866, stressed heredity and the poor constitution of the parents. Montz Gouster, in 1878, added that evidence of moral insanity could be found from early childhood; he stressed the poor judgment often seen in the adult offender, but also mentioned his potential aptitude or skills in certain areas.[36] An American, James J. Kiernan, in 1884, may have been the first to suggest the term moral imbecility. By that time the moral degenerate was fully in place in the literature. Diagnostic terminology for chronic criminals came to include psychopath or psychopathic personality; these terms continued in vogue until very recently, when antisocial personality and antisocial personality disorders replaced them.

The Genius, Insanity, and Degeneration

Psychiatrists were also puzzled by the degenerate who could show isolated pockets of superior abilities. One such case, famous from the early part of the nineteenth century, was Kaspar Hauser. Discovered in 1828 in a state approaching idiocy, he evidenced hyper-acuteness of sight, smell, and hearing, suggesting superior functioning of at least some parts of his nervous system. Similar but more impressive cases were such calculating wizards as Zerah Colburn who could instantaneously and accurately multiply large numbers. This kind of superior ability was reported in people who were otherwise quite undistinguished and, in some cases, retarded. Hence the term of idiot savant.[37] Such persons seemed to have a peculiar kind of genius.

Genius also had a long theoretical connection with insanity, going back to the writings of Plato and Aristotle.[38] In the 1820s, Felix Voisin wrote about the possible association of insanity, genius, and crime. Moreau de Tours, in his 1859 book *La Psychologie morbide dans ses rapports avec la philosophie de l'histoire, ou de l'influence des névropathies sur le dynamisme intellectuel*, extended the issue to questions of degeneration. Shortly thereafter two writers, Galton and Lombroso, started their major contributions to the topic. Galton, stimulated by the work of his cousin, Darwin's *Origin of the Species*, devoted the remainder of his life to a mathematical study of heredity and variations in the human species. His earliest studies, by following the genealogy of famous men, had tried to demonstrate that superior mental abilities were inherited, and led to his 1865 article "Hereditary Talent and Character," and his 1869 book *Hereditary Genius*.

Lombroso had started his studies a little earlier. In 1864 he published his small, forty-six-page book *Genio e follìa* (Genius and Insanity). The subject became a lifetime vocation for Lombroso; he rewrote his book for six editions, ending in 1889 with the greatly expanded 750-page version and a new title, *Men of Genius*. As George Mora has pointed out, all of these writings tended to be anecdotal and prolix. They were designed to buttress Lombroso's point of view and did not respond to the growing chorus of criticism over his scientific methodology.[39] Mora also reviewed the changing concept of genius over the centuries, from an almost mythological trait in ancient times to a God-given one, a view that persisted well into the eighteenth century. This century also saw greater attention paid to the individual human personality as a genius and paved the way for the views of the romantic era and that of biology and degeneration seen in Lombroso's books.

The literature on genius and insanity became extensive and very popular. Martindale, in his review of the topic, found the original writers included many points pertinent to contemporary studies on the creative personality. Too much excitement or too great a sensibility in the genius became a common theme. Moreau, for example, spoke of the brain becoming overexcited. Lombroso, in turn, stressed abnormal sensitivity, a lowered sensory threshold, retarded moral development, and a tendency to maniclike excitement.[40] In 1892, Max Nordau wrote a very popular book, *Degeneration*, reprinted and translated many times. In it he theorized that the higher nervous centers were vulnerable to weakening, thereby allowing the lower centers to take over and dominate. He listed eight basic characteristics: abulia, inability to reject the irrelevant, inane reverie, overemotionality, moral insanity, difficulty in adapting to the environment, pessimism, and, finally, the distress of doubting. Martindale points out that all Nordau's traits involve some form of disinhibition and that the characteristics of "inane reverie" resemble, in many respects, those Freud postulated for his primary process.[41]

In 1898 Eugene S. Talbot wrote an extensive review of degeneration in which he tried to bring order to the mass of theory. Combining evolutionary concepts and a hierarchical organization of the nervous system, he summarized: "The factors of degeneracy affect in the ancestor the checks on excessive action acquired during the evolution of the race, thus producing a state of nervous exhaustion."[42] Disintegration occurs, leading to a simplification in the ordinary degenerate. By contrast, in the genius this process can lead to short-cutting or bypassing the usually developed connections and therefore can produce the different, the original, and the creative.

Nordau, when reprinted in the United States,[43] caused much discussion in the press and among intellectuals partly because his ideas fitted current discussions of neurasthenia, and because of his stimulating and controversial views of famous writers as representing styles of degeneration. His belief that neurasthenia and degeneration were becoming more prominent among the upper classes could hardly pass unnoticed, especially because he did not view it as a slightly perceptible trend, but rather as an epidemic. Nordau said the trend resulted from "the vast fatigue which was experienced by the generation on which the multitude of discoveries and innovations burst abruptly."[44] In this view, degeneration may be seen as the price civilization pays for its enormous spurt of progress.

Nordau quickly came under attack. A fellow German, William Hirsch, answered him in 1894. His book, which became available in an English edition in 1896, did much to refute Nordau. In the same year in the United States, an anonymous work written by A. G. Hake, with an introduction by the future president of Columbia University, Nicholas Murray Butler, also criticized Nordau's opinions. Butler became personal and acerbic when he said that Nordau was pathological; "every large hospital for the insane knows his representative—the one sane man in a world of lunatics."[45] Adolf Meyer was more gentlemanly, but sarcastic, when he called Nordau "a clever journalist who exploited Lombroso's theories of the born criminal and of degeneracy, and who fascinated a wide range of readers with his fatalistic doctrine, which no doubt lingers behind some of the one-sided antikakogenic movements of recent times."[46]

Conclusion

Meyer wrote in 1916. By then the degeneration theory in psychiatry was rapidly dying. Meyer had been critical twenty years earlier (1896), but he had not started the debunking movement. Its roots were varied, but many questions had been raised by those with a more sober view of heredity. John P. Gray, a leader of American psychiatry well known for his conservative and organically-minded attitudes, might have been expected to be a strong supporter of degeneration theory. On the contrary. In 1884, Gray concluded: "an insane diathesis is pure verbal fiction." Disease could not be inherited; an external cause was necessary. For Gray the cause was largely physical in nature. Gray did state that "occupations or crimes that are found to run in families are simply the result of education and training."[47] About the same time, well-balanced views on heredity in psychiatry were presented by the Englishman J. Batty Tuke and the Frenchman Théodule Ribot.[48]

Despite considerable debate about the validity of degeneration theory, parts persisted, although they were gradually absorbed by redefinition. It was frequently noted that certain patients deteriorated during the course of life, while idiots, never able to get started in life, obviously suffered from some form of arrested development. Other people managed to function but suffered from a variety of symptoms that were both puzzling and interesting. Emil Kraepelin, for example, in the seventh edition of his textbook, included "insanity of degeneracy" as a subtitle for his section on constitutional psychopathic states, which included such varied topics as nervousness, despondency, excitement, compulsiveness, impulsiveness, and homosexuality.[49] In his lecture on morbid personalities, he spoke mostly about heredity. Even there he was more positive.[50] Later, in 1918, as Kraepelin looked back in his historical survey of nineteenth-century psychiatry, he still favored a somatic psychiatry, stating that most psychic factors were the product of a disease rather than the cause. He granted possible exceptions to the hysterical disorders, accident or compensation neurosis, and combat neurosis. Heredity was still essential, but he decried careless researchers who indiscriminately included all the potentially defective conditions that they could locate. Newer attitudes and explorations, Kraepelin believed, "discredited the theory of Morel."[51]

After 1900 great demand for clarification arose from the ferment in basic studies in heredity. In that year the original (1866) report of Gregor Johann Mendel was rediscovered. Chromosomes were first described in the early 1880s and by 1901, thirty-four chromosomes in pairs had been described in the human. It was correctly postulated that one set was maternal and the other paternal. In the same year it was proposed that an accessory chromosome determined the male sex. The rearrangement of "chromosomal material" was suspected by 1917 and proven by 1924. These were two exciting decades when blood groups were discovered (1900) and their heredity established (1910). It was a time when the small drosophila fly helped revolutionize the field.[52] No wonder that psychiatrists felt the impact and embarked on more careful observations of their patients.

A psychiatric study written by Otto Diem followed soon after the rediscovery of Mendel. In 1903, Diem demonstrated that many defects were not transmitted at all. More striking was his discovery that if he looked for signs of a hereditary burden from a close study of relatives, 67 percent of the population designated as healthy had such a history. In addition, a study of the insane in institutions raised the percentage to only 78, although he did find evidence that the figures were somewhat higher for certain subcategories.[53] Diem was also cited in the 1924 textbook by the famed Swiss psychiatrist Eugen Bleuler. At that time, degeneration still appeared occasionally as a word, often used only to define recent history and the transformation of concepts into new versions. Stigmata were largely dropped; instead it was realized that there were large variations in the normal population with no pathologic significance. Heredity was still stressed, but Bleuler pointed out that it was far too soon to try to mold the findings into any Mendelian pattern. Certainly the progressive hypothesis of Morel had been discarded.[54] Understanding the role of alcohol changed with the studies of Charles R. Stockard, who, using experimental animals, showed that exposure to alcohol in a pregnant animal could produce sickly offspring, but the effects seemed limited to the next generation.[55]

Clearly, medical degeneration theory had many roots. When Morel's theory emerged, it almost immediately became combined with the new ideas in biology introduced by Charles Darwin and to a lesser degree by Herbert Spencer. The resulting ferment helped to reinforce the biological side of psychiatry as opposed to the psychological and social. At the same time, the proposals of evolution, of natural selection, and of the survival of the fittest came to be applied from a biological point of view as well as from the cultural and political.[56] The latter thinking led to some of the more lurid and extravagant parts of the story of degeneration. Proposals for sterilization of the insane, the mentally retarded, and the criminal seem shocking to us in retrospect, as we recognize that there was not enough knowledge to make such recommendations with any degree of certainty.

Social Darwinism stressed the importance of selection—nature tended to eliminate the unfit through sterility, disease, war, and poverty. The law of nature seemed heartless and inexorable. At the same time writers were inconsistent, for they believed optimistically that the environment could be manipulated to improve the retarded and the criminal while at the same time pessimistically believing they needed to help nature by applying their own social controls. We have seen how fearful people became at the dangers posed by the mentally retarded. The historical hypothesis of social Darwinism is currently being revised by Robert C. Bannister, who concludes from his careful and exhaustive research that it was a myth invented by the liberals of the time to use in their fight against laissez-faire and to support their desire for collective social control.[57] This conclusion may be true in part, but the proposal runs the risk of offering a single explanation for complex human behavior. It is difficult at best to explain why a given individual undertakes a certain course of behavior; to do so for a social group becomes a much more difficult and hazardous task. Degeneration theory and the other proposals and concepts surrounding it provided ammunition for those who wished to criticize, condemn, and defame. It certainly was used that way, and perhaps even for social control, as Stephen Jay Gould suggests in his new book reporting the problems in attempts to develop meaningful tests for studying human intellectual capabilities.[58] Science, after all, is a human endeavor. Even though it strives for accuracy and replicability, constant vigilance is needed to keep it from being diverted from its primary goal by human enthusiasm and by covert and open political and social needs.

The history of degeneration theory illustrates these negative sides. It also must be recognized that the men who proposed it and used it were trying to understand and deal with very real human problems. Their constructive efforts led to no obvious spectacular discoveries, but the debates and research engendered, including those of the opposition, contributed to the growth of knowledge. Positive contributions, sometimes rather indirect, were made to the growth of statistics, to heredity, and especially to the recognition that a single gene could not be used to explain human behavior. Instead a polygenic approach was needed. In psychiatry proper, its greatest contributions were to the development of the understanding of schizophrenia and of personality disorders.

At the same time, the social pathology described in the pioneering studies by Dugdale on the Juke family are still with us and with similar disturbing associations. Recent studies by Samuel B. Guze and his associates indicate that the traditional correlation among poverty, crime, and alcoholism is accurate and shows, in addition, an association with hysteria.[59] Social pathology still runs in families. In their three-generation study in England, Oliver and Buchanan found that the patterns persist despite endless hours of ministrations from seventy-five different social agencies.[60] Why should this be so? Is it social repression, is it simply poverty, or is it heredity? The authors add new and intriguing information from their research on how the children of these families were treated. Dugdale found that the Juke children were neglected and that nearly a quarter were illegitimate. The neglect seen in the children in England appears more vicious, but perhaps not so different from that of the Jukes if we knew all the details. The English children were frequently abandoned, physically assaulted, and sexually molested. It is probably no accident that a quarter of them died. Of those who survived, 75 percent became problem children with hyperactive behavior, frequent screaming, and violent tantrums. These children grew up to be like their parents and, saddest of all, to treat their own children as badly as they were treated. Here is a mixture of social, psychological, and biological factors that cries out for our society to investigate, to understand, and ultimately to prevent. We know now that much of what the nineteenth-century writers considered the inheritance of acquired characteristics was the product of learning. Ironically, the growth of learning and the possibility of cultural evolution does not occur easily in these families. We need to learn how to make it possible for them.

Notes

1. A. E. Carter, *The Idea of Decadence in French Literature, 1830–1900* (Toronto: University of Toronto Press, 1958).

2. René Semelaigne, *Les Pionniers de la psychiatrie française avant et après Pinel* (Paris: J. B. Baillière, 1930), 1:342–351.

3. Morel, "La Dégénérescence du peuple français, ses symptômes et ses causes, Contribution de médecine mentale à l'histoire médicale des peuples," *Annales Médico-Psychologique*, 5th series (1871), 6:291–99.

4. Morel, *La Dégénérescence*, pp. 564–72. The standard history of degeneration theory is by Georges Genil-Perrin, *Histoire des origines et de l'évolution de l'idée de dégénérescence en médecine mentale* (Paris: Leclerc, 1913). Also useful are Erwin H. Ackerknecht, *A Short History of Psychiatry* (New York: Hafner, 1968), and Peter Burgener, *Die Einflüsse des zeitgenössischen Denkens in Morels Begriff der "Dégénérescence"* (Zürich: Juris, 1964).

5. Morel, *Maladies*, p. 515.

6. Exodus 20:5.

7. Daniel J. Boorstin, *The Lost World of Thomas Jefferson*, (Boston: Peter Smith, 1948), pp. 99–104.

8. Philippe Pinel, *A Treatise on Insanity* (Sheffield, England: Todd, 1806), pp. 145–46.

9. Genil-Perrin, p. 26.

10. *Journal of Psychological Medicine*, (1849), 2:428–55.

11. A. H. Sturtevant, *A History of Genetics* (New York: Harper and Row, 1965).

12. Philippe Pinel, *Traité médico-philosophique sur l'aliénation mentale*, 2d ed. (Paris: Brosson, 1809), pp. 13, 46.

13. Jean Etienne Esquirol, *Des maladies mentales* (Paris: Ballière, 1838), 1:64ff.; 2:140.

14. Semelaigne, 2:210–22; Genil-Perrin, pp. 36–38.

15. Genil-Perrin, p. 64.

16. Archibald Church and Frederick Peterson, *Nervous and Mental Diseases* (Philadelphia: Saunders, 1899), pp. 613–14.

17. Colin Martindale, "Degeneration, Disinhibition, and Genius," *Journal of the History of Behavioral Science* (1971), 7:177–82.

18. Adolf Meyer, "A Review of the Signs of Degeneration and of Methods of Registration," *American Journal of Insanity* (1896), 52:344–63.

19. Eric T. Carlson, "Introduction," in Emil Kraepelin, *Clinical Psychiatry*, A. Ross Diefendorf, tr. (1907; rpt. ed., Delmar, N.Y.: Scholars' Facsimiles, 1981).

20. Eric T. Carlson, "George M. Beard and Neurasthenia," in Edwin R. Wallace, IV, and Lucius C. Pressley, eds., *Essays in the History of Psychiatry* (Columbia, S.C.: University of South Carolina Press, 1980), pp. 50–57.

21. Richard D. Walter, "What Became of the Degenerate? A Brief History of a Concept," *Journal of the History of Medicine* (1956), 11:422–29.

22. Martindale, p. 179.

23. William Hirsch, *Genius and Degeneration: A Psychological Study* (London: Heinemann, 1897), p. 142.

24. Isaac Ray, *Mental Hygiene* (Boston: Ticknor and Fields, 1863).

25. Mark H. Haller, *Eugenics: Hereditarian Attitudes in American Thought* (New Brunswick, N.J.: Rutgers University Press, 1963), p. 31.

26. Richard L. Dugdale, *The Jukes: A Study in Crime, Pauperism, Disease and Heredity* (New York: Putnam, 1877) p. 40.

27. Arthur E. Fink, *Causes of Crime: Biological Theories in the United States, 1800–1915* (New York: Barnes, 1962), pp. 92–93.

28. Henry H. Goddard, *The Kallikak Family: A Study in the Heredity of Feeble-mindedness* (New York: Macmillan, 1912).

29. Haller, pp. 107–8.

30. Albert Deutsch, *The Mentally Ill in America* (New York: Doubleday, Doran, 1937), pp. 360–61.

31. Fink, pp. 183–94. As early as 1887, Orpheus Everts recommended castration of criminals, but after 1899 the swing was toward vasectomy. In 1907 Indiana passed the first state law making it possible.

32. George Mora, "One Hundred Years from Lombroso's First Essay 'Genius and Insanity,'" *American Journal of Psychiatry* (1964), 121:562–71.

33. Fink, pp. 106–49.

34. Charles Rosenberg, *The Trial of the Assassin Guiteau: Psychiatry and Law in the Gilded Age* (Chicago: University of Chicago Press, 1968), pp. 244, 246.

35. Rosenberg, pp. 247–48.

36. Sidney Maughs, "A Concept of Psychopathy and Psychopathic Personality: Its Evolution and Historical Development," *Journal of Criminal Psychopathology* (1941), 2:329–56, 465–99.

37. Leo Kanner, *A History of the Care and Study of the Mentally Retarded* (Springfield, Ill.: Thomas, 1964). A. Lewis Hill, "An Investigation of Calendar Calculating by an Idiot Savant," *American Journal of Psychiatry* (1975), 132:557–60.

38. Hirsch, pp. 71 ff.

39. Mora, p. 565.

40. Martindale, p. 177.

41. Martindale, pp. 179–80.

42. Eugene S. Talbot, *Degeneracy: Its Causes, Signs, and Results* (New York: Scribner, 1898); cited by Martindale, p. 178.

43. Max Nordau, *Degeneration* (New York: Appleton, 1895).

44. Cited by Walter, p. 426

45. *Regeneration—A Reply to Max Nordau*, Nicholas Murray Butler, introd. (New York: Putnam, 1896); cited by Walter, p. 426.

46. Adolf Meyer, "The Psychopathic Hospital Laboratory of Social Hygiene," in *The Collected Papers of Adolf Meyer*, Eunice E. Winters, ed. (Baltimore: Johns Hopkins University Press, 1952), 4:130–31.

47. John P. Gray, "Heredity," *American Journal of Insanity* (1884), 41:1–21.

48. J. Batty Tuke, "Insanity," *Encyclopaedia Britannica* (New York, 1881), 13:96–99. Théodule Ribot, *Heredity: A Psychological Study of Its Phenomena, Laws, Causes, and Consequences* (New York: Appleton, 1883).

49. Kraepelin, *Clinical Psychiatry*, pp. 485–514.

50. Emil Kraepelin, *Lectures on Clinical Psychiatry* (London: Baillière, Tindall & Cox, 1904), pp. 282–92.

51. Emil Kraepelin, *One Hundred Years of Psychiatry,* Wade Baskin, tr. (1918; rpt., London: Peter Owen, 1962), pp. 132–35.

52. Sturtevant, *A History of Genetics.*

53. Kraepelin, *One Hundred Years,* p. 133.

54. Eugen Bleuler, *Textbook of Psychiatry* (1924; rpt., New York: Macmillan, 1976), pp. 160, 200–4.

55. Charles R. Stockard, "Hereditary Transmission of Degeneration and Deformities by Descendents of Alcoholized American Mammals," *American Naturalist* (1916); cited by Albert C. Buckley, *The Basis of Psychiatry* (Philadelphia: Lippinott, 1920), p. 121.

56. Stow Persons, ed., *Evolutionary Thought in America* (New York: Braziller, 1956).

57. Robert C. Bannister, *Social Darwinism: Science and Myth in Anglo-American Social Thought* (Philadelphia: Temple University Press, 1979).

58. Stephen Jay Gould, *The Mismeasure of Man* (New York: Norton, 1981).

59. C. Robert Cloninger and Samuel B. Guze, "Female Criminals: Their Personal, Familial, and Social Backgrounds," *Archives of General Psychiatry* (1970), 23:555–58.

60. J. E. Oliver and A. Buchanan, "Generations of Maltreated Children and Multiagency Care in One Kindred," *British Journal of Psychiatry,* (1979), 135:289–303.

7

TECHNOLOGY AND DEGENERATION: THE SUBLIME MACHINE

WILLIAM LEISS
Simon Fraser University

The show-stealing exhibit at the Philadelphia Centennial Exposition in 1876 was the Corliss steam engine, weighing six hundred eighty tons and standing thirty-nine feet high, which provided all the power for the entries in Machinery Hall. According to contemporary accounts, its presence literally overwhelmed all who entered the hall, whether they were ordinary fairgoers, such high and mighty as President Ulysses Grant and the emperor of Brazil, or such well-known writers as William Dean Howells. It excited the popular imagination, as had other such exhibits beginning with the Great Exhibition in 1851, and so outstripped the capacity of ordinary descriptive reporting that only ecstatic metaphorical construction could register the reactions to it. John F. Kasson notes that the fairgoers' descriptions of their experience "frequently became incipient narratives in which, like some mythological creature, the Corliss engine was endowed with life and all its movements construed as gestures. The machine emerged as a kind of fabulous automaton—part animal, part machine, part god."[1]

One guidebook for the Philadelphia exposition offered its readers a lesson in aesthetic judgment. Whereas traditionally poets located the experience of the sublime in our reactions to wild nature or powerful human passions, the guidebook claimed, the modern age recognized the sublime in the design and operation of its great machines. And a newspaper reported that in the presence of the Corliss engine "strong men were moved to tears of joy."

Almost exactly one hundred years later the French "neo-Dadaist" artist Jean Tinguely persuaded the director of New York's Museum of Modern Art to offer the museum's sculpture garden as the site for a spectacular *auto-da-fé* by Tinguely's self-destroying machine. (The performance was named "Homage to New York.") When finished the machine was twenty-three feet long and twenty-seven feet high; its main distinguishable components were a piano, an old Addressograph machine, eighty bicycle wheels, steel tubing, a meteorological balloon, a huge klaxon on wheels, a wide assortment of small mechanized devices, and various chemicals—smoke, flash powders, and foul-smelling substances.

When the main motor was switched on, the piano keys were struck, wheels turned, klaxons sounded, a radio blared, clouds of smoke billowed forth; a number of small constructions broke free and wheeled about; small objects were hurled through the air. Then the piano caught fire, the steel tubing supports began to give way, and the terrified museum authorities ordered in firemen with axes and extinguishers to finish off the machine. Once set in motion, the machine's self-destructive orgy had followed pretty much its own course, rather than the artist's specific sequence of events, and this spontaneity was precisely what Tinguely had hoped most to achieve. To him this machine "was the opposite of the skyscrapers, the opposite of the Pyramids, the opposite of the fixed, petrified work of art, and thus the best solution he had yet found to the problem of making something that would be as free, as ephemeral, and as vulnerable as life itself."[2] The late machine was described as both a beautiful and a terrible thing, and it was reported that at the end some spectators had wept.

All in all the concept of the sublime—the ineffable union of awe and dread, terror and attraction—is as good a guide as any to unravelling the reaction to industrial society and the machine in modern times. The iconography of the machine supports the case. Kasson remarks that many nineteenth-century popular illustrated magazines chose a graphic style and accompanying text for their drawings of large machinery that heightened the sense of "mystery and majesty." One of the most famous illustrations was J. O. Davidson's "Interior of a Southern Cotton Press at Night" (1883). Davidson himself supplied the following explanatory note: "Beneath the converging rays of electronic lamps and reflectors a most weird effect is produced, for the machine assumes the aspect of a grand and solemn demon face, strangely human, recalling the famed genii of the *Arabian Nights*."[3] In the great scene in Fritz Lang's film *Metropolis* (1926), where tier upon tier of identical machines, deep underground, are attended by workers whose rhythmic movements follow those of the levers and dials, the machine's face closely resembles the one engraved by Davidson.

The iconic representation of the machine, in eliciting the feeling of the sublime, was evidence for the darker side of the human experience with large-scale machinery that qualified the popular enthusiasms expressed at the great exhibitions. This deeply rooted ambivalence in the popular mind was mirrored in the struggles by imaginative writers and social thinkers to come to terms with the industrial age.

The majority of nineteenth-century political economists, and virtually all the marginalist economists who created a formalized discipline after them, typified the "happy consciousness" of industrial society; they were satisfied that the abundant and manifest benefits supplied by industrialism and the division of labor overawed whatever negative aspects inevitably accompanied them. They never entirely silenced the dissenting voices, however, who worried about the moral degeneration and degradation of skills in the labor force. Originating in a striking passage in Adam Smith's *Wealth of Nations* (1776), this dissenting strain was kept alive mainly in the socialist movement in the nineteenth century, notably by Robert Owen, Karl Marx, and William Morris. It remains alive in the twentieth-century tradition that runs from Thorstein Veblen to Ivan Illich.

Many of the social thinkers in this dissenting tradition believed, however, that the degeneration characteristic of industrial society was remediable, in most cases by a more or less drastic reordering of economic and political circumstances. It was much different with those who represented the predominant aesthetic sensibility of their time, for among them the prevalent mood ranged from dismay to horror. Beginning about 1830, when the impact of industrialism began to register, major writers entered the lists against the machine and the industrial age: Thoreau, the later Emerson, Melville, and Henry Adams in the United States; Zola, Balzac, and Flaubert in France; Heine, Hesse, and Thomas Mann in Germany; in nineteenth-century England, Carlyle, Dickens, Ruskin, and Morris, and in the early twentieth century, Forster, Lawrence, and Huxley.[4] For some of these it is—at least overtly—a minor theme, but for others the machine becomes the symbol of degeneracy itself. This mood's culminating expression is the great antiutopian novel of the early twentieth century, Yevgeny Zamyatin's *We* (written in 1920).

The antiindustrial sentiment also predominated in the important English and European developments in the plastic and decorative arts, in part as a specific reaction against the direct influence of industrial design on public works and consumer goods. The Aesthetic Movement and Art Nouveau set their faces resolutely against mechanical reproduction and industrial design. Only in the 1920s did architecture and design begin to reconcile themselves to the industrial age.

One can date the aesthetic reaction to the machine from 1829, when Thomas Carlyle's great essay "Signs of the Times" baptized his times the

"Age of Machinery." This reaction is completed almost exactly a century later, with the publication of the two greatest antiutopian novels, *We* (written in Russian, but published first in English translation in 1923) and *Brave New World* (1932). George Orwell was the first to see clearly what Zamyatin had done: "What Zamyatin seems to be aiming at is not any particular country but the implied aims of industrial civilization . . . It is in effect a study of the Machine, the genies that man has thoughtlessly let out of its bottle and cannot put back again."[5] The allusion to the genie, which we have already encountered in J. O. Davidson's commentary on his illustration of the cotton press, is itself one of the most common textual threads in the literary response to the machine age.

The implicit judgment in the aesthetic response in the century after 1830 argued the shallowness of other reactions, especially in political economy and social thought. The latter were, as suggested above, divided into a predominant "happy consciousness" which welcomed industrialization with open arms and a dissenting minority which emphasized the urgency of institutional changes to counteract its deleterious impact on labor and social relations. Most of those in the latter category, however, contended that these negative aspects could be overcome and that the machine age could be turned unambiguously to mankind's benefit.

The dominant literary metaphors appeared to rule out this eventuality. For at its deepest level the matter was one of life and death, considered in terms of the essential determinants of what it means to be human, and there was little doubt that the machine represented the ultimate degeneration, the death of humanity.

In the following pages this theme will be tracked through the series of metaphorical constructions that appear to lead inexorably to the opposition of life and death. This is not necessarily the last word on the subject, however. For Jean Tinguely's self-destructing machine was designed to show precisely that the machine shares with us life's essential attribute, namely mortality, and is thus an affirmation of life rather than its negation.

In a recent article Sander L. Gilman used the idea of "root-metaphor" as a way of understanding both continuities and variations over time in literary expressions that reflect common experiences.[6] It presupposes that we often require a means of synthesizing our perceptions of complex events, especially when faced with radically new circumstances or with those that fall outside the realm of ordinary events. Metaphors allow us to capture the novel or extraordinary event in forms of thought that are well-known to us, thus "domesticating" it, so to speak; furthermore they encourage us to believe that we may be successful in communicating our experience to others. There is a concomitant risk, of course: the metaphorical constructs also limit our ability to assimilate new information and, in conventional discourse, where a certain literalness prevails, they can quickly lose their suppleness and become mere props for unreflective traditionalism.

That established ways of life are challenged by unremitting technological novelty is something of a cliché for us by now; yet however jaded we have become in this regard, we should not forget how profoundly unsettling was the sprouting of large-scale machinery and the factory system for both society and culture in the nineteenth century. For most, common folk and artist alike, it was as if the world itself had come unhinged. Thus it should occasion little surprise that many found they could comprehend its significance only by resorting to metaphorical expressions that were rooted in thoroughly familiar structures of experience. When one recalls the enormity of the changes wreaked in the social and physical landscape in a relatively short time, it is also unsurprising that the search for adequate expressive modes should terminate in the fundament itself: life against death.

No simple scheme can hope to capture all the varieties of expression for such a universally felt experience. The one to be explored here seems to catch a sample of reasonable size and quality, although undoubtedly much that is equally important slips through its mesh. The scheme is composed of three levels of metaphorical construction, internally related to one another, which proceed from the "surface" realm of familiar social experience to the ultimate duality of life and death.

The root metaphor for the surface level of representations of the machine is master and servant. This had two quite obvious advantages. First, it was a relation that was thoroughly familiar in social experience everywhere. Second, and perhaps more important, it is a relation that is readily reversible in imagination. For a long time even the passionate defenders of social hierarchy had conceded that occupying one place or the other in that relation was accidental, and religion had taught that in any case it would not matter at the end, for "the first shall be last, and the last first." The affirmative response to industrialism trumpeted the machine as the perfect servant of human objectives, as the long-sought deliverance from necessity and want. The rejoinder quickly made itself heard: the servant will be master. The imagery of the "sorcerer's apprentice," together with the *Arabian Nights* and its genii, have been favored to make this point.

The root metaphor for the second level is a further development of the master and servant theme. Domination and servitude is an external relation in which each side is necessarily the opposite of the other. At the second level this purely external relation is left behind, and the implicit teleology of the machine itself—its inherent capacity for self-regulation when its own qualities are allowed to fully emerge—is fulfilled on both sides of the man-machine relation: the autonomy of the machine, and man as automaton.

The "autonomous technology" theme is an old and persistent one in Western thought.[7] Conceiving of the machine as autonomous is an extension of the master and servant metaphor. In the latter, for the most part, the machine's role is reversed—servant became master—in the sense that we become so dependent on its productive power in providing desired goods; strictly speaking, then, this is a case of voluntary servitude. In so doing we then set in motion a course of events that results in our losing control over what we have created, in the sense that we can no longer "freely" choose to have it or not. Since we cannot even conceive of turning back, we are beholden to our apparatus, and we begin to adjust our behavior to its *modus operandi;* in Carlyle's words: "Men are grown mechanical in head and in heart, as well as in hand."

What began as an external relation is now an internalized process, whereby the dependent member (the human being) surrenders its own authentic being to its erstwhile instrument. The relation itself, and the tension between its originally opposed sides, dissolves. In *We* Zamyatin gave the most striking representation to the process of internalization and the root metaphor of autonomy/automaton: society is ordered on the model of the machine, and men and women are its subordinate parts whose "functions" are determined strictly in relation to their role in the apparatus as a whole.

The third level of root metaphor was a direct outcome of what preceded it: The concept of automaton led directly to the imagery of life and death.

This metaphor worked on the identification of the machine with the inorganic, necessity, repetition, and identity, and thus death—and the concomitant association of life with the organic, and with contingency, variation, or freedom. The machine as automaton, however, is an entity possessing the characteristics of both the animate and the inorganic; in crossing over the two realms it appears to draw what is living inexorably into the province of the inanimate. Powerful representations of this theme appear in the case studies to be presented later: Melville's "The Paradise of Bachelors and the Tartarus of Maids," E. M. Forster's "The Machine Stops," and Zamyatin's *We.*

For industrialism's defenders machinery had lifted a double yoke from mankind's shoulders, namely subjection to nature's capriciousness as well as to the corrupting influence spread by relations of dependence among persons. Technology would overturn man's age-old subordination to physical forces and deliver the realm of nature holus-bolus into his hands, to do what he would with it. At the same time, material abundance and mechanical aids would do away with the employment of persons in personal service; this was an especially prominent theme in the United States, where industrialism had been linked to republicanism. Two years after

Carlyle's 1829 essay appeared, its message was utterly rejected by a writer in the *North American Review*, Timothy Walker, who entitled his rejoinder a "Defence of Mechanical Philosophy." Of the blessings of technology he wrote, "From a ministering servant to matter, mind has become the powerful lord of matter."[8]

This Baconian theme, both widely sown and deeply rooted by the middle of the nineteenth century, was so successful in its propagation because it represented the relation between human beings and large-scale machine technology as analogous with the completely familiar routine of personal service and dependence. The spreading of egalitarian political philosophy had eroded traditional justifications for relations of personal dependence. The machine appeared in the nick of time; not only could it assume many of the burdensome tasks usually imposed on dependent persons, and in many cases perform more effectively, it could also be seen to be more fitting in this role. Ruskin gave a nice explanation for this point. What a master ordinarily requires of his servants, he remarked, is the maximum output for the least pay (that is, the market value of the servant's labor); and, according to the prevailing economic wisom, this situation will yield the greatest benefits for society as a whole and all its individual members, including the class of servants.

This would be the case, Ruskin objected, "If the servant were an engine of which the motive power was steam, magnetism, gravitation, or any other agent of calculable force." On the contrary, the servant is a human agent whose "motive power is the Soul," and this fact marks an essential difference: "The largest quantity of work will not be done by this curious engine for pay, or under pressure, or by the help of any kind of fuel which may be supplied by the chaldron. It will be done only when the motive force . . . is brought to its greatest strength by its own proper fuel: namely by the affections."[9]

What is most important about Ruskin's distinction is precisely its reinforcing of the metaphor of the master-servant relation as a way of understanding the machine's significance for human life. For always lurking in this relation is the potential reversibility of its terms. Seeing the machine as replacing the dependent human agent in this relation facilitated the transferring of this potentiality—the "reversal of fortune" which catapulted erstwhile servants into their master's place—to the new, quickly multiplying connection between mankind and its mechanical aids.

Melville used the reversal notion in his portrayal of a New England paper mill in "The Paradise of Bachelors and the Tartarus of Maids" (1855): "Machinery—that vaunted slave of humanity—here stood menially served by human beings, who served mutely and cringingly as the slave serves the Sultan. The girls did not so much seem accessory wheels to the general machinery as mere cogs to the wheels."[10] This was to become a favorite image in the critique of industrial society, and especially in the utopian literature that argued the need for a "second reversal," to be achieved by a radical reordering of social relations, that would reestablish mankind's hegemony over the instruments to which it had become enslaved. In his utopian sketch *A Traveler from Altruria* (1894), William Dean Howells suggested this in a way that is especially intriguing because it reinforced the root metaphor; in his imaginary future society "the machines that were once the workman's enemies and masters are now their friends and servants."[11]

The resolution proposed in this notion of "re-reversal" in effect confines the issue under discussion here—the relation between humanity and machinery—to the first level of root metaphors. It finds in effect the representation given by the metaphor to be adequate, and locates the problem solely in reestablishing our right of occupancy in the dominant side of the relation. As we shall see, this was regarded as a rather superficial resolution by those who wished to persuade us to consider the matter in terms of deeper levels of significance and more profound root metaphors. For the re-reversal slips too readily over the circumstances that occasioned the original reversal whereby human agents had become the machine's subjects.

The change in Ralph Waldo Emerson's attitude over a period of twenty years offers a clue to the nature of these circumstances. He began with a robust confidence in the industrial age and its possibilities for improving the human condition: the enormously influential essay "Nature" (1836) trumpets that nature "is made to serve." Illustrating what Leo Marx calls Emerson's "rhetoric of the technological sublime" is the following 1843 entry from his journal: "Machinery and Transcendentalism agree well."[12] *English Traits* (1856) records a different sentiment, however:

> But a man must keep an eye on his servants, if he would not have them rule him . . . (I)t is found that the machine unmans the user. What he gains in making cloth, he loses in general power . . . The incessant repetition of the same hand-work dwarfs the man, robs him of his strength, wit and versatility, to make a pin-polisher, a buckle-maker, or any other specialty; . . . Then society is admonished of the mischief of the division of labor, and that the best political economy is care and culture of men.[13]

Emerson's mention of pin-polishing in his reference to the "mischief" inherent in the division of labor is marvelously appropriate, for the famous opening chapter of Adam Smith's *Wealth of Nations*, which heaped praise on the division of labor, made Smith's own pinmaking illustration a legend in the subsequent political economy literature.

Seventeenth-century Europeans were unable to decide whether the barbarous ways of the New World inhabitants were a degenerate form of earlier civilized conditions or were simply a case of arrested development.[14] Their successors may not have resolved this point, but they were confident at least that they knew the proximate cause: According to Adam Smith the "savage nations of hunters and fishers . . . are so miserably poor" because their labor productivity is so low, and this in turn results from their ignorance of the benefits bestowed by the division of labor.

Smith also knew how to reckon the price paid, however. The mental faculties of everyone in "barbarous societies" remain "acute and comprehensive" and are not "suffered to fall into that drowsy stupidity, which, in a civilized society, seems to benumb the understanding of almost all the inferior ranks of people." The division of labor confines the ordinary worker's activities to routine tasks:

> The man whose whole life is spent in performing a few simple operations . . . has no occasion to exert his understanding, . . . He naturally loses, therefore, the habit of such exertion, and generally becomes as stupid and ignorant as it is possible for a human creature to become . . . His dexterity at his own particular trade seems, in this manner, to be acquired at the expense of his intellectual, social, and martial virtues.

Material progress is won at the expense of a widespread degeneration in mental faculties and the capacity for exercising good judgment in public and private affairs.[15]

The Tory critique of industrial society inspired by Carlyle made much of this theme, claiming that the proponents of industrialism and economic development regarded the working population as nothing but "animated machines."[16] Their opposition lent voice in the political arena to the widespread antimachinery sentiment among the working classes in the early phases of the factory system and the tremendous social disruptions it occasioned. The Tory critique's force diminished as it became increasingly apparent that the necessary concomitant to its attack on industrialism was the preservation of a traditional agrarian economy and social hierarchy. This left sustained opposition effectively in the hands of the radical critics, who also objected to the degradation of labor and skills under industrialism, but who steadfastly maintained that, under radically different social arrangements, the highest possible degree of application of machinery to production was in the worker's interest.

Among all those who were willing to commit themselves to this course, it was Marx who grasped best its profoundest implications:

> In no way does the machine appear as the individual worker's means of labour . . . Not as with the instrument, which the worker animates and makes into his organ with his skill and strength, and whose handling therefore depends on his virtuosity. Rather, it is the machine which possesses skill and strength in place of the worker, is itself the virtuoso, with a soul of its own in the mechanical laws acting through it, . . . The science which compels the inanimate links of the machinery, by their construction, to act purposefully, as an automaton, does not exist

> in the worker's consciousness, but rather acts upon him through the
> machine as an alien power, as the power of the machine itself . . . The
> production process has ceased to be a labour process in the sense of a
> process dominated by labour as its governing unity.

The laborer ceases to be the "chief actor" in the production process and
becomes instead only the "watchman and regulator" over it.[17]

The radical tradition split into two quite different currents in response
to the growing presence of machinery in production and the consequent
deskilling of labor. The most influential current, in which Marx and most
modern socialists are found, accepted the declining role of labor and its
traditional skills in producing life's necessities, and relegated the cultivation of skill and virtuosity to the realm of "free time" or leisure. A much
smaller branch, for which William Morris' utopian tract *News from Nowhere* (1890) is the chief source, drew the opposite conclusion: Reestablish
skilled craft labor as the cornerstone of social life, and limit wants and
satisfactions to what it can provide with the smallest possible degree of
reliance on mechanical assistance.

The factory system methodically undermined labor's autonomy, its very
"substance" as an agent in social life, by eliminating society's dependence
on the rich panoply of craft skills heretofore distributed among the working classes. The historical residue of those skills is absorbed by the system
of machinery, "whose unity"—in Marx's striking formulation—"exists
not in the living workers, but rather in the living (active) machinery,
which confronts their individual, insignificant doings as a mighty organism." In this light it is easy to see why the master/servant metaphor, so
readily applied to the relation between humanity and machinery, was also
so readily reversible: Having appropriated the essential substance of its
putative master, the machine was heir to humanity's accumulated, alienated mastery of its environment; what remained for the "stupid and ignorant" mass of deskilled laborers was only numbing exhaustion in the
service of the machine's imperious rhythm.

The radical critique maintained that the machine could be remastered
and compelled once again to serve mankind's purposes. The system of
machinery confronts the worker as an automaton or as a "living," "mighty
organism" at the level of immediate experience; labor is cowed into submission because it appears as if all skill, initiative, and "virtuosity" have
passed irrevocably from it to another kind of being. Its apparent otherness
and autonomy, however, upon analysis turn out to be just that, namely
mere appearance. In truth it is the same substance: machinery is "objec-
tified labour," the material legacy of past human skill and exertion, that
furthermore has been misappropriated in the form of privately owned
capital. What seemed to be service to the machine was in fact subjection to

another human group that had discovered in large-scale machinery a wondrous device for extracting vast wealth from others' labor. The realization
that labor's enemy was not the machine but the capitalist was, for the
radical critique, the "beginning of wisdom" and the first step toward
reestablishing labor's autonomy.

An implicit rejoinder to this program was made in the period under
review, one that was governed, at what I have called the second level, by
the root metaphors of autonomy/automaton: specifically, the internalization of the machine principle in mankind's own mode of being. From this
perspective labor's victory in wresting control of the industrial system
away from the capitalists would be a pyrrhic one, for this would seal the
fate of society as a whole, which would be committed irrevocably from
that time onward to mechanistic modes of action. The very moment of its
triumph simultaneously would signal labor's final defeat, and its ostensi-
ble autonomy would be a sham. Labor and its skills would be no longer
the heart of the production process, since it had surrendered that role to
machinery; labor—or what was left of it, namely the function of superin-
tendence—would come to occupy the simple role of consumer in relation
to that process.

The contention was that, in accepting machine production as the dominant means for supplying life's necessities, modern society would be
forced as well to adopt a mechanistically oriented routine for life in general:

> The relation in which the consumer, the common man, stands to the
> mechanical routine of life at large is of much the same nature as that in
> which the modern skilled workman stands to that detail machine pro-
> cess into which he is dovetailed in the industrial system. To take ef-
> fectual advantage of what is offered as the wheels of routine go round,
> in the way of work and play, livelihood and recreation, he must know
> by facile habituation what is going on and how and in what quantities
> and at what price and where and when, and for the best effect he must
> adapt his movements with skilled exactitude and a cool mechanical
> insight to the nicely balanced moving equilibrium of the mechanical
> processes engaged. To live—not to say at ease—under the exigencies of
> this machine-made routine requires a measure of consistent training in
> the mechanical apprehension of things.[18]

These comments by Veblen, in *The Instinct of Workmanship* (1914), were
not meant to encourage any hope that this "machine-like process of living" could be overturned: The best one could do was to recommend that it
be taken to its logical conclusion, and place engineers instead of business-
men in charge.

When this concern was first raised, almost a century earlier, it was
possible to surmise that the swelling tide of mechanization might yet
recede again. The great manifesto for those who so believed was Thomas

Carlyle's "Signs of the Times" (1829). For Carlyle the physical instruments rapidly overtaking traditional productive processes were only visible expressions of a deeper malaise, a habit of mind and action he described in precisely the same terms as Veblen would use much later: a pervasive "matter of factness." The machine itself served as metaphor for "the great art of adapting means to ends . . . by rule and calculated contrivance."[19]

Carlyle begins his animadversions by referring to the transformations in the physical environment wrought by the application of machinery to production and transportation; beside its obvious effect in undermining the craftsman's position, mechanization is faulted for being unable to distinguish between appropriate and trivial applications. By these means man seeks to rule Nature, and in doing so pays a heavy price: "Not the external and physical alone is now managed by machinery, but the internal and spiritual also." Here the machine stands for the disappearance of spontaneity, and the rise of a mode of action that first appraises each situation in strategic terms, breaks down ultimate objectives into a manageable series of discrete steps, and appropriates means from whatever quarter to the separate tasks: "Has any man, or any society of men, a truth to speak, a piece of spiritual work to do; they can nowise proceed at once and with the mere natural organs, but must first call a public meeting, appoint committees, issue prospectives, eat a public dinner; in a word, construct or borrow machinery, wherewith to speak it and do it."[20]

By the time he came to write *English Traits* (1856), Emerson had lost his youthful enthusiasm for the industrial age and was ready to echo Carlyle's sentiments: "Mines, forges, mills, breweries, railroads, steam-pump, steam-plough, drill of regiments, drill of police, rule of court and shop-rule have operated to give a mechanical regularity to all the habit and action of man. A terrible machine has possessed itself of the ground, the air, the men and women, and hardly even thought is free."[21] Taken as a metaphorical allusion, the last sentence could do nicely as an epigraph for E. M. Forster's story "The Machine Stops."

Neither Carlyle nor Emerson, however, was yet prepared to concede that all was lost. There was still time to reverse this disastrous course and to reassert the preeminence of the natural and the spontaneous over the mechanical mode of action. Despite its deepening penetration of public and private life, mechanization was not yet triumphant over the old ways. Carlyle advertised this hope in an especially revealing way, namely by suggesting, at the end of his essay, that the fundamental root metaphor governing the first level of representation was still operative: "Indications we do see in other countries and in our own, signs infinitely cheering to us, that Mechanism is not always to be our hard taskmaster, but one day to be our pliant, all-ministering servant."[22]

This curious conclusion seriously undermines the force of the preceding argument. For it suggests that, however widely it had spread, mechanism had not contaminated the original sources of human action, and that it still could be subordinated to individual and collective ends governed by nonmechanical principles. Or perhaps the opposite is nearer the mark: The force of the foregoing argument undermines Carlyle's conclusion.

Matching the uninterrupted march of machine technology in the second half of the nineteenth century was a growing fear that it was indeed out of control. In the relation between humanity and machines, increasingly the former seemed to be the passive partner, and the latter the active agent. The more the system of machinery as a whole assumed labor's erstwhile attributes—skill and indeed "virtuosity" (Marx)—the more the worker appeared "like a machine" in the derogatory sense, fit only for the dull repetitiveness of routine operations. Zola, who on other occasions rhapsodized about modern technology, filled his *Rougon-Macquart* novels with allusions to the machinelike and thinglike character of human action, and correspondingly with the appearance of animate force and autonomous power residing in machinery.[23]

As early as his writings of 1857–58 Marx had referred to an "automatic system of machinery" as the "most complete" and "most adequate" form of the machine itself, "set in motion by an automaton, a moving power that moves itself; this automaton consisting of numerous mechanical and intellectual organs, so that the workers themselves are cast merely as its conscious linkages."[24] The root metaphor of autonomy/automaton, which was to be fleshed out as a favorite device in fiction, alluded not so much to a reversal of roles, as in the case of the master/servant metaphor, but to a complete collapsing of the two sides of a relation into a synthetic entity that transcended both. Its most effective representation was the manlike automaton.

Herman Melville's story "The Bell-Tower" (1855) is thought to be the first fully developed portrayal of such a creature.[25] The story is headed by Melville with an anonymous epigraph, the third passage of which reads: "Seeking to conquer a larger liberty, man but extends the empire of necessity." In the story itself a "great mechanician," Bannadonna, is commissioned to construct a huge belltower; when the tower itself has been completed, he insists on working in secrecy on the belfry, eventually having a large object, concealed in wrapping, hauled up. Bannadonna alone remained in the belfry when the day came to inaugurate the ringing; the entire population waited below, but at the appointed hour, instead of the anticipated booming of the great bell, only a single muffled sound was heard, followed by silence.

Upon entering the belfry the town magistrates found the dead Bannadonna and standing over him an enormous mechanical figure, cast by its creator to run upon a track at each appointed hour and strike the bell with its arms. Bannadonna, intent upon some finishing touches to the bell, had forgotten the hour, and had been struck by the mechanical figure.

Yet this was to have been only the prototype for Bannadonna's ultimate creation, an "elephantine helot" to be produced in great numbers and incorporating all the characteristics of all the animals that mankind had heretofore yoked to its will: "All excellences of all God-made creatures, which served man, were here to receive advancement, and then to be combined in one." And the figure itself was to reinforce the aesthetics of the sublime: Bannadonna's design principle for it was "the more terrible to behold, the better."

Bannadonna had intended to give his "metallic agent" not only the power of locomotion but also "the appearance, at least, of intelligence and will." The terror inspired by the physical appearance of the automaton has its source in a deeper dread, originating in its violation of the border between life and death: inorganic matter, becoming animate by a process of purely mechanical or chemical operations, inevitably produces a reverse effect and draws the living into the realm of the dead. This is the third and final level of root metaphors about the machine.

In another story, "The Paradise of Bachelors and the Tartarus of Maids," published in the same year as "The Bell-Tower," Melville cast the relation between humanity and machinery in these terms. The story's unusual structure is especially interesting, for Melville portrays the degeneracy or sterility of machine-based civilization not by contrasting it to a healthier unmechanized condition, but by juxtaposing it to another kind of sterility represented by traditional culture. The result, while wholly negative in tone, seems to make the point forcefully that there is no succor there.

The "Paradise of Bachelors" section recounts a long and very alcoholic dinner enjoyed by an old group of bachelors in an elegant private club in London; the story then shifts without transition to the "Tartarus of Maids" section, which describes a paper-mill factory in New England that employs a female workforce. Both are based upon visits by Melville, the first at Elm Court in Lincoln's Inn in 1849, the second at Pittsfield, Massachusetts, in 1851.[26]

The "Paradise of Bachelors" is a scene of sedate, well-tempered pleasure. The meal itself, although consisting of many courses, is curiously undistinguished fare; the dominant imagery in the scene is of the bachelors' carefully modulated consumption style: not a one sneezes when the snuff is passed around. The meal itself is, as Dillingham remarks, "a metaphor for their orderly existence." The impression of sterility and lifelessness is transmitted both by their dispassionate overindulgence in food and drink and by the state of lifelong bachelorhood to which all are committed.

The story's structure—the succession of the two sections—employs the first as backdrop for the second: The intrinsically powerful imagery of sterility and death in the second section is heightened further by being presented against what precedes it. This section is saturated with such imagery: the traveler's close brush with death, the pallor in the female workers' faces, the blankness of the paper, the factory ("like some great whited sepulchre"), the setting ("The mountains stood pinned in shrouds—a pass of Alpine corpses"). He sees the apparatus inside the factory:

> Something of awe now stole over me, as I gazed upon this inflexible iron animal. Always, more or less, machinery of this ponderous, elaborate sort strikes, in some moods, strange dread into the human heart, as some living, panting Behemoth might. But what made the thing I saw so specially terrible to me was the metallic necessity, the unbudging fatality which governed it.

It is not just that the machine is the living entity; procreative allusions indicate that it has assumed the generative capacities of life as well. The machine is housed in a room that is "stifling with a strange, blood-like, abdominal heat"; and the elapsed time between the introduction of the pulp and the emergence of the finished paper is "nine minutes to a second." The female workers, on the other hand, are all unmarried virgins whose very substance drains away. In the finished paper the traveler sees "glued to the pallid incipience of the pulp, the yet more pallid faces of all the pallid girls I had eyed that heavy day."

The reference to the "necessity" and "fatality" of the machine reinforces the epigraph to "The Bell-Tower": There is no escape from necessity through machine technology; on the contrary, that way leads to greater bondage.

One can assume that for Melville the world outside the machine's orbit was still vibrant, and that no irreversible commitment to it had been made. By the end of the nineteenth century it seemed to many that such a commitment indeed had been extracted from a society seemingly enthralled by the system of machinery, especially in North America. The dominant opinion seemed to be that whatever unease the machine might evoke paled into insignificance beside the more immediate dangers against which man and machine warred side by side: the power of untamed Nature, wilderness, and the surviving remnants of savage cultures. There is a marvelous representation of this attitude in the Currier and Ives lithograph "Across the Continent" (1868).[27] A train is drawn up before a rough frontier settlement, on the other side of which two mounted native warriors stand; the train itself is the protective hedge for civilization against the yet untamed wilderness.

The imaginative fiction of the early twentieth century recognized this completed commitment—or capitulation—to the machine. The external form of representation that characterizes the first and second levels of root metaphors—the machine confronting mankind as master/servant or as automaton—gave way to imagery of full internalization. Portrayed in its most striking terms, the man/machine symbiosis emerged fully developed, with the inevitable result: degeneration of the physiological and psychological autonomy of the human agent. The machine appeared as metaphor for a human society that was itself organized along the lines of a single machinelike organism.

E. M. Forster described his story "The Machine Stops" as "a counterblast to one of the heavens of H. G. Wells."[28] The human population resides underground, living singly in compartments where, at the pressing of buttons, mechanical devices supply water, food, air, beds, medicine, music, and communicating devices. Travel outside the compartments, although provided for, becomes rare, with a resultant deterioration in skin and musculature: Vashti, the central character, is described as a "swaddled lump of flesh" with "a face as white as a fungus." Originally the interlocking, supportive mechanism that sustained life in the compartments had been directly superintended by its designers; as their dependence became habitual, however, the human agents seemed to lose control over the functioning of the apparatus, which had been supplied with self-repairing mechanical aids. Soon they began to pray to it. That was the beginning of the end: "But Humanity, in its desire for comfort, had overreached itself. It had exploited the riches of nature too far. Quietly and complacently, it was sinking into decadence, and progress had come to mean the progress of the Machine."

Eventually the mechanism collapses, taking with it in its demise the compartmentalized inhabitants. But they were already dead in all but name, the living dead. Kuno, Vashti's son, had tried to explain this to her before the end:

> Cannot you see . . . that it is we who are dying, and that down here the only thing that really lives is the Machine? We created the Machine, to do our will, but we cannot make it do our will now. It has robbed us of the sense of space and the sense of touch, it has blurred every human relation and narrowed down love to a carnal act, it has paralyzed our bodies and our wills, and now it compels us to worship it. The Machine develops—but not on our lines. The Machine proceeds—but not to our goal. We only exist as the blood corpuscles that course through its arteries, and if it could work without us it would let us die.

Hope for regeneration lies only in the rude bands of escapees or natives who exist outside the orbit of mechanized society completely. This theme recurs in the two most famous dystopian novels of the early twentieth century, Zamyatin's *We* and Huxley's *Brave New World*.

In *We*, the individuals—who carry such designations as D-503 and I-330—are described as the "cells" of the "single mighty organism" that is the One State. All live in identical rooms and are nourished by a single industrially produced substance. The Table of Hours regulates all movements, setting prescribed times for eating, work, exercise, and sleep, except for the two Personal Hours each day—which, it is expected, will soon become part of the "general formula" like the others. Zamyatin's imagery is dominated throughout by mathematical allusions. According to the sexual law, for example, each "number" (individual) is entitled to have sexual relations with any other: "You declare that on your sexual days you wish to use number so-and-so, and you receive your book of coupons (pink). And that is all. Clearly, this leaves no possible reasons for envy; the denominator of the happiness fraction is reduced to zero, and the fraction is transformed into a magnificent infinity."[29]

Society itself is the machine, an organism of differentiated and smoothly integrated component parts. A mechanism in the usual sense, the physical object, appears in *We* only as symbol: first as the *Integral*, a spaceship designed to bring the message of "mathematically infallible happiness," achieved in the One State, to other planets; and second as the Benefactor's Machine, a device to cauterize the area of the brain that houses the faculty of imagination. The *One State Gazette* announces to the citizenry:

> Until this day, your own creations—machines—were more perfect than you. . . . The beauty of mechanism is its rhythm—as steady and precise as that of a pendulum. But you, nurtured from earliest infancy on the Taylor system—have you not become pendulum-precise? Except for one thing: Machines have no imagination . . . The latest discovery of State science is the location of the center of the imagination: a miserable little nodule in the brain of the *pons Varolii*. Triple-X-ray cautery of this nodule—and you are cured of imagination—forever. You are perfect. You are machinelike.[30]

As the novel ends, D-503, chief mathematician for the *Integral* project, submits voluntarily to the operation: "It is the same as killing myself—but perhaps this is the only way to resurrection. For only what is killed can be resurrected." Once the operation is universally performed, and the imaginative faculty is genetically blocked in future generations, the mechanism itself will be needed no longer: Society-as-machine will have removed all remaining impediments to its smooth functioning and will be able to reproduce itself identically for all time to come. But, at the city's edge, there is chaos as the remnants of older humanity assault the surrounding Wall.

The matter-of-factness that Veblen identified as the behavioral orientation of the machine age has become the expected routine of everyday life. We are accustomed to quantitative measure in every aspect of social relations. The calculation of benefits and costs in numerical terms pervades our lives—in negotiations between prospective marriage partners as well as between unions and corporations, in setting minimum levels of welfare payments as well as maximum "throwweights" for nuclear missiles. Domestic life is unimaginable anymore without mechanical devices, and more and more persons carry around inside their bodies some testimony to the wizardry of medical technology.

As well, an abundance of automatons in all sorts of horror films and science-fiction literature during the last fifty years has inured us to them; the ubiquitous video games should dissolve whatever remains of the machine's threatening visage. A few scattered souls may still quake at the prospect of self-programming computers becoming obstreperous, and of chess Grand Masters humiliated by an unanswerable gambit, but for most the terror and dread, as well as the sublimity, that fired the nineteenth-century mind is gone. The relation between mind and machine is now grist for the academic mills; the combat in this zone, however fierce it may become, is unlikely to revive that older mood.[31]

The master of the new style is the Polish writer Stanislaw Lem, and the mode of representation is whimsy. *Mortal Engines* introduces us to "electroknights" and "ultradragons," and to a computer which calls itself "Digital Grand Vizier" and insists on being addressed as "Your Ferromagneticity."[32] *The Cyberiad* opens with a story about a machine that suffers with good grace the ridiculous commands of its inventor, although it cannot resist a touch of spite. The stories are infinitely comforting, because Lem's machines have all the pathetic emotions and foibles so readily recognizable as our own.

NOTES

I wish to acknowledge the work of my research assistant, Debbie McGee, who helped in assembling the sources for this essay.

1. John F. Kasson, *Civilizing the Machine: Technology and Republican Values in America, 1776–1900* (Harmondsworth: Penguin, 1976), p. 162. References in the following paragraph in the text are from p. 164.

2. Calvin Tomkins, *The Bride and the Bachelors: Five Masters of the Avant-Garde* (Harmondsworth: Penguin, 1978), pp. 168 ff.; the quotation is from p. 182.

3. Cited by Kasson, p. 171; the illustration is reproduced on p. 167.

4. Cf. Robert Beum, "Literature and *Machinisme*," *The Sewanee Review* (1978), 86:216–44.

5. *The Collected Essays, Journalism and Letters of George Orwell*, 4 vols., S. Orwell and I. Angus, eds. (New York: Harcourt, Brace & World, 1968), 4:72–75. Zamyatin, a naval engineer by training, spent the period 1914–1917 in England.

6. Sander L. Gilman, "Seeing the Insane: Mackenzie, Kleist, William James," *Modern Language Notes* (1978), 93:871–87. Gilman took the idea from Stephen Pepper's *World Hypotheses* (Berkeley: University of California Press, 1966).

7. Langdon Winner, *Autonomous Technology: Technics Out-of-Control as a Theme in Political Thought* (Cambridge, Mass.: MIT Press, 1977).

8. Cited in Leo Marx, *The Machine in the Garden: Technology and the Pastoral Idea in America* (New York: Oxford University Press, 1964), p. 186; see generally pp. 180–90. For the identification of industrialism and republicanism see Kasson, ch. 1.

9. John Ruskin, *Unto this Last* (1862), in *The Works of John Ruskin*, 39 vols., E. T. Cook and A. Wedderburn, eds. (London: George Allen, 1903–1912), 17:29–30.

10. *Selected Writings of Herman Melville*, Modern Library (New York: Random House, 1952), p. 202.

11. Cited by Kasson, p. 228.

12. Leo Marx, pp. 230–32.

13. *Emerson's Complete Works*, 12 vols. (Boston: Houghton Mifflin, 1903–1904), 5:166–67.

14. Ronald Meek, *Social Science and the Ignoble Savage* (Cambridge: Cambridge University Press, 1976), passim.

15. Adam Smith, *An Inquiry into the Nature and Causes of the Wealth of Nations*, E. Cannan, ed., Modern Library (New York: Random House, 1937), pp. 734–36.

16. This paragraph is based on Maxine Berg, *The Machinery Question and the Making of Political Economy, 1815–1848* (Cambridge: Cambridge University Press, 1980), esp. chs. 11–13; the phrase in quotation marks from an 1830 magazine piece is cited on p. 257.

17. Marx, *Grundrisse: Foundations of a Critique of Political Economy* (1857–1858), M. Nicolaus, tr. (Harmondsworth: Penguin, 1973), pp. 692–93, 705.

18. Thorstein Veblen, *The Instinct of Workmanship and the State of the Industrial Arts* (New York: Norton, 1964), pp. 313–34.

19. Thomas Carlyle, *Critical and Miscellaneous Essays*, 5 vols. (London: Chapman and Hall, 1899), 2:59.

20. Carlyle, 2:60, 61.

21. Emerson, 5:103.

22. Carlyle, 2:81.

23. Lewis Kamm, "People and Things in Zola's *Rougon-Macquart:* Reification Re-humanized," *Philological Quarterly* (1974), 53:100–109.

24. Marx, p. 692.

25. H. Bruce Franklin, *Future Perfect: American Science Fiction of the Nineteenth Century* (New York: Oxford University Press, 1966), p. 145.

26. In what follows I am indebted to two recent commentaries: William B. Dillingham, *Melville's Short Fiction, 1853–1856* (Athens: University of Georgia Press, 1977), ch. 8; and Marvin Fisher, *Going Under: Melville's Short Fiction and the American 1850's* (Baton Rouge: Louisiana State University Press, 1977), pp. 70–94.

27. Reproduced in Kasson, p. 179.

28. *The Collected Tales of E. M. Forster* (New York: Knopf, 1964), pp. vii–viii.

29. Yevgeny Zamyatin, *We*, Mirra Ginsburg, tr. (New York: Viking, 1972), p. 22.

30. Zamyatin, pp. 179–80.

31. John Searle, "The Myth of the Computer," *The New York Review of Books*, (29 April 1982), 29(7):3–6.

32. Stanislaw Lem, *Mortal Engines*, Michael Kandel, tr. (New York: Seabury Press, 1977); *The Cyberiad: Fables for the Cybernetic Age*, M. Kandel, tr. (New York: Avon Books, 1976).

8

POLITICAL THEORY AND DEGENERATION: FROM LEFT TO RIGHT, FROM UP TO DOWN

STUART C. GILMAN
St. Louis University

It is understandable, then, that medicine should have had such importance in the constitution of the sciences of man—an importance that is not only methodological, but ontological, in that it concerns man's being as object of positive knowledge.

Michel Foucault, *The Birth of the Clinic*

Degeneracy was one of the most important generic clinical diseases of the nineteenth century. The decline of the individual, group, or race from a "better" condition captured the popular imagination so profoundly that it became an accepted, implicit assumption by most of Western society. Because it reflected the rise of clinical medicine and its ability to objectify disease, degeneracy also profoundly influenced many ontological assumptions. This essay will explore the impact of degeneracy theory on the development of political philosophy in the latter half of the nineteenth century. In carrying out such a study there are two alternatives. One is to cover piecemeal the varying uses of degeneracy by the host of political philosophers during this period. The other, the approach I will use, is to select a few major figures, of vastly different schools, and present an in-depth analysis of how the ontological status of man, read through degeneracy, intertwines itself through their epistemological propositions. The latter approach appears to be both more sensible and more revealing.

I will limit this study to three, disparate figures in nineteenth-century political thought: Friedrich Engels, John Stuart Mill, and Walter Bagehot. Engels represents the socialist tradition, and with his collaborator, Karl Marx, he affected much of contemporary political theory. John Stuart Mill, the ultimate liberal thinker founded in the utilitarian tradition, appears to be the least likely to be infected by degeneracy. However, I will demonstrate that this is far from the case. Walter Bagehot is the least well-known individual of this group, yet he was one of the "fathers" of contemporary political science and one of the most influential social scientists of his day. Countless others were more obviously affected by degeneracy theories, such as the racists Arthur de Gobineau and Hippolyte Taine, existentialist Friedrich Nietzsche, and even pragmatist John Dewey. However, Engels, Mill, and Bagehot represent such radically different traditions that the ontological nature of their thought exemplifies my major premise: the dominance of degeneracy theory in nineteenth-century political philosophy.

The Sciences and the Social Sciences

Where do new approaches and concepts in the social sciences come from? In contemporary political theory they are most often borrowed, sometimes whole, often in part, from the natural sciences and adapted to fit particular theoretical interests.[1] For example, David Easton borrowed the concept of "systems" theory from biologist W. R. Ashby's *Design for a Brain* to formulate his series of works beginning with his classic *The Political System*. This framework dominated two decades of work in political science and is still a popular analytical tool. Other theoretical frameworks, structural-functionalism, cybernetic theory, and coalition theories, all had their foundations in the natural sciences. With the current popularity of such enterprises it is surprising that few political theorists see the same links in thinkers of earlier periods. In fact, political theorists in the nineteenth century also adapted major ideational currents of their day—Darwinism, eugenics, electricity, and chemical discoveries—to describe social phenomena. Thus, Henry Adams uses the metaphor of the electric dynamo to unlock his dynamic theory of history.[2] Yet degeneracy, one of the dominant scientific metaphors in the nineteenth century (and one that unobtrusively fits into many of the theoretical views of the period), is all but unknown to contemporary political theorists and political philosophers.

Degeneracy theory was widely popularized by Bénédict-Augustin Morel, a pious French psychologist.[3] He reinterpreted the fall from grace scientifically, seeing most of the physical and social malaise of his day as a direct result of hereditary degeneracy. Thus, he could observe the degeneration of a single family beginning with alcoholism in one generation, hysteria in the second, insanity in the third, then idiocy, and ultimately sterility. Following the logic that "entire races have the capability of degenerating," he gives as examples alcoholism among the Swedes and opium addiction among the orientals. And, using Buffon, Morel suggests that the very environment of the Negro (who were thought to cook their brains in the hot sun) will lead to their disappearance. Degeneracy became accepted not because it was new, but because it became powerful. It fit, in a special way, into a crucial epistemological gap in nineteenth-century medicine and social science. Its power derived not from its empirical validity, but from the growing societal legitimacy of science and medicine.

Degeneracy also fit the growing desire of theists to join the scientific bandwagon and at the same time retain their religious beliefs. Degeneration appeared to marry the theistic view of the fall from grace to the scientific and medical literature of the day. In so doing, it was an acceptable device for both the secular and religious communities—a type of civil religion taking medico-scientific artifacts and applying them to social problems.[4]

The Generative Metaphor

A preliminary question, yet crucial for this inquiry, is why concepts like degeneracy capture both the scholarly mind and the public imagination. After all, not all major scientific (or pseudoscientific) ideas become popular and dominate public thinking. It is not enough to suggest that they fill a void in the human imagination, much less in academic or public discourse. In fact, such ideas appear to be much more powerful and take on the status of what Donald Schön has called a "generative metaphor."

Schön wants to suggest ways of problem solving, primarily in areas of public policy. His argument is that major difficulties in public policy arise because they emphasize problem solving rather than problem setting. Problem settings are mediated by the "stories" people tell about troublesome situations, "stories in which they describe what is wrong and what needs fixing." It becomes "apparent that the framing of problems often depends upon metaphors underlying the stories which generate problem setting and set the direction of problem solving."[5] Generative metaphors are used in situations where there are dilemmas—social circumstances where there are stubborn conflicts of perspective.

Schön gives a good technological example of the generative metaphor:

> Some years ago, a group of product-development researchers was considering how to improve the performance of a new paint brush made with synthetic bristles. Compared to the old natural-bristle brush, the new one delivered paint to a surface in a discontinuous,

"gloppy" way. The researchers had tried a number of different improvements. They had noticed, for example, that natural bristles had split ends, whereas the synthetic bristles did not, and they tried . . . to split the ends of synthetic bristles of different diameters. Nothing seemed to help.

Then someone observed, *"You know, a paintbrush is a kind of pump!"* He pointed out that when a paintbrush is pressed against a surface, paint is forced through the spaces between bristles onto the surface. The paint is made to flow through the "channels" formed by the bristles when the channels are deformed by the bending of the brush . . .

The researchers tried out the natural and synthetic bristle brushes, thinking of them as pumps. They noticed that the natural brush formed a *gradual curve* when it was pressed against a surface whereas the synthetic brush formed a shape more nearly an angle. (p. 257)

Using this new generative metaphor, "paintbrush-as-pump," the researchers redesigned the synthetic paint brushes to allow them to act as a pump and resolve the puzzle. Schön's primary purpose is to show that the perspective of generative metaphor can be used to displace a problem-solving approach. The generative metaphor allows the researcher to restructure the frame of the conflict by constructing a new problem-setting story. This is accomplished by attempting "to integrate conflicting frames by including features and relations drawn from earlier stories, yet without sacrificing internal coherence or the degree of simplicity required for action." This occurs in its "best" sense, according to Schön, in situations particularly rich in information which provide "access to many different combinations of features and relations" (p. 270).

I will be using this explanatory model in a very different way than Schön intends. I agree with the major thrust of his argument, that generative metaphors can be used to explain why new concepts and ideas are so instantly accepted in both the scholarly and public mind. However, this resolution is not always a positive step in policy making. The generative metaphor can reset the problem, apparently solve a puzzle or paradox, but it does not necessarily do this without error or in the ethically neutral context Schön suggests.

Degeneracy: Its Development as an Idea

The concept of degeneracy took on the character of a generative metaphor in the nineteenth century as a part of the growth of clinical medicine and the technology of classifying diseases. This does not mean that degeneracy was first used in the nineteenth century, but rather its use became enhanced with the rise of scientific empiricism, the popularization of evolutionary biology, and the development of clinical medicine. By the middle of the nineteenth century science became such a dominant *cultural* idea that it rivaled religion in its explanatory power. Clinical medicine attached science and scientific measurement to the role of "healer," and this ultimately led to an unquestioned legitimacy for physicians. Ironically, this also helped to illuminate the role of the medical community in scientific racism.[6]

Degeneracy had been used in many contexts, but none with the scientific precision it ultimately acquired. Its Latin root means "to fall from the genus or stock." It took on the added pejorative connotation of debased or ignoble. Shakespeare's *King Lear* uses the term "degenerate bastard" as early as 1605 and Henry More refers to "this grand degeneracy of the church" in 1664. However, in none of these senses was degeneracy biologically based. It was usually a reference to the debasement of some person of "good or noble stock."[7]

Although Bénédict-Augustin Morel popularized degeneracy theory, one of its most important political uses occurred fifty years earlier. In 1774 Edward Long published *A History of Jamaica,* which used degeneracy to connect his vision of the racial inferiority of the black slave to the developing authority of science. The two-volume work emphasizes both biological and botanical classificatory schemes. Long blends descriptions of flora and fauna with a several hundred page discussion of biological distinctions based on race. For example, he distinguishes between African "herds" and humans because Negroes "are certainly not people." Long argues that Negroes are "void of genius, . . . civility or science" and concludes,

> In so vast a continent as that of Africa and in so great a variety of climates and provinces, we might expect to find a proportionate diversity among the inhabitants . . . But, on the contrary, a general uniformity runs through all these various regions of people; so that, if any difference be found, it is only in degrees of the same qualities; and, what is more strange, those of the worst kind; it being a common known proverb, that all people on the globe have some good as well as ill qualities, except the Africans. Whatever great personages this country might have produced, and concerning whom we have no information, they now are everywhere *degenerated* into a brutish, ignorant, idle, crafty, treacherous, bloody, thievish, mistrustful, and superstitious people. [my italics][8]

It is important to again emphasize that Long tied degeneracy not only to personal characteristics, but also to such permanent physical characteristics as body stature, head shape, hands, color, and even body odor.

Long actually asserts that Negroes are a different species of the same genus, exemplifying the evolutionary character of all things inert, vegetable, and animal (p. 356). He suggests that evolutionary character has two attributes: one progressive and the other degenerate. Using what will become in the nineteenth century a common belief about degenerates, Long concludes that hybrid, black-white children will eventually become infertile, as all violations of "natural" boundaries do. Thus, for Long the

Hottentot woman would be "more honored by the advances of an Orangutang" than a European.

Long was important for many reasons. First, he was seriously regarded as a writer and his opinions were widely quoted.[9] In addition, he gave a moral justification for slavery that was absent in England at the time. The English could easily rationalize justifying enslaving a person who was captured in "war," even a fictionalized war. The noted liberal theorist John Locke also justified slavery in this way.[10] It became the nonexistent justification for keeping the children of slaves in captivity. Even if the slave did something heinous to deserve his condition, it was difficult to transfer this guilt to his children.

The idea of degeneracy allowed this linkage. While carefully avoiding the problem of monogenesis, or the single origin of all men, Long developed degeneracy as a biological concept to justify the condition of slavery for all progeny of the slave. The biological cast to his work might appear to be surprising, for it predates any of Darwin's writings and what we know as contemporary biology. Both evolutionary and devolutionary theory have been a consistent theme in various forms since the time of Aristotle.[11] In addition, the writings of Buffon, Jean Lamarck, and Erasmus Darwin were highly popularized versions of evolutionary theory, all of which were available to Long.

Both Darwin and Long were trying to win a "war" of theoretical dominance against the medical/sociological school which emphasized the curability of race. Samuel Stanhope Smith's *Essays on the Causes of the Variety of Complexion and Figure in the Human Species* (1787) was one of the most important works of this school. Henry Moss, an exslave, popularized this theory when he developed white patches on his skin and became a traveling curosity.[12] However, the *pragmatic* necessity of justifying slavery made degeneracy more popular, and eventually dominant.

As a medical metaphor it rationalized the ethical and political contradictions growing from inequalities in the nineteenth century. For Long, the prime example of degenerate inequality, that is permanent, fixed, intergenerationally transmitted inferiority, was the Negro slave. Degeneracy became a commonly accepted assumption in nineteenth-century popular culture, and its appearently scientific and clinical origins allowed it to be applied to a host of other circumstances. All of this fifty years before Erasmus Darwin's grandson Charles embarked on *H.M.S. Beagle*.

Degeneracy and the Rise of Clinical Medicine

However much we explore the pervasiveness of degeneracy in nineteenth-century culture, it cannot be considered a true generative metaphor unless it resolves an apparent paradox or puzzle. A picture of the circumstances surrounding the rise of degeneracy cannot be completed unless its place in clinical medicine is understood. Not until the nineteenth century did medicine take on the trappings of empirical science. From the late Middle Ages through the eighteenth century medicine was viewed as art, much like pottery making and silversmithing. In addition, medicine was often opposed on religious grounds, because many theologians viewed disease as either just punishment from God or the malicious work of Satan.[13] Medical science was truly an *art* at this time and one should not confuse it with the contemporary medical practices which appear to exploit all aspects of scientific discovery. This was still the medicine of "leeching" and body humors. Most common men believed, and with good cause, that it was far more dangerous to go to the doctor than to do without one. Hospitals were merely places to *speed up* death. It was not until clinical medicine became associated with the extraordinary advances of scientific inquiry and measurement that it gained new legitimacy. By using the new procedure of "statistical evidence" it took on the role of healer for both physical and *social* disease.

The primary emphasis of clinical medicine during the last century was developing taxonomies of diseases using empirical data. These disease taxonomies were made to fit the fundamental suppositions of nineteenth-century medicine which were as much theological as scientific. Charles Rosenberg argues that the basis for understanding medicine during this period was the biblical edict "like begets like." As innocent as such an aphorism appears to be, it led to four basic assumptions by both physicians and laymen:

(1) Acquired characteristics were inherited.
(2) An assumption that heredity was a dynamic process beginning with conception and ending in weaning.
(3) A belief that character, disease, and temperament were inherited in the form of tendencies and predispositions.
(4) Most physicians agreed that the sexes played a necessarily different role in heredity.[14]

It is important to elaborate on each of these because the lacuna in clinical knowledge which these assumptions produced naturally led to the general acceptance of such diseases as degeneracy, and the use of degeneracy theory as an implied cultural assumption in much of nineteenth-century political philosophy.

The vision of heredity at this time was that it was "plastic," totally mutable, from the time of conception through weaning. The implications of this belief, tied to the notion that acquired characteristics were inherited, changed a great number of social relationships and political beliefs. As late as 1885, a professor of medicine at the University of Pennsylvania warned that the "indulgence of a man's grandfather at his [the grand-father's] wedding feast [may] be written upon his body in the unmistak-able characters of a debilitated and dyspeptic stomach."[15] One reason for the disappearance of wet nursing was the widely held belief that a lower-class wet nurse might impart in her milk the germs of libertinism, crimi-nality, and alcoholism.[16] Even the similarity of twins to each other, more than to other siblings, was credited to the time differences during which the parents' physical attributes had changed.

The third element—a belief that character, disease, and temperament were inherited—was called diathesis or, more commonly, a constitutional bent. This view saw disease as the result of the total interaction of the person with the environment. A person was comprised not only of his own interactions but the interactions of his ancestors. Depending on the moral and physical conduct of one's ancestors, this could lead to atavism, a natural deterioration of the individual's constitution. Thus, tuberculosis, cancer, and mental illness were diathetic conditions. And the patient's constitutional type was viewed as determining of his physical and moral health.[17]

Last, men and women were believed to give different traits to the child—the mother gave stamina and the father intellect, for example. This gave rise to the notion of "sex-limited" ills, or ills that resulted from the dominant sex partner. When a woman violated her "constitution" by be-ing aggressive, her progeny might be color blind and hemophiliacs. This belief is important in understanding the opposition to the franchise for women or equalizing their role in society. It was feared that changing the constitutional bent of women would radically change the biological and *moral* health of a nation. This perception would color the political dis-course about the value and role of women in governance.

Degeneracy had been used as a biological concept much earlier than the 1840s, and it was an accepted metaphor when applied to race, sex, and class differences. However, it was not until Morel's publication of *Degeneracy* that it became a popular clinical metaphor. As this point de-generacy changed from what can be called a "common metaphor" to a generative metaphor.[18] The clinical notion solved a series of apparently unresolvable problems both for the physician and the layman. It was possible to explain diseases (and inequalities) in terms of class distinc-tions, racial difference, and sexual inequalities and to investigate them through empirical evidence and scientific principles. The abrupt appear-ance of an "objective" standard was incredibly persuasive, and this ap-parently benign clinical tool was suddenly crucial for legitimizing prejudice.[19]

In a sense degeneracy theory filled a conceptual void once the four medical presuppositions are understood. It was necessary to have a clini-cal notion of the range of diseases to which these circumstances would lead. (I specifically distinguish clinical from medical. By "medical" I mean the identification, morphology, and cure of disease. By "clinical" I follow Foucault in suggesting the institutional and psychological elements of disease as a linear series of morbid events.) Degeneracy was one of the major generic diseases that apparently resolved a puzzle in medical knowledge. It describes the propensity of people to contract diseases, both physical and moral, and to pass them on to other generations. Even the development of germ theory had little impact on the persuasiveness of degeneracy theory. It was argued that the accuracy of germ theory buttresses diathesis—degeneracy being one aspect. People simply had a constitutional bent to attract such germs which in turn caused disease.

Degeneracy and Political Philosophy

Degeneracy was successful because it married cultural, scientific, religious, medical, and social beliefs by apparently allowing all of them to have an explanatory "truth." As with most generative metaphors its closeness of "fit" with accepted perceptions of reality makes it acceptable, and, in a sense, makes it generative. It is perhaps ironic that the generative metaphor must rely heavily on previous forms to make the claim about its radical character.

It would be wrong to assume from the above discussion that *all* political philosophers during the nineteenth century used degeneracy theory in the ways suggested above. Rather, in arguing about the political status of men, and women, their rights, their equality, and even their humanity, political philosophers during this age felt it was necessary to deal with questions often seen as arcane today. In some cases, they assumed degeneracy and tried to argue around it or incorporate it in their theories. In other cases, political thinkers would adapt and even transmogrify degeneracy so that it would fit more neatly within their epistemological perspective. No matter the approach, an understanding of this dominant generative metaphor is crucial for a full appreciation of much of nineteenth-century political philosophy.

Friedrich Engels and the Degenerate Society

Friedrich Engels is most noted as the collaborator of Karl Marx. Engels was born a petit bourgeois, and somewhat ironically was the owner of a small industry. He supported Marx, financially and spiritually, and enabled him to complete the scientific research that would be necessary to justify communism. Engels contributed markedly to the literature of communism, and many of his works are considered to be crucial foundations for contemporary Marxist-Leninism. There is no question about the friendship of Marx and Engels, nor of their feelings that theirs was the correct road to socialism.

Still, the raging debate in the last decade among Marx scholars has centered around Engels' contribution to Marxist theory. Some philosophers have suggested that Engels was a "second-rate" mind who bastardized and corrupted much of Marx's work. Others counter that such a close collaboration between the two could not have taken place if Marx had detected the so-called inferiority of Engels. Even more important, if Marx was brilliant, which both sides concede, then why did he not detect the perversion of Marxism with which Engels is charged?[20] In either case, I think a reasonable argument can be developed for looking at the special attention Engels paid to his study of "nature" and its incorporation in the corpus of his writings. I do believe that large segments of Engels' writings on evolution and nature directly contradict, or substantially change, concepts previously written by Marx, and in some cases by both Marx and Engels.[21]

In fact, the sum of my argument is that Marx and Engels constantly disputed the application of Darwin to socialist theory, and that Engels (known or unknown to Marx) married evolution to degeneracy theory in order to provide a *justification* for socialism. The non-Hegelian nature of this integration demonstrates why these arguments appear to violate much of the epistemological grounding of Marxism.[22]

The tension between Marx and Engels on the subject of Darwinism, and more important Engels' insistence on extrapolating from it to the work of Morgan and other anthropologists, can be most clearly seen in Marx's ethnological notebooks.[23] Marx spends an extraordinary amount of time critically appraising Morgan, Phear, Maine, and Lubbock. In all cases he found them lacking a clear historical perspective or the ability to fully understand the ethnological foundations of society in historical materialism. Criticizing them in the same light as Darwinism, Marx concludes that they "internalized social prejudices, ethnocentrisms, and uncritical borrowings of the pre-conceptions of their social origins."[24] The critiques Marx levels against Morgan are often ignored, because they appear to so undermine Engels' arguments, especially *The Origin of the Family, Private Property, and the State*. This book is simply a rewriting—some sections less rewritten than others—of Henry Morgan's *Ancient Society*. The clear paradox here has often led more traditional Marxist scholars to go to great lengths to conceal it.[25] Marx saw the perversions available if the permanence of biological "status" could be married to even the most liberal ethnological assumptions. Marx's concern becomes more apparent in his dialogue with Engels over Darwin.

Although Marx was living in England at the time, it was Engels who wrote Marx with great excitement about the *Origin of the Species*. And in a series of fascinating letters in the summer of 1866 the worth of Darwin is debated by these two seminal figures. Engels becomes Darwin's defender. Marx appears to be trying to coax his friend away from the brute empiricism and apparent determinism in Darwin. This exchange has been called "a bizarre intellectual episode" by one current commentator.[26] Yet it demonstrates beyond question the profound intellectual foundation Engels found in Darwin.

Both Marx and Engels accepted the idea of degeneracy theory, as did most intellectuals of their age. However, Marx linked degeneracy to environment and Engels founded his notion in the determinism of evolving man—an early version of the nature vs. nurture controversy.[27] The controversy begins in a letter to Engels from Marx on August 7, 1866, in which he highly recommends Pierre Trémaux's *Origine et transformations de l'homme et des autres êtres* (Paris, 1865) as an "important advance over Darwin." Trémaux argues that there was a high correlation between the type of soil—the physical basis of human survival—and racial/national character. Therefore, a study of soil samples would result in a corresponding racial character.

> Progress, which in Darwin is purely accidental, is here a necessity, on the basis of periods of development of the earth; degeneration which Darwin cannot explain, is here simple; ditto the rapid extinction of mere transitional forms, compared with the slowness of the development of *espèces* types, so that gaps in palentology, which bother Darwin, are here a necessity . . .
>
> For certain questions, such as nationality, etc., a natural basis is found only in his work. For example . . . the Russians are not only not Slavs but, rather Tartars, etc., but also that on the existing soil formation of Russia the Slavs become Tartarized and Mongolized, just as he (he has been in Africa for a long time) proves that the common Negro type is only a degeneration of a much higher one.[28]

Engels writes a slashing critique of Trémaux suggesting that "there is nothing to his whole *theory,* since he neither understands geology nor is capable of understanding the most ordinary literally-historical critique."[29] Marx replies the next day suggesting that Engels' attack was reminiscent of Georges Cuvier's disputation of the pre-Darwinian notion of variability of the species.[30] Interestingly, Marx concludes that "Trémaux's basic idea . . . is an idea that only has to be *expressed* in order to earn for ever a citizen's right in science."[31]

What Marx appears to be doing here and elsewhere in his correspondence with Engels during this period is dissuading him of the importance of Darwin. Engels readily admits his enchantment with Darwin and Marx appears to be attempting to get Engels to view Darwin's work with more detachment. One senses in Marx's critiques of Darwin, and his suggestion of alternative biological theorists such as Trémaux, and in 1868 Karl

Nikolaus Fraas,[32] that Marx was steering Engels away from Darwinian determinism. Although Marx was fascinated by Darwin, he understood the *historical* basis of natural selection and the Malthusianism that was inherent in it. Marx was more Lamarckian in his biology, which some critics with little knowledge of contemporary biology consider damning.[33] Engels' work during this period became harshly deterministic. And after the death of Marx, Engels openly tried to adapt Darwin to Marxist theory.

Both Marx and Engels held views of degeneracy largely based on the burgeoning of degeneracy theories in medicine. Marx's view was affected by those who emphasized the ecological origins of degeneracy, having befriended Edwin Ray Lankester.[34] Lankester was one of the most important degeneracy theorists of the time and edited the *Quarterly Journal of Microscopical Science* for almost fifty years. However, even though he thought Lankester a friend, there is no hint of "Darwinian degeneracy" in any of Marx's later works. It appears profoundly insubstantial to suggest that his friendship with Lankester caused "the last vestige of the Hegelian dialectic of progress" in Marx's work to disintegrate.[35] In Engels' case there is an entire body of literature published by him to support the contention that he read much of Darwinian degeneracy into Marxist theory.

Engels and Dialectical Materialism

Engels originated the term dialectical materialism, a concept Marx never used.[36] First coined in the "Anti-Dühring," five years before Marx's death, Engels fully fleshed out the significance of dialectical materialism in the *Origin of the Family, Private Property and the State* and in the *Dialectics of Nature*. These two volumes are filled with evolutionary and degeneracy terms, images, and themes. Most of Engels' "later" works reflect his fascination with science, and especially with attempts to justify the "science" in scientific socialism.

The "Anti-Dühring" was the result of what Engels called "his inundation for two years in the natural philosophy and science of his day." In the first chapter, he attempts to distinguish himself (and Marx) from the nineteenth-century natural philosophers and include Marx's work in the body of natural science. Engels concludes that to understand dialectics one must understand that the dialectical method is evolution, and that evolution is the prime case in any proof of dialectics. He emphasizes that dialectical materialism accounts for both "progressive" and "retrogressive" changes in society.[37]

The marriage between dialectics and evolutionary theory is what links socialism to science. It is not surprising then that Engels describes Dühring's work as "irresponsibility due to meglomania" when he reads Dühring's suggestion that Darwinism is "a piece of brutality directed against humanity." Engels insists that Darwin's evolutionary theory is the greatest advance since Marx, placing anthropologist Lewis Henry Morgan third on his list. He characterizes the development of historical socialism as "evolutionary . . . in its main features."[38] To emphasize this evolutionary commitment Engels actually outlines the evolution of materialism in the appendices: from Bacon, to Hobbes, to Locke, to Priestly, and finally to Marx.

Evolutionary theory offered a clinical context for Engels' beliefs about degeneracy. It not only destroyed the fantasy of a supreme being, but provided a logic for the development of humankind. "This history of mankind no longer appeared as a wild whirlwind of senseless deeds of violence, all equally condemnable at the judgement seat of nature, but as the process of the evolution of man himself."[39] Thus, the idea of evolutionary theory was not merely a positive innovation for Engels, it was a dominant world view. Darwin had not merely discovered an important scientific artifact, but had provided an explanatory paradigm through which all scientific theory—including scientific socialism—could be understood.

Degeneracy fit very well into the perceptions of evolutionary theory held in the nineteenth century. It is implied throughout *The Origin of the Family, Private Property and the State* that there are both progressive and degenerate conditions in society.[40] However, in the little known essay "The Part Played by Labor in the Transition of Ape to Man," Engels most fully elaborates his degenerative perspective. This essay begun in 1876 is unfinished. Editors usually attach it to the *Origin* because it is reflective of the same anthropological bent. It is also Engels' most original anthropological piece.

The argument in this essay is primarily sociobiological, that is, it uses biological elements to explain behavioral characteristics. Thus, Engels can conclude that the development of the human hand naturally leads to an emphasis on labor. It is this fundamental change from ape to man, caused by a decline in the feeding grounds, that makes man a predator. The character is the human hand developed out of this sociobiological *need*. The availability of the hand as a tool allowed men to plan for the future; instead of killing off all animals available to them, man develops a "predatory economy": "This 'predatory economy' of animals plays an important part in the gradual transformation of species by forcing them to adapt themselves to other than the usual food, thanks to which their blood acquires a different chemical composition and the whole physical constitution gradually alters, while species that have remained unadapted die out."[41] The predatory economy led naturally to the development of tools. The first available tool for man was fire, which allowed primitives to "half digest meat." With the introduction of tools "the hand had become free." It is not only the organ of labor, but the product of labor.

This evolutionary movement also contained a devolutionary element. Men can degenerate back toward animals. However, there is a limit to how far a man can fall. As degenerate and savage as a man becomes he will never be an ape. "The lowest savages, even those in whom regression to a more animal-like condition with a simultaneous physical degeneration can be assumed, are nevertheless far superior to these transitional beings."[42] Engels believed that savages not only live in a more animal-like world but experience a resulting physical degeneration. Both Marx and Engels use the term degeneracy when referring to savages, but Engels built the idea of degeneracy into his view of social evolution.

In order to integrate degeneracy into socialism Engels had to shift the level of analysis. That is, degeneracy was recast so that it no longer occurred at the individual or racial level, but at the socioeconomic level. By placing degeneracy at the level of societal analysis, Engels succeeds in turning something apparently antithetical to Marxism into a theory that significantly compliments it. Degeneracy might occur at the individual level, but it was symptomatic of societal deterioration. Thus, both the savage and the civilized man were caught in the natural process of social evolution.

How can one tell a degenerate society from a progressive one? Capitalism was degenerate and would die out, precisely because in its final development it exhibited all of the barbarism of the most savage condition. "Darwin did not know what a bitter satire he wrote on mankind," writes Engels, "and especially on his countrymen, when he showed that free competition, the struggle for existence, which the economists celebrate as the highest historical achievement, is the normal state of the *animal kingdom*. Only conscious organization of social production . . . can lift mankind above the rest of the animal world . . . Historical evolution makes such an organization daily more indispensible, but also with every day more possible."[43] Evolutionary theory is therefore a reflection of societal degeneration. Capitalism's crisis is suddenly shifted from the Hegelian dialectic to the metaphor of devolutionary and degenerate societies.

Engels' major criticism of Darwin was that he had lumped together "natural selection" and "survival of the fittest."[44] In fact, Engels argues that in some cases adaptation can mean regress as well as progress. Degenerate conditions, such as capitalism, can become apparently viable. But in its viability, adaptation determines what will follow it and precludes a host of other possibilities. Or, in Engels' words, "each advance in organic evolution is at the same time a regression, fixing *one-sided* evolution and excluding evolution along many other directions."[45]

For Engels capitalism takes on the same clinical and metaphorical images as the degenerate. It is impotent. That is, capitalism is incapable of evolving beyond itself. As a socioeconomic system it will become more and more barbaric, and will resort to incredible measures to maintain stability.

These tactics for survival will include violence as well as fetishism. Ultimately, this savage state is beyond rehabilitation, and it is implicitly dangerous. The longer any degenerate condition was allowed to manifest itself the more severe it would be, and the greater potential disaster it boded for society.

In essence the above argument demonstrates that Engels constructed a generative metaphor from degeneracy theory and Darwinism to allow him to explain Marx's Hegelianism. This generative metaphor not only fit into socialism, but apparently added scientific veracity to the claims of scientific socialism. The clinical-biological model filled out the abstraction of the Hegelian dialectic and interfaced Marx's dialectical *Aufhebung*. It apparently explained for Engels the essence of the socialist moment: "Thus at every step we are reminded that we by no means rule over nature like a conquerer over a foreign people, like someone standing outside nature— but that we, with flesh, blood and brain, belong to nature, and exist in its midst, and that all our mastery of it consists in the fact that we have the advantage over all other creatures of being able to learn its laws and apply them correctly."[46]

John Stuart Mill and Modern Liberalism

The degeneracy theories of the nineteenth century, even in the more sympathetic light that Engels tried to cast them, still appear to be totally alien to contemporary liberalism. John Stuart Mill, in his defense of liberty and equality, women's rights, and minority rights, seems to epitomize the staunch opponent of everything that degeneracy theory suggests. Yet a major current in Mill's thought can be traced to degeneracy.

In the writings of John Stuart Mill there is a consistent dichotomy, a liberal and conservative side. This has nothing to do with periods of his life, but rather distinctions between a "conservative" approach toward culture and a "liberal" emphasis on social rights throughout his life.[47] This distinction is important because it colors Mill's approach to government and explains his reticence about democracy. Mill was also profoundly influenced by the biological science of his day, which tended to lend credence to very conservative cultural assumptions.

This cultural conservatism is clear in Mill's methodological approach to utilitarianism. In fact, he substantially changes the essence of Bentham's felicific calculus so that a utilitarian could account for qualitative as well as quantitative changes in happiness. Bentham's dictum "the greatest happiness of the greatest number" is replaced by "the greatest happiness *per se*." As Dante Germino points out, this change was necessary because not all are equally qualified to judge the *summum bonum*. Rather, Mill reflects the same judgment as Aristotle about the *spoudaios*, the fully developed individual, who through appreciating and enjoying "both the physical and intellectual pleasures can judge their relative qualities."[48] There is a sense of elitism in such an approach and some scholars actually read Mill as attacking the common man.[49] I believe they are wrong. However, it appears just as misleading to suggest that Mill's vision aimed at the fusion of "quality" and participation.[50] Although education might lead to the elevation of human character, Mill was not naive enough, as some have suggested, to see it as a universal panacea, much less a justification of complete equality.

Rather than retrace the essence of Mill's liberalism, I want to emphasize his objections to democracy and the origins of those objections in degeneracy theory. It is often assumed that democracy and civil liberties are inseparable. Not only is this a relatively current idea, but in Mill's case it is wrong. Mill was a passionate defender of civil liberties and human rights, but it does not follow that he supported mass participation in the governmental process. It is unfortunate that some scholars, in order to make Mill more readily interface with contemporary notions of liberalism, have assumed that one naturally grows out of the other.[51] Mill has also been criticized for his bourgeois ethic, which I believe is justified, but too often simplistically drawn.[52] Other scholars have tried to save Mill from this criticism by basing their reinterpretation on what they characterize as a nineteenth-century view of human potential.[53] In no case is there an attempt to understand Mill's view of human nature within the context of nineteenth-century clinical science.

Mill was fascinated with the scientific discoveries of his age. He hails Darwin, who "has found (to speak Newtonially) a *vera causa*, and has shown that it is capable of accounting for vastly more than had been supposed; beyond that, it is but the indication of what may have been, though it is not proved to be, the origin of the organic world we now see."[54] He uses Darwin's work extensively and points to it as a model of scientific inquiry in *A System of Logic*.

His impression of Darwin was formed by his good friend Herbert Spencer. Mill not only socialized with Spencer, but also had an extensive correspondence with him. In that correspondence, as well as in other writings about Spencer, Mill showed him only the highest admiration. In a letter responding to a criticism of Spencer, Mill writes:

> You ask my opinion concerning Mr. Spencer's "First Principles" & "Principles of Biology" as contributions to the advance of thought. I answer that I attach to them, in that respect, the very highest value. . . . They seem to me to hold a most important place in the scientific thought of the age. Within the present generation several large and comprehensive generalizations have made their way into Science—the Unity and conservation of Force, the Darwinian theory of

organic development, and (though this is a branch of the last) *the hereditary transmission of acquired faculties.*[55]

It is not by coincidence that Mill includes a hereditary theory of acquired characteristics: precisely what Spencer and the degeneracy theorists were trying to marry to Darwinian theory.[56] The inheritance of acquired characteristics was absolutely crucial to make Spencer's case about the biological basis of society. Without this "scientific" artifact attached to Darwinism, social Darwinism and degeneracy would have no biological basis. An intensive reading of Mill can only lead one to conclude that he understood most of Darwin's writings through the work of Spencer.

For example, he concludes his evaluation of Spencer's work:

> At this critical period in what will probably turn out to be one of the great transformations in Science, nothing could be more fortunate than that some person, with faculties so peculiarly adapted to the purpose as Mr. Spencer should have taken up the explanation of Nature on the new principles synthetically, setting out from them as true, & working out in detail what sort of an explanation they are capable of affording of the complicated world in which we live. Until this attempt was made, the theories in question, considered as universal laws of nature, could be neither verified nor disproved. And arduous as the attempt is, no one who studies these works of Mr. Spencer is likely to deny that it has been made by a mind equal to it, & that it will mark a step in the progress of thought.[57]

Spencer was the great synthesizer, precisely because he brought Mill's own beliefs about human nature into focus. In a letter to Spencer, Mill warmly compliments him on the primacy of biology and psychology in his work.[58] Any familiarity with Spencer's work during this period, especially *Social Statics* and the later *First Principles,* will demonstrate the reliance of Spencer on theories of degeneracy.[59] The point of our argument is that Mill not only read Darwin through Spencer, but understood most of what he grasped about the interrelationship between biology and human nature through Spencer's works.

Because Mill was not as interested in natural phenomena as Engels, only a few works directly allude to degeneracy theory. The most detailed examination is found in his *A System of Logic,* especially in his remarks on political ethology. Mill's fascination with this subject often puzzles scholars. However, it makes excellent sense within the context of Spencer's impact and the dominance of degeneracy theory.

Mill believed that no ethological science could be absolutely precise. He did believe that certain aspects of the human character could be measured consistently. He even suggested scientific methods through which such an ethological sketch could be developed. Such a sketch of human characteristics could detail mental characteristics of certain "races": English, Italian, and French. Each of several characteristics of men could be used to develop a political ethology from which broad generalizations could be made.[60]

Mill believed that all historical events are really dependent upon psychological and ethological laws. He criticized Vico's work[61] for not recognizing these underlying laws and emphasizing a "trajectory" of progress. Rather, Mill emphasized that progress is not "to be understood as synonymous with improvement and tendency to improvement. It is conceivable that the laws of human nature might determine, and even necessitate, a certain series of changes in man and society, which might not in every case . . . be improvements."[62] These degenerate aspects would haunt Mill and apparently would be one cause for his rejection of democracy.

Mill did not believe his "ethology" would, or should, be perfectly empirical. He defended his position in a series of correspondence with positivist Auguste Comte. Comte believed that a sophisticated phrenology would make it possible to "perfectly" measure each individual's character. On the other hand Mill emphasized the development of ethology as an intermediary between biology and sociology. Ethology would determine "the sort of character produced, conformable to the general laws of the character, by the entire and interrelated force of physical and moral circumstances on the individual."[63] This branch of study presupposed general charcteristics, not only of individuals but of entire nations. If these nations were to maintain their freedom they must guarantee it by appreciating the great character that brought them to their peak and the degenerative aspects that could destroy civilization. This view was profoundly influential in Mill's political philosophy.

Certainly Mill was a civil libertarian, but was he a democrat? I believe that the answer is no, and my reason is linked to the dominance of nineteenth-century degeneracy theory. J. H. Burns argues that Mill "was never able to assent without reservations to the straightforward democratic principle of majority rule . . . because he remained convinced that men were not in fact equally endowed with the qualities which make for sound political judgment."[64] In order to circumvent the majority Mill advocated a number of governmental devices for dampening the effect of democratic rule.

First, he proposed a professionally trained civil service, made up of the "best and the brightest" individuals in society. These men and women would be apart from the political fray and allowed to ignore the majority will in pursuing a greater good. Second, he advanced the notion of "personal representation," or "a single-transferable vote," that would allow an elite to govern through a multitiered quota system.[65] Mill believed that such a system also strengthened minorities, whose favored candidate might lose in the election. In effect, such a system protects—Mill recognized this—the interests of the propertied and the educated. Mill also suggested second chambers, rejection of voting by ballot, and the establishment of an expert legislative commission.

However, the most controversial proposal by Mill was his scheme for plural voting which involved totally disenfranchising some groups in society and giving several votes to others, all under the guise of the principle of competence. This latter principle was technically based on intelligence and experience. However the groups to be disenfranchised, those who could not read, write, or do simple arithmetic, who paid no taxes, or who received any form of welfare, did not obviously fit under the rule of competence.[66] Mill's justification was that these groups do not take even a minimal interest in taking care of themselves, let alone an interest in the general welfare. Mill had great difficulty in deciding upon the criteria for extra votes, other than gradations of intelligence. He recognized that even this would be highly speculative, but in the best spirit of contemporary meritocracy,[67] Mill believed that it would enshrine the principle of competence in the constitution of the people.

This antidemocratic tendency is closely tied to Mill's theories on "historical deterioration." Mill believed that there is a constant threat of deterioration in any society, and, therefore, any changes in society must occur gradually. The threat of majoritarianism was that such a government constantly kept society at the edge of the abyss of deterioration. Without an elite to direct "the wise and noble" things, no society can survive. "The honor and glory of the average man is that he is capable of following that initiative; that he can respond internally to wise and noble things, and be led to them with his eyes open."[68] This is not an advocacy of dictatorship, but rather a glorification of the "natural" elite in a liberal society. Societies willing to take advantage of the "genius" in their midst are most likely to avoid historical deterioration.

For Mill historical deterioration takes on the same characteristics as degeneracy. Clinical deterioration once begun cannot be reversed. It is carried from generation to generation and manifests itself either through tyranny or radical democracy. The only dam to this natural flood is the elite of society who carry with them both a moral and intellectual superiority:

> We ought not to forget, that there is an incessant and ever-flowing current of human affairs towards the worse, consisting of all the follies, all the vice, all the negligence, indolence, and supinenesses of mankind; which is only controlled, and kept from sweeping all before it, by the exertions which some persons constantly, and other by fits, put forth in the direction of good and worthy objects. . . . A very small diminution of those exertions would not only put a stop to improvement, but would turn the general tendency of things towards deterioration; which, once begun, would proceed with increasing rapidity, and become more and more difficult to check, until it reached a state often

seen in history, and in which many large portions of mankind even now grovel.[69]

Deterioration is a direct outcome of the political ethology of various nations. The character of those nations inevitably leads them more readily, or more hesitantly, to accept the tide of deterioration.

Mill often reflects a subtle racism in looking for cases of decline. In a letter to Gustave D'Eichthal[70] Mill agrees with D'Eichthal's suggestion for greater contact between the white and black races. They are exactly opposite in character to Europeans "in their love of repose and in the superior capacity of animal enjoyment and consequently of sympathetic sensibility, which is characteristic of the negro race." The racial stereotyping reflects much of Spencer's early work, but also demonstrates the interrelations between Mill's view of deterioration and the study of political ethology. He uses these offhandedly to justify a colonialism of Southern Europe.[71]

Mill reflects the historical biases of his age. He distrusts the masses of people because they tend to degenerate society. He also views certain peoples as incapable of contributing to the intellectual and material value of culture. Finally, he believes in a general tendency toward deterioration of all nations which is almost impossible to stop. Dennis Thompson notes that through a "distinctly Manichean synthesis" Mill combines the classical theme of degeneration with the theme of improvement through human effort. It is perhaps an unstable mixture, but it hardly justifies ascribing a high degree of optimism to Mill.[72] I believe that Thompson is correct in attributing a degenerative aspect to Mill's theory of history. However, it is far from a classical theory of degeneracy. Rather, it fits into the rise of degeneracy theory in the nineteenth century. Mill acknowledged the influence of Spencer and the preeminence of Darwinian biology in his own intellectual development. It is not surprising to find these dominant scientific ideas reflected in his political thought.

In summary Mill, like Engels, adapted degeneracy theory to his own political ends. Although not explicit, he wove degeneracy into much of his political theory. His theory of historical deterioration is too close to degeneracy, in both content and structure, to ignore the parallels. Mill found Spencer's work comfortable, precisely because it allowed him to justify elitism within a pragmatic democratic structure. This was the only "practical" means of democratic government, even though Mill recognized that it could not be morally justified. Like many others in the past one hundred and fifty years, Mill fell back on scientific justification to buttress morally unpalatable beliefs. The science of his day presupposed degeneracy. John Stuart Mill was a nineteenth-century man, with the same beliefs, attitudes, and prejudices as his peers. Given the dominance of degeneracy theory, it should not be surprising to find even the father of modern liberalism swayed by this powerful generative metaphor.

Walter Bagehot: The Prosperous Victorian

Walter Bagehot is usually categorized as a social Darwinist. In 1922, sociologist Harry Barnes placed Bagehot among the English circle of brilliant minds of the nineteenth-century "including among others Acton, Buckle, Darwin, Gladstone, T. H. Green, Huxley, Maine, Maitland, Mill, Ruskin, Spencer, Tyler and Wallace. Perhaps he [Bagehot] possessed a higher degree of genius than any of the others of that company."[73] He has been variously described as an essayist, literary critic, and political analyst. Bagehot was a graduate of the University of London and spent his life as a small-town banker and the editor of the famous financial magazine the London *Economist*. He was the author of a number of books that had an enormous influence on the intellectual life of his contemporaries.

Bagehot is included here for several reasons. First, his theories reflect the main currents of degeneracy theory. Second, Bagehot was not only one of the greatest intellectual "stars" in Victorian England, but is often credited with influencing the beginning of the eugenics movement in England. Last, he had a profound influence on the origins of political science as an academic discipline in the late nineteenth century. His *The English Constitution,* is still studied as one of the classic works on British government by political scientists over a century after its publication. And his emphasis on the use of biological frameworks and positivism for the study of politics was apparently an inspiration to one of the most important empirical political scientists of today, David Easton.

Although Bagehot's name is little known in contemporary political science, many of his ideas retain their currency; many stem from nineteenth-century notions of degeneracy and his ties to the intellectual currents of the medical community of his day.

Woodrow Wilson, one of the founders of American political science and later to be President of the United States, idolized Bagehot in two essays in the *Atlantic Monthly.* Wilson suggested using Tocqueville and Bagehot as models for political research. Not only was his political analysis considered important, but it was the classic example of the historical approach to politics: "Occasionally, a man is born into the world whose mission it evidently is to clarify the thought of his generation, and to vivify it, to give it speed where it is slow, vision where it is blind, balance where it is out of poise . . . such a man was Walter Bagehot.[74] Wilson hailed Bagehot for his originality in the study of politics and his ability to integrate racial theories within political analysis. It was Bagehot who argued that the study of "race origins" and political development had to be combined to understand the progress of man.[75]

More recently David Easton has extolled Bagehot's commitment to Comtean positivism. Although he disclaims the conservative conclusions of Bagehot, Easton believes that Bagehot "was one of the first liberals to recognize the contribution" of "positivism, in the broadest sense of scientific method."[76] Through positivism Bagehot founded *elitist* theory (later elaborated by Pareto and Mosca), which Easton characterizes as "liberal realism." Elitists believe that "true democracy" can only function within a governmental structure that allows a small group to govern. Bagehot's "fear of the results of popular suffrage inspired him to inquire into the nature of this liberal value and to use psychology and biology as the scientific instruments of his analysis."[77] The use of positivism and biology was viewed as a crucial methodological insight by Easton. Easton's fame, not suprisingly, comes from his own combination of a biological approach, systems theory, and positivism. I am not suggesting that Easton's work mirrors the writings of Bagehot, but rather that Bagehot's influence continues even today.[78]

Bagehot was himself influenced by his intellectual foundations. His primary mentor was James C. Prichard. Prichard was Bagehot's uncle and one of the most important British physicians and ethnologists of his day. He was a prolific author, and much of his research appears to stem either from Morel's degeneracy theories, or to anticipate them. For example, in his two-volume work *Researches as to the Physical History of Man* (Edinburgh, 1826), Prichard argued that the white race was not the original race of the Old Testament.[79] Rather, all of man's descendants were black, and as civilization advanced people became more and more white. He sees the Italians as being more "swarthy," because with the decline of the Roman Empire they were "degenerating from civilization." He also believed that the decline of civilization led to severe diseases of the brain. This led to the destruction of races because of their natural degenerate tendencies.[80] The study of diseases of the brain was Prichard's medical specialty and he was a primary advocate of "leeching" for curing headaches. In his later life he was appointed Commissioner of Lunacy for the City of London, a post he held until he died in 1848. Many of Bagehot's biographers, including Woodrow Wilson, credit Prichard with Bagehot's fascination with race.

Walter Bagehot's most profound contribution to social Darwinism and degeneracy theory is his *Physics and Politics*. In modern terminology, the title is clearly a misrepresentation of the content of the book. Its primary focus is on the application of natural selection and inheritance to the understanding of political society. For Bagehot there was a clear link between physics and biology, and ultimately politics. Physics was the model of scientific inquiry which, as Easton pointed out, takes on a positivistic character.

Using the anthropological and biological evidence available to him, Bagehot concluded that there are three periods in the evolution of political community: custom-making age, nation-making age, and the age of discussion. In the custom-making age imitation of mores leads to initial cohesion and stability. He designates this the "cake of custom."[81] During such a period national standards and characteristics guide conduct along uniform lines of activity. This period does not distinguish between crime and sin. Even such a simple form of government is considered the first element of human progress. During the nation-making or state-making stage there is a struggle for existence among groups with different "cakes of custom." and an elimination of groups with less effective customary procedures. War is the dominant feature of such a period, and the sophistication of military equipment is the "most conspicuous fact in human history." The age of discussion is the culminating period which destroys mythology and secularizes the world. Discussion means free and open discussion by the elite, who put a premium on intelligence and "animated moderation." "By animated moderation Bagehot means that rare combination of a mental constitution or a cultural condition which is receptive to suggestions of change with one which is sufficiently reflective to avoid impulsive and reckless approval of innovations."[82]

Societies survive because they are willing to succumb to discipline. Discipline is what makes even the most wild of men tame. Bagehot believed, much like Hobbes, that man in any natural state was wild and evil. Even the most merciless, tyrannical state is better than no state at all, and through a natural selection of such states progress is achieved. Once "polities are begun," writes Bagehot, there is no difficulty in explaining why they lasted. Whatever may be "said against the principle of 'natural selection' in other departments, there is no doubt of its predominance in early human history. The strongest killed out the weakest, as they could."[83] Primitiveness, which he equated with many of the "rights" doctrines of liberalism, might be poetic and romantic but totally unrealistic.

Bagehot believed that liberalism was based upon a false belief in an innate human reason. Human beliefs and actions result from imitation, which is the most fundamental part of human nature. He believed that Spencer was wrong to emphasize rational self-interest. Men simply render blind obedience to the institutions and myths handed down by their ancestors.[84] Such a reverence for these "superstitions" allows nations to grow in a stable fashion. The most stable nations are termed "deferential communities." These are nations where "the numerous unwiser part wishes to be ruled by the less numerous wiser part."[85]

England is an ideal deferential democracy because the English were too stupid to take advantage of their freedom. Democracy worked well in Britain, but only because the masses of England were submissive to their social and economic betters. The business of life is dull and it requires dull men to live it well. Irritable, far-seeing originality leads to vice in business and government.[86] Thus the dull Englishman who is not enamored with the lure of the intellect is the ideal political subject.

The Americans and the French were not as intimidated by law, so they lived in far less stable societies. "The trouble with the French is that they are not stupid enough to govern themselves. They are an impatient peo-

ple, interested in ideas, devoted to the fascinating possibilities of tomor-
row instead of the routine obligations of today."[87] Americans were
victimized by an erroneous imitation of the English constitution which
emphasized the separation of powers. Bagehot believed that American
government was unwieldly because it artificially separated administrators
and legislators. In addition it discouraged the natural selection of able
men for political leadership and made it impossible to develop responsible
public opinion. For Bagehot government by elite, in the interests of the
masses, was the only responsible way to have a democratic polity.

Thus far there is little to distinguish Bagehot from other social Darwi-
nists, except for his interesting twists on the natural selection of governments. However, in *Physics and Politics* he went beyond social Darwinism
and developed a series of corollaries from degeneracy theory and applied
them to the political environment. These corollaries capture the essence
of his mentor's (Prichard) work and allow the contemporary reader an
encapsulated example of the impact of nineteenth-century clinical medicine on political thought.

Bagehot began with the social Darwinist presupposition that not only
do the strong destroy the weak, but they always do so for the greater good
of humanity. These successful groups dominated through custom and the
demand for absolute uniformity. Persecution of "alien" groups naturally
develops from this. Initially, prejudice and persecution were necessary to
prevent developing disloyalty in the society. Ultimately, persecution was
its own natural selection, bringing both material and moral progress.[88]
Because of this process societies develop beneficial "characters" which in
turn create two historical forces: "Once the race-making force which,
whatever it was, acted in antiquity, and has now wholly, or almost, given
over acting; and the other the nation-making force, properly so called,
which is now acting as much as it ever created."[89] The races and character
of men are molded through the governmental process under which they
develop.

One alternative to war might be miscegenation of races. However, there
is no guarantee that such unions might succeed. First, in "Jamaica and
Java the mulatto cannot reproduce itself after the third generation." Second, there are both successes and failures so that the result cannot be
relied upon. In cases where a race develops and its *character* is better
suited to its place and time, it will dominate its parents and supplant both.
When a mixed race is not as good it will degenerate, and "passes away soon
and of itself."[90]

Bagehot criticizes Galton for not realizing that natural selection among
nations was precisely the kind of process that Galton's eugenics advocated.
Societies create the character of their people through natural selection.
Unsuccessful nations are destroyed or absorbed and successful countries

internalize natural selection. "Nature disheartened in each generation the ill-fitted members of each customary group, so deprived them of their full vigour, or, if they were weakly, killed them.[91] Social problems are a natural, clinical part of this process. For this reason he vehemently criticizes "radicals" like Charles Dickens who excite the masses " to discontent and repining." Dickens merely creates instability of society without ever explaining how social evils are to be removed.[92]

Bagehot fears instability. He likens stable societies to cones balanced on their points and believes the slightest "breeze" will topple them. What civilization hides is the barbarous nature of all men and societies which are masked by our most sacred customs. When these myths are attacked they are capable of unleashing horrible forces and of *degenerating* civilizations back to the most primitive of societies.[93] Bagehot believed that the experiences of the French in the first half of the nineteenth century gave empirical validity to this claim that all civilizations can degenerate.

Much like Hobbes, Bagehot believed that Leviathan was far preferable to the sleeping Behemoth. In his *Letters on the Coup d'État* in 1851 he used this as a justification for the dictatorship of Napoleon III. He fully defended Napoleon's actions, "stoutly supporting the use of military violence, attacking the freedom of the press and maintaining that France was wholly unfit for parliamentary government."[94] France had degenerated from a society that could afford a "government by discussion" to the natural stage of a military dictatorship.

The lesson of the French is that no society is exempt from deterioration. All nations exist at the precipice. Human nature will progress, but only if the masses of people are taught to be submissive and compliant. "If human nature was to be gradually improved, each generation must be born better tamed, more calm, more capable of civilization—in a word, more *legal* than the one before it. . . . Though a few gifted people may advance much, the mass of each generation can improve but very little on the generation which preceded it; and even the slight improvement so gained is liable to be destroyed by some mysterious atavism—some strange recurrence to a primitive past."[95] For Bagehot the essential lesson of history is that it is a clinical metaphor. Nations are not only forever involved in a process of natural selection, but are also prone to degeneration.

For Bagehot political development and all political processes were in a constant war with potential savagery. He succeeded in placing this Hobbesian analysis in a biological setting. But his synthesis combined the Spencerian thesis of natural selection with the commonplace of degeneracy. As David Easton sums up Bagehot's thought: "The progress or degeneration of Western nations had depended on the rise of a rational *elite* and the subordination of the masses, a relationship which had been assured by the laws of biology and psychology, the transmission of acquired imitation."[96] Walter Bagehot clearly saw that the malaise of degeneracy, which so victimized individuals, was also a disease of the polity; the cause of all great civilizations' fall toward barbarism.

Degeneracy and Nineteenth-Century Political Theory

Political theories are seldom the result of a single social artifact, nor do they ever develop in a vacuum. Degeneracy theory had a broad impact on the political philosophy of the nineteenth century, but it was by no means the *only* relevant concept. However, its impact is so broadly interwoven during this century that degeneracy sometimes appears pervasive. For example, William Graham Sumner directly embraced degeneracy. He ridiculed those who argue that Western societies "civilize lower races." Rather, they degenerate to the point that they disappear. The choice is liberty, inequality, survival of the fittest—or degeneracy. Degeneracy was the vital image, along with the survival of the fittest, in the American age of industrialism. They were the dominant themes in the writings of Andrew Carnegie and John D. Rockefeller.[97]

Racism was also a theory that built directly upon degeneracy theory, perhaps more closely than any other during the nineteenth century. Its primary advocates were Hippolyte Taine, Houston Stewart Chamberlain, and Arthur de Gobineau. All of these writers used degeneracy to explain the impact of impure races on nations. However, Gobineau's *The Inequality of the Human Races* uses it as the dominant theoretical perspective.

> Societies perish because they are degenerate, and for no other reason. This is the evil condition that makes them wholly unable to withstand the shock of the disasters that close in upon them; and when they can no longer endure the blows of adverse fortune . . . then we have the sublime spectacle of a nation in agony. . . .
>
> The word *degenerate*, when applied to a people, means (as it ought to mean) that the people has no longer the same intrinsic value as it had before, because it has no longer the same blood in its veins, continual adulterations having gradually affected the quality of that blood.[98]

Racism and its offspring, Fascism and Nazism, would carry degeneracy theory into the twentieth century where its implications, and suggested cures, would have their most nightmarish impact.

Another area where degeneracy theory had an obvious influence was upon the burgeoning social sciences in the late nineteenth century. Although these are treated elsewhere in this volume, we should note that degeneracy in sociology, psychology, and anthropology had a profound impact on both the political thought and politics of the period. Ludwig Gumplowicz and Karl Pearson led the way in sociology, while William McDougall, Lewis Terman, Robert Yerkes, and Henry Goddard added the eugenic bent to psychology.[99] This social scientific analysis was buttressed by a spate of such popularizers as Lothrop Stoddard. Stoddard's *The Rising Tide of Color* and *The Revolt Against Civilization* were extremely popular in the early twentieth century.[100]

In a less direct manner degeneracy theory found its way into the political philosophy of pragmatism and early existentialism. For instance, John Dewey's remarkable essay *The Influence of Darwin on Philosophy* reconstructs degeneracy theory so that it supports the ideology of the welfare state, rather than laissez-faire. But Dewey's method of analysis comes very close to justifying permanent inferiority for degenerates because of deference to the demands of the current community in devising pragmatic ethics. Lee C. MacDonald appears to be correct when he argues that Dewey comes close to a "frightfully reactionary position."[101] Friedrich Nietzsche also deals indirectly with degeneracy theory. His vision of *Übermensch* towering over the commonness of modern civilization is a clear enough allusion. Yet Nietzsche's purpose was to overcome Darwin and the racists who "think they inquire, without being already in possession of a standard of values.[102] The tragedy of his aphorisms is that they only overcome "ethics" through an analysis of how values degenerate in society. For Nietzsche this act occurs existentially and politically as civilization reaches decadence and the *Übermensch* rises out of its ashes like a phoenix.

Degeneracy was pervasive throughout most of the political thought of the nineteenth century. Perhaps it was so little noticed by historians because it was so ubiquitous. This broad acceptance gave testimony to the power which coincided with the rise of clinical medicine and the legitimacy of science in the nineteenth century. The creation of a powerful generative metaphor so widely accepted that it "melts" into the background of most of the political theory of an age is no small feat. It is perhaps suggestive of our own innocence when dealing with the "facts" of science and medicine.

The Impact of Political Philosophy and Degeneracy

It would be a mistake to leave the impression that degeneracy was an innocent tangent in the ultimate advancement of science. Rather, it must be seen as an ideological belief from which incredibly persuasive conclusions about the human condition can be drawn. Degeneracy also has a history. It has been used as an excuse for mass murder, prejudice, and every other sort of villainy.

In the United States it has affected not only the political ideas of the nation but its political actions as well. Degeneracy is closely tied with the racism of the last century and most of this century. Supreme Court cases including the Civil Rights cases and *Plessy v. Fergusen* often reasoned from principles of degeneracy, or cited "contemporary" medical and anthropological research to justify discrimination. The infamous Tuskegee experiments, where blacks were injected with syphilis by physicians and allowed to "become terminal," grew out of a belief that the American black was so morally degenerate that the disease would soon be contracted anyhow.[103]

Degeneracy theory was used to victimize the poor as well as the black. Justice Holmes in his dissent in *Lochner vs. New York* argued that the case made it appear that the "14th Amendment" enacted "Herbert Spencer's *Social Statics.*" In addition, so-called criminal families were institutionalized in insane asylums and prisons, and were persecuted by local authorities and religious zealots, all on the grounds of degeneracy. As the case of *Buck v. Bell*[104] so graphically illustrates, degeneracy beliefs can very easily lead to public policy solutions. In 1927 it was sterilization. Tens of thousands of the insane—many whose only disease was being poor—were castrated or sterilized with the blessing of both the state and federal governments. (The court's argument in *Buck vs. Bell* appeared to be beneficent: Sterilization made "these unfortunates more equal" because they could now leave the asylum!)

Degeneracy theory became a vital part of the eugenics movement and ultimately became part of national policy. The Johnson Immigration Act of 1924, in force until 1964, resulted from eugenics work by Terman, Yerkes, and Goddard who used the "new" Binet I.Q. test. Rather than using the test to detect what it was designed for, learning problems, it was crafted to separate the degenerate classes who were destroying American democracy. As Calvin Coolidge wrote as Vice President in 1922, "the laws of biology had demonstrated that Nordic peoples deteriorate when mixing with other races."[105] The Johnson Act effectively eliminated the immigration of Eastern Europeans. Between 1935 and 1945 hundreds of thousands of Eastern European Jews were denied entry permits, leading most of them to death in the concentration camps.[106]

Most studies of political theory in the nineteenth century emphasize the major philosophical schools and their impact on one another. They sometimes even suggest that Darwinism had an impact. However, few studies have ever attempted to re-create the major intellectual metaphors of the nineteenth century. This essay has demonstrated the broad impact of clinical science on political thought. More specifically it has demonstrated the pervasiveness of degeneracy theory in nineteenth-century thinking, and the power of such concepts when they become dominant generative metaphors. These perspectives are still with us today. They are found in George Gilder's currently popular *Wealth and Poverty* (New York: Basic Books, 1981) and in the order of Judge E. Albert Morrison in Tacoma, Washington, in June 1982 to castrate a child molester. The latter order was based on a 1909 law which empowered law enforcement officials to sterilize degenerate persons.[107]

Conclusion

Engels, Mill, and Bagehot absorbed degeneracy theory as a metaphor and applied it to their various philosophies. What is important is not the common source of these adaptations, but the general dissimilarities in the thrust, direction, and purpose of their political philosophies. My point in this essay is to demonstrate the ubiquitous nature of degeneracy theory in nineteenth-century political theory, and therefore its character as a generative metaphor. What is so fascinating about this dominant medical metaphor is that the majority of great minds of the nineteenth century concentrated on adapting degeneracy to their own theoretical view rather than challenging it. Degeneracy was dominant precisely because it was so seldom questioned. It was also flexible enough to fit into most of the prevalent theoretical approaches during this era. Where it would not fit precisely, it was modified to eliminate its most negative attributes.

The three thinkers treated here tended to unobtrusively weave the thread of degeneracy through their own political visions. For Engels it made "sense" of Hegel's dialectic, for Mill it provided a reason for protecting degeneracy from the majority, and for Bagehot degeneracy explained the advance of civilization. In all three cases degeneracy was not used literally as it was in the clinical circles of the time. Rather, as a generative metaphor it could be used to describe a sense of process that seems imperative in much of modern political theory. It was an image that grasped in a limited way how forces in society worked.

This essay's purpose was to view the impact of degeneracy on the thought of Engels, Mill, and Bagehot. Generative metaphors like degeneracy are important precisely because political theory is not written in a vacuum. Engels, Mill, and Bagehot, as timeless as some of their work is, are nineteenth-century men. It can only add to our understanding of their writings if we appreciate the elements of their context. As an element, degeneracy provides that engine of process in these theories which Hannah Arendt sees as unique in contemporary political theory:

> The modern concept of progress pervading history and nature alike separates the modern age from the past more profoundly than any other single idea. To our modern way of thinking nothing is meaningful in and by itself, not even history or nature taken each as a whole, and certainly not particular occurrences in the physical order or specific historical events. There is a fateful enormity in this state of affairs. Invisible processes engulf every tangible thing.[108]

NOTES

1. See Michael Weinstein, *Systematic Political Theory* (Columbus, Ohio: Charles E. Merrill, 1971).

2. Henry Adams, *The Education of Henry Adams* (Boston: Houghton Mifflin, 1961), ch. 25.

3. Morel, *Traité des dégénérescences physiques, intellectuelles et morales de l'espèce humaine* (Paris: Ballière, 1857). However, the notion of degeneracy is much older and richer. "Language, Medicine, and Politics: The 19th Century Impact of Medicine and Politics," presented at the International Conference for the Study of Language and Public Policy, Cancun, Mexico, December, 1981.

4. See Dan Nimmo and Christopher Combs, *Subliminal Politics* (Englewood Cliffs, N.J.: Prentice-Hall, 1981), pp. 64–68.

5. Donald Schön, "Generative Metaphor: A Perspective on Problem-Setting in Social Policy," in Andrew Ortony, ed., *Metaphor and Thought* (Cambridge: Cambridge University Press, 1979), p. 255.

6. Stuart Gilman, "Language, Medicine and Politics."

7. Eric Partridge, *Origins* (New York: Macmillan, 1963), p. 250.

8. Edward Long, *A History of Jamaica*, (rpt., London: Frank Cass, 1970), vol. 2, book 3, p. 353.

9. Michael Banton and Jonathan Harwood, *The Race Concept* (New York: Praeger, 1975), ch. 2. See also Elsa V. Goveia, *A Study of the Historiography of the British West Indies to the End of the Nineteenth Century* (Mexico: Instituto Panamericano de Geografia e Historia, 1956).

10. John Locke, *The Second Treatise on Government*, book 2, ch. 4, para. 23.

11. Stuart C. Gilman, "A Biology of Equality," presented at the Southern Political Science Association Meeting, Atlanta, Georgia, November, 1980.

12. Marvin Harris, *The Rise of Anthropological Theory* (Ithaca, N.Y.: Cornell University Press, 1968), pp. 86–87.

13. Michel Foucault, *The Birth of the Clinic* (New York: Vintage, 1975); see also L. S. King, *The Medical World of the 18th Century* (Chicago: University of Chicago Press, 1958); and David Riesman, *Medicine in Modern Society* (Princeton: Princeton University Press, 1938).

14. Charles Rosenberg, "The Bitter Fruit: Heredity, Disease, and Social Thought in Nineteenth Century America," *Perspectives in American History* (August 1974).

15. Rosenberg, p. 192.

16 See, e.g., Joesph E. Winters, "The Relative Influences of Maternal and Wet Nursing on Mother and Child," *Medical Record* (1896).

17. Constitutional "types" were dominant in the medical literature throughout the eighteenth century. The biological and clinical developments of the nineteenth century did little to change this theory. Rather, constitutionalism was adapted to fit the more scientific theory (and terminology) of the age, and empirical evidence was gathered to support it.

18. See George Lakoff and Mark Johnson, "Conceptual Metaphor in Everyday Language," *The Journal of Philosophy* (Spring 1980). Cf. Max Black, "More About Metaphors," in Anthony Ortony, ed., *Metaphor and Thought*.

19. The persuasiveness of "empirical" evidence, no matter its origin, has been and continues to be a problem in the social sciences. See Stanislaw Andrewski, *The Social Sciences as Sorcery* (New York: St. Martin's Press, 1972), p. 127.

20. For a detailed discussion of this debate, see Z. A. Jordan, *The Evolution of Dialectical Materialism* (New York: St. Martin's Press, 1967); Norman Levine, *The Tragic Deception: Marx Contra Engels* (Santa Barbara: CLIO Books, 1975); Louis Althusser, *For Marx* (New York: Vintage Books, 1969); Shlomo Avineri, ed., *Marx's Socialism* (New York: Lieber-Atherton, 1973).

21. See Lewis Feuer, "Marx and Engels as Sociobiologists," *Survey* (Autumn 1977–1978), 23(4).

22. Avineri, p. 17, n. 26.

23. Lawrence Krader, ed., *The Ethnological Notebooks of Karl Marx: Studies of Lewis Morgan, Phear, Maine, and Lubbock* (Atlantic Highlands, N.J.: Humanities Press, 1972).

24. Krader, p. 84.

25. One of the strangest is given by Eleanor Burke Leacock in her introduction to the *Origin of the Family . . .* (New York: International Publishers, 1972): "Engels sharpened the implications of the comparison Morgan drew between primitive communal and class society, using it as an argument for socialism. Therefore, both Morgan's and Engels' work have had checkered careers, and opinions about them have shifted as the political atmosphere has changed. . . . When more inquisitive students read some of Marx's and Engels' works, they commonly end up distorting the ideas they have gleaned therefrom, as they search for modes of discourse acceptable for the publications which are the means of successful entry into the academic brotherhood. Morgan's *Ancient Society* too is seldom read, and when mentioned in college classes is often distorted and rejected out-of-hand" (p. 15).

26. See Feuer, p. 120. However, several of Feuer's interpretations of Marx and Engels in this context appear strange. For example, when arguing that Marx was a converted Darwinian as early as 1860, Feuer explains Marx's subsequent, and bitter, critiques of Darwin by suggesting that he was "disquieted" by the Malthusian implication. In any case, his essay raises many more questions than it resolves.

27. See John C. Loehlin, Gardner Lindzey, J. N. Spuhler, *Race Differences in Intelligence* (San Francisco: W. H. Freeman, 1975).

28. Saul Padover, *The Letters of Karl Marx* (Englewood Cliffs, N.J.: Prentice-Hall, 1979), p. 215.

29. Engels to Marx, October 2, 1866, p. 220.

30. Georges Cuvier, *Discourse on the Revolutions of the Surface of the Globe* (Paris, 1826).

31. Padover, p. 220.

32. Karl Nikolaus Fraas, *Climate and the Vegetable World Throughout the Age: A History of Both* (Landshut, 1847); see Marx's letter to Engels of March 25, 1868, in Padover, pp. 247–48.

33. See Feuer, p. 127. In contrast, many discoveries in the contemporary synthetic theory of biology have adapted or adopted much of Lamarck's work. See S.

Gilman, R. Simon, S. Zegura, "Evolution, Ethics and Equality," in M. Darrough, R. Blank, and D. Green, eds., *Biological Differences and Social Equality* (Westport, Conn.: Greenwood Press, 1983).

34. E. Ray Lankester, *Degeneration: A Chapter in Darwinism* (London, 1888).

35. Feuer, p. 128.

36. Z. A. Jordan, *Evolution of Dialectical Materialism*.

37. F. Engels, *Herr Eugen Dühring's Revolution in Science* (Chicago: Charles Kern, 1935), pp. 20 and 21.

38. Engels, p. 29 and part 3, ch. 2.

39. Friedrich Engels, *Socialism: Utopian and Scientific* (New York: International, 1972), p. 49.

40. *The Origin* reflects the degenerative biases of the day for several reasons. The most notable is that it is a page by page rewriting of Lewis Henry Morgan's *Ancient Society*. Engels uses Morgan's work and rewrites conclusions so that they intersect Marxist theory. Engels, *The Origin of the Family, Private Property and the State* (New York: International, 1972).

41. Engels, *The Origin*, p. 256.

42. Engels, *The Origin*, p. 252.

43. Friedrich Engels, *Dialectics of Nature* (New York: International, 1971), p. 19.

44. Engels, *Dialectics of Nature*, p. 236. Engels was wrong in this accusation. "Survival of the fittest" was the invention of Herbert Spencer and Darwin was very reticent about applying it to natural selection. See Gilman, Simon, and Zegura for detailed treatment.

45. Engels, *Dialectics of Nature*, p. 236.

46. Engels, *Origins*, p. 21.

47. See C. L. Ten, "Mill and Liberty," *Journal of the History of Ideas* (January–March 1969), 30:47–68.

48. Dante Germino, *Modern Western Political Thought* (Chicago: Rand McNally, 1972), p. 240.

49. E.g., Shirley Robin Letwin, *The Pursuit of Certainty* (Cambridge: Cambridge University Press, 1965), pp. 301ff.

50. Germino, p. 241.

51. See Norman Kretzmann, "Desire as the Proof of Desirability," *Philosophical Quarterly,* (July 1958), 8(32):256–58.

52. See Richard Lichtman, "The Facade of Equality in Liberal Democratic Theory," *Inquiry* (1969), vol. 12.

53. Graeme Duncan and John Gray, "The Left against Mill," in *New Essays on John Stuart Mill and Utilitarianism*, Wesley E. Cooper, Kai Neilsen, and Steven C. Patten, eds. (Guelph, Ontario: Canadian Association for Publishing in Philosophy, 1979), pp. 203–29.

54. F. E. Mineka and D. N. Lindley, *The Later Letters of John Stuart Mill, 1849–1873* (Toronto: University of Toronto Press, 1972), pp. 1553–54 in a letter to H. C. Watson, January 30, 1869.

55. Mineka and Lindley, p. 1,570. My italics.

56. See J. C. Greene, *The Death of Adam* (Ames: Iowa State University Press, 1959), or T. A. Goudge, *Ascent of Life: A Philosophical Study of the Theory of Evolution* (Toronto: University of Toronto Press, 1961).

57. Mineka and Lindley, p. 1,570.

58. Mineka and Lindley, p. 1,555; a letter to Herbert Spencer dated February 3, 1869.

59. For a discussion of Spencer's contributions see Stanislav Andreski, *Herbert Spencer: Structure, Function and Evolution* (New York: Scribner's, 1971), pp. 7–32.

60. John Stuart Mill, *A System of Logic* in *The Collected Works of John Stuart Mill,* J. M. Robson, ed. (Toronto: University of Toronto Press, 1974), p. 874–75, 904–10.

61. Giovanni Battista Vico, *Principi di una scienza nuova* (Naples: Mosca, 1725).

62. Mill, *A System of Logic,* p. 913.

63. Iris Wessel Mueller, *Mill and French Thought* (Freeport, N.Y.: Books for Libraries Press, 1968), p. 108. For an indepth insight see Mill's letter to Comte dated January 28, 1843) in Francis E. Mineka, *The Earlier Letters of John Stuart Mill, 1812–1848* (Toronto: University of Toronto Press, 1963), pp. 556–58.

64. "Utilitarianism and Democracy" in Samuel Gorovitz, ed., *Utilitarianism: John Stuart Mill with Critical Essays* (Indianapolis: Bobbs-Merrill, 1971), pp. 269–72.

65. See Paul B. Kern, "Universal Suffrage without Democracy: Thomas Hare and J. S. Mill," *Review of Politics* (July 1972), vol. 34.

66. See Dennis Thompson, *John Stuart Mill and Representative Government* (Princeton: Princeton University Press, 1976), pp. 98–101.

67. See Stuart C. Gilman, "The Problem of Seeing Equality: Herbert Spencer and the Meritocratic Position," in Masako Darrough and Robert Blank, eds., *Biological Differences and Social Equality* (Westport, Conn.: Greenwood Press, 1983).

68. John Stuart Mill, *On Liberty* (New York: Bobbs-Merrill, 1956), p. 81.

69. John Stuart Mill, *Representative Government,* quoted in Thompson, p. 149.

70. See D'Eichthal's *Lettres sur la race noire et la race blanche* (Paris, 1839).

71. Mineka, *The Earlier Letters of John Stuart Mill,* p. 404.

72. *Thompson,* pp. 149–50.

73. Harry Barnes, "Walter Bagehot and the Psychological Interpretation of Political Evolution," *American Journal of Sociology* (March 1922), 27:573.

74. Woodrow Wilson, "A Literary Politician," *Atlantic Monthly* (November 1895), 76 (457):670. See also Woodrow Wilson, "A Wit and a Seer," *Atlantic Monthly* (October 1898), 82:527–40.

75. Wilson, "A Literary Politician," p. 672.

76. David Easton, "Walter Bagehot and Liberal Realism," *American Political Science Review* (February 1949), 42:20.

77. *Easton,* p. 20.

78. Easton is one of the most lauded contemporary political scientists. He has written numerous works including *The Political System* (New York: Knopf, 1953), *A Framework for Political Analysis* (Englewood Cliffs, N.J.: Prentice-Hall, 1965), and *A Systems Analysis of Political Life* (New York: Wiley, 1965).

79. See Prichard's *Natural History of Man* (1885) and *Physical History of Man* (1813).

80. James C. Prichard, *On the Extinction of Some Varieties of the Human Race* (Birmingham, 1839).

81. Walter Bagehot, *Physics and Politics* (New York: Knopf, 1948), p. 29.

82. *Barnes,* p. 578.

83. Bagehot, *Physics and Politics*, p. 26.

84. See William M. McGovern, *From Luther to Hitler* (London: Harrap, 1946), pp. 464–65.

85. Norman St. John-Stevas, *Walter Bagehot* (London: Eyre and Spottiswoode, 1959), from *The English Constitution*, p. 385.

86. St. John-Stevas, p. 388.

87. Crane Brinton, *English Political Thought in the 19th Century* (New York: Harper, 1962), p. 183.

88. McGovern, p. 469.

89. Bagehot, *Physics and Politics*, p. 91.

90. Bagehot, *Physics and Politics*, pp. 72 and 73.

91. Bagehot, *Physics and Politics*, p. 151.

92. Bagehot, "Charles Dickens," in Norman St. John-Stevas, *The Collected Works of Walter Bagehot* (Cambridge: Harvard University Press, 1965), pp. 101–02.

93. Bagehot, *Physics and Politics*, p. 159.

94. McGovern, p. 472.

95. Bagehot, *Physics and Politics*, p. 225.

96. Easton, "Walter Bagehot," p. 31.

97. Richard Hofstadter, *Social Darwinism in American Thought* (Philadelphia: University of Pennsylvania Press, 1944), pp. 31–32.

98. Arthur de Gobineau, *The Inequality of the Human Races* (New York: Putnam, 1915), pp. 24–25.

99. For an indepth analysis see Allan Chase, *The Legacy of Malthus* (Urbana: University of Illinois Press, 1980). See also William Ryan, *Blaming the Victim* (New York: Vintage Books, 1976), esp. pp. 304–09.

100. See McGovern, pp. 487–90.

101. Lee C. MacDonald, *Western Political Theory* (New York: Harcourt, Brace and World, 1968), p. 560.

102. Friedrich Nietzsche, *The Will to Power* (New York: Vintage Books, 1968), p. 226.

103. James Jones, *Bad Blood* (New York: Free Press, 1981).

104. 274 U.S. 200 (1927). See Stephen Jay Gould, *The Mismeasurement of Man* (New York: Norton, 1981), p. 335.

105. Quoted in Richard Kluger, *Simple Justice* (New York: Vintage Books, 1975), p. 307.

106. Ryan, pp. 304–9.

107. *St. Louis Post-Dispatch*, June 3, 1982, p. 4a.

108. Hannah Arendt, *Between Past and Present* (New York: Viking, 1968), p. 63.

9

LITERATURE AND DEGENERATION: THE REPRESENTATION OF "DECADENCE"

SANDRA SIEGEL
Cornell University

It is questionable whether any single idea can be said to have dominated any age, as Mill thought "comparing" had dominated modernity.[1] Darwin's *Origin* (published within two decades of Mill's essay) demonstrated considerably greater scrutiny than simple acts of comparison. We can be certain, though, that during the second half of the century classification and comparison, kindred activities, increased. Kindred, but not identical: unlike the more detached act of classifying, the act of comparing, when exercised habitually, usually elicits judgments. By 1900, the Victorians had placed nearly every act, whether social or literary, on one or another side of a great divide. No matter was too small for scrutiny. They evaluated. They took positions. And no matter was too large. While the social scientists celebrated how far contemporary civilization had advanced, social and literary critics lamented how far civilization had declined. This would not have been strange—differences have always prevailed—if attentiveness to each other's views, frequently published in the same periodicals, had led them to controversy as most other issues did. But on this issue, where one would have expected vigorous debate, there was silence.

It is worth recalling Ruskin's remark of the 1860s that "progress and decline" were "strangely mixed in the modern mind."[2] That "mix" became stranger as the Victorians classified events according to their power to carry them forward or cast them backward in time. In the discussion that follows I want to take up two questions: how are we to account for the ease and satisfaction with which readers assimilated opposing assessments of the same facts? And how are we to account for silence where we would have expected bitter conflict? My purpose here is to illuminate the time itself by turning to certain arguments *about* progress and decline. Those arguments constitute events which, like other events that historians explain, are of interest because they need not have occurred. It will become clear in the course of considering how the Victorians presented their arguments that they might have presented them differently. (Let me say at once that a fuller discussion than space allows here would require comment on my method as well as my selection of representative examples.)

The writings of anthropologists, folklorists, and other antiquarians, the young James Frazer, Andrew Lang, Max Müller, for example, who contrasted modernity with antiquity, the urbane with the barbarous, were understandably self-congratulatory. Frazer's cartographies of primitive customs, beliefs, institutions, and behavior were sketched from the point of view of the superiority of the more advanced over the inferior, less advanced savage. He exalted his contemporaries. He flattered them. His vivid accounts provided readers with descriptions of what others, mostly social critics, characterized as decadent. The antiquarians' lurid accounts made available to the critics, whose muted interest in the past was equalled by their insatiable curiosity, ample imagery, abundant examples, and a powerful idiom for interpreting themselves and their contemporaries. In exchange they offered their antiquarian contemporaries animated descriptions of "decadence." They envisioned the possibility of becoming, by way of a backward movement in time, exactly like the savage—a condition that had long been likened to the natural condition of women and children. With that fear hovering over them, the social critics' descriptions intensified the anthropologists' desire to affirm progress, and, insofar as they did affirm that desire, subdued their worry that the condition of savagery might recur.

If the antiquarians took satisfaction in distinguishing "Us" from "Them," their need to preserve that difference increased as they acknowledged their fear. For as Frazer well knew, in spite of the persistence with which he affirmed how far civilization had traveled, civilization remained merely a fragile surface: savage survivals, ordinarily dormant, were a potential hazard. The social critics who were convinced that their time was "decadent" thought that they had erupted. The reciprocity the critics and antiquarians enjoyed drew them into a silent yet complicitous dependence from which both enclaves profited. To better understand their dependence as well as their silence we need to consider the unbounded optimism that characterized certain accounts of decadence—and the covert fear that prompted and sustained them.

The place of language in culture; the origin of religion; the significance of magic; the meaning of myth, ritual, and custom: on these subjects Victorian ethnographers were divided. Yet on two other issues—whether ethnography was a science, and whether it represented the newest evidence of progress—they were in agreement. Not all antiquarians who were influenced by Darwin actually read his work, but the young Frazer, whose first articles prefigured the copious volumes he produced over the next forty years, certainly did. All Frazerian anthropology recapitulated the general argument of *The Descent of Man:* animals evolve from lower (simple) to higher (complex) forms of life; humans evolve according to stages, from a position of moral and intellectual weakness to moral and intellectual strength; and, as part of the human species, women are superior to lower forms of life, but men are intellectually, physically, and morally superior to women. Two consequences followed: Anthropology presented itself as authoritative because it studied human institutions as a "science"; second, Frazer relied on the analogy of the development of the fetus in order to interpret social arrangements. The imaginative richness of his language, which constantly likened social institutions to something else— the fetus, for example—readily deferred conclusions. Such deferral, combined with his authoritative tone, helps to explain why Victorian anthropology is as hopeful—it was scientific—as it is fearful of failure. Ethnography's typically authoritative tone replaced definitive authoritative statements even as such statements were themselves necessarily cast in metaphor. One set of observations was presented, but only to be understood in terms of yet another about something different. As Darwin, throughout his writings, but especially in *The Descent of Man*, drew frequently on the analogy between the development of the fetus and the evolution from lower to higher forms of life, so Frazer extended the analogy to the domain of "social institutions." Darwin had argued that the human embryo repeats the history of the evolution of mankind: traces of previous stages survive.

The structural derivatives of Frazer's thought, the influence Darwin exerted, and the origins of Victorian ethnography are subjects of interest that have yet to be fully explored. Here, however, I want simply to point out that Frazer's argument delineated the boundaries that separate civilization from savagery by distinguishing between the primitive past and the present. At the same time, Frazer alerted his contemporaries to traces—I shall call them embryonic survivals—the existence of which were not only essential to anthropology, but made possible the study itself. Needful as traces were in order to see how far we had come, they were also a constant reminder of the "fragile surface" of civilization. Their exis-

tence threatened to dissolve the distinction between savagery and civilization, which made preserving the concept of difference all the more
important. Ethnography promised to preserve those boundaries. Survivals were visible, provided one looked at the human fetus closely, as
Darwin had. *The Expression of Emotions in Animals* extended consideration of survivals to the more ambiguous domain of gesture. Following
Darwin, Frazer found that rather than being lost, moments of the past, or
"stages" of the past, were preserved in social life even though the species
(or social life) advanced. Darwin had turned to embryology for evidence
of previous stages of development. Frazer applied this method to the
study of primitives. Each relied on the embryonic model, the one to map
the evolution of humans from lower forms of life, the other to map the
evolution of civilization from savagery. Social life passed through stages
similar to those through which the embryo passed. Frazer, who was fearful that evidence for charting the development of human cultures would
vanish, admonished anthropologists to study existing savages. Even if
survivals were lost—if existing savages were to perish before their customs
and characteristics were recorded—survivals exist in social life (social
equivalents of fetal survivals): "Embryology shows that the very process
of evolution, which we postulate for the past history of our race, is sum-
marily reproduced in the life history of every man and every woman who
is born into the world."[3] If the life history of every man and every woman
repeats the past history of the human race, then the child bears the same
relation to the savage as the adult does to civilization: savagery and civilization stand in opposition to each other as the child does to the adult.
The child, who represents an arrested stage of human development, provided a readily accessible embodiment of the vision of the savage in Victorian social science. Frazer described "Social Anthropology" as "the
embryology of human thought and institutions."[4] Where savages were
inaccessible one could turn to contemporary civilization: The savage past
persists in the present.

Readers of *The Descent of Man* will recall that Darwin evokes the quadrumana, a half-bestial, half-human creature, so frequently, why it oc-
cupies so special a place in his account of how man came into being invites
speculation. After his own laborious effort, Darwin must have been astonished by his vision of the mentally superior creature whose triumphant
emergence from the animal world represented the culmination of a long
process of evolution. Although the triumph of the quadrumana was no
different in kind from those of other superior species, it was of considerably greater significance and interest as the essential link in the unfolding
of events that led to the emergence of the fully human savage, the existing
savage, and, finally, civilized man. For Darwin the quadrumana represented the end of the line. At precisely that juncture, Frazer began his
inquiry. "Well handled," Frazer wrote, "the study of the evolution of

beliefs may become a powerful instrument to expedite progress if it lays bare certain weak spots in the foundations of which modern society is built. At present, we are only dragging the guns into position: they have hardly yet begun to speak."[5] There is more to be noticed here than Frazer's confident tone, or, even, the magnitude of the task he set for anthropology. Indeed, for Frazer the long-range effect of recovering the origin of civilization was the promise of expediting progress; but the immediate effect was to call attention to the differences that separate savagery from civilization.

Apart from the lurid pleasures of that empirical subject, really more speculative than empirical, the more fully the social scientists amplified the differences that separated "Them" from "Us," the more readily could they congratulate themselves on the progress of civilization: Modern western man was physically, mentally, and morally superior; his social arrangements and institutions were more complex; his religion and his science were more advanced. For Frazer and others the clearest sign that civilization had indeed approached the threshold of far-reaching advance was the development of the science of anthropology, the latest example of civilization. The immediate practical gain of an otherwise recondite subject was not negligible: turning to the savage was a means of reassuring contemporary culture of how far it had advanced. The further back in time one traveled, the further civilization could be said to have progressed.

"All *existing* savages," Frazer wrote, "are probably far indeed removed from the condition in which our remote ancestors were when they ceased to be bestial and began to be human."[6] Our contemporary habits of thought have diverged far enough from this typically Frazerian turn of mind that it may be a little difficult to recognize the implicit analogy that Frazer is drawing here. We may need to remind ourselves that because Frazer was simply applying Darwin's theory to social life he imagined an unrecognizably bestial, but equally unrecognizably human creature, whose successors were increasingly more advanced. Frazer admonished anthropologists not to confound the existing savage—"human documents"—as he called them, with his more remote ancestors.[7] The existing savage differed as greatly from his ancestor as he did from civilized man. Although Frazer did not delineate the differences sharply, he brought into clear focus a world inhabited successively by bestial creatures; half-bestial, half-human creatures; fully human savages; and, finally, by civilized man who represents the present threshold beyond which, armed with the new guns of anthropology, civilization might now advance further.

It is, perhaps, merely a striking coincidence, yet interesting nevertheless, that the two pairs of oppositions—human/beast and male/female—around which Darwin organized *The Descent of Man* are also played out, but to different purposes, by the later generation of social critics in their discourse about decadence. While the first third of Darwin's *The Descent of Man* takes up the question of the differences that separate humans from lower forms of life, and accounts for the superiority of man, the balance of the book takes up the question of the differences that separate male from female, and accounts for the superiority of men over women. Although these are distinct considerations, as it turns out, the same qualities Darwin ascribes to men (as opposed to women) are also those that separate man from beast. While woman was thought to be finely wrought by nature, the formation of her skull indicated her intermediate position between the child and man.[8] As the quadrumana gained supremacy over lower forms of life through the principle of natural selection, males gained supremacy over females through the principle of selection according to sex. Darwin not only explains the ways in which women are inferior to men; he also explains the origin of their inferiority. In the course of fighting for the possession of their women, men rivaled other men. Through the law of battle he became greater in strength and in intelligence. Those who were successful in possessing and keeping their women triumphed. Thus civilization evolved and continued to progress.

Darwin repeatedly reminds his readers that man's greater physical, mental, and moral strength is due to his inheritance from his half-human male ancestors. During the "long ages of man's savagery" these characters would have been preserved, or even augmented, "by the success of the strongest and boldest men, both in the general struggle for life and in their contests for wives; a success which would have insured their leaving a more numerous progeny than their less favored brethren." The characteristics of primeval male progenitors—physical strength, perseverance, courage, intellectual vigor, the power of invention, and determined energy—are precisely those qualities that continue to separate male from female.[9]

Not everyone who had opinions about Darwin read *The Descent of Man*, but echoes of Darwin are strong and clear in *The Golden Bough*. "Even where the system of mother-kin in regard to descent and property has prevailed most fully, the actual government has generally, if not invariably, remained in the hands of men. Exceptions have no doubt occurred; women have occasionally arisen who by sheer force of character have swayed for a time the destinies of their people. But such exceptions are rare and their effect transitory; they do not affect the truth of the general rule that human society has been governed in the past, and human nature remaining the same, is likely to be governed in the future, mainly by masculine force, and masculine intelligence." That force and intelligence, as Darwin plainly said, is responsible for civilization: Frazer's language and thought resemble Darwin's so closely his own voice is often indistinguishable: "In the struggle for existence progress depends mainly on competition: the more numerous the competitors the fiercer is the struggle, and the more rapid, consequently, is evolution."[10]

The Golden Bough, twelve volumes in all, is animated by the contrast Frazer draws between the "childlike mind of the savage and his childlike interpretation of the universe" and the "forward thrust of civilization toward religion and science."[11] Frazer substitutes the "child" for the savage more often and more vividly than he emphasizes the affinities savages and children share, ignores the differences that separate them, and uses the words "child" and "savages" interchangeably to evoke the same imaginative configuration. Whatever "They" are like, "We" are different.

By 1890, the denigrated condition of children provided familiar evidence for the analogy to function effectively. Frazer had no interest in the child as such, at least if one is to judge from his writings. In the context of his anthropological writings, however, the invocation of the child enabled him to describe the obscure, and necessarily imaginary, past of the savage as though the savage he was describing were familiar. To trace how far civilization had advanced, the figure of the child mediated access to the savage. One could, by contrast with the savage, see more clearly what was not valued within and by civilization. "We must constantly bear in mind that totemism is not a consistent philosophical system, a product of knowledge and high intelligence, rigorous in its definition and logical in its deductions from them. On the contrary it is a crude superstition, the offspring of undeveloped mind, indefinite, illogical, inconsistent." The savage, like the child, "is probably indeed much more impulsive, much more liable to be whirled about by gusts of emotion than we are."[12]

At the turn of the century discussions of primitive man were invariably conducted from a moral point of view. That difference was neither neutral, as might be the difference between chairs and tables or circles and squares, nor was it abstract. Each time it was invoked it was recharged with meaning: unless we kept "Them" in clear focus, "We" could not understand ourselves—and vice versa. But the same difference that separates "Them" from "Us" separates the adult from child; higher from lower, vigor from pallor, strength from weakness, courage from cowardice, patience from frivolity, perseverance from capriciousness, intellect from passion, reason from emotion, idea from instinct, and science from magic. Yet such pairings, which were understood as part of a hierarchical design, originated from a more inclusive difference that distinguished men from women. The reverse was true too: discussion about the difference (of "masculine" and "feminine") preserved the validity of those oppositions, each one of which was gender marked.

The later Victorians associated the idea of culture—civilization was an interchangeable term—with "masculine force and masculine intelligence."[13] The answers that were given to two questions—what kind of education, if any, was appropriate for women; and what women's role in political life should be—which were debated at length during the second half of the century—depended on certain presuppositions about the sexes: controversy intensified and positions became explicit as the traditional view of woman was reaffirmed more vigorously than ever before. It may seem that I am crediting Darwin with having exerted more influence than he properly deserves. While Darwinian science weakened biblical theology, which is well known, it strengthened the biblical view of the place of woman in the world.

In *The Descent of Man* Darwin produced evidence that supported the traditional view of the physical, mental, and moral superiority of male over female, evidence on which Frazer also relied to support his assumptions, assumptions that were so infused in the social thought of the tradition there was no need to address them unless one set out to challenge, or to meet the challenge, they posed. Rather than controvert or augment the traditional view, Darwin simply restated it and, in light of the evidence he gathered, proposed the principle of selection according to sex with fresh authority. To the degree that Darwin's thought confirmed the traditional view of gender, those who read or read about *The Descent of Man* may well have become less rather than more self-conscious about the presuppositions that justified the exclusion of women from cultural life. Although controversy over the natural equality of the sexes was vigorous by the 1980s, when cast in the metaphorical language of "separate spheres" or "woman's place," the issue inspired less controversy.

Arguments about "woman's place" had the effect of warning women— but men, too—about crossing conventional social boundaries. Women who trespassed ran the risk of becoming like men, while men ran the risk of becoming like women. Some social critics, particularly those who were fearful that such confusion was about to occur, attached the epithet "effeminate" to the time itself (and it has remained a salient figure in subsequent historiography). Although the idioms drew attention to "woman's place," there were comparable consequences for men. While the antiquarians set their sights on remote regions, yet confirmed the "masculinity" of their own civilization, others ranged over the local exotic. I will return to this subject shortly, after we observe the way the word "decadent" behaved in Victorian discussions about their own time, the fullest one of which was conducted by Max Nordau, German Hungarian physician and author. He argued, in a book that had the appearance of being scientific, that artists are insane and called them interchangeably "degenerated" or "Mattoids": persons of erratic mind, compound of genius and fool.

The first English translation of Nordau's *Degeneration* appeared in February 1895 and before the end of the year at least seven impressions had been printed. Nordau predicted that "after some centuries art and poetry will become pure atavisms and will no longer be cultivated except by the most emotional part of humanity—by women, by the mad, perhaps even by children." In his reply to *Degeneration*, George Bernard Shaw circumvented the issue of art and madness by singling out the excess that characterized *Degeneration*.[14] He did not accuse Nordau of all the phobias and manias he had identified as signs of decadence. But he did accuse him of graphomania. With characteristic shrewdness, Shaw pointed out that in his inveterable effort to name the disease Nordau had overreached his purpose, exceeded the boundaries of rationality. He might have said that Nordau enacted his own phobia about disorder, exhibited a mania to put things in place. To enumerate all of the late Victorians' self-dramatizing acts, and to account for them, would divert us. Enough to take note of their penchant for shaping images of themselves, not as they were, but as they imagined they were (or might be), by rewriting the history of the past, and by inventing a past of their own. The idea of "comparing," whether of oneself with another or of one's own time with past times, encouraged this. Nordau's *Degeneration*, which belongs to the same genre of activity as Frazer's *Golden Bough*, provided a new idiom for discourse about decadence.

It would be foolish to describe either book as phobic or manic, although it should be kept in mind that both were guided by the same wish and motivated by the same fear. Nordau, who imagined that civilization was edging toward collapse, and who regarded much of contemporary life as threatening, scrutinized nearly every aspect of it. He searched as though with untoward acquisitiveness for phobias and manias. The need to order (according to which everything is one thing or the other, mania or phobia), was itself a sign of his fear of chaos—a phobia about chaos that quickly became a mania for ordering: he classified phobias and manias with manic excess. Although Nordau was not exemplary of the social critics who described decadence, nonetheless he represents the limiting instance of a prevailing attitude toward disorder. Pivoting on the twin ideas of restraint and manliness as the distinguishing characteristics of civilization, his argument, like the more general discussions of progress and decline, is governed by fear and lacking in restraint.

In the 1890s "decadent" typically referred to style, in its widest range of meanings. In the most pointed account Arthur Symons comments, defines, and describes the word. Where others were silent, he invoked the perfect sanity, and perfect proportion of classical Art as the measure of comparison for contemporary literature. Des Esseintes, the hero of Huysmans' *A Rebours*, is made to stand for the representative "decadent" in whom Symons finds "the sensations and ideas of the effeminate, over-civilized, deliberately abnormal creature who is the last product of society." He describes the novel as "barbaric in its profusion, violent in its emphasis, wearying in its splendor."[15] Although Symons stresses the excess, rather than the complexity, or even the madness of decadent art, more was at stake for him and for his readers than simple aesthetic judgment. Symons was less Arnoldian than many of his more conservative contemporaries: like them however, he thought Art and Civilization reflected each other, thought the moral worth or health of the one was identical to that of the other.

Culture, Symons imagined, followed a circuitous path (not Frazer's linear pattern), eventually returning to its original condition. He pointed to the attributes shared by the "new barbarism," of which he did not entirely disapprove, and the "old barbarism," which Frazer's notion of savagery readily evoked. Symons' and Frazer's evaluations differed, but their descriptions, the one of contemporary life and the other of savagery, were remarkably similar. One singled out order, restraint, rationality, and faith to which he contrasted savagery; the other singled out excess, self-absorption, chaos, and effeminacy to which he contrasted the masculine ideal of the Victorian version of Greek culture. By conflating decline and effeminacy, Symons elaborated his idea of decadence in opposition to that imagined Greek ideal: his conclusions, different from Frazer's, were guided by the same conceptual frame and gender marked language. Moreover, the political consequences were identical, too, whether one wrote about the savage, or about the decadents, about progress or decline. Victorian ethnography and social criticism justified the power and privilege men held over women. At the same time, the emergence of feminism (and the political and social gains women made in the second half of the century), increased men's need to confirm their position.

Arthur Waugh, frequent contributor to the periodical press, described decadence with characteristic urgency, lamenting that "freedom of speech is degenerating into licence. . . . The writers and critics of contemporary literature have, it would seem, alike lost their heads." Waugh made explicit what a significant number of others of his generation believed: "The man lives by ideas; the woman by sensations; and while the man remains an artist so long as he holds true to his own view of life, the woman becomes one as soon as she throws off the habit of her sex, and learns to rely upon her judgment, not upon her senses. . . . It is unmanly, it is effeminate, it is inartistic to gloat over pleasure, to revel in immoderation, to become passion's slave; and literature demands as much calmness of judgment, as much reticence, as life itself."[16]

The Victorian poetic allowed for an easy allegiance between social and literary critics. If art represented the time, then the time could be understood by way of the literature it generated. Social critics, who addressed themselves as readily to literature as they did to the politics of social life, evaluated one as easily and authoritatively as the other. Frederic Harrison, who commanded a prominent position in letters, will serve as a representative example: "It is the lady-like age: and so it is the age of ladies' novels. Women have it all their own way now in romance . . . Up to a certain point, within their own limits, they are supreme. Half the modern romance, and many people think the better half, is written by women . . .

Let us accept what the dregs of the nineteenth century can give us, without murmuring and repining." When asked to amplify his position, Harrison responded: "I have spoken of a certain decadence. It is true that I have been showing examples of a certain slackness in creative force, sundry morbid tendencies, and an obvious state of chaos, and some false prophets in our midst: . . . Decadence in art is a sure sign of some organic change taking place in our moral sense. Healthy art is the outward and visible sign of an inward and spiritual growth."[17]

If healthy art was a sign of inward and spiritual growth, as Symons had said it was as early as 1893, unhealthy art was a sign of disease. That issue was explored tirelessly in the periodical press. In an unsigned article in *The National Observer,* for example, the issue was reiterated somewhat differently, but the terms in which the subject was conceived remained constant: the author distinguishes between the decadents of earlier generations who were *men,* whereas the new decadent is an "invention as terrible as, and in some ways more shocking than, the New Woman." The new decadents "have been tolerated, why one does not know, and have presumed on toleration. The time has surely come when there should be an end of this, and when every man who cares for the manhood of literature should lift his pen against so disgustful a crew."[18]

This is an extreme position, but not an unreasonable one. So long as the words "civilization" and "masculine" were conceived as conceptual cognates, the New Woman *was* shocking and the new decadents *were* "an invention as terrible." The New Woman, like her mirror image, the new decadent, who was always male, confused what was essential to her nature. She not only moved in the public sphere, but behaved like a man, even as the new decadents, in their self-absorption and inaction, behaved like women, lost their masculine vigor. For the Victorians, any confusion of gender was bound to have implications for "civilization." Of the many consequences one was the elaboration of "separate spheres." Neither the idea—that woman is a thing apart—nor the figure of speech was new. But there can be no doubt that as women's sphere of activities widened, as gender roles overlapped, and as the separation of the "spheres" appeared precarious, the phrase was used more frequently than ever before. These considerations account for the surge of interest at the century's turn, chiefly on the part of men, in confirming and justifying the social reality that lay behind the figure of "separate spheres." If women had access to higher degrees in education, to the professions, and to property; if they rode bicycles, abandoned constrictive modes of dress, and moved freely in the public sphere—if all this were possible, how could it be said that the spheres were separate? And if they were not separate, what would justify the position of power and privilege men enjoyed? It is understandable that fresh arguments should have been articulated with a new sense of importance in order to eliminate the new decadents and the New Woman. Therefore, men argued that the spheres always had been separate, and were intended by Nature and God to remain that way. What men claimed was at stake, however, was neither their own power nor their privilege, but civilization itself.

Frederic Harrison talked about the question in an address he gave at Newton Hall in a lecture, appropriately, in honor of August Comte.

> We come back to this—that in body, in mind, in feeling, in character, women are by Nature designed to play a different part from men. And all these differences combine to point to a part personal not general, domestic not public, working by direct contact not by remote sugges- tion, through the imagination more than through the reason, by the heart more than by the head . . . and all this works best in the Home. That is to say, the sphere in which women act at their highest is the Family, and the side where they are strongest is Affection. The sphere where men act at their highest is in public, in industry, in the service of the State; and the side where men are strongest, is Activity.[19]

To point to the different roles women and men are by Nature designed to play; to delineate what those are and why they need to be separated according to gender—the one belonging to the sphere of the Family or Home, and the other to the State or to Activity—were commonplace arguments in Victorian periodicals, although Harrison was more impas- sioned and more eloquent than many of his contemporaries. Neither his eloquence nor his passion prompted him to pause to consider the meta- phoricity of his language. On the contrary, the transfer of the language of science to discourse about social life served much the same function as Frazer's transfer of the "New Biology" to the domain of social institu- tions. If Harrison had simply stated that increased opportunities for women in education and in the professions would cause the social order to collapse, he would not have been as persuasive: his persuasiveness, which derived from his authoritative tone rather than the cogency of his argu- ment, depended on the notion that the spheres of social life are *like* the heavenly spheres. Harrison evoked this arbitrary analogy—of social life to the heavens—with such ease that the force of the figure eludes notice.

If the adjective "separate" had not been attached to the word "sphere," if the word "sphere" simply referred to the space occupied by women, as distinct from men, we would probably feel inclined to identify the two spheres as an orientational metaphor that designated some variety of spa- tial hierarchy. We might think, for example, of earthly and celestial space. But "separate spheres" implied two—perhaps more—spaces, set apart, neither one of which was necessarily preferable. Rather than suggest to their readers the outer limit of space—that is, the hollow globe that en- closes the earth—or, the concentric, transparent, hollow globes astrono- mers of earlier centuries thought surrounded the earth, the phrase suggested the orbit of a planet, as well as the spherical planets themselves, both of which moved within naturally designated boundaries. The use of metaphor, which involves understanding one thing in terms of another, necessarily evinces correspondences. The attributes of the second acquire those of the first. In this instance, the social order acquired the characteristics of the physical universe. To be understood each needed to be thought identical to the other, as though it were the other. Moreover, as Woman was thought to be the ordering principle of the Family, the Family was referred to as belonging to her; and, similarly, as Man was thought to be the ordering principle of the State, the State was referred to as belonging to him. Through a process that resembles understanding one thing in terms of another, as by a quantum leap, a part was also made to stand for the whole: "Woman" came to stand for one Sphere while "Man" came to stand for the other. Woman's activity, Harrison argued, should retain its home-like beauty, and should be "womanly and not mannish. All that we ask is that women, whether married or unmarried, whether with families of their own or not, shall never cease to feel like women, to work as women should, to make us all feel that there are true women amongst us and not imitation men." Before I consider the connections between "sameness" the notion of women as "imitation men," it will help to notice a few more passages from Harrison's talk:

> We are only seeking to assert a paramount law of human nature. We are defending the principle of the womanliness of women against the anarchic assertors of the manliness of woman. . . . In the name of mercy let us all do our best with the practical dilemmas society throws us. But let us not attempt to cure them by pulling society down from its foundations and uprooting the very first ideas of the social order.[20]

Harrison could count on his auditors to understand by the words "social order" and "society" the word "civilization." To uproot the foundations meant to uproot the two institutions, the Family and the State, that distinguished civilization from savagery. He appealed to his listeners, undoubtedly sympathetic to his view to "teach [women] that this specious agitation must ultimately degrade them, sterilize them, unsex them." Women's higher duties, Harrison argued, were neither to compete with men in professions, to participate in public life beside them, nor to engage in the strenuous labor required by work outside of the home. "The higher duties of love, beauty, patience, and compassion, can only be performed by women, and by women only so long as it is recognized to be their true and essential field." Thus, Harrison concluded: "It is impossible to do both together. Women must chose to be either women or abortive men. They cannot be both women and men. When men and women are once started as competitors in the same fierce race, as rivals and opponents, instead of companions and helpmates, with the same habits, the same ambitions, the same engrossing toil and the same public lives, Woman will have disappeared, society will consist of individuals distinguished physiologically, as are horses or dogs, into male and female specimens. Family will mean groups of men and women who live in common, and Home will mean the place where the group collects for shelter."[21]

Harrison makes two claims: That unless women remain within their sphere, they will become "imitation" or "abortive" men; and, second, crossing from one sphere to another will bring about the ruin of civilization, return all of us to a condition of "Barbarism." Turn-of-the-century journals, letters, minutes of meetings, and articles in the periodical press by Mona Caird, Janet Hogarth, Millicent Fawcett, Emmeline Pankhurst, and others confirmed that conventional gender roles were being blurred. In addition to women's accession to political organization, their participation in the labor force and in the professions, which coincided with the social dislocation of the family, threatened to undermine their place in the home. In retrospect it is easy to see how arbitrary Harrison's conclusions were. Only one already convinced of his ideology would be persuaded that overlapping gender roles would dissolve gender differences or that civilization verged on collapse. Harrison understood that the changing social realities challenged the adequacy of the figure of "separate spheres." Conversely, invoking that metaphor served to stabilize increasingly precarious conventions about gender. But not without competing views.

While Harrison argued that women ran the risk of "sameness," which he thought was undesirable, there is little evidence that women were fearful of becoming like men. On the contrary, many were fearful that if they continued to be restricted by roles convention had assigned them, their capacity to realize themselves would continue to be aborted. Women willingly risked being different from what they were, perhaps because for them, being different held the promise of becoming more, rather than less like "women." But in Harrison's view when women crossed from one sphere to another, they violated "natural laws," challenged the natural order. If *women* were not fearful of becoming "abortive men," whose fear was Harrison addressing? And why did the prospect of women's widening sphere excite terror in men?

It does not seem farfetched to say that the power of Harrison's own rhetorical move engendered his fear. In arguing that men and women are different, he elided something as remote and abstract as the "heavenly spheres," and as immediate and particular as the social order. By likening social life to the galaxies, by conflating two separate spheres, Harrison enacted linguistically what he eschewed sociologically. His elision of Nature and social life enabled him to argue that unless spheres are kept separate, unless women remain in their place, civilization would revert to savagery. That difference *can* be dissolved seems to be true imaginatively, if not virtually. If social life could be thought of as being identical to the Heavenly galaxies, then women *could* be thought of as being identical to men. On the one hand Harrison argues against the power of metaphor to shape images of the world that exist apart from the metaphors themselves;

on the other, the metaphorical frame of his argument against the imminent dangers of confusing gender identity regenerates the force of metaphor against which he argues. Metaphor permits the possibility of imagining likenesses that cannot be imagined apart from metaphorical thinking. Harrison may well have been addressing women, but the women he addressed had no existence apart from his own imaginings. If *he* were a woman, he would not want that woman to *be* like him. He spoke as though he were that woman, from an imagined woman's point of view, yet one of his own making. To be *like* a woman imaginatively, was to have realized that possibility. He might have been less fearful (or not fearful at all) had he restrained himself from acting out that possibility. Having enacted what he feared, he became his own adversary. Other issues, one of which concerned sameness, undoubtedly contributed to Harrison's fears and accounts for the tone of panic that competed with cogent discourse about the vexed political issues that occupied the later nineteenth century.

From Harrison's point of view—and from Darwin's, Comte's, and Frazer's, for example—gender differences, marked according to a moral hierarchy, were congruent with privilege and power. If it were possible to eliminate physical, moral, and intellectual differences, if women could "disappear," as Harrison feared they might, that hierarchy would disappear too.

By now it should be evident why a "falling away" from civilization was thought to be "effeminate," and why "effeminacy" was thought to represent a decline: Darwin had confirmed, and Frazer after him had reconfirmed, that civilization was a result of masculine vigor and intelligence. A man who had failed to be sufficiently masculine (or a culture that failed to be sufficiently civilized) was thought to be less than itself. A woman who falls away from herself, however, is not less than what she naturally is; she is more womanlike: more excessive, irrational, impulsive, intuitive, child-like.

Moreover, the idea of "decadence" depended upon thinking about culture as though it were identical with the organic world of plants and animals which pass through their cycle of birth, growth, deterioration, death, and decay; Darwin's (and Frazer's) conceptions depended on the analogy of the fetus; the legend of "separate spheres" depended on the language of astronomy. Yet, such "facts" as "excess," "irrationality," "effeminacy," and such likenesses as those drawn between the galaxies and social institutions, or the fetus and the evolution of social arrangements, are of a very different order of truth than, for example, that in the year 1895, Justice Wills declared Oscar Wilde had been "the centre of extensive corruption of young men of the most hideous kind"; or, that in the year 1910, King Edward died; or, that in the same year there were strikes of mine and dock workers; or, even that, in the year 1908, Arthur Balfour, in exasperation over the failed attempts to define the word "decadence," finally proposed that it "was rather like digestion: we knew it took place, but couldn't quite say how."[22] The failure to define "decadence" did not inhibit social critics, who appeared to be innocent of the conventions their language conserved and of the fictions they shaped, from using the word. They were at least as innocent as the ethnographers who might have observed—but they too failed to take note of themselves—their own repetitive descriptions, their fascination with the lurid, their interest in Magic and Naming, in the very notion of retrieving the arcane origin of mankind in order to uncover "weak spots" in modernity. It is not difficult to see that their own ethnographic enterprise had as fragile yet complex a surface as that of the civilization they imagined. Nor is it difficult to see why, in light of their arguments, they found descriptions of decadence useful. Each discourse enacted the same ideology.

In spite of the effect Frazer's anthropology had—of confirming that we were civilized and therefore superior—the impulse to confirm, and to confirm so loudly and insistently combatted the fear that "We" were, indeed, like "Them." While the presence of savage survivals—existing "human documents"—made the "science" of anthropology imaginable, it made equally imaginable the imminent eruption of the savage self. Children, the mad, and women were constant reminders of the condition from which civilization had evolved and to which civilization could revert. Adult and manlike behavior were salient signs of progress. But the threat remained: adults could become like children; men could become like women.

The enactment of the science of anthropology was one means of confronting the threat. It would not be an exaggeration to say that the Victorian savage was an elaboration of what the Victorians feared they might too easily become if they were not "civilized." Among the many uses of nineteenth-century anthropology, it reiterated those attributes of civilization that needed to be conserved if the Victorians were not to become like savages, children, or women.

The energetic ordering and arranging of the past assuaged the uneasiness the later Victorians felt about their time and themselves: the idea of comparison enabled them to differentiate themselves from what they feared they might be or might become. The subject of primitive man, which absorbed the attention of anthropologists, led them to anticipate the consummation of their wish to establish a science that would assure them of remaining civilized, although their method required postponement of their practical ambitions. Many undoubtedly felt themselves to be on the threshold of a perpetually deferred discovery throughout their lives. Although the controversy over the priority of "language" or "will," generated by Max Müller's hypothesis, persisted into the nineties, none disputed that what needed to be understood about the world of primitive man was Magic.[23]

The ethnographers initiated their pursuit of origins with the study of Magic because they believed Magic, particularly the magic of transformation through power of naming (and all of the accompanying rituals, customs, and habits that arise from this wish), represents the initial stage of human activity. There is more to be said about why the early ethnographers selected this aspect of primitive experience when other questions might easily have absorbed their attention. The pertinent parallel I wish to draw here is that neither the early ethnographers nor their successors noticed, perhaps because they were straining to be scientific, the affinities between their own pursuit and the activities they described, classified, and scrutinized. To name primitive man, to identify him properly, would enable them to transform modernity. Their interest in Magic, particularly in naming, is especially strong, although seeing their own ambitious enterprise as being, in itself, a Magical activity, did not occur to them.[24] They reserved their wonder for the study of the primitive, whose history promised full knowledge of their own origins, seeking the knowledge of which obscured their own fear. The savage they imagined, more fictional than real, served to order and control the intellectual life of Victorian anthropologists: An imaginary double of their own making whose existence was mediated by accounts as lurid as the arcane world they described. The savage was a fearful version of what they suspected they might actually be. If others could be shown to be different, they could not be like those others.

Frazer's explorations into arcane origins is shrouded in astonishing excess. The study of myth and ritual that had begun earlier in the century culminated in 1889 with the publication of the first volume of *The Golden Bough*. The proliferation of articles about the subject during the second half of the century can be accounted for in a number of ways. It would be foolish to diminish the political context that nurtured the emergence of anthropology. Ethnographic and folklore studies aided colonialism even as the Celtic revival confirmed that such studies stirred national feeling. But apart from these considerations, there is something noteworthy about the individuals who devoted their sedentary lives to writing books about strange customs and beliefs, translating myths, fairytales, and epics, and finding vestiges of arcane rites in classical literatures without moving from the confines of their studies in Oxford, Cambridge, and London. Their studies are informed by a nostalgia for the past, a lament for the absence of myth and ritual from modern life, and a desire to recover something felt to be lost which science would remedy. The practical social-mindedness was oddly modulated by their pursuit of exotic excess in their most astonishingly excessive accounts. At rest in their libraries, they were buoyed by their imaginative energies to remote regions of the world. When they returned, they proceeded to prepare fastidious descriptions of cannibalism, incest, self-affliction, headhunting, nakedness, marriage customs, and much other less-forbidden but equally unfamiliar behavior. In spite of their lurid subjects, their books are often tedious exercises in repetition, books about books, more than equal in their strangeness to the customs they described so laboriously. Their convictions about the possibility of amassing enough information to arrive eventually at significant conclusions, and their ambition to find a cure, need to be seen in the context of the enchantment with which they described modes of existence different from their own. Their sedulous descriptions, which were designed to recuperate and classify the strangeness, gave them a certain authority to speak with the confidence they needed to describe still more. The unselfconsciousness with which they undertook veritable descriptions separated them from their avowedly literary contemporaries and from the social critics who were describing "decadence." But the ethnographers whose lives were austere, whose descriptions were as inflated as their imaginations were vivid, flattened their exotic subjects. The titles of their books were often beguiling, but the books themselves are ponderously inclusive and tedious. Their peculiar deflation of their exotic subjects contains an excess of its own no less lurid and peculiar than the lives they described.

If the anthropologists' excessive accounts of primitive man were self-protective, the social critics' descriptions of contemporary "decadence" could only have exacerbated their fear, heightened their desire to delineate differences more sharply, and strengthened their convictions about progress. They, in turn, provided the social critics with a conceptual analogue for describing "decadence": the world of the primitive was insufficiently controlled, measured, and developed by masculine vigor and masculine intelligence; the world of the "decadents," having "fallen away" from civilization, mirrored the world of the primitive. Whether one argued the mark of the age was "progress" or "decline," each made the same claim on the imagination. Literary activity, whether of reading or of writing, inspired traffic with the lurid and, simultaneously, assigned to that activity a privileged place apart. But like all privileges, this one appears to have been in perpetual need of confirmation. Whether one was imagined to differ from or to resemble the savage, each polemical move demarcated "Them" and "Us." Savages—"They"—were repeatedly likened to women in the writings of the anthropologists. In the writings of the social critics, "We" had become like "Them." Rather than controvert each other, or engage in bitter conflict over the issue of "progress" or "decline," each confirmed for the other that civilization was "masculine." And each eschewed, with equal fear, the "feminization" of civilization.

The threat to "masculinity"—examples were found in the lives of individuals, literature, and the wider realm of the "spirit of the age"—were countered in various ways, one of which involved identifying such signs through repeated comparisons with yet other signs. Such social critics as Harrison engaged in eloquent lament, while such anthropologists as Frazer engaged in tedious affirmation: because they shared the notion that civilization was "masculine," gender mediated their discourse. As Frazer thought the savage self within culture might erupt at any time—existing savages were a constant reminder of what reversion might mean—for others, women, particularly women who moved out of their proper sphere, were a constant reminder of the possibility of what might occur if civilization reverted to barbarism, or became "effeminate."

I have argued that the legend of "separate spheres" was revived in the later part of the century as a response to anxieties about sexuality, which were acted out and intensified in discussions of "decadence" and "savagery." Both words were inseparable from political considerations. When sexuality itself became a distinct topos, men enacted their fears more boldly, yet with greater resistance to clarifying their own confusions.

Havelock Ellis and John Addington Symonds were responsible for having introduced the subject into British social thought and they, rather than Freud, or Krafft-Ebing, published the first articles about "sexual inversion," as Symonds, who borrowed the term from Italian social theory, called the phenomenon.[25] We can fairly suppose that Ellis' studies, which recounted the details of anonymous individuals' erotic lives and habits, like the anthropologists' studies of anonymous savages, activated a dormant interest in picturing the marginal world more vividly. If fear of inversion in themselves and in those around them prompted Ellis and Symonds to describe narcissism (as Ellis was the first to call it), reading and writing about this subject could be regarded as salutary acts which, joined as they were to anthropological discourse about the "savage" and to social criticism about "decadence," contributed to the Victorian idea of civilization as a masculine invention.

Would the Victorians recognize themselves in the picture I have constructed here? We might imagine they would have chosen to present their arguments differently according to how we answer this question. More importantly, their choices would have had different consequences.

NOTES

1. "The Spirit of the Age," reprinted in *Essays on Politics and Culture*, Gertrude Himmelfarb, ed. (Garden City, N.Y.: Doubleday, 1962). I wish to acknowledge my debt to Jerome Buckley whose work, most particularly *The Triumph of Time* (Cambridge, Mass.: Harvard University Press, 1966), is among the most illuminating and provocative studies on this subject. It would be impossible to acknowledge my indebtedness to all of the other studies that have influenced my thinking and made it possible to bring together aspects of social thought that have generally remained isolated from one another. I want, nevertheless, to single out the work of J. W. Burrow, Linda Dowling, Karl Beckson, Richard Ellmann, Tom Gibbons, Sandra Gilbert, Barbara Gelpi, Susan Gubar, Gertrude Himmelfarb, Walter Houghton, Samuel Hynes, John Lester, John Reed, Martha Vicinus, and Judith Walkowitz. A shorter version of this paper was presented at the Fifth Berkshire Conference on the History of Women, Vassar College, April, 1981.

2. Ruskin, *Modern Painters*, as quoted in Buckley, p. 58. For a fuller discussion see *Modern Painters* (New York: International Publishers, n. d.), vol. 3, ch. 16.

3. Frazer, "The Scope and Method of Mental Anthropology," *Science Progress*, (April 1922), 64:583. Although I have drawn in some instances from works of Frazer written after 1900, his earlier writings are cast in similar language and contain the same conceptual frame.

4. Frazer, "The Scope of Social Anthropology," *Psyche's Task* (London: Macmillan, 1913), p. 162.

5. Sir James George Frazer, *The Golden Bough* (Macmillan, 1911), "Preface to the Second Edition," September 1900, 1:xxvii. Andrew Lang echoes the passage in *Magic and Religion* (London: Longmans, Green, 1901), p. 7.

6. Sir James George Frazer, *Totemism and Exogamy* (London: Macmillan, 1910), 4:17. See also *Questions on the Customs, Beliefs, and Languages of Savages* (Cambridge: Cambridge University Press, 1907), pp. 5–10. My emphasis.

7. See n. 4, above; p. 172.

8. Charles Darwin, *The Descent of Man* (New York: Collier, 1902), p. 717. Subsequent quotations are from this edition.

9. Darwin, pp. 724–25.

10. *The Golden Bough*, 2:209; *Totemism and Exogamy*, 1:93.

11. *Totemism and Exogamy*, 1:xiii–xiv; *The Worship of Nature* (London: Macmillan, 1926), 1:6. Compare Darwin, part 3, ch. 19.

12. *Totemism and Exogamy*, 4:4; *The Belief in Immortality* (London: Macmillan, 1913), 1:265–66.

13. *The Golden Bough*, 2:2.

14. Max Nordau, *Degeneration* (New York: Appleton, 1895), especially book 1, p. 543; George Bernard Shaw, *The Sanity of Art* (New York: Tucker, 1908).

15. Arthur Symons, "The Decadent Movement in Literature," *Harper's New Monthly Magazine* (November 1893), 87(522):866.

16. Arthur Waugh, "Reticence in Literature," *The Yellow Book* (April 1, 1894), pp. 356–57, p. 355.

17. Frederic Harrison, "The Decadence of Romance," *Forum* (1894), 17:223–24; "Art and Shoddy: A Reply to Criticisms," *Forum* (1894), 17:718–19.

18. *The National Observer*, February 23, 1895.

19. Frederic Harrison, "The Emancipation of Women," *Fortnightly Review*, (October 1, 1891), 198:447, 448.

20. Harrison, "Emancipation," p. 448.

21. Harrison, "Emancipation," pp. 451–52.

22. *The Westminster Gazette*, May 27, 1895; Arthur Balfour, *Essays: Speculative and Political* (New York: Doran, 1921), p. 208.

23. See, for example, Andrew Lang, *Modern Mythology* (London: Longmans, Green, 1897), which is, in part, a response to Max Müller, *Chips from a German Workshop* (London: Longmans, Green, 1875), p. 4. See also E. B. Tylor's commentary on his exhibition of *Charms and Amulets Displayed at the Folk-Lore Congress*, Joseph Jacobs and Alfred Nutt, eds. (London: David Nutt, 1892), pp. 387–93. Among the countless examples, see *The Golden Bough*.

24. See Frazer, *Bibliography and General Index*, twelve, "Name," "Names," "Namesakes" and "Naming": 12:383; Edward Clodd, *Tom Tit Tot: An Essay on Savage Philosophy in Folk-Tale* (London: Duckworth, 1898), especially chs. 5 and 6.

25. Havelock Ellis and John Addington Symonds, *Sexual Inversion* (London: Wilson and Macmillan, 1897), pp. 26–29.

10

ART AND DEGENERATION: VISUAL ICONS OF CORRUPTION

PATRICK BADE
Christie's, London

In a lecture entitled "The Ideas of Progress and Their Impact on Art," E. H. Gombrich said, "If one can name one idea that dominated that great and creative nineteenth century, it is the idea of progress." Without doubt the idea of progress has greatly influenced the way in which twentieth-century art historians have seen the history of nineteenth-century art. They have tended to present it as a triumphal and inevitable progress from Romanticism through Realism, Impressionism, Post-Impressionism to Fauvism, Cubism, and Abstract Art in the early twentieth century. This idea of inexorable progress in modern art can be seen in embryo in Paul Signac's *D'Eugène Delacroix au néo-impressionisme*, published in 1899; it found definitive form in Julius Meier-Graefe's *Die Entwickelungsgeschichte der modernen Kunst* published in 1904.

To nineteenth-century artists and writers on art the situation looked very different. With the exception of Pissarro and his Neo-Impressionist friends, few protagonists of Signac's and Meier-Graefe's accounts of nineteenth-century art would have accepted the idea of progress in the arts and the positions in this progress which these writers assigned to them. The utterances of nineteenth-century artists and the writings of contemporary critics are frequently marked by an extraordinary pessimism. Artists as diverse as Delacroix, Ingres, Burne-Jones, and Gauguin lamented that they were born into an age unfavorable to the arts. It would seem that in matters of art, the nineteenth century was afflicted with a painful sense of inferiority and decline.

Decadence in the arts was attributed to a variety of causes. Ingres blamed the frequency of and size of art exhibitions; Baudelaire, the influence of photography; Edmond de Goncourt thought that realism and the fashions for rococo and Japanese art, which he had done so much to propagate, were "three steps towards decadence." The painter and art historian Eugène Fromentin blamed bad education; Delacroix worried about increasing luxury and the poisonous effects of alcohol, tobacco, and opium.[1] Ruskin and Morris blamed the evils of capitalism. Others, following the ideas of Gobineau and of "decadent" men of letters, spoke of racial exhaustion or the "Latin decadence." Max Nordau pointed to the nervous hysteria brought on by industrialization and the growth of the cities. The most common complaint was simply that civilization was growing old and senile. Whatever their political and artistic creeds these men were united in the belief that in the nineteenth century the arts were not progressing but declining. Indeed, it was this sense of decline that inspired many of the art revivals of the nineteenth century; the Nazarenes, the Pre-Raphaelite Brotherhood, Pugin's Gothic revival, the arts and crafts movement, and Art Nouveau.

By the 1880s the idea that the arts were declining was a fashionable platitude and was lampooned by W. S. Gilbert in his libretto for the operetta *Patience*. The aspiring aesthete was advised:

Be eloquent in praise of the very dull old days
Which have long since passed away,
And convince'em, if you can, that the reign of
Good Queen Anne was culture's palmiest day
Of course you will pooh-pooh whatever's fresh
And new, and declare it's crude and mean.
For Art stopped short in the cultivated court of the
Empress Josephine.

Scientific Progress and Artistic Decadence

Progress in the arts was not believed to be necessarily attendant upon progress in other areas of human activity—industry, science, and the improvement of living standards. For many, in fact, the opposite was the case: Progress in industry and science was the chief cause of decadence in the arts. Edmond and Jules de Goncourt wrote, in 1854: "Industry will kill art. Industry and art are two enemies which nothing will reconcile, no matter what one does or says." Baudelaire was convinced that the "purely material developments of progress have contributed much to the impoverishment of the French artistic genius which is already so scarce."[2]

Though speaking from a very different political viewpoint, Ruskin and Morris would have shared both the belief that industrialization was inimical to progress in the arts and a profound suspicion of machines and scientific inventions. The attitude of nineteenth-century artists to industry and science was often suspicious, fearful, and hostile. The Goncourts

approvingly quote Gavarni's contemptuous dismissal of scientific progress. Delacroix's *Journal* shows his hostility to the "merciless machine"
and "those fiendish contraptions, railway trains." He wrote "I have a
horror of the usual run of scientists," and complained of "these American
inventions to make people go faster."[3] Puvis de Chavannes had nightmares
after visiting the Hall of Machines at the Paris Universal Exhibition of
1889 and told his students despairingly, "there is no more art to be done."[4]

Few nineteenth-century artists would have been able to paint that other
great symbol of industrial progress produced for the 1889 Exhibition, the
Eiffel Tower, with the uncritical delight of Seurat's beautiful small painting. Even Turner, who painted some of the earliest and most memorable
images of the industrial age, was skeptical of its new inventions. In his
famous painting "Rain, Steam, and Speed—The Great Western Railway"
of 1844, he irreverently painted a hare scampering along the track in front
of the steam engine, and in "The Fighting Téméraire Tugged to her Last
Berth to be Broken Up—1838," Turner's sympathies clearly lie with the
spectral beauty of the old ship rather than with the gleaming black tug in
the foreground.

Eighteenth-Century Background and the
Legacy of Jean-Jacques Rousseau

The concept of decadence in the visual arts was already well established
in the mid-eighteenth century with the critical reaction to the excesses of
the rococo style. Writers such as La Font de Saint-Yenne, in his "Réflexions sur quelques causes de l'état présent de la peinture en France,"
published in 1741, and Diderot in his *Salons* attacked the frivolity and
hedonism of contemporary French painting and hankered for the noble
grandeur of art in the age of Louis XIV, Poussin, and Le Brun. Diderot
saw moral and aesthetic decadence in the art of Boucher: "The degradation of taste, of colour, of composition, of character, of expression, of
drawing, is a consequence of the degradation of morals."[5]

With his influential works *Thoughts on the Imitation of Greek Works of
Art in Painting and Sculpture* (1755) and the *History of Ancient Art*, Johann
Joachim Winckelmann impressed his contemporaries with their mental
and physical inferiority to the ancients and with the decadence of their
arts. But it was Jean-Jacques Rousseau who did the most to undermine
confidence in modern civilization. In 1750, when Rousseau, answering the
question put by the Dijon Academy, "Has the restoration of the arts and
sciences been conducive to the purification of morals?" came to the conclusion that civilization and the arts and sciences were corrupting rather
than improving influences, he initiated a train of thought that runs
through the nineteenth century.

Delacroix was troubled by Rousseau's ideas and makes many references to them in his *Journals*. An entry for May 1, 1850, seems to reject Rousseau's thesis: "Is everything that derives from man's intelligence a snare, a disaster, or a sign of corruption? But if this is so, why does not Rousseau blame the savage for painting and ornamenting his rude bow, or decorating with feathers the apron with which he hides his nakedness?" When in a more pessimistic frame of mind, Delacroix would echo the sentiments of Rousseau: "How Civilization, as we understand it, dulls our natural feelings!"[6]

The critic Théophile Thoré reviewing the Salon of 1861 thought that a little barbarism would be a healthy antidote to the debilitating effects of civilization: "A little savagery or rather barbarity is not at all ill-suited to decadent periods. When the Roman Empire was dying of consumption, the northern barbarians often came to awaken it from lethargy. Art is sick in France, and does not like these country doctors who come with solid recipes and unshakable health." The "country doctors" were the Realist painters Courbet and Millet. "They come from the forests and mountains. That is why they don't have the same taste as the charming artists who paint with pink in the midst of boudoirs."[7]

The nineteenth-century artist who most fully embodied the ideas of Rousseau was Paul Gauguin. "Your civilisation is your disease, my barbarism is my restoration to health," Gauguin wrote to Strindberg in 1895.[8] Gauguin liked to present himself as a "savage from Peru," a "wolf without a collar," a man who had thrown off the influence of corrupt European civilization and reverted to healthy barbarism. Of course, Gauguin no more became a savage when he went to Tahiti than Marie-Antoinette became a milkmaid when she played in her dairy at Rambouillet. Gauguin's hatred of civilization was part of his European cultural inheritance and had nothing to do with his Peruvian ancestors. His art was the product of a highly sophisticated Parisian culture. Meier-Graefe recognized this when he compared Gauguin with Van Gogh: "He lacked the Dutchman's healthy peasant blood; his was a mixed Parisian fluid." Gauguin occasionally dropped the image that he had created for himself. In *Noa Noa* he describes himself as "almost an old man in body and soul, in civilised vices and lost illusions."[9] When he lusted after an androgynous Tahitian boy, he explained that "a whole civilisation had been before in evil and had educated me."

Political Viewpoints

Artists and writers who were committed to revolution and the transformation of society also felt that they were in a period of decadence and corruption. "England, like France is rotten to the core," wrote the anarchist Camille Pissarro to his son Lucien. Pissarro saw the Symbolist art which bloomed in the latter part of his life as "the art of orange blossoms which makes pale women swoon" and a sign of the corruption of French culture. "The bourgeoisie frightened, astonished by the immense clamour of the disinherited masses, by the insistent demands of the people, feels that it is necessary to restore to the people their superstitious beliefs. Hence the bustling of religious symbolists, religious socialists, idealist art, occultism, Buddhism, etc., etc. . . . May the movement be only a death rattle, the last."[10]

Pissarro's Neo-Impressionist friends Georges Seurat and Paul Signac shared his revolutionary political views. According to Signac, Seurat had "a lively feeling for the degradation of our era of transition" and for this reason he chose to represent "the pleasures of decadence: balls, kick-choruses, circuses."[11]

In England such political idealists as John Ruskin and William Morris also saw decadence in the arts and blamed it upon the effects of capitalism. According to Walter Crane, it was this sense of artistic decadence that led Morris to socialism in the first place.[12] Morris himself wrote: "The old art is no longer fertile, no longer yields us anything save elegantly poetic regrets; being barren, it has but to die, and the matter of moment now is, as to how it shall die, whether with hope or without it."[13]

For such radicals as Pissarro, Signac, Morris, and Henri van de Velde, however much they might lament current decadence, there was the hope of social revolution which they believed would reverse the degeneration of the arts. In *The Aim of Art* Morris wrote: "I think we who have learned to see the connection between industrial slavery and the degradation of the arts have also learned to hope for a future for these arts; since the day will certainly come when men will shake off the yoke, and refuse to accept the mere artificial compulsion of the gambling market to waste their lives in ceaseless and hopeless toil; and when it does come, their instincts for beauty and imagination set free along with them, will produce such art as they need."

Some, of course, took the contrary view that it was desire for political change and the encroachments of democracy that were the root cause of decline in the arts. Ingres said, "men are in love with change, and in art change is often the cause of decadence." The Goncourt brothers attacked the philistinism of democracy in *La Révolution dans les mœurs*, published in 1854. They believed that the increasing power and prosperity of the masses would lead to art becoming a "parasitic and suspicious activity" subsidized by the state.

Art and Sickness

It was a common belief throughout the nineteenth century that there was a connection between ill health and creativity, and, more specifically, between nervous disorder and genius. An element of sickness or neurosis was frequently singled out as being the specifically modern component in an artist's work. It was believed that the artist was like the madman in that he experienced sensations and emotions more intensely than ordinary men. The increasing sense of alienation from normal society felt by many artists in the course of the nineteenth century also led them to identify themselves with the insane. It is this sense of close sympathy and self-identification that lends powerful intensity to Géricault's portraits of mad people.

Romantic artists were fascinated by madness. Goya's paintings of mad-houses are the most memorable among many nineteenth-century depictions of such scenes. Such literary or historical figures as Hamlet, Ophelia, Marguerite, and Tasso, who suffered from madness, were popular with Romantic painters.

The connection between genius and insanity was given scientific respectability by a number of nineteenth-century scientists, among them Moreau de Tours, Lombroso, and J. F. Nisbet. In *The Insanity of Genius* (1891), Nisbet asserts that "all the available evidence . . . points clearly to the existence of nerve-disorder as a fundamental element of genius in relation to colour and form." He supports his assertion with a list of painters whose lives, he claimed, show evidence of mental and physical degeneration.

Nisbet was not alone in seeking a connection between physical illness and artistic sensibility. Illness and a weak constitution were often cited as a proof, if not the cause, of artistic creativity. Delacroix harped constantly upon his ill health in his journal. He made an interesting analogy between his ill health and his imagination, which he considered the source of his talent; "My health is not good—as temperamental as my imagination." The connection is made more explicit by Dargenty in *Eugène Delacroix par lui-même*, published in 1885. He says that Delacroix's violent works "are the result of an exhausted blood." Burne-Jones' wife, in her biography of the artist, stresses the importance of his ill health, saying that it "must take its place as one of the understood influences of his life. With him, as with other sensitive natures, body and mind acted and reacted on each other. . . . In times of physical weakness he could upon occasion flare up with nervous energy of an astonishing kind."[14] Edmond de Goncourt clearly believed that Degas's physical and mental weakness was an integral part of his talent and a sign of his modernity as an artist. After a visit to Degas's studio in 1874, he wrote in his journal: "An original fellow this Degas, sickly, neurotic, ophthalmic to such an extent that he is afraid he will lose his sight, but on that very account an exceptionally sensitive being who feels the subtle character of things. Of all the painters I have seen up to now he is the one who best catches the spirit of modern life in his depictions of that life."[15]

In a letter of 1895 to his son Lucien, Camille Pissarro rejected the painting of Burne-Jones on the ground that it was "too sick." Pissarro was out of step with many of his contemporaries who liked the painting of Burne-Jones and other Symbolist artists just because it was sick. A tradition of nineteenth-century art criticism going back to Baudelaire saw sickness and neurosis as signs of modern sensibility. In his Salon review of 1845, Baudelaire described his hero Delacroix as "a great genius sick with genius." The following year he enthused about Delacroix's depiction of women "sick and gleaming with a sort of interior beauty." In his review of the Exposition Universelle in 1855 he again celebrated Delacroix's ideal of female beauty: "These women, sick at heart or in mind, have in their eyes the leaden hue of fever, of the strange sparkle of their malady."

This taste for the unhealthy was inherited by the man who was, after Baudelaire, perhaps the most gifted and perceptive French art critic of the century, Joris Karl Huysmans. In 1884, in his novel *A Rebours*, he described Gustave Moreau as having the "morbid perspicuity of an entirely modern sensibility" and Odilon Redon's drawings as "a new type of fantasy, born of sickness and delirium." Redon's drawings remind Des Esseintes, the novel's hero, of the effects of typhoid fever. In an article on Whistler, Huysmans described the artist's work as "convalescent painting, exquisite, completely personal, completely new."[16]

By the 1880s the idea of the artist as someone sickly and morbid was well enough established for Gilbert and Sullivan to make use of it in their operetta *Patience*, which made fun of the aesthetic movement. The aesthete is characterized as:

A pallid and thin young man—
a haggard and lank young man—
a greenery-yallery, Grosvenor Gallery
Foot-in-the-grave young man!

It was the meteoric success of Beardsley and Lautrec in the 1890s and the growing fame of Van Gogh and Gauguin at the turn of the century that firmly established the image of the artist as morally, physically, and mentally degenerate. A cartoon of 1910 in the satirical German magazine *Simplicissimus* shows an impoverished German artist with wife and children to support, lamenting: "Actually if one were a Frenchman, or dead, or a pervert—best of all: a dead, perverted Frenchman—then one could live!"

Julius Meier-Graefe asserted that Beardsley was one of the most characteristic figures of the age and that a true understanding of the culture of the time was quite impossible without a knowledge of Beardsley's work. Meier-Graefe might have said the same of Lautrec, who seemed to be as representative of fin-de-siècle Paris as Beardsley was of fin-de-siècle London. It was the infirmity of these two artists as much as the perversity of their subject matter that gave them this position.

On September 15, 1894, the painter Paul Signac complained in his diary of the neglect of his mentor Georges Seurat and of what he saw as the excessive and unwarranted admiration for Van Gogh, who, he said, "is interesting only because of his aspect as an insane phenomenon . . . and whose only interesting paintings are those which were done at the time of his sickness in Arles."[17] It was no doubt true that Van Gogh's madness made him an object of interest and helped to establish his reputation before those of the other great Post-Impressionists. Albert Aurier, in the only article to be published on Van Gogh during his lifetime, harped upon the neurotic aspects of his art in a way that now seems absurdly exaggerated and typically fin-de-siècle. Aurier characterized Van Gogh's art as "almost always on the edge of the pathological." He wrote, ". . . . he is a hyperaesthete with obvious symptoms who perceives with abnormal and possibly even painful intensity the imperceivable and secret character of lines and forms, and even more of colours, of light, of the magic iridescence of shadows, of nuances which are invisible to healthy eyes and that is why his realism, the realism of this neurotic, why his sincerity and his truth are different from the realism, the sincerity and truth of those great petits bourgeois of Holland, so sound of body and well balanced in mind, who were his fathers and his masters . . .[18] Aurier goes on to describe Van Gogh as "this robust and true artist with brutal hands of a giant, and the nerves of a hysterical woman."

Van Gogh was somewhat puzzled and embarrassed by this effusion. He was not in sympathy with the conscious perversity and preciousness of the "decadents" and with the cultivation of ill health. In November 1889 he wrote his brother that he preferred Puvis de Chavannes and Delacroix to the Pre-Raphaelites because they painted "more healthily."

Not surprisingly though, Van Gogh's illness led him to ponder the relationship between madness and creativity. He often returned to the subject in his correspondence with his brother Theo. Van Gogh wished to be healthy and to produce a healthy art that would be comprehensible to normal and simple people. But he accepted his illness with resignation. Before going to the asylum at Saint-Rémy, he wrote: "I am beginning to consider madness as a disease like any other and to accept it as such." A few months later, in September 1889, he wrote, "Well, with the mental disease I have, I think of the many other artists suffering mentally and I tell myself that this does not prevent one from excercising the painter's profession as if nothing was amiss." His letters also show that he thought his painting could be of help to his illness, and his illness of help to his art. Work, he said, was "the best lightning conductor for my disease." In May 1889 he wrote to his sister-in-law Johanna: "It is those who love nature to the extent of becoming mad or ill who are painters." The following month there was a touching and revealing exchange of letters between the brothers Vincent and Theo. Theo expressed the fear that Vincent had pushed

his art to the point that endangered his sanity. After congratulating his
brother on the boldness of his work, Theo continued: "But how your head
must have laboured, and how boldly you ventured to the furthest point,
where dizziness is inevitable. For this reason, my dear brother, when you
tell me you are working again, though I am delighted in one way, since this
gives you a means of avoiding the condition into which so many of the
unfortunate people fall who are having treatment where you are, nevertheless I feel a little uneasy when I think of it, because before you are completely cured you must not venture into those mysterious regions where it
seems one can skirt past, but not enter with impunity." Vincent's answer
shows that he felt that his madness was not merely a personal affliction
but something that resulted from the age in which he lived: "Do not fear
that I shall ever of my own will rush to dizzy heights. Unfortunately we
are subject to the circumstances and the maladies of our own time,
whether we like it or not."[19]

Van Gogh's longing for health and his sad acceptance of his illness is in
marked contrast to the way in which the great Norwegian painter Edvard
Munch cherished and cultivated his ill health and mental instability. He
wrote: "I must retain my physical weaknesses, they are an integral part of
me. I don't want to get rid of illness, however unsympathetically I may
depict it in my art." Munch exulted in his tainted ancestry, describing his
mother as "eaten away by the worm of consumption" and his father as
"tainted with a tendency towards degeneracy." "Sickness, insanity and
death," he wrote, "were the black angels that hovered over my cradle and
have followed me throughout my life." Curiously, Munch deeply resented
it when anyone else described his art as sick. He wrote: "I do not think my
art is sick—despite what Scharffenberg and many others believe. Those
kind of people do not understand the true function of art, nor do they
know anything about its history."[20]

After his nervous breakdown in 1908 and the partial resolution of his
mental problems through medical treatment, Munch adopted a calmer
life-style and a less introspective and neurotic kind of art. But he continued to worry that these changes for the better in his mental and physical health would impoverish his art. In 1913 he wrote: "My health is
getting better and better, and I find myself increasingly able to enjoy the
company of my fellow men. But strangely enough that does not help my
art. In fact, my earlier invalid's mentality had a very favorable effect on
my work."[21]

Anthropomorphism and the Latin Decadence

It was a widespread belief in the nineteenth century that civilizations
had a limited lifespan, following a process of growth and decay similar to
that of man. Baudelaire, in his review of the 1855 Exposition Universelle,
put the idea succinctly.

As far as the arts are concerned, this idea was certainly not new to the nineteenth century. Ancient writers, describing the development of Greek sculpture, were the first to give it expression. Later, Vasari in his account of the Renaissance in the *Lives of the Artists* and such eighteenth-century theorists as Winckelmann and Giovanni Battista Vico exhibited a similar belief.

What was new in the second half of the nineteenth century was the racial interpretation given to this anthropomorphic view of civilizations. Borrowing their terminology from Darwin, writers on art spoke of different European nations and cultures as though they were separate species. Cultural rivalries were discussed in terms of a battle for the survival of the fittest. There is an interesting parallel between these cultural rivalries, which found expression in the pages of art magazines in the 1890s, and the international political rivalries of these years. The idea that each culture had its allotted lifespan found particular favor among German writers, who believed that Germany was at the beginning of hers, whereas the older European "Kultur-Völker" were already in decline.[23] According to Georg Fuchs, *Deutsche Kunst und Dekoration*, England, France, and Belgium had already exhausted their creative powers. It was now the turn of Germany and it was important to make the most of the opportunity as it was Germany's fate to be superseded by the peoples of the New World (10:534).

The idea of the decadence of the Latins, borrowed from literature, was ever-present in German art magazines of the period, either openly expressed or tacitly implied. It was often stated that the most interesting developments in the decorative arts came from the Germanic lands. Hermann Muthesius complained that Northern European innovations in the arts were caricatured and corrupted by their Latin imitators.

Comparisons of German and French art stressed the healthy virility of German art and the sickly effeminacy of French art. In describing the German wine restaurant at the Paris 1900 Exhibition, Meier-Graefe compared French and German taste in the decoration of restaurants. "The Restaurant [the German wine restaurant] belongs to the stronger sex just as those in Paris belong to the weaker; the Parisian builds his restaurant as a boudoir for 'cocottes.' So that the German restaurant is yet again one of the many signs of the difference between the two races, which always comes to expression in the development of the decorative arts in the two countries" (5:386). A writer in *Deutsche Kunst und Dekoration* said of the Bing pavillion in the same exhibition: "For us Germans it is in any case a little too effeminate, too playful and coquettish. For the French perhaps, for this reason perfectly suited" (6:569).

It is strange to find Meier-Graefe wholeheartedly accepting the myth of Latin decadence. One of the most influential propagandists for French art, he was responsible more than anyone else for the introduction of modern French painting into Germany. He lost control of the magazine

Pan, which he had launched in 1895, in a notorious incident triggered by his inclusion of Lautrec's lithograph of Marcelle Lender. Apparently it was the whiff of decadence that attracted Meier-Graefe to French art in general and to Lautrec in particular. In an article in *Dekorative Kunst* he described Napoleon as "the last and most colossal hero of the Latin race," and his period as the last great age of Latin culture: "Roman form which had once already conquered the Gothic, the expression of the Germanic peoples, appeared for the last time; a farewell that goes back over two hundred years, the farewell of a race that goes under; and of an art which had reached the highest peaks of human achievement" (6:90). He described modern France in melodramatic terms: "France, the lovely, unlucky land, is today like a ruined ballroom in which the vilest crimes and the most heroic deeds are carried out side by side, by almost the same men. Already the ballroom burns on all sides and inside it, the muse of Lautrec dances with brilliant contortions, the last diabolical cancan."(4:1,899).

The Expression of Pessimism in Nineteenth-Century Art

The underlying pessimism of nineteenth-century thought found clear expression in its art. It was a period in which many artists liked to see themselves as seers and prophets and throughout the century artists made ambitious attempts to paint and sculpt works that presented a broad philosophical view of the human condition and of the history of mankind and civilization. By and large the artists who presented a pessimistic viewpoint carried the most conviction and expressed most profoundly the preoccupations of the age—Géricault and Delacroix in their "Grandes Machines," Rodin in the "Gates of Hell," Munch in the "Frieze of Life" and Gauguin in "Where do we come from? What are we? Where are we going?"

When Delacroix was painting "Virgil Presenting Dante to Homer" for the cupola of the library of the Palais du Luxembourg in the 1840s, he said that he was trying to paint an Elysium where great poets and sages "enjoy a happiness which is not merely trivial." Ingres, painting his mural of the "Golden Age" at the Chateau of Dampierre at the same time, made a similar attempt. Despite the beauty of individual figures the picture was, as a whole, unsuccessful. Very few nineteenth-century artists succeeded in painting a "happiness which is not merely trivial." The serene visions of Puvis de Chavannes, the strange hieratic Sunday afternoons of Seurat, Hans von Marées' Naples frescoes, and the exotic paradise of Gauguin's South Sea paintings are perhaps exceptions. But even these masterpieces exhibit a degree of melancholy and a strange sense of lethargy. It has frequently been pointed out that it was the destruction rather than the dawn of civilization that fired Delacroix's imagination when he painted the library of the Palais Bourbon. "Attila the Hun and His Hordes Overrun Italy and the Arts" is vastly more successful and compelling than the corresponding "Orpheus Brings the Arts of Peace to the Primitive Greeks."

Countless public buildings and monuments of the nineteenth century are adorned with mural paintings or sculptural friezes which celebrate progress and present optimistic and patriotic views of history. Almost inevitably the artists deemed appropriate for such commissions were the dullest and most academic. On the rare occasions when such projects fell into the hands of artists of originality and imaginative power—Delacroix's Palais Bourbon ceiling, and Klimt's Vienna University ceiling—the artist transformed and subverted the positivist theme to produce something far more complex and equivocal. We see Delacroix's subversion of his ostensibly optimistic theme most clearly in the scene representing science. It shows Pliny the elder recording the eruption of Vesuvius, which was about to destroy him along with the towns of Pompeii and Herculaneum. It is not so much the power of science that is demonstrated as its impotence in the face of hostile nature.

A yet more radical subversion of positivism was perpetrated by Gustave Klimt in his Vienna University ceilings. The professors who devised the scheme intended it to be a celebration of knowledge and progress. Klimt was asked to illustrate philosophy, medicine, and jurisprudence, three pillars of civilization. In the words of Carl E. Schorske, Klimt represented jurisprudence as "an erotic nightmare in a clammy hell." Instead of representing medicine with the achievements of Lister and Pasteur, Klimt "confronted the culture of scientific progress with an alien and shocking vision. He presented medicine's field of action as a phantasmagoria of half-dreaming humanity, sunk in instinctual self-surrender, passive in the flow of fate."[24]

It is interesting to compare Klimt's representations of knowledge and science with those of Puvis de Chavannes at the Sorbonne and the Boston Library. Puvis's lack of faith in the positivist doctrine he was preaching is evident in the pedantry of the Sorbonne mural and the disastrous ineptitude of the images he devised to symbolize "Physics" in the Boston Library.

A recurring theme in nineteenth-century painting is the decline or destruction of civilizations corrupted by wealth and luxury. Parallels were frequently drawn between nineteenth-century Europe and the decadent periods of the empires of Carthage, Rome, and Byzantium; and such pictures as Turner's "Decline of the Carthaginian Empire," John Martin's "Fall of Ninevah," Couture's "Romans of the Decadence," and Rochegrosse's "Last Day of Babylon" were intended to warn against the dangers of wealth and luxury, a danger Delacroix took very seriously, as we know from his journal. When Delacroix came to paint "The Death of Sardanapalus," however, the opportunity to draw a moral was entirely lost in an orgy of sadism and sensuous color. Despite the censorious statements of his journal Delacroix too obviously sympathizes with the decadent voluptuary Sardanapalus.

A similar ambivalence compromises the stern warning offered by Couture's enormous painting "The Romans of the Decadence," which many took to be a comment on the morals of mid-nineteenth-century France. The painting is an incitement as much as a warning. Théophile Gautier described it: "Statues with severe expressions, and solemn gestures, representing the great Romans of the glorious epochs, witness impassively, from the heights of their pedestals, the debauches of their degenerate descendants." It was with the degenerate descendants rather than with the stern representatives of the glorious epochs that Gautier and his circle identified. In 1861 Gustave Boulanger painted a strange picture of the interior of Prince Napoleon's neo-Pompeiian villa in the Avenue Montaigne, with Théophile Gautier and various actors dressed as Romans. The entertainments offered in Prince Napoleon's villa were evidently more sedate than those depicted by Couture. Nevertheless Boulanger's picture says a great deal about the fantasies of the ruling class during the Second Empire.

Delacroix, Baudelaire and Chenavard

Delacroix and Baudelaire must be regarded as central figures in any history of nineteenth-century art and particularly so in one that sees nineteenth-century art in terms of development and progress. Their attitudes on the question of progress or decadence in the arts were extremely complex. Both were intensely pessimistic and their pessimism showed in the affectation of the pose of a dandy and of an aristocratic and fastidious contempt for the culture of their time and all its products. Surveying contemporary art in his *Salon of 1846* Baudelaire saw only "a swarming chaos of mediocrity." He wrote "all is turbulence, a hurly-burly of styles and colours, a cacophony of tones, enormous trivialities, platitudes of gesture and pose, nobility by numbers, clichés of all kind." Delacroix complained of the "miserable little pictures we produce to match our mean little dwellings." He wondered if the nineteenth century were capable of producing beauty. "Can a debased society enjoy lofty things of any kind? Probably not. Moreover, in our present state of society, with our hide-bound customs and mean little pleasures, the beautiful can only occur by accident, and this accident never assumes sufficient importance to change public taste and bring back the majority to an appreciation of beauty."[25]

Baudelaire, too, links the debasement of art with that of society in the opening sentence of his famous essay on the "heroism of modern life." "Many people will attribute the present decadence in painting to our decadence in behavior." Both he and Delacroix explicitly rejected the concept of progress in the arts. In the introduction to his review of the Exposition Universelle in 1855, Baudelaire described the concept of progress as "this grotesque idea, which had flowered upon the rotten soil of modern fatuity," and warned, "if this disastrous folly lasts for long, the dwindling races of the earth will fall into the drivelling slumber of decrepitude upon the pillow of their destiny."

While apparently accepting the concept of "progress," Delacroix wondered whether it was not harmful rather than beneficial. "From all the signs that have been staring us in the face during the past year, I believe it is safe to say that all progress must lead, not to further progress, but to the negation of progress, a return to the point of departure. . . . It is not very clear that progress, that is to say, the onward march of things good as well as evil, has brought our civilisation to the brink of an abyss into which it may very possibly fall, giving place to utter barbarism." Baudelaire asked whether indefinite progress was not a "most cruel and ingenious torture," whether it would not turn out to be a "perpetually renewed form of suicide."

Delacroix and Baudelaire shared a profound distrust of material progress and its products—machines, new luxuries, and conveniences. Baudelaire castigated those simple-minded people who equated progress with "steam, electricity, and gas—miracles unknown to the Romans." Delacroix expressed similar misgivings in his journal; "I have no need to point out how harmful to morality and even to health many of his [man's] so-called improvements have been."

The two also shared in a cyclical view of civilization. They believed that even genuine progress could not continue forever. Periods of achievement must alternate with periods of decadence. Delacroix wrote: "No sooner do nations reach a certain stage of civilization than they find themselves growing weaker."[26] Baudelaire believed that civilizations follow the same process of growth and decay as living organisms: "It must never be forgotten that nations, those vast collective beings, are subject to the same laws as individuals."

Several entries in Delacroix's journal indicate that he believed that there is a point of perfection in the arts beyond which no progress is possible and that in the arts of music and painting this point had already been reached. In 1850 he wrote: "Mozart is undoubtedly the creator—I will not say of modern art, since none is being produced at the present time—but of art carried to its highest point, beyond which no further perfection is possible."[27] As far as painting was concerned, Delacroix believed that "all the great problems of art were solved in the sixteenth century."[28] In some notes made for a projected dictionary of fine arts in January 1857, Delacroix wrote gloomily: "Since the height of their perfection in the sixteenth century, the arts have shown a steady decline." This belief in the inability of the modern artists to go beyond the perfection of the old masters brings Delacroix surprisingly close to his great rival and opponent Ingres, who said: "Nothing essential remains to discover in art since Phidias and Raphael."

Delacroix was prompted to take a different and less pessimistic line in the discussions he had with the painter Chenavard, even though Chenavard's theory of decadence clearly bothered him considerably. He wrote: "His devastating doctrine of the inevitable decay of the arts may well be true but we must not allow ourselves to think of it."

The name and reputation of Paul Chenavard are irrevocably linked with the Revolution of 1848 and the brief-lived Second Republic. It was the leaders of the Second Republic who gave Chenavard the opportunity to realize his ambition of creating a vast decorative scheme in the Panthéon, which would have enabled him to express his philosophy and his view of world history. It was the fall of the Republic that thwarted Chenavard's scheme.[29] But Chenavard did not share the utopian optimism of the Second Republic's leaders. In his predictions for civilization he was far more gloomy even than Delacroix and Baudelaire. Like Baudelaire, Chenavard believed that civilization followed a course similar to the lifespan of man. Unlike Baudelaire, he did not see a possibility for renewal or for more than one lifespan. The whole history of man from the dawn of civilization to man's final extinction would, he believed, follow the pattern of a single human life. Chenavard thought that civilization had reached maturity in the time of Christ and was already far advanced in senility. As the contemporary critic Théophile Silvestre put it: "He came to adopt this idea, so tragic for an artist, that painting had stopped expressing elevated thoughts and was weakened through the affectation of technique to a point where it was no longer able to render the type of all human art, the image of man, and, no longer animated by social thought, it had come in our time to exhaust its last insignificant manifestation: landscape."[30]

Art Criticism

Julius Meier-Graefe wrote: "The amount of talking and writing about art in our day exceeds that in all other epochs put together."[31] In nineteenth-century France most of the talking and writing was done by literary men rather than by art critics in the modern sense or by men with any professional or practical involvement in art. Much of the most memorable and influential art criticism in nineteenth-century France came from Romantic and Symbolist writers: Baudelaire, Huysmans, and the self-styled decadents of the second half of the century. Max Nordau spoke of "the reign of terror of decadent critics." There is no doubt that this tendency in French art criticism led to a certain amount of distortion. From Delacroix to Redon, Van Gogh, and Gauguin, artists were often irritated by the literary critics who lavishly praised their work and felt they were misinterpreted. Pissarro, while grateful for Huysmans' support, felt that he had only a very partial understanding of Impressionism and its aims and wrote his son Lucien: "We can't all be sick like Huysmans." Redon was puzzled by what the critics read into his mysterious images and Puvis rejected the label of "Symbolist" which they gave him. Gauguin was moved to write an article of protest against men of letters who presumed to set themselves up as art critics.

Moreau, Puvis, and Redon, the three artists most praised by the decadent novelist and critic Péladon, resolutely refused to be associated with his Salons de la Rose + Croix. It is strange to find Rossetti and Moreau, who were so much admired by the decadents, criticizing other artists for being decadent. In 1864 Rossetti dismissed the French Realist school as "simple putrescence and decomposition.[32] Moreau, criticizing the sculpture of Rodin, said: "Rodin—the dream of Michelangelo flitting through the soul and brain of Gustave Doré . . . inevitably with the sadism of Rops, the decadence of the modern spirit, and the mindlessness of beerhouse mysticism mixed with boulevard pornography, but with talent, a great deal of talent."[33] For these two "decadent" artists then, decadence seems hardly to have been a desirable quality.

Decadent critics frequently annexed artists who seem to us to have had very little to do with their aims and tastes. Teodor de Wyzewa could discuss Manet, Monet, and Degas under the heading of "La peinture Wagneriènne." Huysmans gave a perverse and decadent interpretation to Whistler and Degas. Whistler's "Nocturnes" became opium-induced hallucinations and Degas's ballet dancers, who now seem so innocuous, even pretty, presented to Huysmans an image of "moral decay" painted with "a lingering cruelty, a patient hatred." This view of Degas was repeated some years later by Meier-Graefe: "Out of the faces of courtesans, out of defiled flesh that rages in silence, out of the smiles of meagre ballet-dancers, out of the pain that is almost pleasure again, he creates a new and grandiose world of form. . . . His form is a monstrous mask, like the devils heads of the Japanese, but more human—more bestial."[34]

Max Nordau and Oswald Spengler on Art

Max Nordau's *Entartung*, first published in 1893–94 and translated into English in 1895 as *Degeneration* has acquired an extremely dubious reputation. It does indeed present an extraordinary mixture of pseudoscience, misinformation, and wild prejudice, which seems all the more sinister in the light of later German history. Nevertheless, George Bernard Shaw took it seriously enough to write a short book in reply to it, and in his day Nordau was widely read and influential.

Shaw neatly summed up the central idea of Nordau's book: "His message to the world is that all our characteristically modern works of art are symptoms of a disease in the artists, and that these diseased artists are themselves symptoms of the nervous exhaustion of the race by overwork."[35] Many of Nordau's thoughts are neither very original nor very sinister. His warnings against the dangers of alcohol, tobacco, drugs, pollution, the adulteration of food, and the effects of big city life echo ideas expressed by Delacroix in his journal and would be topical and unexceptionable today.

What made Nordau's book so remarkable was the vehemence and vividness with which he wrote. Nordau's overheated imagination, his spicy prose style, and his ability to find perversity and decadence in almost anything remind one of Huysmans. It is amusing to find Nordau picking out as symptoms of degeneracy in other writers the features that are so characteristic of his own writing: long-windedness, inconsistency, and the excessive use of scientific jargon. Of Huysmans in particular Nordau says, his "employment of technical expressions and empty phrases, scientific in sound, is peculiar to many modern degenerate authors and to their imitators."[36]

The greater part of *Degeneration* is concerned with literature rather than art. As Shaw pointed out, Nordau's knowledge of painting was extremely limited and he makes some surprising mistakes. (Neither Nordau, nor Shaw, seems to have been very clear about who the Impressionists were or what they were trying to do.) Nordau, for example, was quite out of touch with recent developments. As representative of modern art he chose Besnard, Puvis de Chavannes, Raffaelli, and Manet. He says nothing of Gauguin, Van Gogh, Munch, Lautrec, and Seurat, who might have lent themselves rather better to his thesis. As far as the visual arts are concerned, the principal targets in *Degeneration* are the doctrine of "art for art's sake," the Impressionists, the Pre-Raphaelites, and the Symbolist painters.

Nordau classifies the aesthete's doctrine of art for art's sake as "egomania" and sees it as an excuse for immorality. He writes: "It never occurs to us to permit the criminal by organic disposition to expand his individuality in crime and just as little can it be expcted of us to permit the degenerate artist to expand his individuality in immoral works of art. The artist who complacently represents what is reprehensible, vicious, criminal, approves of it, perhaps glorifies it, differs not in kind but only in degree, from the criminal who actually commits it" (p. 326).

The Pre-Raphaelites are discussed under "Mysticism." Nordau asserts that mysticism is a principal characteristic of degeneracy. "To cite authorities for this is about as unnecessary as to adduce proof for the fact that in typhus a rise in temperature of the body is invariably observed" (p. 45). Nordau first attacks Ruskin. Grossly misrepresenting Ruskin's ideas, Nordau describes Ruskin as "a Torquemada of aesthetics." "To the service of the most wildly eccentric thoughts he brings the acerbity of a bigot and the deep sentiment of Morel's 'emotionalists.'" The Pre-Raphaelite painters are criticized for the obscurity of their symbolism and their excessive attention to detail. "This uniformly clear reproduction of all the phenomena in the field of vision is the pictorial expression of the incapacity for attention" (p. 83).

Impressionist and Symbolist painters are used as examples when Nordau discusses the symptoms of degeneracy. He claims that the stylistic innovations of the Impressionists and of Puvis de Chavannes and Carrière are the result of defects of vision brought on by nervous disorders. "The curious style of certain recent painters—Impressionists, Stipplers, or Mosaists, Papilloteurs, or Quiverers, roaring colourists, dyers in gray and faded tints—becomes at once intelligible to us if we keep in view the researches of the Charcot school into the visual derangements in degeneration and hysteria" (p. 27). The Impressionist use of violet in shadows is also attributed to sickness: "painters suffering from hysteria and neurasthenia will be inclined to cover their pictures uniformly with the colour most in accordance with their condition of lassitude and exhaustion. Thus originates the violet pictures of Manet and his school, which springs from no actually observable aspect of nature, but from a subjective view due to the condition of the nerves" (p. 29).

Nordau was not alone in believing that the eccentricity of Impressionist color was due to defective eyesight. It was a criticism often repeated. Much to the disgust of Pissarro, even Huysmans wrote that the overuse of blue by the Impressionists was due to a "disease of the visual organ."[37] By contrast, the "decadent" writer Laforgue believed that "the Impressionist eye is, in short, the most advanced eye in human evolution."

Degeneration was not Nordau's last word on the subject of the visual arts. In 1907 he published a book entitled *On Art and Artists*. Compared to the fireworks of *Degeneration* it is a rather tame performance. Nordau had still not caught up with modern art. It seems remarkable that in 1907 Munch and Van Gogh were still unknown to him. However, his views on many of the artists discussed in *Degeneration* had undergone an extraordinary transformation. Monet and Degas are praised and Pissarro congratulated on the sharpness of his retina. Carrière, whose pictures were previously described as "suffused in a problematical vapour, reeking as if with a cloud of incense," now became "one of the noblest, chastest, most deeply-feeling artists of today."[38]

The one artist who receives the full blast of Nordau's eloquence is Rodin. Rodin he says has been "raised to the dignity of a test for decadent ways of feeling." "You do not admire Rodin?" Nordau asks rhetorically,

"You are no decadent. No beauty with her hair combed in the Botticelli style will love you: Mallarmé will not write poems, nor will Nietzsche philosophise for you. Nobody will invite you even to a black mass." Of the "Gates of Hell" Nordau says: "Fits of hysteria shake and twist these bodies, every motion of which betrays shocking aberration and eager sadism. . . . Rodin's demoniac women have swallowed pills of Spanish-fly. Thus it is clear that Rodin must be dear to all wanton schoolboys, impotent debauchees, and incipient spinal sufferers." Other sculptures of Rodin, Nordau says, "hint at other forms of morbid sensuality on which I am reluctant to dwell."[39]

It is interesting to compare Nordau's description with that of a contemporary admirer of Rodin, Gustave Geffroy, and to find a remarkable similarity in the imagery used. Geffroy wrote: "Mouths open as if to bite, women run with swelling breasts and impatient buttocks; equivocal desires and tormented passions quiver under the invisible whip-lashes of animal rutting."

Max Nordau's ideas on art clearly influenced those of Oswald Spengler in his *Untergang des Abendlandes*, published in 1918 and translated into English as "The Decline of the West." Spengler replaces Nordau's pseudoscience with a fatuous philosophizing. It is difficult to draw much sense from his opaque prose, and his knowlege of modern art is apparently even more limited than that of Nordau, but the judgments and conclusions are similar. For Spengler, Wagner and Manet (two of Nordau's bêtes noires) marked the final stage in the history of Western art. "The bitter conclusion is that it is all irretrievably over with the arts of form of the West. . . . What is practised as art today—be it music after Wagner or painting after Cézanne, Leibl and Menzel—is impotence and falsehood."[40]

Foolish and ignorant though they now seem, the pronouncements of Nordau and Spengler on modern art fell on fertile ground and provided an unhappy legacy from the nineteenth century to our own.

NOTES

1. Henri Delaborde, *Ingres, sa vie, ses travaux, ses doctrines* (Paris: H. Plon, 1870). "To remedy the overflow of mediocrity which has caused the disintegration of the French School, to counteract the banality which has become a public misfortune, . . . [which sickens taste and overwhelms the state administration of the arts, fruitlessly wasting its resources,] it is necessary to renounce exhibitions."

Charles Baudelaire, *Art in Paris, 1845–1862: Salons and Other Exhibitions Reviewed by Charles Baudelaire*, J. Mayne, tr. and ed. (London: Phaidon, 1965). "I am convinced that the ill-applied developments of photography, like other purely material developments of progress, have contributed much to the impoverishment of the French artistic genius which is already so scarce" (p. 153).

Edmond de Goncourt, *The Goncourt Journals, 1851–1870*, Lewis Galantière, tr. and ed. (Garden City, N.Y.: Doubleday, Doran, 1937).

Louis Gonse, *Eugène Fromentin: Painter and Writer* (Boston: J.R. Osgood, 1883): "We are all—will the acknowledgement be too harsh?—the product of a worthless instruction or a detestable education."

Eugène Delacroix, *The Journal of Eugène Delacroix: A Selection*, Hubert Wellington, ed., Lucy Norton, tr. (Ithaca, N.Y.: Cornell University Press, 1980), September 21, 1854: "We borrow from nature such poisons as tobacco and opium and make them into the instruments of our gross pleasure, and we are punished by loss of energy and the degradation of our minds."

2. Edmond and Jules de Goncourt, *La Révolution dans les mœurs* (Paris: E. Dentu, 1854); Charles Baudelaire, *Salon of 1859.*

3. Delacroix, *Journal*, June 6, 1856; May 6, 1852; August 27, 1854.

4. M. Vachon, *Un Maître de ce temps, Puvis de Chavannes* (Paris: Société d'Édition Artistique, 1900), p. 61.

5. Quoted by Anita Brooker, *Jacques-Louis David* (New York: Harper and Row, 1980), p. 17.

6. Delacroix, *Journal*, January 3, 1857.

7. Théophile Thoré, *Salons de W. Bürger, 1861 à 1868* (Paris: Libraire de Vᶜ Jules Renouard, 1870), p. 145.

8. *Paul Gauguin: Letters to His Wife and Friends*, Maurice Malingue, ed.; Henry J. Stenning, tr. (Cleveland: World, 1949), p. 197.

9. Paul Gauguin, *Noa Noa* (Paris: A. Ballard, 1966), p. 17.

10. Camille Pissarro, *Letters to His Son Lucien*, John Rewald, ed., with assistance of Lucien Pissarro; Lionel Abel, tr. (New York: Pantheon Books, 1943), June 13, 1883; July 8, 1891; May 13, 1891.

11. Paul Signac, "Impressionistes et révolutionnaires," *La Révolté*, June 13–19, 1891.

12. Walter Crane, *An Artist's Reminiscences* (London: Methuen, 1907), p. 258.

13. William Morris, *The Aim of Art*, 1887.

14. Lady Burne-Jones, *Memorials* (New York: Macmillan, 1904), 2:3.

15. Edmond de Goncourt, *Journal: Mémoires de la vie littéraire* (Paris: Flammarion, 1872–96), February 13, 1874.

16. Joris Karl Huysmans, *Certains* (Paris: Tresse and Stock, 1889).

17. John Rewald, ed., "Extraits du journal inédit de Paul Signac," *Gazette des beaux-arts* (July–September, 1949), p. 104.

18. Albert Aurier, "Les Isolés, Vincent van Gogh," *Mercure de France*, January 1890.

19. *The Complete Letters of Vincent Van Gogh* (Greenwich, CN.: New York Graphic Society, n.d.), 3:536.

20. Ragna Stang, *Edvard Munch*, Geoffrey Calverwell, tr. (New York: Abbeville Press, 1979), pp. 36 and 123.

21. Stang, p. 202.

22. See E. H. Gombrich, *The Ideas of Progress and Their Impact on Art* (New York: Cooper Union School of Art, 1971).

23. *Deutsche Kunst und Dekoration*, 11:91, and 10:528. Page and volume numbers hereafter given parenthetically in the text.

24. Carl E. Schorske, *Fin-de-Siècle Vienna: Politics and Culture* (New York: Knopf, 1980), pp. 251 and 240.

25. Delacroix, *Journal*, January 1, and February 4, 1857.

26. Delacroix, September 21, 1854.

27. Delacroix, March 3, 1850.

28. Delacroix, 1847 notebook, undated, p. 85.

29. See Joseph C. Sloane, *Paul Marc Joseph Chenavard: Artist of 1848* (Chapel Hill: University of North Carolina Press, 1962).

30. Sloane, p. 73.

31. Julius Meier-Graefe, *Modern Art* (New York: Putnam, 1908), 1:5.

32. D. G. Rossetti, *Letters of Dante Gabriel Rossetti*, Oswald Doughty and John Robert Wahl, eds. (Oxford: Clarendon Press, 1965), letter to his mother, November 12, 1864.

38. Quoted by Jean Paladilhe and Josbe Pierre, *Gustave Moreau*, Bettina Wadia, tr. (New York: Praeger, 1972), p. 134.

34. Meier-Graefe, p. 278.

35. George Bernard Shaw, *The Sanity of Art: An Exposure of the Current Nonsense about Artists Being Degenerate* (London: New Age Press, 1908), p. 17.

36. Max Nordau, *Degeneration* (New York: Appleton, 1895), pp. 302–03. Page numbers hereafter given parenthetically in text.

37. Camille Pissarro, May 13, 1883.

38. Max Nordau, *On Art and Artists* (New York: 1907), p. 176.

39. Nordau, *Art*, p. 275.

40. Oswald Spengler, *The Decline of the West*, Charles Francis Atkinson, tr. (New York: Knopf, 1926–28), p. 293.

11

THEATER AND DEGENERATION: SUBVERSION AND SEXUALITY

SIMON WILLIAMS

University of California,
Santa Barbara

For Max Nordau the drama of the European modernists was aberrant. Like the pictorial and decorative art of the day, it aimed not at energizing and instructing its audiences, but at "exciting the nerves and dazzling the senses."[1] Nordau attributes the appeal of such material to various causes, from widespread indulgence in narcotics and stimulants, to residence in large cities, to fatigue from a world where the pace of life is constantly accelerating. He fervently advocates return to a society where order, obedience, and regular habits are the rule, describing fin-de-siècle culture as the result of a "practical emancipation from traditional discipline, which theoretically is still in force." One of these disciplines he rigorously upholds is marriage and the regulation of sexual conduct within it, as contemporary degeneracy makes itself evident in "unbridled lewdness, the unchaining of the beast in man."

Nordau's reactionary assault on contemporary culture arises in part from his inability to adapt to a post-Darwinian world in which moral absolutes were being undercut by an awareness that man's biological nature did not dwell happily in a condition of constant social restraint. But for the theater historian who has observed the centuries-long campaign against theatrical performance, conducted primarily by conservative divines of many sects and denominations, Nordau seems to be saying little that is new.

Although on the continent by the start of the nineteenth century attacks from the pulpit on the theater were in decline, in England the flood of such sermons had reached its peak.[2] For the Evangelical preachers, the very existence of theater was evidence of the persistence of pagan impulses in man, as the stage appealed solely to his love of the world and the flesh; hence, attendance at its productions was incompatible with a love of God. Evangelical suspicion was caused partly by a belief that most plays staged were actively anti-Christian, with tragedy exalting "pride, ambition, and revenge,"[3] giving "splendour to the worst of passions," and comedy encouraging audiences to laugh with vice and to scorn virtue. Earnestness of mind was dissipated, people were led to become "light, trifling, and profane," and cleverness rather than honesty was applauded. But in addition to the supposedly immoral purpose of the drama, performance on stage per se was considered to subvert the supremely rational tenets of a Christian society. Performance enthroned the world. As the theater's splendid spectacles encouraged audiences to delight in the transitory beauties of life, the treacherous imagination was inflamed, which in turn obscured the sound moral precepts preachers imposed on their congregations. This led automatically to confusion and submission to lower instincts. As the Reverend Thomas Best of Sheffield, an indomitable antitheatrical campaigner, warned, "Images and ideas have been communicated which, working their way into the very recesses of the heart, have there taken root, and have at length produced the deadly harvest of a licentious conversation and a profligate life."[4]

If merely watching theatrical presentations had such deleterious effects, those responsible for them, the actors, were of necessity dissolute and unregenerate. As preachers were unable to distinguish between the performer's personality and the roles he played, they considered the actor to have no character or will. As a result, they argued, he would automatically practice in life those misdemeanors he represented on stage. Actresses, of course, were de facto harlots, as nightly they allowed themselves to be embraced in public by strange men. Their very presence on stage was an act akin to prostitution. "As most of their exhibitions are of the amorous description, you will generally see the dress of the actress loose in the extreme: and indeed it is the only livery that suits her part; while she appears to represent a character that is wanton and impure, her dress, her attitude, her language, must all conjoin to bring matters forward to the same *delicious* point." Performers of both sexes were described as giving rise to "all those impure sensations which can scarcely be equalled in any place but a brothel!" Aroused spectators were assumed to "retire from their meetings to the house of debauchery to gratify [their] ungovernable lusts."[5] All in all, Evangelical preachers found theater to be a hideous product of luxurious living, encouraging tendencies to unbridled sensuality, leading to the corruption of young men, the ruin of young women, the destruction of the Christian household, and the downfall of an enervated and profligate nation. Its offerings were, in the words of Tertullian, a frequently quoted authority, "honey dropping from the bowels of a toad, or the bag of a spider."[6]

In some respects it must be granted that the preacher's insights into theater were apt. To the Evangelical, who envisioned a progressive, morally regimented society, there *was* much that could be subversive in theater. For a start, for the first half of the nineteenth century, theaters in London, and Paris too, were situated in disreputable neighborhoods, surrounded by "a halo of brothels,"[7] pickpockets' dens, and moldy slums. Audiences were often unruly, so that Charles Dickens could describe the Drury Lane auditorium as "a beargarden, resounding with foul language, oaths, shrieks, yells, blasphemy, obscenity, a truly diabolical clamor."[8] Prostitution flourished, and there was probably much truth in preachers' claims that box office receipts would fall off if ladies of the night were not permitted to do business in the precincts of the theater. The Evangelicals' perception of the nature of drama was also not entirely inaccurate. In essence comedy is anarchic and, while not completely immune to ethical considerations, often champions the victory of vital spirit over systems that might attempt to contain it. Normative structures commonly recommended by the preachers could be represented as forces to be overcome rather than submitted to. Then tragedy has rarely been exclusively concerned with man's salvation in a Christian universe, as it examines the harsh necessities determining his freedom without paying too much attention to their specifically theological implications. Finally, the Evangelicals may have been partially right in their judgment of actors. The very conditions of the acting profession do not encourage a quiet domestic life. Furthermore, the desire to act no doubt arises in part from the desire to exhibit oneself, a trait that runs against the self-effacing ethic of a Christian society. As will be seen, in England fervent efforts were made by actors to deny public perception of them as morally lax, but on the continent, above all in Paris, where, as members of the city's *bohème,* actors lived free of the moral restraints binding bourgeois families, they capitalized on risqué reputations. Indeed the century abounds in colorful tales of actresses who flamboyantly violated sexual taboos, from the voluptuous Mlle. George (1787–1867), one-time mistress of Napoleon, through to the exotic Sarah Bernhardt (1845–1923).

But while the Evangelical antitheatricalist had some right on his side, he was blind to features of the theater peculiar to his time. As the century progressed, in London rougher elements of the audience were excluded, so the auditorium became quieter, more decorous, and more subject to the Victorian cult of Respectability. While incidents of soliciting did not cease entirely, by the end of the century a high-minded father could take his daughter to the theater without too much fear for her blushing at her fellow audience members. Henry James found this audience dull. "It suggests," he wrote, "domestic virtue and comfortable homes," composed as it was of "mild, fresh-coloured English mothers . . . wrapped in knitted shawls . . . rosy young girls, with dull eyes and quiet cheeks . . . handsome and honorable young [men] . . . in evening dress."[9] Instead he

preferred the less exclusive audiences of Paris, the "clever, cynical multitude that surges nightly out of the brilliant boulevards," whose concern
was not to show off clothes or to display to a wider public graces acquired
in the drawing room. Their more raffish conduct and lack of reverence
toward the stage made for a livelier evening in the theater. In London
somnolence reigned.

The Evangelicals can be excused for their misconceptions about audiences as the middle classes possessed the theater only after the antitheatrical attacks had passed their peak. Preachers were, however, strangely
ignorant of the moral tone of the average play. During the eighteenth
century, much of the amoral spirit of the drama had been purged when
dramatists shifted its domain from kingly courts where ambition and
corruption held sway to more domestic settings. In these plays the indus-
trious merchant and his dutiful family had been treated with sympathy,
while the dramatic action underscored homely virtues such as honesty,
scrupulous consideration for others, diligent attention to one's duties both
in familial and professional spheres. Any personal good fortune, such as
marriage to a young and beautiful heiress, was seen as the reward of virtue
rather than as a consummation only to be achieved by intrigue. One could
be erotically fulfilled only if one was good. Melodrama, the most ubiquitous of all popular nineteenth-century theatrical genres, was, for all the
hurly-burly of its action, essentially heir to the moralistic plays of the
previous century. Impulses that were natural and amoral were accounted
for in terms of good and evil, the action normally ending with the victory
of virtue and a spectacular, terminal defeat for any forces that opposed it.
Unquestioned absolutes were loyalty to family and community, honesty in
all one's dealings, obedience to legitimate authority, and, above all, sexual
purity. If it were not for the surface violence of its actions, undoubtedly a
key factor in its appeal, melodrama should have been met with the approval of the most devout Evangelical.

The nineteenth-century theater was also marked by a distinct rise in the
social status of the actor. In Britain, mindful of the public suspicion
against them, leaders of the profession such as William Charles Macready
(1793–1873), Helena Faucit (1817–1898), and Charles (1811–1868) and Ellen
Kean (1806–1880) went to great pains to demonstrate the unblemished
respectability of their private lives and to assert the noble nature of their
calling. Actors came to be seen more and more in fashionable salons, and
when Henry Irving (1838–1905) was knighted in 1895, the profession acquired official approval. On the continent there was equivalent progress
in the fortunes of actors. In 1849 the Catholic church in France declared
once and for all that actors had full rights to receive the sacrament, and
some decades later in the 1880s, select members of the Comédie Française, as distinct from actors in the commercial boulevard theaters, were
being awarded the *Légion d'honneur*. In German-speaking countries, where
theater had been patronized by governments since the late eighteenth

century, actors had less difficulty in winning social acceptance; indeed, in Vienna, as the influence of the aristocracy waned, they became setters of fashion for the city's population. Knighthood also dignified the profession when, in 1881, Adolf Sonnenthal (1834–1909), a leading actor at the Burgtheater, the Austrian national theater, was elevated to the hereditary peerage. By the end of the century, in both Britain and continental Europe, leading actors were enjoying a social *éclat* and a sizeable salary undreamed of a hundred years before.

As long as the theater was less than respectable, there was little hope it could be accepted as a forum for the discussion of issues important to the day. Throughout the century, public attitudes, which often differed little from those of the Evangelicals, forced upon the theater the task of reflecting social and ethical norms, a pressure it responded to positively, as if to deny its reputation for subversiveness. Nowhere is this clearer than in its treatment of themes of sexuality. As a general rule, both the plays and the manner in which they were performed reflected broadly held views on the dangers of indulging one's sexual desires more than is strictly necessary to ensure the continuation of the race. Victorian prudery can be attributed to several causes, both economic and psychological, but perhaps the commonest reason for this fear of sex can be identified in the writings of William Acton, a London doctor, whose books were read widely both in Britain and on the continent. For Acton man was a creature of limited vitality who would inevitably suffer disease, nervous collapse, insanity, even death, if he failed to exercise rigorous control over his sexual desires. As if to ensure his survival, women were seen as totally quiescent. "The majority of women," Acton wrote, "(luckily for them) are not very much troubled with sexual feeling of any kind."[10] Acton saw woman as a moral ideal, a fantasy world of purity, embodying those virtues men should, in the best of worlds, possess. But conveniently she has been given just enough tolerance for sex so that she can make an "unselfish sacrifice" of her body to her husband when necessity dictates.

Popular melodrama almost invariably reflected this highly idealized view of women. Occasionally illicit relations do occur in it, when the forces of evil need to be painted in specially dark colors, but never with intent to determine the attractions that bind the partners. Adultery was rarely treated until late in the century, and when it was, as in Benjamin Thompson's immensely popular *Stranger* (1798), an adaptation of August von Kotzebue's *Misanthropy and Repentance* (1789), the heroine's adultery, which has taken place years before, is viewed only as the temporary lapse of a virtuous woman. Whatever drove her to it is never examined, focus being placed entirely on her repentance and on the charity of those men who come to accept it. Gothic melodrama, which flourished in the early decades, deals at times with sexual passion, though never as part of the normal human condition. For example, in plays such as Charles Nodier's *Vampire* (1820), which went through several adaptations in the course of the century, sexual desire is exhibited as supernatural possession that causes the heroine to wander deliriously in caverns and shady places in search of her demon lover. But once she returns to consciousness, she is totally unaware of the dark forces that have briefly taken over her body. The melodramatic heroine is rigorously chaste, quite unable to conceive the possibility of submitting to the advances of admirers. She is the prototype of the Victorian woman Acton described, devoid of interest in and knowledge of sex. To the closing years of the century, she held sway on stage.

In the melodrama, of which she is so typical a figure, psychology counts for nothing, morality is all. Characters have little life; they are not so much human beings as moral emblems, with traits fixed and given, not acquired and mutable. They are sealed units in a world that demonstrates moral norms, a world in which nothing changes, in which deviation by someone who is basically "good" is exploited to preach a sermon, not to indicate mainsprings of action that might challenge the legitimacy of the norm. Characters are saved or damned not by their own efforts but by the force of circumstance, wielded by a moralistic providence. They affirm a view of man as an element in a system, whose personal experience has no value in itself. To the end of the century, theater perpetuated the model of man as a morally motivated being, a unit in a rational organization, stalwart, unchanging, "monopathic."[11]

Despite the prevalence of the monopathic view of man, it did not go unchallenged on the stage. In tracing the origins of the malaise of modernist art, Max Nordau identifies degenerate elements in the plays of the French Romantics of the 1820s and '30s, which were characteristic of a culture striving to be "free from moral and mental restraints." His primary objection, above all to the drama of Victor Hugo (1802–1885), was the way in which "the aesthetic prevailed over the useful, and the fantastic over the rational." Undoubtedly Hugo was little concerned with perpetuating the clichés of melodrama, already firmly ensconced in both the London and Parisian theaters. In fact he aimed to create precisely their opposite. In his famous "Preface to *Cromwell*" (1827), he advocated a drama whose action was impelled by conflicts caused by the struggle of dualistic forces within the individual, who was described as "double . . . composed of two beings, one perishable, the other immortal, one carnal, the other ethereal, one enchained by the appetites, the other borne on the wings of enthusiasm and dreams."[12] Hugo's vigorous and replete language, his opulent Renaissance settings, and his extravagant characters are all designed to create in the audience an ambiguous response; the beauty of the surface never reflects moral worth in conventional, melodramatic manner. *Lucrèce Borgia* (1833), the greatest success of his playwriting career, was written specifically to reverse audiences' moral expectations, as by mixing "the most unrelieved moral deformity . . .

with . . . a single pure sentiment . . . the sentiment of maternity,"[13] he managed to make the "monster" of Lucrèce sympathetic to his audiences. Despite the woodenness of many ancillary characters, Hugo successfully sustains an equivocal response to Lucrèce throughout the play, counterpoising sympathy toward her as a mother and a victim of others' cruelty with antipathy toward the Lucrèce who revenges herself on all who stand in her way. Unfortunately his fellow playwrights signally failed to achieve an equivalent ambiguity. Though such celebrated popular shockers as Dumas père's *Tower of Nesle* (1832) introduced on stage horrendous themes of infanticide, incest, and the like, characterization remained monopathic, so the result was merely sensational drama that might justify many antitheatricalist suspicions.

French Romantic drama had little immediate influence on the development of the nineteenth-century theater, but toward the end of its dominance of the Parisian stage, an actress appeared whose ability to invest classical roles with an unnerving sense of physical corruption provided an analogy in acting to Hugo's dramaturgy. Known simply as Rachel, from the summer of 1838, when, as an eighteen-year-old she made her debut at the Comédie Française, to her early death from consumption in 1858, she was unquestionably the most idolized actress, first of Paris, later of all Europe. Her private life, spectacular even by Parisian standards, earned for her a notoriety that undoubtedly enhanced her presence on stage, especially as her demure, severely classical beauty suggested virginal purity. The suggestion was belied, however, not only by her reputation, but by her ability to use simple, quiet speech to intimate the presence within her characters of malign forces. She allowed these forces slowly to rise to the surface, so that the character eventually fell prey to them. Her fascination came about through her establishing an antithesis between a cool, seemingly unchangeable exterior and, behind it, an intensely felt physicality that was subject to laws of biological change. The marmoreal and the physical seemed to infect each other, resulting in a portrayal of moral and physical decline. As Phèdre, for example, through "her reddened eyes in the pale marble mask, her lips discolored where the violets of death [seemed] to have replaced the roses of life, Mlle. Rachel [had] the fatal and sinister air of a victim devoured by some terrible expiation."[14] In one way this was a characteristically Victorian portrayal of sexuality as a debilitating force, but in another it was not, for this moral and physical degeneration could appear strangely attractive. Her acting was able to arouse in the audience a sense of exhaustion cognate to that in the character, but one that was exciting. As George Henry Lewes observed of her Phèdre, this woman "standing on the verge of the grave with pallid face, hot eyes, emaciated frame" also possessed "such . . . amazing variety and compass of . . . expression that when she quitted the stage, she left us quivering with . . . excitement."[15]

Rachel's acting was a rare exception for most of the nineteenth century. The three greatest Romantic actors, Edmund Kean (1787/90–1833), Fréd- érick Lemaître (1800–1876), and the German Ludwig Devrient (1784–1832) all in different ways represented the disquieting influence unconscious forces exercise on the human psyche, but such acting was unusual for women. Most admired of all mid-century actresses of the time was the English Helena Faucit, whose interpretations of Shakespeare were praised for "the happiest combination of archness and attraction of man- ners with unvarying maidenly refinement of demeanor."[16] She had the ability to transmute any physical response to her into a sentimental one, through "the power she possesses of rousing those sympathies which men need not be ashamed of, though their eyes dim with tears." Interestingly, Faucit's husband, Sir Theodore Martin, in a monograph on Rachel, recog- nized the French actress's power on stage, but refused to grant her true greatness as an actress as "to rise to the level of great art and to keep there, the inner life and the habits of the artist must be worthy, pure and no- ble."[17] While Faucit cleansed her audience, Rachel was clearly regarded as besmirching them.

Nevertheless, by mid-century sexual themes were emerging as topics in the drama; by century's end sex was so widely discussed on stage that George Bernard Shaw could complain that adultery was the only theme that could guarantee a full house. Such discussion was hardly ever, of course, affirmative. The first *succès de scandale* on the theme of the "fallen woman," which would eventually become ubiquitous, was *The Lady of the Camelias* (1849, prod. 1851) by Alexandre Dumas *fils*. Despite its popular success, the play was capable of turning the most liberal of mid-century thinkers into prudish reactionaries; even George Henry Lewes, not known for the conventionality of his private life, considered it a profoundly sub- versive work. Primarily this was because Dumas not only treated a de- praved character, the courtesan Marguerite Gautier, sympathetically, but in contrast to Hugo he presented her not in a glamorous Renaissance setting but in contemporary life. Then the realism of Dumas' dialogue and his facility at characterization make it difficult to distinguish the whole- some from the corrupt; in fact the play appears to call such distinctions into question. In *The Lady of the Camelias*, the world of the courtesan is presented as though it were totally normal; at the end it is invested with pathos as Marguerite is elevated to the level of a pseudosaint. But her death cannot help but strike an attentive audience as gratuitous as it is neither causally nor thematically related to the earlier action. Dumas' motive behind it is difficult to divine from the play text alone, but in a later drama, *The Demi-Monde* (1855), his most sustained analysis of the courtesan class, he explicitly condemns sexual congress outside marriage. Through his mouthpiece character Olivier de Jalin, he upholds a society, preserved by the code of marriage, in which the disease of infidelity, seen as a specifically feminine trait, should be stamped out by the assertion of moral right as represented by masculine rationality. After initially adopting a liberal attitude toward sexual matters, Dumas recasts the old formulas with a melodramatic axis now spanning the sexes rather than the more abstract conceptions of good and evil. Might not the death of Marguerite have been a covert judgment on her, a first formulation, not entirely realized, of a masculine claim to dominate woman, apparently in the name of moral order, though perhaps more out of fear of his sexual feelings toward her?

Dumas *fils'* treatment of Marguerite was paradigmatic for the representation of the fallen woman on the late nineteenth-century stage. The increasing obsession of dramatists and audiences with the figure indicates a shift in the melodramatic sensibility. While Emile Augier in *Olympe's Marriage* (1855) has his errant heroine shot at the final curtain, later dramatists would devise less sensational, more touching deaths. Like Letty in Henry Arthur Jones' *Saints and Sinners* (1884), the fallen woman might die of exhaustion after spending years nursing the sick in atonement for her past errors, or, like the pitiful adultress in Mrs. Henry Wood's *East Lynne* (1864), she might just "die of sin."[18] This increasing sympathy extended toward her was a tacit concession to the concept of a mixed human condition, a slight advance from the Actonian position on female sexuality. By mixing the saintly with the sinful, the fallen woman came to be someone to be both pitied and mistrusted. Her death would often occur with the man she had offended keeping watch by her bedside, extending to her the benevolence of his forgiveness. In this way, piquancy of dramatic situation was preserved while the essential rightness of the masculine ethic was unambiguously asserted. Even when the presence of active sexual forces in woman were admitted, they were subject to a rigidity of outlook that insisted on the absolute inviolability of marriage and the maintenance of sexual continence.

As the parting shots were being fired from the pulpit in the war against the theater, plays began to appear on the stages of London and continental cities which would have confirmed the worst fears of the Evangelical preachers and, as has already been mentioned, aroused the wrath of reactionaries such as Max Nordau. These plays, first produced in private theaters financed by subscription audiences, did not attempt to appeal to the broadest possible audience, nor to reflect commonly held moral assumptions, above all on human sexuality. Nevertheless, by the end of the century, they had found their way onto the stages of subsidized theaters in central Europe and were even beginning to make some headway in the commercial systems of London and Paris. The plays of the Naturalist and Symbolist schools, which compose the "Modernist" wave of the European theater, established the stage as a platform upon which the fallacies of conventional morality could be exposed. For Nordau, of course, they were the product of a segment of society that had lost its values and sense of purpose, a segment composed of people devoted to the worship of the arcane, the perverse, and the scatalogical.

It is impossible to summarize satisfactorily the work of playwrights as diverse as Henrik Ibsen (1828–1906), August Strindberg (1849–1912), George Bernard Shaw (1856–1950), Anton Chekhov (1860–1904), Gerhart Hauptmann (1862–1946), Arthur Schnitzler (1862–1931), Frank Wedekind (1864–1918), and a host of minor dramatists whose work is part of the modernist movement. Modernism in the theater was distinguished by the variety of backgrounds from which the playwrights came and for the individuality of each playwright's reaction against the formal and thematic conformity of run-of-the-mill drama. But one standpoint that does unite them is their view of man as one who is prompted by physical, biological impulses, and their constant insistence that sexuality in both man and woman is the norm rather than the deviant exception. If, by the end of the century, victories in the war between science and religion were all to the scientists, these dramatists were clearly on the winning side. Strindberg, for example, considered those plays he wrote during the 1880s to be paradigms for a new drama that demonstrated Darwin's theory of natural selection and the survival of the fittest. A little later Freud, whose researches into the components of the human psyche revealed it to be a biological complex of contradictory needs, sublimations, and repressions, all working in reaction to or in concert with the sexual drive, claimed that Schnitzler's plays had anticipated or paralleled his own findings. Freud also found in Ibsen's work perfect psychological types, embodying psychic patterns that only appeared in modified form in everyday life.

With their preeminently biological view of man, the Modernists tended to represent the conventions of bourgeois life as unnatural, coercive forces on the individual, limiting his potential freedom of action and his postulated right to self-determination. If the individual's needs were nonsocial in origin, then society's claim to ascendancy over him could be viewed as an arbitrary violation of his very nature. So, that which in theater had been represented as degenerate in man's nature, now came to be seen as intrinsic to his condition. From the Naturalistic viewpoint, one held at times by Ibsen, Strindberg, Hauptmann, and Emile Zola (1840–1902), whose main contribution to the theater was the seminal essay "Naturalism in the Theater" (1879), man was a creature formed mainly by forces of heredity and environment. As the environment, by the late nineteenth century, involved for many people life in the slums of large industrial cities or in the tightly structured bourgeois family, society itself could be regarded as having a degenerative influence upon man's natural organism. The accusation of who or what was degenerate could therefore be reversed.

The Modernist dramatists did not, of course, find easy acceptance. Nordau saw people's growing interest in their work as a sign that the energy of an otherwise healthy society was being sapped, a way of thinking that clearly parallels the opinions held by the Evangelicals earlier in the century on the theater in general. Ibsen, the first of the new dramatists to capture public attention, was Nordau's prime target, as he was for the conservative establishment in general, spearheaded in London by the dramatic critic Clement Scott, whose famous review of *Ghosts* described the play as "a dirty act done publically."[19] This was an extreme example of the vitriol initially poured on Ibsen's plays in London and, to a lesser degree, elsewhere. Strindberg too had difficulties in having his plays produced, not only because of the technical problems they posed, which were considerable, and for the obscurity of many of his themes, but also because of the way in which they reflected his highly publicized marital problems and his distressing mental collapse, which seemed to argue the inadequacy of the human frame to withstand the newly posited biological freedom. Schnitzler, despite his reputation as an inimitable recorder of the graceful Viennese way of life, in fact met opposition in his city, finding it easier to have his plays produced in the more liberal Berlin. Then Wedekind, from a solid bourgeois family, was widely considered a renegade and little more than a sexual pervert, an accusation that penetrated him so deeply that the latter half of his creative life was crippled by his need to justify, not always with effect, his early views on the need for sexual freedom.

Given the Modernists' pivotal interest in sexuality as a norm, it is notable that their theater, unlike the theater of our own day, is in fact entirely lacking in plays that advocate unfettered sexual freedom. No doubt this was due in part to the watchful eye of the censor and to the greater inhibition of late nineteenth-century audiences. But it may also have been reflective of deep-seated doubts in the playwrights themselves over the possibility of living up to the new norms. In some ways, despite their recognition of sexuality, they never entirely freed themselves from conventional views of it as a degenerative force.

This can be seen in the great *cause célèbre* of the Modernist theater, Ibsen's *Ghosts* (1881). Nordau reviled the work, claiming that Osvald was the paragon of the play, his final words "the sun . . . the sun" being typical of the enervated fin-de-siècle spirit Ibsen was glorifying. This strange judgment is caused partly by Nordau's infuriating tendency arbitrarily to read, without any concern for the dramatic context, chosen characters as mouthpieces for the playwright. Ibsen, however, had little interest in delivering messages; rather his purpose was to expose the contradictions and paradoxes of life. As if to emphasize this, *Ghosts* begins as though it were a thesis play, intended to demonstrate the truth of a given dogma or opinion on life. From the very start, the phrase "the joy of life" is on characters' lips. When introduced by Osvald early in the play, it refers to the spontaneous outpouring of energy in sexual and creative endeavors. The idea is then taken up by Mrs. Alving, who, in the interests of the "joy of life" and in a hopeless attempt to counteract Osvald's decline into imbecility, is prepared to sanction an incestuous union between him and Regine. As she recalls her past, she comes to realize that her husband too once had the joy of life within him and that she unwittingly caused his own and the present tragedy by denying him the right to express it. Ibsen then might seem to be advocating sexual liberty at all costs. But there is an important countercurrent. Osvald, recently back from Paris, is a creature of limited vitality, with little of the energy that had invigorated and destroyed his father. He, even more than Pastor Manders, understands the virtues of a quiet, enclosed family life. Such an outlook is, of course, partly the result of his mother's implanting within him ideals of domesticity, but it is obviously intensified by the syphilis inherited from his father. In *Ghosts*, Ibsen, while exploring Darwinian ideals of biological inheritance, uses them ultimately to reflect a distinctly Actonian view of the consequences of sexual freedom. While his characters aspire toward freedom in the new dispensation, their physical contributions keep them tied to the limited, domestic world. Osvald's physical degeneracy drives him back into the arms of the stifling family and imbecility.

The most ambivalent of all Modernist dramatists on sexual matters was August Strindberg, who, during his Naturalist period in the 1880s, saw sexual relationships as little more than a feral battle between two irreconcilable species, male and female. At this point in his career, Strindberg, for all his claims to be in the forefront of contemporary thought, seems to be doing little more than perpetuating the ideas of Alexandre Dumas *fils* on the relationship of the sexes. Strindberg's men initially appear to display rational patterns of thought, concern for objective truth, and a strong sense of morality. Women, on the other hand, are represented as egotistical, lacking in any sense of responsibility, irrational in their actions, and often promiscuous. But Strindberg, unlike Dumas *fils*, was all too aware of the impossibility of man and woman being reconciled within marriage. No legal sanction was capable of containing the sexual battle in which man and woman fought for supremacy over each other and which consequently did not allow them to find a center of repose in which they could live at harmony with each other and the world around them.

In such plays as *The Father* (1887), *Miss Julie* (1888), and the later *Dance of Death* (1901), sexual relationships within or outside marriage do not indicate a will to unity in the partners, and after the first passionate collision, sex increasingly becomes used as a means to possess and control the other. But the outcome is not automatically the victory of the male, as, given the distinction between the sexes, logically it should be. While Jean, the aggressive, proletarian servant might prevail over his mistress Julie, whose energy has been sapped by years of inbreeding, in *The Father*, the

Captain succumbs to madness after his wife has, apparently without intention, planted in his mind the suspicion that he might not be the father of his daughter Bertha. The Captain's stance of regulating his life by principles that can be scientifically proven—in this case obvious similarities between himself and his daughter—is undercut by an inner weakness of will and a fatal inclination to surrender to doubts that challenge his rational posture. This process, as the Captain describes it to us, is fueled by his desire for his wife, which at times is so overpowering that he has been led to abandon all faith in a world of absolute value. He is therefore rendered powerless to exercise control over either himself or those around him. Sex in Strindberg is often represented as a destructive force, dissolving rather than strengthening the bond of marriage.

At first sight, the most revolutionary play on the subject of sex in this period is Wedekind's *Spring's Awakening* (1892), possibly because of the unprecedented representation on stage of sexual acts such as flagellation, masturbation, and an incipient homosexual encounter. As a result, the play was not seen until 1906, in Berlin, in a severely cut version. But despite the surface sensationalism, Wedekind's view of sex is not entirely radical. Certainly he attacks effectively the repressive German education system and the hideous prudery of teachers and parents, who insist on regarding the growth of sexual feelings in their adolescent charges as manifestations of gross degeneracy. He also contrasts the frigid educational world with a persuasive vision of sexual activity as a benign function of nature, so that his adolescents, both boys and girls, appear to possess a vitality that is potentially unlimited. They are therefore foils to the incipient weaklings of the Victorian imagination. But not entirely so. Nature is not a benign force only. The young girl Wendla intuits in it a power that can destroy. Also, in the pathetic figure of Moritz, a clammy-handed specimen of Acton's imagination, Wedekind gives credence to the idea that human beings can quickly sap their sources of energy. While Moritz's suicide, which is caused by his inability to face up to his sexual yearnings, is an indictment of the world of adults for not helping him come to terms with his sexuality, at the same time it seems to reflect Actonian fears about limited vitality. The adolescents are unwitting victims in a conflict between society and nature, and, given the establishment society's indifference to or fear of dealing with this problem, the only solution is to adopt a posture of cold and isolated superiority. This is the way taken by Wedekind's hero, Melchior, whose acceptance of life through the figure of the Man in the Mask, indicates a willful rejection of such virtues as compassion and altruism, in favor of a harsh egoism that admits the demands of neither nature nor society. To survive, it is implied, one must constantly and ruthlessly assert oneself.

Wedekind's later plays on sexual themes have similar conclusions. The sexually unquenchable child of nature, Lulu, in *Earth Spirit* (1893) and *Pandora's Box* (1902), is finally dispatched by Jack the Ripper in a grim variation on the fate of the fallen woman, while the writer Buridan's mistress, Kadidja, in *Censorship* (1908), throws herself out of the window to avoid final rejection by her lover. In both cases, the assertive male survives. For all his reputation as an advocate of sexual freedom, Wedekind frequently reveals a callousness toward women, who are creatures that can ultimately be dispensed with. Perhaps Wedekind rather than Strindberg can be seen as the true heir to Dumas *fils*.

But Wedekind is not characteristic of the Modernist movement. Other playwrights, while expressing doubts at the possibility of complete sexual fulfillment, did admit the imperative of the sexual drive and even came to find in it important ethical dimensions. This came about through their recognition first that women lived more contentedly with their sexuality than men did, second that they accordingly had an ameliorative, occasionally transformational effect upon a society dominated by men. Take, for example, Ibsen. In his early prose plays, and even in some later works such as *Little Eyolf* (1894) and *John Gabriel Borkman* (1896), familiar Dumasian distinctions seem to be at work as he depicts the relationship of the sexes, but values conventionally associated with them are qualified, and conventional judgments are either nullified or reversed. Men tend to indulge in a rhetoric replete with the phrases of orthodox morality, but by ironies created through the action, this is revealed to be nothing more than an evasion of facing up to the requirements of any given situation. Men in Ibsen can be intolerably inflexible in their ideals. They are monolithic—"I'm the same as I always was," says Pastor Manders in *Ghosts*[20]— not unlike the sealed characters of melodrama. Women, in contrast, can be dynamic, changeable, and unpredictable. They discover and assert responses to life which are individual and independent, they learn through experience rather than from precept, and they follow with ease the promptings of their feelings. Their warmth and spontaneity call into question the authenticity of the male pose. They are intuitors of the biological impulse, agents of life, change, and movement in an ossifying world.

As a general rule, this view of woman holds good for most Modernist playwrights. Shaw's women, for example, are "biologically" motivated in contrast to their male companions, who are far more concerned with social considerations when deciding on a course of action. In Schnitzler's plays, women are consistently protesting, not always with much avail, against an impersonal and hypocritical society dominated by men who are concerned mainly about the appearance of respectability, even if their conduct is far from living up to that appearance. Women become the bearers of truth.

Identification with the woman's point of view, with one who had for most of the century been the underdog in the European drama, was a salient feature of the Modernists' work. At its most extreme point of development, in the later plays of Ibsen and Strindberg, it involved a basic rethinking of the distinction between the sexes and an inquiry into the very nature of sexual identity. Although *Ghosts* and *The Father* viewed sex in a relatively conventional way, the immediacy of the sexual impulse was shown to be so strong that a significant proportion of Ibsen's and Strindberg's later writings was devoted to coming to terms with it. But as domestic stability and sexual fulfillment were seen to be incompatible, their final plays represent a withdrawal from the reality of the everyday world, often becoming flights into the more insubstantial, phantasmal realm of poetry, a realm seen, both by male characters within the play and by the playwright himself, through the consciousness of woman.

A key play in this transformation was Ibsen's *Rosmersholm* (1886). This describes how a pastor who had once been a pillar of the conservative factor in his small Norwegian town renounces his beliefs in order to preach a more liberal gospel. He wishes to create a society in which all men will be united not by forced allegiance to an external authority, but by their own will and inclination. His admirable though quixotic mission is, of course, opposed by the conservatives he has deserted. They have a powerful weapon against him as Rosmer's wife, Beate, sister to the leader of the conservative faction, has committed suicide, apparently as the result of a developing liaison between Rosmer and their housekeeper, Rebekka West. The play covers the last twenty-four hours of Rosmer's and Rebekka's lives, which they end in a double suicide. Their suicide is caused by their discovery that the changes that have come about at Rosmersholm have not been activated by rational causes, as Rosmer initially thought. Instead, Rosmer comes to realize that the change in his ideology was caused by his growing attraction toward Rebekka, especially after she admits that she half consciously drove Beate to her death in her own scarcely admitted desire to possess Rosmer. Their suicide is ambiguous, for, despite their ecstatic claims that only in death have they achieved a "true marriage," it can also be regarded as a refusal to face up to the changes caused by sexual desire.

Rosmersholm is a difficult play. It does not have the clear contours of the earlier prose plays, while the final defeat suggests that Ibsen is questioning the validity of ideals with which he was associated in the public imagination. But the very difficulty of the play, lying in unconscious motivations of necessity only sensed by the characters, is the reason for its importance. Like Victor Hugo before him, although with far greater subtlety, Ibsen is seeking not to reflect contemporary mores but to confound clarity of moral vision in his audience. In *Rosmersholm*, not only has the sense of moral value been destroyed, but the very constitution of the human being, who both creates and abides by those values, has dissolved. Once the rational facets of Rosmer's life appear to him to have been solely illusions, sublimations of unconscious forces he could not initially recognize, he loses his sense of identity, and the only reality he can cling to is the sense of being possessed by the person who created the crisis. Rosmer, therefore, has become the creation of Rebekka, and, as she so aptly points out, she has become his creation, for both he and his gloomy house have worked upon her, sapped her vitality, as if they were a disease. But Rosmer and Rebekka do not end the play at poles opposite to the ones from which they started; rather they enter into a limbo in which they feel themselves subject to demonic influences, not part of themselves, akin to both the destructive powers of nature and the coercive agencies of tradition. These are given expression in the symbol of the white horses, which are both part of the Rosmersholm tradition and descriptive of natural, especially sexual urges. As the symbol gathers to itself the contradictory meanings of the play and states more clearly than either Rosmer or Rebekka can their true condition, the couple begin to lose all sense of self-determination. That the final meaning of the horses is death, caused by the irreconcilability of social and biological demands, is clear only at the climax, as the lovers throw themselves into the foaming millstream.

Although the central symbol of *Rosmersholm* can only be grasped fully by the audience, the horses have always been vaguely present in some characters' consciousness. Only Rebekka has always been acutely aware of their immanence and crucially so. Hers is the mind that feels the workings of natural forces, that understands and accepts the dictates of the biological, that can sense meaning in the natural world. This leads Ibsen himself into a dilemma, because the poetic symbols that realize the natural world and increasingly become the focal points of his plays are only grasped directly through the female mind and imagination. Hence the means by which he, as a creative artist, perceives and represents the world is alien to his masculine nature. The artist himself then, must, of necessity, be androgynous.

As if he were aware of this, Ibsen's next play, the attractive *Lady from the Sea* (1888), deals in part with the contrast between spontaneous creativity, which, in the figure of Ellida, is aligned with a love of nature and a desire for sexual freedom, and barren, labored creativity, exhibited in the sculptor Lyngstrand, who is sexually devitalized and given to uttering the most fulsome pomposities about the inferiority of women to men. Ellida's is "one of those rare, intensely poetic natures whose every thought is a metaphor," whose perception of life goes beyond "the logical nucleus of our thought"[21] to an imaginative vision that sees life in natural terms. That this is alien to and destructive of masculine perception is clear from Lyngstrand's slow dying as the result of an illness he contracted when he was once immersed in the sea for several hours. As the sea, which is Ellida's element, has been presented as symbolic of all that gives life vitality, it is clear that an existence bounded totally by social and moral conventions will degenerate as it is no longer fed by the natural sources of life. Although the play ends with Ellida ultimately resisting the forces of nature, their potent existence is fully acknowledged.

Ibsen's later plays are centered around two conflicts, the need for the individual to hold the balance between the demands of convention and the promptings of nature, and, more personally for him, for the creative artist to reconcile the necessity of forcing the vital stuff of life into form with his recognition through the eyes of woman that form violates the stuff of life. The human condition is extraordinarily tense. The mind is no longer a tightly structured unit, parameters of experience cannot be clearly defined, masculine identity, formerly so sure and defined, is now ductile in the hands of woman—"I am beginning to think," says Master Builder Solness to Hilda Wangel, "no part of me is safe from you."[22] But the moment the tension snaps and the individual surrenders to one of the two forces pulling him, disaster is inevitable. Either he will capitulate to domesticity, to an undemanding social life, and live out a pitiful existence of physical and psychic degeneration, or, prompted by woman, he will abandon himself to forces of nature in the illusion that he is about to reach the peak of his creative and sexual potential. Such moments lead instantly to his death, symbolized in *The Master Builder* (1892) and *When We Dead Awaken* (1899) as a fall from a high place. Man holds the balance between degeneration and impossible fulfillment and growth. If he surrenders to either, he is lost. Life and art, society and nature, morality and biology can never be reconciled.

A man who did succumb to the tensions was August Strindberg, whose mental breakdown, the "Inferno Crisis" between 1893 and 1897, was activated in part by his inability to reconcile contradictory impulses within himself, split as he was between a desire to live within traditional structures and his troubling experience of sex, which taught him that such structures were no longer authentic. For Strindberg, the interpenetration of souls was a more immediate and physical sensation than it was for Ibsen. He imagined identities flowing into and mingling with each other, transforming each other so radically that ultimately he could recognize no point of contact between life as he experienced it and the regulative systems that attempt to order that life. At no time was this more apparent than during sexual congress. Hence, women appear in Strindberg's later plays either as demonic females intent solely on destroying male identity, or, when he could accept this confusing state of fluidity and see within it a truth greater than that offered by the rational world, women appear as highly idealized figures, releasing within him creative powers that are suppressed in more normal, outwardly stable relationships.

Strindberg's experience of psychic formlessness influenced inevitably the composition of his plays and methods of stage presentation. The stage is no longer "another world" which, it is implied, had an independent existence. Ibsen, with the possible exception of *When We Dead Awaken*, always created with painstaking detail the appearance of everyday life upon his stage and so remained within the conventions of the nineteenth-century theater. Strindberg, however, abandoned such representation as well as a linear action that traced the workings of cause and effect. In their place he provided ambiguous settings, which at times were used to communicate literally the experience of mental disturbance. Scenic features were often just fragments in a strangely ordered collage, presented sometimes as objects in their own right, at other times as symbolic emanations of the protagonist's mind. Even characters on stage might be present solely as facets of the central character. The fascination of *To Damascus*, a strange trilogy of plays, completed in 1904, lies in the confusion created by this ambiguity. What has an objective existence? What is merely a figment of the protagonist's imagination? What is part of himself? What is the objective world? As the Unknown, the central figure of the trilogy, says to the Beggar, who has been haunting him throughout: "Where am I? Where have I been? Is it spring, winter, or summer? In what century am I living, in what hemisphere? Am I a child or an old man, male or female, a god or a devil? And who are you? Are you you, or are you me? Are these my own entrails I see about me? Are these stars or bundles of nerves in my eye; is that water, or is it tears?"[23]

With Strindberg, the stage changed from being a place where an action is represented under the assumption that it has an objective existence to one in which personal psychic states are reproduced. In such drama, clearly defined, recognizable, accepted social principles are no longer dramatized, discussion and conflict are no longer key determining features of the drama. Stage performance moves away from action toward a more static condition, closer in nature to the lyric poem. Although Strindberg was not the only playwright to remove dramatic and objective elements from the stage, no dramatist explored its lyric potential as far as he did. And constantly at the apex of his plays, as if to acknowledge her importance and inspiration, stands the idealized figure of woman. In what is possibly Strindberg's finest work, *A Dream Play* (1902), the Daughter of Indra, who acts as a mother, wife, and muse respectively to the three souls of the play's creator, the Officer, the Lawyer, and the Poet, is eventually portrayed as the sole means by which man can finally intuit an ideal beauty and order that lie behind the confusion of his present condition. So, while woman causes psychic confusion, she can also point, if not to its solution, at least to its cessation.

This brief inquiry into the later work of Ibsen and Strindberg has gone slightly beyond the limits originally set of examining sexuality as an aspect of degeneracy. Ibsen and Strindberg did not change the century's thinking on sexuality, rather they heightened it in order to emphasize the imperative of the biological. They did not conceive of a new superman who had sufficient vitality to respond to the powerful urges of nature, though many of their characters have superhuman aspirations. Frequently they depicted social conditioning as a cause of man's limitations and, in contrast to the popular drama of their time and earlier, often represented society as having a degenerative effect on the human frame. At other times, human beings themselves were inadequate. Therefore, in order to examine the biological imperative in a context where it was not confined, infected, and destroyed by forces opposing it, they turned their attention toward the way in which it fueled their creativity. In doing so they evolved, in different ways, highly personal forms of drama. In these, meanings became expressed less through words, more through highly complex symbols, or, in Strindberg's case, also through a dramatic form, which, while always structured, was flexible enough to allow for the representation of fluid experience. For both playwrights, women, originally the underprivileged sex of the European drama, were leading spirits as their perceptions led to a formulation of poetic meaning. From the sexual impasse of their earlier plays, Ibsen and Strindberg evolved new dramatic forms and so regenerated the theater.

Max Nordau would have disagreed. He wrote little on Ibsen's late plays and only mentioned Strindberg in passing, claiming rather inaccurately, as we can see now, that his works were totally in opposition to Ibsen's. But if Nordau had written on Strindberg, there can be little doubt that he would have categorized his writings as nothing more than examples of egomania and mysticism. Seeing no moral purpose in them, he would have deplored the obfuscation of meaning and the intent of the plays to work upon the audience's mind tactilely and through suggestion, rather than through clear, easily understood statement.

Here we can turn once more to the Evangelicals. "Images and ideas have been communicated which, winding their ways into the recesses of the heart, have there taken root and have at length produced the deadly harvest of a licentious conversation and a profligate life." So preached the Reverend Thomas Best back in the 1820s. Best, like so many who spoke against the theater, abominated it for its tendency to confuse the rational judgment and to call into question the clear precepts of a moral system. As I have shown, throughout the century, the commercial theater avoided such a subversive purpose, and, especially in its treatment of sexuality, reflected the moral norms of society. I have not mentioned all occasions when dramatists challenged this proclivity of the theater, but from Victor Hugo on we can see a progression, halting and broken until the final years of the century, toward a theater that presented life in terms that were not made simple by automatic reference to a conventional moral system. In those plays, whatever the system condemned and marked as degenerate, was looked at with new understanding, with a regard for its legitimacy. Consequently the fallacies of conventional morality were exposed. The Modernists completed the process. Although they did not always champion the degenerate above the normal, although at times they reflected rather than rejected current thinking on sexual matters, in their view of the composition of personality, their recognition of the primacy of the sexual urge, and their elevation of the status of woman, they challenged many of the assumptions that society and the formers of its opinions held. They were not, unfortunately, an irresistible force in the theater. Even today in our own theater and on our cinema and television screens, we can see all too often the continuation of moralistic melodrama. But where the theater is still vital, the resonant "images and ideas" so feared by the Reverend Best, but consistently cultivated by serious dramatists from Hugo on, are still capable of confounding our judgments. At the same time, they bring to our minds a strange enlightenment.

NOTES

1. Max Nordau, *Degeneration*, tr. from 2d German ed. (New York and London: Appleton, 1912), p. 11.

2. J. W. Arnott and J. W. Robinson, in *English Theatrical Literature, 1559–1900: A Bibliography* (London: Society for Theatre Research, 1970), list over 150 separate publications on the stage/church controversy between 1800 and 1850, in comparison to 40 publications between 1750 and 1800 and 85 publications between 1850 and 1900.

3. Rowland Hill, *A Warning to Professors, Containing Aphoristic Observations on the Nature and Tendency of Public Amusements* (London: Hartnell, 1805), p. 13.

4. Rev. Thomas Best, *Sermons on the Amusements of the Stage* (Sheffield: Ridge, 1831), p. 14.

5. Alexander Sutor, *An Essay on the Stage* (Aberdeen: Chalmers, 1820), p. 108.

6. Quoted by Rev. Tho. Thirlwall, *Royalty Theatre: A Solemn Protest* (London: Plummer, 1803), p. 14.

7. *The Theatre: Its Injurious Influence on the Morals of the Community* (Edinburgh: Ogle, Allardyce, & Thompson, 1820), p. 11.

8. Quoted in Brian Dobbs, *Drury Lane* (London: Cassell, 1972), pp. 123–24.

9. Henry James, *The Scenic Art*, Allan Wade, ed. (New Brunswick, N.J.: Rutgers University Press, 1976), p. 101.

10. William Acton, *The Function and Disorders of the Reproductive Organs* (Philadelphia: Lindsay & Blakiston, 1865), p. 133.

11. Peter Brooks, *The Melodramatic Imagination* (New Haven: Yale University Press, 1976), p. 291.

12. Victor Hugo, "Préface de 1827," *Cromwell*, in *Œuvres complètes* (Paris: Martel, 1949), 4:21. My translation.

13. Victor Hugo, "Préface de 1833," *Lucrèce Borgia*, in *Œuvres complètes* (Paris: Martel, 1951), 13:188. Translated in Victor Hugo, *Dramas*, I. G. Burnham, tr. (Philadelphia: Barrie, n.d.), 5:9.

14. Théophile Gautier, *L'Histoire de l'art dramatique* (Leipzig: Hetzel, 1859), 3:225. My translation.

15. George Henry Lewes, *On Actors and the Art of Acting*, 2d ed. (London: Smith, Elder, 1875), p. 27.

16. Sir Theodore Martin, *Helena Faucit (Lady Martin)* (Edinburgh and London: Blackwood, 1899), p. 165.

17. Sir Theodore Martin, *Monographs* (New York: Dutton, 1906), p. 195.

18. Michael Booth, *English Melodrama* (London: Jenkins, 1965), p. 156.

19. *Ibsen: The Critical Heritage*, Michael Egan, ed. (London: Routledge & Kegan Paul, 1972), p. 190.

20. *The Oxford Ibsen*, James W. McFarlane, ed. (London: Oxford University Press, 1961), 5:385.

21. Hermann Weigand, *The Modern Ibsen* (New York: Holt, Rinehart & Winston, 1925), p. 233.

22. *The Oxford Ibsen,* James W. McFarlane, ed. (London: Oxford University Press, 1966), 7:421.

23. August Strindberg, *The Road to Damascus: A Trilogy* Graham Rawson, tr. (New York: Grove, 1960), p. 177.

12

IMAGES OF DEGENERATION: TURNINGS AND TRANSFORMATIONS

J. EDWARD CHAMBERLIN
University of Toronto

"Progress is a comfortable disease." This modern phrase, from a poem by e. e. cummings,[1] expresses a skepticism about the idea of progress that has been chronic since ancient times and became acute sometime around the eighteenth century, when economic and social progress generated an enslavement to seemingly insatiable material wants and needs. The twentieth century, in its turn, has acknowledged its inheritance of a belief in progress with everything from elegant irony to blunt condemnation. But it was the nineteenth-century imagination that was most preoccupied with this uneasy issue, and most enchanted by its ambiguities.

Throughout the nineteenth century, there was a tradition of rendering the idea of progress by means of a logic of growth, which included a pathology of decay. But for many, the idea had a very uncertain locus of authority, despite—or perhaps because of—its association with the natural sciences. What the Russian poet Vyacheslav Ivanov described (in the 1920s) as "the feeling, at once oppressive and exalting, of being the last in a series,"[2] could apply either to degeneration and decay (which was his intention) or to progress, for both the idea of progress and the idea of degeneration could be either prospective or retrospective, and could celebrate either loss or gain. It was the unsatisfactory character of any simple logic of contraries—and of any simple-minded contrast between the healthy and the unhealthy, say, or between virtue and vice—that Oscar Wilde was emphasizing when he remarked that "what is termed Sin is an essential element of progress. Without it the world would stagnate, or grow old, or become colourless."[3]

Both progress and degeneration had to do with change, and they might be acknowledged according to quite different logics: a logic of changes in form, or a morphologic; and a logic of changes in purpose, or a teleologic. It was quite possible that progress in morphological terms would be looked upon as degeneration from a teleological perspective, and vice versa. Indeed, much literary and artistic analysis during the 1800s turned around these very contradictions. An increasing subtlety or idiosyncracy in artistic effect might be recognized as a considerable formal advance, a heightened achievement; or as an indication of an indulgent decline, a loss of force and direction, a diminishment.

There were some traditional paradoxes, such as the convention of the progress of the spirit accompanied by the degeneration of the flesh. At their best, nineteenth-century figurations of the traditional trope intensified the paradox. For example, Gerard Manley Hopkins fashioned his poem "That Nature is a Heraclitean Fire and of the Comfort of the Resurrection" by using a contrast between a degenerative beauty and the regenerative truth; between a (morphological) change to the primal forms of earth, air, water, and finally fire, and a (teleological) change to an embrace of Christ as "the mark of man's sake."[4] The poem is easily read as a celebration of an apocalyptic moment; but it is important to feel the ambivalent energies of degeneration and regeneration—energies that do not so much oppose as reinforce each other—in the juxtaposition of the burned ash and the immortal diamond.

> Flesh fade, and mortal trash
> Fall to the residuary worm; world's wildfire, leave but ash:
> In a flash, at a trumpet crash,
> I am all at once what Christ is, since he was what I am, and
> This Jack, joke, poor potsherd, patch, matchwood, immortal diamond,
> Is immortal diamond.

It is in this moment of complex ambivalence that nineteenth-century art and thought achieved some of their most compelling effects. Many of these are not sacred, but secular, as with Ernest Renan's vision of the philosophical consciousness which combined this ambivalence with a profound sense of its compelling mystery.

> The pearl-oyster seems to me to provide the most apt image of the universe and the degree of consciousness which is to be supposed pervading it as a whole. In the depths of the abyss humble forces of life create an intelligence singularly ill-served by its organs and yet extraordinarily skilful in attaining its end. What is called a sickness of this little living cosmos brings about a secretion of striking beauty, on which men put great value. The intelligence pervading the universe is, like that of the oyster, vague, obscure, singularly unsure of itself and consequently slow in its workings. Suffering creates spirit and intellec-

tual and moral progress. Sickness of the world, in reality pearl of the world, spirit is the goal, the final cause, the ultimate and undoubtedly the most brilliant product of the universe in which we live.[5]

Renan's "sickness of the world, in reality pearl of the world" has a more than superficial analogy to the Puritan consciousness that informs Nathaniel Hawthorne's *The Scarlet Letter* (1850). There, the ambiguities surrounding the degeneration of the flesh and the transcendence of the spirit are concentrated in Pearl herself, Hester Prynne's daughter and the embodiment of her sin of adultery with the Rev. Dimmesdale, as well as of her paradoxical promise of salvation through suffering and grace.

But when all was said and done by the manipulators of ideas, it was still true that one of the most familiar models of degeneration and decay was not at all ambiguous. Disease might in a sense be a tentative category to those decadent artists for whom unhealthiness was a virtue in a world dominated by the healthiness of industry, probity, and thrift. But old age and death could never for long be the plaything of subtle minds. They were part of a reality that nobody could refute; and this reality was widely generalized, for the stages of growth and decay were easily perceived as applicable to corporate as well as to individual life.

The biological understanding of degeneration was crucial in all of this, and it was entangled with the nineteenth-century logic of types, and of stereotypes. In 1857, B.-A. Morel characterized degeneration (in *Traité des dégénérescences physiques, intellectuelles et morales de l'espèce humaine*) as a morbid deviation from an original type. His was one of the first attempts to delineate the relationship between abnormal mental states and processes of a degenerative environmental and hereditary determinism. Its appeal as a causal notion—like the notion that something called gravity causes apples to fall—was considerable. But just as the idea of gravity was an idea about relationships between apples and stars, so the idea of degeneracy was essentially an idea about relationships on the one hand between normality and abnormality and on the other between growth and decay, with all of the problems involved in establishing agreement with regard to the notions of normality and growth. There were a variety of ambivalences within these relationships, which often appealed more (or were more apparent) to the literary than the scientific mind, and in a sense obscured some of the differences between degeneration conceived as a scientific pathology and degeneration conceived as an aesthetic or ethical anarchy, or between disorderings and perverse orderings. The idea of degeneration hovered between allegiances to concepts of change as a process and as a force; and this in turn implicated the imagination in ways that defied any simple-minded distinctions between aesthetic, scientific, or moral structures.

The idea of degeneration as a diminishing or reversing or perverting of the processes of generation, by a declension to a lower type or by a morbid change in structure, relied on images of generative vitality and structural

complexity or beauty which it celebrated even—or perhaps especially—as
it denied them. One of the most familiar accounts incorporating these
generative images was provided for the second half of the nineteenth
century by Charles Darwin. Naturally, then, it was in the context of the
ideology of evolution that many of the definitions of degeneration took
shape. In 1875, Anton Dohrn pointed out some limitations of the standard
post-Darwinian assumption "that all the change of structure through
which the successive generations of animals have passed has been one of
progressive elaboration," and proposed "that degeneration or progressive
simplification of structure may have, and in many lines certainly has,
taken place." In his entry on "Zoology" written for the ninth (1890)
edition of the *Encyclopaedia Britannica,* E. R. Lankester quoted Dohrn,
and proceeded to describe the geological record as providing evidence of
two kinds of "progress": "progressive elaboration" and "progressive simplification," which he called "degeneration." Elsewhere, he elaborated on
this.

> It is clearly possible for a set of forces such as we sum up under the
> head "natural selection" to so act on the structure of an organism as to
> produce one of three results, namely these: to keep it *in statu quo;* to
> increase the complexity of its structure; or lastly, to diminish the com-
> plexity of its structure. We have as possibilities either Balance, or
> Elaboration, or Degeneration.[6]

This is very close in principle to Herbert Spencer's formulation (originally
in an essay called "Progress: Its Law and Cause," which was published in
1857) of the general principle of evolution as "the transformation of the
homogeneous into the heterogeneous." He modified this in *First Principles* (1862) to read "a change from an indefinite, incoherent homogeneity
to a definite, coherent heterogeneity." In Lankester's words, elaboration,
or degeneration . . . or balance. Going forward, or backward, or standing
still.

And yet, beyond the precision of scientific classification, beyond the
familiar chronology of the ages or stages of living organisims, or the
phases from the simple to the complex and back again, degeneration came
to have a kind of magical significance conjuring up forces and processes
which the word did not make that much more comprehensible. Arthur
Balfour gave a sense of this when he spoke of the word "decadence":

> The unknown [does not] become less unknown merely by receiving a
> name. . . . We have not an idea of what "life" consists in, but if on that
> account we were to abstain from using the term, we should not be
> better but worse equipped for dealing with the problems of physiol-
> ogy: while on the other hand if we could translate life into terms of
> matter and motion tomorrow, we should still be obliged to use the word
> in order to distinguish the material movements which constitute life or
> exhibit it, from those which do not.[7]

Degeneration was in many respects a word for something of which both the morphology and the teleology were elusive. We are inclined to think that because many people used the term, they knew what it meant. That was manifestly not always the case with the word degeneration. It was a particular item of rhetoric, and a general type of image. The more deliberate its use, often the more uncertain its significance. Its most certain characteristic was that it was the opposite of something else. But even this is a bit too tidy, for nothing was more characteristic of the creative—including of course the scientific—imaginations of the nineteenth century than a tendency to transform a precise idea of degeneration into the elusive reality of metaphor or metonymy. This was in one sense part of the economy of literary or scientific discourse, but it tended to implicate the figures of speech in the meanings of degeneration, and to intensify an awareness of the moments as well as the conditions of change in a way that centered on the paradox of their degenerative vitality. The poets, experts in metaphor and metonymy and therefore in deviations from original types, often located their subject as well as their language in the complex changes and energies of transformation, of which degeneration was the most familiar image.

"C'est Elle! noire et pourtant lumineuse" (It is She! black and yet luminous.) Tenebrae . . . with a decadent priest. The ritual is sacrilegious, and the flowers on the altar are evil; but the spirits visit anyway. Their allegiance is uncertain. It is the shadowy, obscure world of Charles Baudelaire, *de profundis*, writing four sonnets of degenerate despair under the title *Un Fantôme* (A Spectre).[8] The first describes—or is it prescribes?—a somber encounter in "Les Ténèbres" (The Darkness), and ends in this haunting line, with its ambiguous image of transcendent power. The elements of the visitation are familiar enough, combining an intensely individual lyricism with a casually traditional typology. The year is 1860. Baudelaire is with his strange mulatto paramour, Jeanne Duval, and both are profoundly ill. She, who was his mistress, has now become his sick child—*sa chère fille*—for whom he cares with frantic hopelessness. He is himself sick at heart . . . literally, eating his heart out: "cuisinier aux appétits funèbres,/ Je fais bouillir et je mange mon cœur" (a cook with morbid appetites, I boil and eat my heart). And he knows that only in dreams and in visions is there any life remaining.

But the feeling of what is left, and the intimation of what has been or what might be, are all that poetry has ever offered; and this sonnet relies for its power on the substantial traditions of poetry, and of the imagination. These became obsessions for Baudelaire, these traditions of the poet—the seer and the sayer—as one of the jests of God who reigns over the realms of silence and darkness: "Je suis comme un peintre qu'un Dieu moqueur/ Condamne à peindre, hélas! sur les ténèbres" (I am like a painter that a derisive God condemns to paint, alas, on darkness). This is the world of impressionist feeling and symbolist thought, a world in which, as Arthur Symons suggested, "the visible world is no longer a reality, and the unseen world no longer a dream."[9] It is a world of shades and specters, a world of profound ambivalence where poetic structures of transcendence become confused with imminent psychological realities.

In the sonnet entitled "Le Portrait" (The Portrait), the fourth in the sequence, the poet begins with a personification of the emblems of degeneration, "la Maladie et la Mort." Sickness and death, in the imagery of the poem, "font des cendres/ De tout le feu qui pour nous flamboya" (make ashes of all the fire that blazed for us). The sonnet and the sequence conclude with a description of Time as "noir assassin de la Vie et de l'Art" (black assassin of life and art). It is not an uncommon figuration, to be sure, but is enriched—and the uneasy affiliations of the poem as a whole are confirmed—by the poet's defiant assertion to that "noir assassin": "Tu ne tueras jamais dans ma mémoire/ Celle qui fut mon plaisir et ma gloire!" (You will never destroy in my memory that which was my pleasure and my glory); and by the previous association of black with the poet's "belle visiteuse . . . noire et pourtant lumineuse" (beautiful visitor . . . black and yet luminous). Are sickness and death included in this ambivalence, this ambiguity of loss and gain from which memory derives its power? Are sickness and death then invested with a similar sort of luminous particularity, a transcendent mutability? Is the imminence of "la Maladie et la Mort" analogous, or perhaps identical, to the presence of "la belle visiteuse"? Or to her absence? C'est Elle! La Maladie? La Mort?

Like the poetry, these questions hover between the particular and the universal. Furthermore, they tempt a reader—certainly they tempted nineteenth-century readers—to various sorts of reductive analysis, many of them apparently trivial but nevertheless powerful in their hold on the popular imagination, because informed by a notion of degeneration that was in a sense a reflection of the poetic imagery. Thus Baudelaire himself, or his society, were viewed as deviant and decadent, and the poem their morbid offspring.

Behind such responses, there was fear, to be sure, but also the compelling instinct to supply causes for effects. This instinct had profound psychological and sociological roots, and it was sustained by the general enthusiasm—especially regarding anything to do with generative processes or forces—for a teleology of final causes and a morphology of efficient causes. Thus, the mechanism of natural selection became a teleology of Natural Selection. So too, there were such achievements as the great logical figurations of Hippolyte Taine, with his compelling accounts of the relationship between events (literary or artistic, broadly cultural, historical) and their location in time and place.

> Every event, whatever it may be, is conditioned, and, its conditions
> being given, when these conditions are present, it never fails to oc-
> cur. . . . Human history is a thing of natural growth like the rest; its

direction is due to its own elements; no external force guides it, but the inward forces that create it; it is not tending to any prescribed end but developing a result.[10]

This is Taine, writing of the *ancien regime*. He recognized, as would any good historian, that along with the generative forces there must be some consideration of those external factors that might effect events. Indeed, his best known formulation is of the importance of the factors of race, milieu and moment, a formulation that gave to his *History of English Literature* (1863–73) (where it appeared in its most complete form) an impressive coherence. Taine's sustaining interest was in degenerative and regenerative processes; he once described his account of contemporary circumstances as analogous to a medical consultation, in which the patient was France whose political constitution had caused the country to suffer from an illness comparable to an attack of syphilis.[11] In the French Revolution, Taine recognized a model of degeneration, and he identified it both as a process, connected with intellectual and social transformation, and as a force, providing its own compelling apocalyptic images of change. Fusing the notions of change and of transformation was in some ways the stock in trade of much nineteenth-century speculation, and gave rise to paradoxical formulations. Renan, for example, referred to revolution as a sickness of the body politic, an eruption from the depths, a malady . . . but a sacred malady, in which the spirit shows itself through a fevered illness.

The images of degeneration which were familiar in the nineteenth century followed a pattern that was indebted sometimes to theology, sometimes to biology, and often to a kind of hybrid rhetoric drawn from what Frederic Harrison called "the very silliest cant of the day, the cant about culture."[12] Cultural health was most often measured by its evidence of disease—its symptoms of decline, its morbid tendencies, its unbalanced disposition, its subversion or perversion; and in a world in which there was little basis for agreement on what constituted the common wealth of a particular culture, it was perhaps natural that most observers turned to what John Ruskin called (in an 1862 coinage in *Unto This Last*) its "illth." One of the best known of these nineteenth-century observations, at least in the English-speaking world, was Matthew Arnold's *Culture and Anarchy*. Arnold's analysis was fiercely polemical and at times disagreeably precious, but it supplied an etiology of cultural growth and decay along with an aesthetic of cultural order and chaos. His enthusiastic lamentation of the conditions of degeneration and darkness was evangelical in its passion; it was matched, in a way, by his celebration of the possibilities for regeneration—sweetness and light. Arnold's analysis was essentially negative, however, and contrasted with the scheme posited by Harrison, in *Order and Progress* among other places. Harrison was one of Auguste Comte's most admirable English disciples, and one of the few with a mind of his own. Even with his optimistic belief in a schedule of social improvement, he was not insensitive to the degenerate condition of things. With his Comtian view that the smallest substantive organism of which society is composed is the family, not the individual, he promoted the growth of society toward a better state with an enthusiasm that was far from untroubled by contemporary social conditions and tendencies, especially since the values he cherished were so clearly different from the ascendant utilitarian social philosophy, with its belief that social habits and values derive from (and therefore need to be sustained by) the needs and wants of individuals. Arnold, for all of his passion for the sordid and the shallow, did offer one of the most compelling nineteenth-century analyses of a hierarchy of sensibilities within a hierarchy of classes, and one of the most convincing celebrations of the possibilities of a certain kind of cultural order. Both Arnold and Harrison are interesting not so much for what they said—though Arnold's phrase-making has held its own—as for the way in which they circled around each other and around the notions of progress and degeneration. As Balfour noted in his essay on "Decadence," "if current modes of speech take decadence more or less for granted, with still greater confidence do they speak of progress as assured. Yet if both are real they can hardly be studied apart, they must eventually limit and qualify each other in actual experience, and they cannot be isolated in speculation."

Again and again, such speculation mirrored the qualifications out of which it arose, as in Thomas Carlyle's forecast in *Past and Present* (1843) of an apocalyptic change in the condition of England: "the eternal stars shine out again, as soon as it is dark *enough*." It is not only the tradition of historical discourse, but the tradition of figurative language and imagery—the tradition of imaginative discourse—that determines this kind of description. Or that of Renan, when he described Paris as "a sickness, but a sickness like that of the pearl."[13] "Noire et pourtant lumineuse," perhaps. It is clear that conceptual translations of this sort are radical transformations, or deviations from one type to another. It is not so easy to tell the direction of change. It never is with metaphor.

The trope is a formidable literary device, literally a "turn" of phrase—from the Greek *tropos*, turn—a figure of speech in which a word or phrase is used in a deviant sense, a sense other than that which is usual, or reasonable. It comes to refer to figurative, especially metaphorical, language in general, and to the embellishment of artistic (in particular, musical) forms. A turning or transformation is, of course, a change; and in 1865 Rudolph Clausius, who together with William Thomson (later Lord Kelvin), was one of the key figures in the development of the science of thermodynamics, proposed the concept of *en-tropy* to describe the "transformation-contents" of a system (on the somewhat mistaken etymological analogy of the word en-ergy as work-content).[14] Clausius' interest was in thermodynamic processes; and entropy was the name he gave to a quantity that describes the degree to which the energy of a system ceases to be available energy—the degree to which (thermal) energy ceases, that is, to have the potential to be transformed (or is unavailable for conversion) into (mechanical) work. When entropy increases, this means that available energy decreases. The system runs down.

In the early nineteenth century, heat was identified as a form of energy, and then the statistics of molecular motion were established, and so the branch of physics called thermodynamics was formulated. The first law of thermodynamics established conservation of energy as the principle that energy may be transformed from one kind to another—heat energy to mechanical energy, for example—but it cannot be created or destroyed. The total amount of energy is constant. The second law of thermodynamics, which comes in many versions, all logically equivalent, is the significant one as far as the idea of entropy is concerned. Heat energy, according to the second law, always flows from a relatively hot body to a relatively cold body when two bodies are in contact; it never flows from the cold body to the hot body without the expenditure of work—which is, of course, how refrigerators operate, and why they sometimes break down exhausted from all that work. All of this is simply to say that the process of heat transfer from a hot to a cold body is inevitable and irreversible. Another version of the second law states that if any physical system is left to itself and allowed to distribute its energy in its own way, it always does so in a manner such that the quantity called entropy increases; that is, the available energy of the system, or its ability to do work, decreases. Now, energy becomes heat when it is disordered; for instance, the disordering (by fission, or breaking apart) of an atom of uranium, containing intensely ordered energy, releases enormous quantities of heat. So heat is disordered energy; and disorder, which can exist without energy, becomes heat as soon as it is energized. Entropy is a measure of the quantity of disorder in a total system, or of the unavailability of the energy in the system to turn this disorder into heat.

Finally, most physical processes can be characterized as beginning and ending in equilibrium states, and passing through states of nonequilibrium. A reversible process is one in which the state of the system is changed by a continuous succession of equilibrium states. It is an ideal, such a reversible process, though it can be closely approximated in reality; and in 1824 Sadi Carnot proposed a theoretically important reversible process now called the Carnot cycle. The change of entropy in a reversible process is zero. But all natural processes are irreversible, and involve an increase in entropy. What Clausius affirmed was that the second law of thermodynamics is equivalent to the statement that the entropy in the universe is increasing. That is, any system plus its environment—or any closed or complete system, of which the universe is an obvious example—

becomes increasingly and irreversibly less organized, more chaotic, over time. Less ordered, more disordered. Less able to do work. Running down. Degenerating. The second law of thermodynamics was the most powerful figuration of degeneration that the nineteenth century proposed. But it was never easy to translate.

The logic of thermodynamics and its second law derived from a general anatomy of relationships between order and disorder in various areas of inquiry. The power of this logic depended in part on its authority as a structural counterpart to the reality to which it referred, and in part on its authority as a hovering presence uniting the particular phenomena and a universal condition. As with other scientific figurations, such as the law of gravity, the second law of thermodynamics conjured up a reality in which there were no clear distinctions between the moment and the condition of change, or between cause and effect. This was a reality that science both delighted in and abhorred, for it was a reality in which its ideas were acknowledged as beautiful before they were accepted as true. It was a reality in which the idea of degeneration, like the idea of progress, held sway. Its appeal was ultimately to the imagination, which in turn gave it convincing expression.

A boggy wood as full of springs as trees.
Slowly she slipped into the muck.
It was a white dress, she said, and that was not right.
Leathery polished mud, that stank as it split.
It is a smooth white body, she said, and that is not right,
Not quite right; I'll have a smoother,
Slicker body, and my golden hair
Will sprinkle rich goodness everywhere.
So slowly she backed into the mud.

If it were a white dress, she said, with some little black,
Dressed with a little flaw, a smut, some swart
Twinge of ancestry, or if it were all black
Since I am white, but—it's my mistake.
So slowly she slunk, all pleated, into the muck.

These are the opening stanzas of "The Idea of Entropy at Maenporth Beach," a poem by the contemporary British poet Peter Redgrove.[15] Its epigraph is from Baudelaire: "C'est Elle! noire et pourtant lumineuse." With tentative exuberance, the poem celebrates a complex ambivalence, as the figure disappearing into the muck is described in the language of disconcerting associations. "Slunk," for example, with its reptilian etymology, is picked up later in the final lines of the poem as new colors "slither" to the sea; and "swart," a word of older meanings, is repeated to reinforce the intensity of the following passage, but also marks a Botticellean turning.

The mud spatters with rich seed and ranging pollens.
Black darts up the pleats, black pleats
Lance along the white ones, and she stops
Swaying, cut in half. It is right, she sobs
As the fat, juicy, incredibly tart muck rises
Round her throat and dims the diamond there?
It is right, so she stretches her white neck back
And takes a deep breath once and a one step back.
Some golden strands afloat pull after her.

The mud recoils, lies heavy, queasy, swart.
But then this soft blubber stirs, and quickly she comes up
Dressed like a mound of lickerish earth,
Swiftly ascending in a streaming pat
That grows tall, smooths brimming hips, and steps out
On flowing pillars, darkly draped.
And then the blackness breaks open with blue eyes
Of this black Venus rising helmeted in night
Who as she glides grins brilliantly, and drops
Swatches superb as molasses on her path.

The poem closes with an orchestration of black and white, of the dark and
the luminous, and of the language of deliberate vision and the language of
casual humor.

Who is that negress running on the beach
Laughing excitedly with teeth as white
As the white waves kneeling, dazzled, to the sands?
Clapping excitedly the black rooks rise,
Running delightedly in slapping rags
She sprinkles substance, and the small life flies!

She laughs aloud, and bares her teeth again, and cries:
Now that I am all black, and running in my richness
And knowing it a little, I have learnt
It is quite wrong to be all white always;
And knowing it a little, I shall take great care
To keep a little black about me somewhere.
A snotty nostril, a mourning nail will do.
Mud is a good dress, but not the best.
Ah, watch, she runs into the sea. She walks
In streaky white on dazzling sands that stretch
Like the whole world's pursy mud quite purged.
The black rooks coo like doves, new suns beam
From every droplet of the shattering waves,
From every crystal of the shattered rock.
Drenched in the mud, pure white rejoiced,

From this collision were new colours born,
And in their slithering passage to the sea
The shrugged-up riches of deep darkness sang.

It is a fine poem, powerful in its ambiguities, and in its final conjunctions: the song and the shore; the disintegrating (shattering waves, shattered rock) and the whole (droplets, crystals); laughing and crying; the intimations of darkness and silence and the luminous celebrations of light and song. The turning of sea and land—as "new suns beam/ From every droplet of the shattering waves,/ From every crystal of the shattered rock"—is achieved within a frame in which the images of both (waves and droplets, rock and crystal) become intertwined, and in which she becomes the singer, literally "the shrugged-up riches of deep darkness," and sings of the sea, the origin and end of this "black Venus rising helmeted in night/ Who as she glides grins brilliantly."

It is a poem in which the availability of energy—"riches," in the language of the poem—is the subject, embodied in images which have in common suspended affirmations and denials, their precarious condition caught between one state and another, sustained by the central image of intermittence, the beach. The poem belongs in a tradition that, along with Baudelaire's sonnet sequence, includes Walt Whitman's "Out of the Cradle Endlessly Rocking," with its haunting final dissolution an image of degeneration.

A word then, (for I will conquer it,)
The word final, superior to all,
Subtle, sent up—what is it?—I listen;
Are you whispering it, and have been all the time, you sea-waves?
Is that it from your liquid rims and wet sands?

Whereto answering, the sea,
Delaying not, hurrying not,
Whisper'd me through the night, and very plainly before daybreak,
Lisp'd to me the low and delicious word death,
And again death, death, death, death,
Hissing melodious, neither like the bird nor like my arous'd child's
    heart,
But edging near as privately for me rustling at my feet,
Creeping thence steadily up to my ears and laving me softly all over,
Death, death, death, death, death.

Which I do not forget,
But fuse the song of my dusky demon and brother,
That he sang to me in the moonlight on Paumanok's gray beach,
With the thousand responsive songs at random,
My own songs awaked from that hour,

And with them the key, the word up from the waves,
The word of the sweetest song and all songs,
That strong and delicious word which, creeping to my feet,
(Or like some old crone rocking the cradle, swathed in sweet
    garments, bending aside,)
The sea whisper'd me.[16]

From the same imaginative tradition comes Matthew Arnold's great celebration of dissolution, and of the assertions of love against dissolution, "Dover Beach." The beach is described as "a darkling plain/ Swept with confused alarms of struggle and flight,"[17] and the poem is sustained by a rhetoric that may have lost some of its magic but still retains its sense of tension and ambivalence. Anthony Hecht, in his devious parody "The Dover Bitch: A Criticism of Life," catches this in a modern idiom, complete with its disintegrating etceteras.

So there stood Matthew Arnold and this girl
With the cliffs of England crumbling away behind them,
And he said to her, "Try to be true to me,
And I'll do the same for you, for things are bad
All over, etc., etc."[18]

But the poem from which Redgrove's meditation on "The Idea of Entropy at Maenporth Beach" most obviously turns is Wallace Stevens' "The Idea of Order at Key West,"[19] with its compelling shoreline configurations upon which the notions of order and chaos depend for their imaginative power. Stevens, who wrote a poem entitled "Metaphor as Degeneration," often played upon these paradoxes: "death is the mother of beauty," runs one of his most familiar phrases.

Redgrove's poem is in an important sense about degeneration as the nineteenth-century imagination conceived it, about its ideas and images of entropy, and the complex relationship of the idea of degeneration to ideas of order, of which progress is one . . . and degeneration is another. The poem celebrates a female consciousness and power of startling and yet familiar aspects. Against this is implied a notion of masculine rationality, according to which these sibilant transformations are degenerate. In another of Redgrove's poems, "Water-Witch, Wood-Witch, Wine-Witch," the central figure—a *femme fatale* of sorts, who "uncaps jars of venemous honey"—appears "wet all through . . . shivering on an abyss," and speaks:

       look, you know
The language we call "Crossing the River", do you speak
The older tongue called "Wallow"?

The language of such dark and yet luminous feminine authority provided one form in which the nineteenth century embraced the chaotic, the
disordered, the disintegrating—the sources of power and genius. Walking
on those beaches, as Prufrock discovered, held promise of enchantment,
and of death. Black, and yet luminous; the nineteenth century seemed to
admire literature and art of hovering allegiances and haunting transformations, of which androgyny was one of the most compelling images.

Others were not so enchanted. Some observers saw all of this as nothing
more than a kind of imaginative indigestion, and saw such art and literature as unhealthy deviations from an original in which clarity and precision reigned. This was implicit in Walter Bagehot's distinction between
the pure, the ornate and the grotesque in poetry,[20] and there were an
increasing number of classifications of this sort around the turn of the
century. A. E. Orage predicted in 1914 "a classical revival . . . and the
return of the spirit of the masculine eighteenth century."[21] And Irving
Babbitt, in 1919, described romanticism as "wonderful rather than proba-
ble . . . it violates the normal sequence of cause and effect in favour of
adventure. . . . The uncultivated imagination in all times and places is
romantic."[22]

To some extent, these were all simply qualifications of Goethe's troublesome remark, that "I call classical all that is wholesome and romantic all
that is sickly," which was widely quoted in the nineteenth century to
denounce the pathologies of romanticism—*les fleurs du mal*, as well as the
more vulgar enthusiasms of the hoi-polloi, and the general excesses of all
revolutionary modes, whether artistic or political.

For many observers, all of this presented both a diagnostic and a prescriptive challenge. Max Nordau, for example, applied his ruthlessly reductive logic to determine the morbid causes of the works of art. "The
fashions in art and literature . . . have their source in the degeneracy of
their authors, and the enthusiasm of their admirers is for manifestations of
more or less pronounced moral insanity, imbecility, and dementia."[23]
Having diagnosed the cause of the affliction, the prescription was simple:
eliminate the cause (which was indistinguishable from the symptom), and
the disease will soon disappear.

Morel's account of degeneration as a morbid deviation from an original
type provided the basic scheme for this kind of argument, if for no other
reason than that it was a nice way to illuminate a morphology of diminishment and a teleology of despair. Nordau's contribution was essentially
rhetorical: a listing of the traits of degeneration, including such characteristically "romantic" features as emotionalism; dejectedness; disinclination
to action; predilection for inane reverie due to an inability to grasp, order,
and elaborate impressions into ideas and judgements. In fact, there was
much attention paid to these afflictions long before Nordau brought his
pedantry to bear, and throughout the century there were typical accounts

of the present age as precious and paltry, and typical comparisons with ages of heroic ideals and larger-than-life leaders. The virtues of heroic determination and civilized decorum were matched with the vices of insipidity and extremism. Writing of a recognizable group of "degenerate" nineteenth-century figures, Jean Carrière caught both the spirit and something of the letter of late nineteenth- and early twentieth-century formulations in his book *Les Mauvais Maîtres* (1921), translated in 1922 by Joseph McCabe as *Degeneration in the Great French Masters*. The "masters" under condemnation were Rousseau, Chateaubriand, Balzac, Stendahl, Sand, Musset, Baudelaire, Flaubert, Verlaine, and Zola. In part, it is a somewhat dreary antiromantic sermon, of the sort that was popular in literary critical circles in England about the same time. Carrière ended his book with the obligatory chapter on "The Renaissance of the Classical Spirit," bringing to a conclusion a long harangue against all that is uninformed by sweetness and light. He proposed a familiar association of the solar with the classical, and demonstrated a complementary suspicion of all that is done by the light of the moon. Combining an enthusiasm for what he referred to as "sunny and limpid" work with an admiration for "strength and light," he specialized in mocking the surrender to weakness, the exaltation of gross pleasures, and the essential triviality of emotion in the work of those whom he castigated, paying more attention to substance than (as did Bagehot, for example) to style. Writing of Musset, Carrière provided a typical rejection of the diminished figurations of nineteenth-century art and life.

> It is a great sorrow when Prometheus makes the mountain ring with his anger at the evils which torment his beloved humanity; when Priam and Achilles, in face of mourning Troy, weep together over the long line of corpses on the shore and over all the misfortunes that threaten both peoples; when Aeneas tells Dido of the sack of Troy and the destruction of his race; when the exiled Dante, forgetting his personal misfortunes, thinks only of Italy torn by civil hatreds and calls it *di dolore ostello;* when the Hebrew poets, by the river in a strange land, hang their harps on the willows and lament the loss of Jerusalem; when on Golgotha, lit by lightning, Christ utters his supreme cry to the humanity that will suffer for ever. But to speak about a great sorrow, to weep out one's soul in desperate sobs, to conjure up the most tragic figures, to call to witness all the forces of nature and all the ages of human history, to declare oneself a victim of the gods just because Dame Sand has gone off with the solid Pagello, really—I must say it, though I be disgraced for ever in the eyes of all girls in the first flush of puberty and all young men of erotic dreams—it is a mockery of human misery, a sacrilege of sorrow.[24]

Oscar Wilde describes this sacrilege in terms that turn the blasphemy around, as he translates the image of the Man of Sorrows and

> hears in much modern Art the cry of Marsyas. It is bitter in
> Baudelaire, sweet and plaintive in Lamartine, mystic in Verlaine. It is
> in the deferred resolutions of Chopin's music. It is in the discontent
> that haunts the recurrent faces of Burne-Jones's women. Even Matthew
> Arnold, whose song of Callicles tells of "the triumpth of the sweet
> persuasive lyre," and the "famous final victory," in such a clear note of
> lyrical beauty—even he, in the troubled undertone of doubt and dis-
> tress that haunts his verse, has not a little of it.[25]

The foolish Marsyas, master of the flute and associated with Dionysus and
Cybele, challenged Apollo, the patron god of the lyre, and in defeat was
flayed alive for his affront. (He was first awarded victory by Midas, who
was overruled by the Muses, and in turn was punished for his stupidity.)
The cry of Marsyas, who in his contest with Apollo was also known as
Pan, was a cry of almost comic despair, a perverse confusion of victory and
defeat. Pan is dead. Or, in Nietzsche's terms, "Die Tragödie ist tot."

The opposite of degeneration, in such a scheme, is progress conceived
as a certain high purpose, a commitment to Apollonian standards, to the
winner's song. This imaginative opposition was especially important later
in the nineteenth century, when the apostles of moral or financial or
national uplift recognized in their "decadent" contemporaries just this
kind of enervated and enervating grotesquerie, a descent from an original
type drawn from images of classical heroism or high lyric melancholy.
Eliot's Prufrock, singing his debilitated love song, is very much intended
as a parody of this typology, whatever his more polemical affiliations. And
the image of fatal desire with which Eliot's poem closes follows a tradition
in which, to return to my original theme, there is a confusion of regenerative and degenerative power. Moderism inherited much of its imagery
from nineteenth-century degeneracy, and its imagination was fostered not
by beauty and fear as much as by what Carrière called "a mind overcast
and senses quivering." When W. B. Yeats included Walter Pater's description of Leonardo's Mona Lisa (from his *Studies in the History of the Renaissance* (1873)) at the beginning of his *Oxford Book of Modern Verse* in 1936,
and set it as a poem, he was doing something more than playing ty-
pographical tricks; for the passage, in all of its purple, catches the spirit of
the complex ambivalence in which the idea of degeneration was implicated
and out of which the twentieth-century modernists fashioned their particular imagery of dissolution.

Being archetypal, like Lady Lisa—"expressive of what in the ways of a
thousand years man had come to desire"—was one thing. Being untypical
was quite another. Extremes of individuality were alternately celebrated in
the nineteenth century as constituting admirable originality, the leading
evolutionary edge of the human species, as it were, or as demonstrating a
process of degenerate disinhibition and unchecked egotism. This latter
was the pattern of analysis presented by such enthusiastic chroniclers of

egomania as Max Nordau, but it had a complex place in the neuro-logic of degeneracy that was developed by E. S. Talbot (in books such as *Degeneracy: Its Causes, Signs and Results* (1898) and *Degeneracy and Political Assassination* (1901)), and earlier by J. H. Jackson, and others. The analytic model was quite simple: a distinction between low and high functions—or what Talbot called the primary (instinctual) ego and the secondary ego (concerned with "checking" the instincts, and therefore with ethical, aesthetic, and abstract notions); an excessive stimulation of activity within the higher center; a state of nervous exhaustion, a collapse of the inhibiting function leading to an egotistical wallow and the triumph of the lower instincts. There is an implicit distinction here, applying to both simple and complex organisms, between functions of force and those of process. If the forces are either too weak or too strong, the organism stops growing or burns itself out. If the processess are not integrated, the organism develops with more or less morbid deviations from the norm. In either case, degeneration has set in.

In all of this, the idea of what Lankester called balance had a persistent, and in a sense classical, appeal. The importance of balance was emphasized in Geoffrey Saint-Hilaire's theory of organic balance and the proper subordination of the parts to the whole, a principle that Taine adopted in his analysis of national cultures. In another field, Philippe Pinel's important early work on the treatment of insanity—*Traité medico-philosophique sur l'alienation mentale* (1788, 1801)—was premised on the Aristotelian doctrine of balancing the emotions. Somewhat later, Comte focused on the etymology of alienation to emphasize the idea of being uncertainly centered, as it were. Unbalanced. For Pinel, the proper treatment for "mental alienation" was what he called (with somewhat antique grace) "moral." Since insanity itself was deemed to have "moral" causes—overbearing emotions, crudely speaking—its treatment should address these causes, and work toward a moral balance—which is to say, a balancing of the passions. This idea spanned the nineteenth century. From Moreau de Tours in *La Psychologie morbide* (1859), with his analysis of genius as a disease caused by overexcitation of the brain, to Cesare Lombroso in *L'Uomo di Genio* (1888), translated into English by Havelock Ellis in 1891, proposing that genius is characterized by abnormal sensitivity—especially by a tendency to alternate between excessive energy and excessive indolence—there was a consistent refrain which located the conditions of degeneration in imbalance, in whatever direction, and found many of its images in those dark grottos of the mental landscape from which grotesque art took its inspiration.

It is easy to see how an excess of passion, or particular narrow enthusiasms—just the sort of things that poets and politicians specialize in—would eventually reinforce the categorizing of certain kinds of poetic and public activity as degenerate (though Pinel, for instance, in fact praised the description of extreme emotional states that were characteristic of much eighteenth-century literature). Although Pinel's analysis was one-sided in its emphasis on the emotional, he was still in the minds of thoughtful people late in the nineteenth century. During the 1870s, for example, when Oscar Wilde was at Oxford, the study of pathological and degenerate behavior took its cue from this tradition of psychological inquiry; Wilde's notebooks make clear both his own interest in Pinel, and also the general interest in abnormal behavior deriving from the early work of Pinel and others. J. F. Nisbet's book on *The Insanity of Genius*, published first in 1891 and subtitled "the general inequality of human faculty physiologically considered," used "insanity" as synonymous with "unsoundness," while describing the "man of genius" as one who

> overflows with ideas; countless memories are stirred in his brain and he discovers combinations and affinities in facts, tones, and colours, that lie beyond the scope of the ordinary mind. In all these accomplishments the madman is his equal . . . Genius, insanity, idiocy, scrofula, rickets, gout, consumption, and the other members of the neuropathic family of disorders, are so many different expressions of a common evil—an instability or want of equilibrium in the nervous system.

The lunatic, the lover, and the poet, of imagination all compact . . . and all loony, operating by the light of the moon. Nothing sunny and limpid here. (Nisbet was drama critic for the *Times;* Victorian melodrama took its toll.)

All of this pathological speculation had its most general application in the differing views about the evolution of mankind. Essentially, there were two perspectives in the nineteenth century: a view of man as having advanced, and a view of man as having regressed. But even this was not straightforward. When Darwin entitled his book on "the origin of man and his history" *The Descent of Man*, he was deliberately complicating the notion of evolutionary progress with provocative language that drew attention to man's descent from some ape-like creatures. He wrote at the end of the book that "the main conclusion arrived at in this work, namely, that man is descended from some lowly organized form, will, I regret to think, be highly distasteful to many." And he was quite conscious that his central argument turned against "that arrogance which made our forefathers declare that they were descended from demi-gods."[26] As Dean Inge once noted, "the Greeks prided themselves on being the degenerate descendants of gods, we on being the very creditable descendants of monkeys." So an argument informed by an idea of progress is imaged by means of an idea of degeneracy. It is, as one early reviewer noted,

> a new doctrine of the fall of man. (Darwin) shows that the instincts of the higher animals are far nobler than the habits of savage races of men, and he finds himself, therefore, compelled to reintroduce,—in a form of the substantial orthodoxy of which he appears to be quite unconscious,—and to introduce as a scientific hypothesis the doctrine

that man's gain of knowledge was the cause of a temporary but long-enduring moral deterioration as indicated by the many foul customs, especially as to marriage, of savage tribes. What does the Jewish tradition of the moral degeneration of man through his snatching at a knowledge forbidden him by the highest instincts assert beyond this?[27]

The notion of man as an advanced animal form—either naturally evolved or divinely inspired or both—was received wisdom in the nineteenth century, before and after Darwin. And so, of course, was the notion of fallen man. Fallen in various respects. There was, for instance, the conviction that was especially popular in the eighteenth century that it had all been downhill from the beginning. Lord Chesterfield, in the 1780s, suggested that,

If we give credit to the vulgar opinion, or even to the assertions of some reputable authors, both ancient and modern, poor human nature was not originally formed for keeping. Every age has degenerated; and from the fall of the first man, my unfortunate ancestor, our species has been tumbling on, century by century, for about six thousand years.[28]

The vision of William Blake, in which contemporary man has degenerated from his original Titanic form and has disintegrated from the corporate being which defines a true imaginative unity, gave a powerful form to this idea, a form which has several analogues not only in the Bible, but in the Scandinavian myths which were popular during the period. Blake's conception depended upon several degenerative processes: the division of the self into a neurotic subject-object duality; the fall from a lively and active creativity to an enervated and reactionary passivity, and, related to this, the imaging of a power outside the self, usually as some kind of enchanting female will; the transformation of an imaginative order into a chaos of realities. All of these changes are contradicted in the notion of an integrated vision; and the astonishing nonsense of Blake's "Auguries of Innocence" merely confirms how disintegrated is not only our vision but also our capacity to acknowledge a vision that is whole.

To see a World in a Grain of Sand
And a Heaven in a Wild Flower,
Hold Infinity in the palm of your hand
And Eternity in an hour.[29]

And so Nebuchadnezzar browsing on grass becomes an image of the descent of man and his kingdoms, a descent that has the inevitability of natural process and the irreversibility of apocalyptic or even quotidean force. The appeal of this image is ambivalent, like the appeal of one of the great visions of regeneration in the Bible, the vision of Ezekiel (which Blake incorporated into "Night the Ninth: The Last Judgment" of the Four Zoas).

And he said unto me, Son of man, can these bones live?

And I answered, O Lord God, thou knowest.

Again he said unto me, Prophesy upon these bones, and say unto them, O ye dry bones, hear the word of the Lord . . .

So I prophesied as I was commanded; and as I prophesied, there was a noise, and behold a shaking, and the bones came together, bone to his bone . . . and the breath came into them, and they lived, and stood up upon their feet, an exceeding great army.

Then he said unto me, Son of man, these bones are the whole house of Israel.[30]

But the dry bones, not the great army or the whole house, hold the imagination.

Leaving aside such grand metonymies, images of degenerate or fallen man were common in the early nineteenth century and they typically ranged from images of the insane and later the criminal to more generalized descriptions of so-called savage races as representing a degraded type. Insofar as the imaginative figurations of change were controlled by an Edenic ideal—which is to say, insofar as paradise was deemed to have been lost rather than not yet found—the notion of degeneration was bound to prevail. There were complications, to be sure. Since the primitive peoples were so obviously morally inferior to the European civilizations, they were taken to provide proof of a degeneration from which civilization had found (in Christian morality) a mode of regeneration. The affiliations of primitive peoples were assumed to be more strongly with animals than with the higher species of man. The language that was used to describe native people in North America in particular often included bovine imagery—speaking of them as "ringed, streaked, spotted and speckled cattle"; or of being weaned away from their primitive habits and indigenous affiliations. The use of the land by hunters and gatherers was looked upon as idle, a sort of "browse" over the territory; and it was compared with civilized uses—cultivation of the soil, agriculture, the basis of human culture.[31]

But since primitive peoples also seemed, according to other perspectives, to have more closely discovered, and governed themselves according to, the laws of nature, there was some considerable disagreement about just who had descended, and from what. The skeptical reassessment of cultural "elaboration" which began in the eighteenth century reinforced this perspective, whether celebrating savage nobility or setting regenerative simplicity ahead of degenerative luxury. It was never a simple story. Robert Chambers, in his *Vestiges of the Natural History of Creation* (1844), raised a considerable fuss by insisting that the original state of mankind was barbarous rather than civilized, and by providing a resolutely materialist account of the origins of language, according to which human (beginning with primitive) language was a refinement of the gesture and sign language of animals.

For many nineteenth-century writers and thinkers, the questions surrounding language—and especially primitive languages—gave the idea of degeneration one of its most intriguing formulations. The notion was that the once vital relationship between signifier and signified which supposedly enlivened primitive language—which gave it (to turn a phrase of Ezra Pound), a "luminous particularity," in which every word was a metaphor, the naming of a presence, the acknowledgment of a wonderful encounter—that this relationship had degenerated into a set of arbitrary codes, with vitality replaced by convention. This attitude seriously complicated Champollion's deciphering of Egyptian hieroglyphics; against his argument that ancient writing was essentially phonetic, others posited a view of such language as pictographic, an embodiment of a direct and pure relationship between subject and object. Richard Chenevix Trench, one of the most notable proponents of this view of language, wrote in his book *On the Study of Words* about how originally "many a single word (was) in itself a concentrated poem, having stores of poetical thought and imagery laid up in it." Trench argued that language began "not with names, but with the power of naming," and that this power had been all but lost.[32] Therefore, along with other philologists such as Joseph de Maistre and Julius Charles Hare, Trench was committed to a form of the doctrine that the tendency of civilization is toward barbarism, and away from primitive "revealed" wisdom. The radical distinction here was between the primitive and the savage. In terms of language specifically, insofar as it had moved away from its primitive origins, modern language had become a cluster of dead metaphors, "fossil poetry," to use Emerson's designation.[33] This notion of language—as something from which the magic has gone—always had a popular appeal, of course, with contemporary usage being routinely condemned as a falling away from the standards of an earlier time, a decay of principles, morals, national purpose and vitality, and so forth. Arnold applies a particularly distasteful version of it to his description of the plight of a girl named Wragg who left the workhouse in Nottingham with her illegitimate child and was arrested on a charge of murder after the infant had been found strangled.

> *Wragg!* If we are to talk of ideal perfection, of "the best in the whole world," has anyone reflected what a touch of grossness in our race, what an original short-coming in the more delicate spiritual perceptions, is shown by the natural growth amongst us of such hideous names—Higginbottom, Stiggins, Bugg! In Ionia and Attica they were luckier in this respect . . . by the Ilissus there was no Wragg, poor thing.[34]

One does not have to look far for comments on the relationship between degeneration and language. Lankester, for example, was quick to shift from biological discussion to a discussion of how "true Degeneration of language is only found as part and parcel of a more general degeneration of mental activity." There were a number of variations on the idea of degeneration in language, of which one of the most prominent had an ironic twist. Trench and others celebrated the original autonomy of the single word, though they lamented the contemporary diminishment of its once powerful logic. But it was that autonomy itself, particularly insofar as it was at the cost of larger and more heterogeneous linguistic structures, such as the phrase or the sentence or the paragraph or the page, that became the focus of attention as symptomatic of the contemporary degeneration of language.

This kind of analysis was controlled both by Herbert Spencer's model of progress from the simple to the complex, and by a specific analogy with the federation of cells in a healthy organism and the proper subordination within any organism of the parts to the whole, or of the individual to society. A literary style in which this sort of lieutenancy was defied was sometimes condemned, sometimes celebrated. In an essay on Baudelaire written in 1868, Théophile Gautier described how

> the poet of the *Fleurs du Mal* loved what is improperly called the style of decadence, and which is nothing else but art arrived at that point of extreme maturity yielded by the slanting suns of aged civilization: an ingenious complicated style, full of shades and of research, constantly pushing back the boundaries of speech, borrowing from all the technical vocabularies, taking colour from all palettes and notes from all keyboards, struggling to render what is most inexpressible in thought, what is vague and most elusive in the outlines of form, listening to translate the subtle confidence of neurosis, the dying confessions of passion grown depraved, and the strange hallucinations of the obsession which is turning to madness. The style of decadence is the ultimate utterance of the Word.[35]

Some time later, Paul Bourget took up the topic with a more specific acknowledgment of a scientific analogy, and a muted enthusiasm.

> If the energy of the cells becomes independent, the lesser organisms will likewise cease to subordinate their energy to the total energy and the anarchy which is established constitutes the *decadence* of the whole. The social organism does not escape this law and enters into decadence as soon as the individual life becomes exaggerated beneath the influence of acquired well-being, and of heredity. A similar law governs the development and decadence of that other organism which we call language. A style of decadence is one in which the unity of the book is decomposed to give place to the independence of the page, in which the page is decomposed to give place to the independence of the phrase, and the phrase to give place to the independence of the word.[36]

The magazine *transition*, as important as any in the development of modernism, gave over much of its space in the late twenties to celebrations of the revolutionary independence of the word, picking up just this degenerated inheritance. The paradoxes were still there. What T. E. Hulme and other early modernists referred to as the appropriate subordination of the parts to the whole—or the appropriate deference to tradition, a version of the same thing—was a norm that conditioned the celebrations of its defiance. When Friedrich Nietzsche, for example, described a degenerate style such as that which Gautier praised, the effect is typically ambivalent, especially given Nietzsche's own characteristically disintegrating aphoristic style.

> Decadence (is) characterized by the fact that in it life no longer animates the whole. Words become predominant and leap right out of the sentence to which they belong, the sentences themselves trespass beyond their bounds, and obscure the sense of the whole page, and the page in its turn gains in vigour at the cost of the whole—the whole is no longer a whole. This is the formula for every decadent style: there is always anarchy among the atoms, disaggregation of the will.[37]

On these terms, the idea of degeneration determined the styles of modernism, and its subjects as well. Progress is a comfortable dis-ease. Virgil's *otium*—or true ease—is to be found in simplicities, in deviations from a civilized typology, more like the prescriptions of Jean-Jacques Rousseau than those of Herbert Spencer. As the contemporary poet Derek Walcott has asked, "where else to row but backward?"[38] Perhaps the genius of it was to be going in two directions at once. That was, in a way, what gave the idea of degeneration such a powerful appeal. "Noire et pourtant lumineuse."

NOTES

1. 'pity this busy monster, manunkind,' from 1×1 (1944). See *Complete Poems*, e. e. cummings, G. J. Firmage, ed. (London: MacGibbon and Kee, 1968), 2:554.

2. Quoted in Renato Poggioli, *The Theory of the Avant-Grade*, Gerald Fitzgerald, tr. (Cambridge, Mass.: Belknap Press, 1968), p. 75.

3. "The Critic as Artist," first published in the *Nineteenth Century* in 1890. See *Complete Works* (London: Methuen, 1908), 8:134. James Joyce commented of Wilde's aesthetic attitude that "at its base is the truth inherent in the soul of Catholicism: that man cannot reach the divine heart except through that sense of separation and loss called sin." "Oscar Wilde: The Poet of *Salome*," *The Critical Writings of James Joyce*, Ellsworth Mason and Richard Ellmann, eds. (New York: Viking, 1964), p. 205. Ernest Renan's version of this same paradox was that "pain is the great agent of progress" tr. from *Dialogues philosophiques* (1876).

4. This phrase is from "The Wreck of the Deutschland," stanza 22, written in 1875–76. "That Nature is a Heraclitean Fire . . ." was written in 1888. See *Poems of Gerard Manley Hopkins*, 4th ed. W. H. Gardner and N. H. Mackenzie, eds. (Oxford: Oxford University Press, 1970), pp. 58, 105–06.

5. Ernest Renan, *Examen de conscience philosophique* (1888), *Feuilles detachées*, *Œuvres complètes*, Henriette Psichari, ed. (Paris: Calmann-Lévy, 1947–61), 2:1181–82. Quoted in (and translated by) H. W. Wardman, *Ernest Renan* (London: Athlone Press, 1964), p. 214.

6. *Degeneration: A Chapter in Darwinism* (London: Macmillan, 1880), pp. 28–29. The *Encyclopaedia Britannica* quotation is from 24:811. For a further discussion, see J. E. Chamberlin, "An Anatomy of Cultural Melancholy," *Journal of the History of Ideas* (Oct.–Dec. 1981), 42(4):691–705.

7. Arthur Balfour, *Decadence* (Cambridge: Cambridge University Press, 1908); originally delivered as the Henry Sidgwick Memorial Lecture at Newnham College in January 1908. It was a topic that had long interested Balfour, and for which he had a considerable audience. In his Preface to his own book on *The Idea of Progress: An Inquiry Into its Origin and Growth* in 1920, J. B. Bury gives prominence to the fact that "the doubts (regarding progress) which Mr. Balfour expressed nearly thirty years ago, in an address delivered at Glasgow, have not, so far as I know, been answered." The address referred to was entitled "A Fragment of Progress," delivered at Glasgow University on November 26, 1891, and published in *Essays and Addresses* (Edinburgh: David Douglas, 1893), pp. 241–82. W. R. Inge, Dean of St. Paul's, picked up Balfour's theme at the beginning of his essay on 'The Idea of Progress' (delivered as the Romanes Lecture at Oxford on May 27, 1920), noting that "the theory of progress and the theory of decadence are equally natural, and have in fact been held concurrently wherever men have speculated about their origin, their present condition and their future prospects." I am grateful to Stephen Regan for drawing my attention to Balfour's 1908 lecture.

8. First published in *L'Artiste* on October 15, 1860; the poems were written earlier that year. The sonnet sequence appeared in *Les fleurs du mal*, 2nd ed. (Paris: Poulet-Malassis et de Broise, 1861), from which the quotations are taken.

9. Arthur Symons, *The Symbolist Movement in Literature* (London: Heinemann, 1899), p. 6.

10. Taine, *The Origins of Contemporary France*, J. Durand, tr.; *The Ancient Regime* (London, 1881), pp. 176, 179. Quoted (and the translation revised) in Leo Weinstein, *Hippolyte Taine* (New York: Twayne, 1972), p. 123.

11. From a letter to Ernest Havet of March 24, 1878; referred to by Weinstein, p. 124.

12. From an essay entitled "Our Venetian Constitution," which appeared in the *Fortnightly* (March 1867); reprinted as "Parliament before Reform" in *Order and Progress* (London: Longmans, Green, 1875), p. 150. The remark was quoted by Matthew Arnold in his "Introduction" to *Culture and Anarchy*, which along with the chapter entitled "Sweetness and Light" constituted his final lecture as professor of poetry at Oxford in May 1867. This and five succeeding articles (under the general title "Anarchy and Authority") were published in *Cornhill* between 1867 and 1868; and then gathered together as *Culture and Anarchy* and published as a book by Smith, Elder, in London in 1869.

13. In "La Monarchie constitutionnelle en France," published in *Revue des Deux Mondes*, Nov. 1, 1869. Quoted in Wardman, p. 215.

14. Clausius' German word was *entropie*. The word was first used in English by Peter G. Tait in 1868, who (as though to confirm its ambivalence) used it in a sense opposite to that of Clausius. Tait's usage was followed (with some variations) by Clerk Maxwell; but then both Tait and Maxwell, in company with other writers on the topic, reverted to Clausius' definition, which is, of course, the one now accepted.

15. From Peter Redgrove, *Dr. Faust's Sea-Spiral Spirit and Other Poems* (London: Routledge and Kegan Paul, 1972), pp. 20–21. "Water-Witch, Wood-Witch, Wine-Witch," quoted below, also appears in this volume, pp. 11–12.

16. First published in a somewhat different version under the title "A Child's Reminiscence" in the Christmas number (December 24, 1859) of the New York *Saturday Press*. Included in *Leaves of Grass* (Boston: Thayer and Eldridge, 1860). The text here is from *Leaves of Grass* (Boston: James R. Osgood, 1881).

17. "Dover Beach" was probably written in the early 1850s, though the date and occasion of composition have not been certainly established. It was first published in *New Poems* (London: Macmillan, 1867). See *The Poems of Matthew Arnold*, Kenneth Allott, ed. (London: Longman's, 1965), pp. 239–43.

18. From Anthony Hecht, *The Hard Hours* (New York: Atheneum, 1967), p. 17.

19. From *Ideas of Order* (New York: Alcestis Press, 1935). "Metaphor as Degeneration" was included in a later volume, *The Auroras of Autumn* (New York: Knopf, 1950). See *Collected Poems of Wallace Stevens* (New York: Knopf, 1954), pp. 128–30, 444–45.

20. Walter Bagehot, "Wordsworth, Tennyson and Browning; or, Pure, Ornate and Grotesque Art in English Poetry," which first appeared in the *National Review* in November 1864.

21. A. E. Orage, *New Age* (August 27, 1914), 15:397. Quoted in David S. Thatcher, *Nietzsche in England 1890–1914* (Toronto: University of Toronto Press, 1970), p. 254. See also Tom Gibbons, *Rooms in the Darwin Hotel: Studies in English Literary Criticism and Ideas 1880–1920* (Nedlands: University of Western Australia Press, 1973).

22. Irving Babbitt, *Rousseau and Romanticism* (Boston: Houghton Mifflin, 1919), pp. 4–5.

23. The English translation of the second edition of Nordau's *Entartung* (Berlin: Duncker, 1892–93) appeared in London early in 1895 under the title *Degeneration* (Heinemann). (A French translation, *Dégénérescence*, was published in Paris by Alcan in 1894.) Nordau had dedicated the book to Cesare Lombroso, and this passage is from the letter of dedication, p. viii.

24. Jean Carrière, *Degeneration in the Great French Masters*, Joseph McCabe, tr. (London: T. Fisher Unwin, 1922), pp. 135–136.

25. From *De Profundis*, Wilde's letter to Lord Alfred Douglas from Reading Gaol, written in 1897. Although versions appeared as early as 1905, it was first published in a complete (though somewhat inaccurate) form in 1949. The most accurate text is in *Letters of Oscar Wilde*, Rupert Hart-Davis, ed. (New York: Harcourt, Brace and World, 1962), p. 490. For a more extensive discussion of this theme, see J. E. Chamberlin, *Ripe Was the Drowsy Hour: The Age of Oscar Wilde* (New York: Seabury, 1977), especially ch. 5 ("The Cry of Marsyas").

26. Darwin, *The Descent of Man* (London: John Murray, 1871). The first quotation begins the penultimate paragraph; the second is the penultimate sentence of the first chapter.

27. Anonymous, in the *Spectator* on March 12, 1871. Quoted in S. E. Hyman, *The Tangled Bank: Darwin, Marx, Frazer and Freud as Imaginative Writers* (New York: Atheneum, 1974), p. 49.

28. *The Lounger* (1787), 1(19):172. Quoted in Lois Whitney, *Primitivism and the Idea of Progress in English Popular Literature of the Eighteenth Century* (Baltimore: Johns Hopkins University Press, 1934), p. 43.

29. Written around 1800. See *The Complete Writings of William Blake*, Geoffrey Keynes, ed. (London: Oxford University Press, 1966), p. 431. The mention of Nebuchadnezzar is a reference to Plate 24 of *The Marriage of Heaven and Hell*, with its subscription "One Law for the Lion and Ox is Oppression." Emerson uses the same image of Nebuchadnezzar in his essay on "Nature" (1836), arguing in a similar vein that "man is a god in ruins . . . man is the dwarf of himself." (*Works*, 1:74) With regard to the idea of an original and ultimate unity from the perspective of which the present state is degenerate, compare (as Blake undoubtedly did) John Milton's comment that "a Commonwealth ought to be but as one huge Christian personage, one mighty growth, and stature of an honest man." ("Of Reformation Touching Church Discipline in England," book 2, introduction.) Quoted in Northrop Frye, *Fearful Symmetry: A Study of William Blake* (Princeton: Princeton University Press, 1947), p. 43.

30. Ezekiel, 37:3–4, 7, 10–11.

31. The quotation describing Indians as cattle is from H. H. Breckenridge, a particularly unenlightened eighteenth-century observer. The reference to weaning Indians away from their anomalous and anachronistic attachment to mother nature was a staple of nineteenth-century social, economic, and political commentary on such matters. See J. E. Chamberlin, *The Harrowing of Eden: White Attitudes Towards North American Natives* (Toronto: Fitzhenry and Whiteside, 1975); and Elemire Zolla, *The Writer and the Shaman: A Morphology of the American Indian*, Raymond Rosenthal, tr. (New York: Harcourt, Brace, Jovanovich, 1973).

32. R. C. Trench, *On the Study of Words* (London: J. W. Parker, 1851). The quotations are from pp. 14 and 24.

33. From "The Poet" (1842–44). See *The Works of Ralph Waldo Emerson* (Boston: Houghton, Mifflin, 1883), 3:26.

34. From "The Function of Criticism at the Present Time," *Essays in Criticism,* 1st Series (London: Macmillan, 1865). George Watson, in his book *The English Ideology: Studies in the Language of Victorian Politics* (London: Allen Lane, 1973), makes reference to this passage, and to this kind of disengagement.

35. Quoted by Havelock Ellis in his essay on J. K. Huysmans in *Affirmations* (London: W. Scott, 1898), p. 178.

36. Quoted by Havelock Ellis in "A Note on Paul Bourget" (1889), reprinted in *Views and Reviews* (London: Desmond Harmsworth, 1932), 1:52.

37. "The Case of Wagner: A Musician's Problem," Anthony M. Ludovici, tr., in *Complete Works*, Oscar Levy, ed. (London: T. N. Foulis, 1909–13), 8:19–20.

38. Derek Walcott, *Another Life* (London: Jonathan Cape, 1973), p. 75.

DEGENERATION:
Conclusion

Degeneration was part of the rhetoric of nineteenth-century science. Its power was the power that science claimed for both the objectivity and the analogical validity of its descriptions of natural phenomena. From its first application in the sphere of biology the idea of degeneration was transferred to a variety of other areas, and derived much of its authority from the structure of scientific explanation. But like science itself, these explanations were metaphorical and used the concept of degeneration with all of the metaphorical power of those metaphysical abstractions, such as the fall from grace, which they replaced.

The idea of degeneration was a powerful and sometimes pernicious figurative device for the organization of knowledge in the nineteenth and twentieth centuries. It relied for something of its power on being contrary to the idea of progress, which had its own overwhelming authority, not always beneficent. For example, the concept of progress led, through the application of Marx's philosophy of progress, to the gulags; and through the perversion of Nietzsche's superman, to the rise of fascism in Italy and Germany. To complete the picture from a political perspective, the idea of degeneration was used as a means of classifying and circumscribing those who would not or could not progress.

The particular political configurations that employed the structures of progressive and degenerative change sustained a range of political agendas, from the relatively casual in twentieth-century Britain to a thoroughly malignant expression in twentieth-century Germany. The German experience suggests the complex authority which the idea of degeneration could claim for itself, as it informed speculation in both the sciences and the arts, and determined courses of political action. As an example, the concept of the mentally ill as degenerate became part of a perception and a rhetoric of difference, which in turn sustained a powerful if perverse idea of progress.

One of the most widely held views of mental illness during the nineteenth century was that the madman was a throwback to a more primitive stage of human development. This view dominated Charles Darwin's understanding of madness and colored his perception of the madman in his scientific explanations. Indeed, he drew on this concept in his work on human emotions to show that madmen (or in his case madwomen) were much closer to the beast than to civilized man in their expression of emotions. The image of the madman as a degenerate throwback cut across all the categories of mental illness, from hysteria to neurasthenia, and from the general paralysis of the insane to dementia praecox. But the status of difference ascribed to madness, and to the madman as a throwback to a more primitive type, also assumed a role in determining the identity of another group, that of the artist. The identification of these two groups as similarly degenerate became a particular preoccupation in Germany during the Third Reich.

In the opening decades of the twentieth century German art and indeed most of European art revelled in its difference, picking up the romantic legacy of the artist as outcast or outsider. But it took on a special character. Having discovered the art of Africa, modern art rediscovered the creativity of the mentally ill. While the medical establishment in Germany looked upon the mentally ill as "primitives" who had to be locked up in order to protect society, the artistic avant-garde looked upon them as kindred souls, like themselves incarcerated within the walls of an oppressive society. Thus, such writers as Ernst Stadler, Georg Trakl, Carl Einstein, Alfred Döblin, and the Dadaist Richard Huelsenbeck all used the voice of the madman as the poetic alter ego of the avant-garde.

Wieland Herzfeld, publisher, poet, and essayist, stated this quite directly in 1914 in a polemic published in the expressionist periodical *Action*. For him the madman was the model artist: "They keep their own language—it is the statement of their psyche, and yet orthography, punctuation, even words and turns of phrase, which do not reflect their feelings, they avoid. Not out of forgetfulness but out of unwillingness." The avant-garde in Germany accepted the mask of the madman and of the primitive—and hence of the degenerate—since this status provided the artist who understood himself as different with the freedom of a new and different discourse. This was, of course, a conceit, incorporating a benign use of the idea of "degeneration" within the figurative structures of modern art.

Yet in appropriating the label of "degenerate" the avant-garde entered into an unholy alliance with those who had developed the label of "degenerate" as a means of qualifying difference. Item: in Europe, especially in France and Germany, Jews were considered to be especially prone to mental illness. The giants of European psychiatry from Jean Martin Charcot to Emil Kraepelin and Richard von Krafft-Ebing, shared the view that Jews, because of generations of inbreeding, evidenced a much higher risk for mental illness than other groups in the general population. Jewish thinkers such as Cesare Lombroso and Max Nordau accepted this view

and attempted in their scientific (or popular scientific) writing to rationalize the madness of the Jew. The Jew was especially prone to madness, they
thought, but this was not a product of his biology but of the social pressures, the persecutions, he experienced. The Jew was different, was more
primitive, than his Christian neighbor. This view was only the medicalization of the rhetoric of difference as stated by Hegel, who saw the Jew as a
remnant of a past age, out of phase with the progress of history. And so
both groups of outsiders, the artist and the Jew, were associated through
an analogy with the degenerate, the primitive, the throwback. This association held throughout the early twentieth century in Europe especially,
with attacks on the avant-garde as both "crazy" and "Jewish."

In 1924, in the prison at Landsberg, the leader of a failed coup d'état
against the young Weimar Republic dictated his political philosophy. Adolf Hitler took the seemingly benign associations of the mad, the Jew, and
the avant-garde all as degenerate, and placed them within a political context. "Sixty years ago an exhibition of so-called dadaistic 'experiences'
would have seemed simply impossible and its organizers would have ended
up in the madhouse. This plague could not appear at that time, because
neither would public opinion have tolerated it nor the state calmly looked
on. For it is the business of the state, in other words, of its leaders, to
prevent a people from being driven into the arms of spiritual madness."
For Hitler, dictating *Mein Kampf,* the success of the avant-garde was a sign
of the degeneracy of the state. The stage was set for the culmination of a
hundred years' war between the contrary but complementary logics of
degeneration and progress. Madmen produce art which is glorified; and
rather than controlling these madmen, rather than placing them in
asylums, the state purchases their works and places them in museums. It
seemed to Adolf Hitler like a vicious foolishness.

And who were these madmen? According to one of the wall posters
produced by the Ministry of Propaganda during 1936, they were the
"hacks, the psychopaths, the Jews, and the Jew-lovers." The Nazis organized a show of "Degenerate Art" in 1937. The 750 objects were exhibited
in the Munich Anthropological Museum as examples of primitivism and
were contrasted with works of art by the mentally ill. The artists who were
exhibited, artists such as Ludwig Kirchner, Emil Nolde, Otto Müller, and
Marc Chagall, were all labeled as "degenerate," and therefore as "Jewish."
The program for this exhibit cited Hitler on the degeneracy of Jewish
modernism, but also quoted Wieland Herzfeld as proof of the self-conscious "madness" of the avant-garde. Suddenly, what had been an analogy
between "madness" and "creativity," organized in the figurative logic of
degeneration, took on a real political dimension. The works of these madmen were removed from the galleries and either auctioned off in Switzerland or burned. Then the madmen were removed.

In seeing the primitive and the degenerate as a pernicious influence in the state, Hitler noted the need for a program of action. The state must defend itself from "regression," from the "symptoms of decay in a slowly rotting world." Art must be purified, but so must the body politic. Thus one of the first undertakings in the Nazis' program of applied eugenics was the killing of inmates of mental hospitals in Germany, at least until the Catholic Church in the person of Cardinal von Galen interceded in 1939, shortly after the program had begun. But still, of course, the mad, the Jew, and the avant-garde were linked through the model of degeneration.

To be sure, this perception was given some credibility by the avant-garde labeling itself as mad and primitive, just as the nineteenth-century avant-garde had labeled itself useless and unhealthy. But the shift in the implication of these labels, and the awesome authority of scientific rhetoric during this period, led the Nazis to create the fiction of a community of outsiders, all of whom were dangerous to the health and integrity of the state, and all of whom had to be removed in order to prevent environmental or hereditary contagion.

In this program, degeneration served as the indicator of difference, whether applied to the Jew, the insane, the homosexual, or the artist. It was the most radical and the most terrible example of the translation of a descriptive metaphor into the prescriptive logic of political action. The power of the idea of degeneration lay in its appropriation of the rhetoric of scientific discourse, and thereby of the rhetoric of truth. And this was a nineteenth-century legacy, as the literal truth of being different was translated into the figurative truth of being degenerate. Both truths were given equal status.

There were complex relationships between the idea of degeneration and the way it was used to define certain kinds of difference. Initially, degeneration brought together two notions of difference, one scientific—a deviation from an original type—and the other moral, a deviation from a norm of behavior. But they were essentially the same notion, of a fall from grace, a deviation from *the* original type. Degeneration is a genetic disorder; and its prototype is appropriately found in the Book of Genesis. As the locus of belief shifted from religion to science, the discussion incorporated a new scientific rhetoric, which was in turn incorporated into the discourse of the social sciences and the humanities. The logic of degeneration became an instrument of analysis, and in due course, a reason for action. The diagnosis came first, and the cure . . . But there was no cure. The degenerate could not be helped; his condition was immutable. The best that could be done was to identify and isolate him. And then eliminate him, one way or another.

The idea of degeneration became a monstrous intellectual legacy, something like the idea of progress. Degeneration as a word became so soiled by the realities that sprang from it, by the Holocaust and other inhumane actions, that it could no longer be used except as a term of opprobrium. To speak of a work of art as degenerate, to label the mentally ill as degenerate, is now possible only in a kind of tabloid rhetoric. Science has moved in new directions. We have seen in a little more than a century the birth and death of a powerful idea. Its natural history may provide us with some sense of the complexity of our own discourse, as well as some suspicion about the validity of all structures of human perception.

Index